The Convoluted Universe

Book Four

Dolores Cannon

OZARK
MOUNTAIN
PUBLISHING

PO Box 754
Huntsville, AR 72740
479-738-2348 or 800-935-0045
Fax 479-738-2448
www.ozarkmt.com

For permission, serialization, condensation, adaptions, or for our catalog of other publications, write to Ozark Mountain Publishing, Inc., P.O. Box 754, Huntsville, AR 72740, ATTN: Permissions Department.

Library of Congress Cataloging-in-Publication Data
Cannon, Dolores, 1931 - 2014
    The Convoluted Universe – Book Four, by Dolores Cannon
Ongoing series continues to explore unknown metaphysical theories and concepts.

1. Evolution of Consciousness 2. Beginning of the Earth 3. Creation of Humans 4. Changing and Color of DNA 5. Life After Death
6. Metaphysics
I. Cannon, Dolores, 1931- 2014 II. New Consciousness III. Metaphysics
IV. Title

Library of Congress Catalog Card Number: 2007920151
ISBN: 978-1-886940-21-5

Cover Art and Layout: Victoria Cooper Art
Book set in: Times New Roman; Baskerville Old Face
Book Design: Julia Degan

Published by:

OZARK
MOUNTAIN
PUBLISHING

PO Box 754
Huntsville, AR 72740
479-738-2348; 800-935-0045; fax 479-738-2448
www.ozarkmt.com

The important thing is not to stop questioning. Curiosity has its own reason for existing. One cannot help but be in awe when he contemplates the mysteries of eternity, of life, of the marvelous structure of reality. It is enough if one tries merely to comprehend a little of this mystery every day. Never lose a holy curiosity.

Albert Einstein, 1879-1955

TABLE OF CONTENTS

Foreword   i

Part One – Beyond the Veil

Chapter   1   My Own Past Lives   3

2   The Evolution of Consciousness   17

3   The Spirit Side   35

4   Life As Other Creatures   41

5   Many Choices   79

6   The Planning Stage   91

7   A Short Life   111

8   A Difficult Assignment   129

9   Balance In Life   143

10   Traveling   151

11   Accumulator of Information   167

12   Carrying Guilt   175

13   Changing the Past   183

Section – Murder and Suicides

14   Murder and the Resting Place   197

15   Fear Is Carried Over   207

16   Murder and Suicide   221

17   A Suicide   233

18   A Heartbroken Suicide   241

19   A Suicide Repays Karma   255

Part Two – The Convoluted Universe Keeps Expanding

Section – The Beginning of Earth

20   Back To The Beginning   273

21   "Tweaking"   289

22   The Creation of Humans   307

23   Separating From the Source   323

24   Too Much Too Soon   347

Section – Energy

25   The Pink Energy From
the Crystal Planet   365

26   Creating Energy   381

27   An Energy Being   399

28   Unknown Energy   407

29   The Sun   413

30   Activation of the New Light Energy   419

Section – Time and Dimensions

31	The Depot	435
32	The Village That Is Out Of Time	449
33	The Embodiment of An Aspect	469
34	Changing DNA	475
35	The Color of DNA	489
36	Working With the Systems of Earth	507
37	The Healing of Ann	525
38	The Backdrop People	553
39	The Fragments Reunite	567
40	The Pictures	579
41	Finis	587

FOREWORD

Welcome everyone! Welcome, new readers to this series, and welcome back, the others who have been following my adventures in hypnosis through the past years. When I began the *Convoluted Universe* series I mistakenly thought it would only be one book. I had been working on the information that became *The Custodians*, my twenty-five years of investigations about UFOs and abductions. I had gathered a great deal of information and I thought I had covered everything anyone would want to know about the phenomenon. Then the information began to take an unexpected turn. It was moving away from extraterrestrials into metaphysical concepts and theories that I had never heard before. That was when I knew I would have to finish that book and start another one. I didn't know how it would be accepted because it was a departure from my normal writing about hypnosis and the search for lost knowledge. Although this is also considered "lost" knowledge, it was going in a different direction. I called the first book "a book that was intended to bend your mind like a pretzel." I thought it might appeal to those who have followed and read my books over the past thirty years, and they would be able to see my evolution in this field. Yet I was pleasantly surprised when I found that the first book of this series was being read by first time readers of my work. I didn't know if people would be able to understand it if they just jumped right into the deep end of the pool. I always suggested that they start with my first books and move up to this work gradually. But I began to get mail that suggested the readers were more ready than I could ever have imagined. Some wrote, "I may not understand it, but it really makes me think." And that was my intention. In the books, I say to treat these books like "mind candy." New concepts and theories to be enjoyed and pondered over, and then put aside so the reader can continue their own life. Just an interesting sideline or detour from the norm.

When I was getting *The Convoluted Universe* ready for publication I suddenly decided to add *Book One* to the title. At that point I really didn't know if there would ever be another book in that series. I thought I had put everything possible in the first book. But something made me call it *Book One*. I should know by now that "they" were behind it. "They" knew I had just scratched the surface and now that I had embarked on this new journey, there would be tons of new information to be brought forth. And thus it has been. Each book in the series has introduced more and more strange concepts for people to think and wonder about. At the end of *Convoluted Universe, Book Three,* I truly thought they had given me everything possible. That there was nothing left to learn and be exposed to. They had told me everything. But as I was putting the book together I had one last session in Montreal that brought forward yet another mind-bending concept. At the end of that chapter I said, "Now I know there is nothing more to discover." And they said, in their infinite wisdom, "Oh, no! There is more! There is more!" And on that note I was able to finally finish the 700 page book and get it published. They then allowed me to rest for a few months as the book went into production. All my hypnosis sessions were "normal," just the usual therapy to help people with their physical and personal problems. Then the information began to come in again, and I knew there would indeed be a fourth book. When I called the first book *Book One*, I laughed because I thought, at the most there might be one more book. Now I have no idea how many there will be. I just keep writing and they keep exposing me to new information. As I put this book together, I find I have enough material for three sections on different subjects. So the journey continues.

For those who are just now joining us, welcome to the adventure and the journey. For those who have been part of the entire journey, welcome back and I hope you find more interesting concepts as we continue the adventure. So read with an open mind and be prepared to have your minds bent some more. After all, pretzels are an interesting shape. They really resemble the symbol for infinity, don't they?

PART ONE

BEYOND THE VEIL

Chapter 1

MY OWN PAST LIVES

W henever I am giving a lecture I am invariably asked the same question, "Do you know about any of your own past lives?" I think it would have been impossible to have been working in this field for over forty years and not try to find out about yourself. In the early days I had past life regressions done by various hypnotists. I was as curious as anyone else. That was how I discovered what I *did not* want my own clients to experience. There were many things about their various techniques that left me feeling uncomfortable, uneasy, upset and disturbed. It was not always a pleasant experience. I obtained information, but the session was not always done in a professional manner. I realized that they were only doing what they had been taught, and had never questioned why they were doing it that certain way. Yet *I* questioned it. If I was uncomfortable during or after the session I tried to understand why. Then over the years as I developed my own technique, I built in safeguards so none of my own clients would ever have to experience the same unpleasant feelings. This is another reason I always recommend that my students experience their own past life regression, so they will know how to deal with their clients. How can we practice something if we have never experienced it?

During the early years I found out about eight of my past lives. It was important in the fact that I discovered my relationships with my family members, and why we had to come back together again. And I found out why I am doing the work I do. That was very important in itself. Now I no longer need to look for past lives because I think I have discovered all

I need to know. It is a valuable tool, but that is all it is, a tool. When you begin to evolve and know yourself then you no longer need to continue going back into the past. To some people it is done more for entertainment value than for therapy. Then it does not serve a good purpose. They can become like "past-life junkies," looking for the next "fix" out of curiosity. That defeats the whole meaning of past life therapy, that the person becomes comfortable in *this* life. The past memories are good and valuable information, but they must be put to use in the present body, especially family relations. We have to weave it all together the same way we have woven the memories of our own childhood and other experiences. For good or bad, they are the story of our life and must be dealt with and reconciled. The other lives are only extended memories, and should also be incorporated into our present life. This helps to make the individual a well-rounded and sane personality.

To go back to the story, I discovered about my purpose (the eternal question) in this life. At the time it happened I didn't even know the rest of my life would be devoted to helping people through exploring their past. I enjoyed the work, and had just begun to write my first book (*Jesus and the Essenes*), but there was no way I could foresee how vast my work would become. When I had the regression in the home of a friend I had no idea what would come out.

I regressed back to the days of the huge Library at Alexandria in Egypt. All my life I have been fascinated with books. I could read before I entered school, and grammar was easy and second nature to me. I was a child during the Depression so money was very tight. My sister and I did not have any luxuries. There were lots of hand-me-downs and clothes bought at thrift stores. In those days you had to make do with what you had. If it cost money, forget it, you weren't going to get it (except at Christmas when there were a few toys). That was why I was so excited during the first grade when someone came to our class and talked about the huge library that was not far from our school in St. Louis. They were encouraging us to get library cards and gave us a paper to take home to apply for one. I had already devoured all the books available in our class, and my hunger was at a fever pitch when I heard we could go to a library where hundreds of books were available. The very best part was that it was *FREE*. I couldn't believe my ears. Free. I ran all the way home with the paper in my hand to show my mother. My excitement must have been contagious when I showed her the paper and went on and on about how I could get a card to read any book I wanted to and it was *free*. To make a long story short, my mother got the card, and every few days she would take me the several blocks to the gigantic library where I could check out books. I remember walking the aisles between the shelves and I was in pure heaven as I realized there was no limit to what I could read. Later when I could go by myself I spent hours there, and always carried armloads of books home. I was never without a book, and I spent many hours escaping into the wonderful world of imagination that books presented. In high school if I wasn't in a class I was in the school library pouring through the encyclopedias. I had a rather strange compulsion that I developed about that same time. In my spare time in study hall I would keep occupied by copying all the words in the dictionary. Each time I would mark where I had left off and continue the next day, just copying word after word in my notebook. I could say that this came from my love of books, but I later discovered through my past life regressions that I had a previous life as a monk in a monastery where my job was to copy manuscripts and texts by hand. But it was a good compulsion because it imbedded the use of words and language into my psyche.

I read everything I could get my hands on, and this love of books and the desire to learn continued all my life. Even today when I write one of my books, I research it "to death." After I have completed the sessions and the real work of writing the book begins, I spend hours (and sometimes all day) in a library gathering my facts. To me that is heaven to search for hours, and finally come up with the treasure of finding one elusive fact. When I wrote my three books on Nostradamus: *Conversations With Nostradamus*, I read every book ever written on the great master. Some of them were out of print and the only copy would be available from the Library of Congress, which was obtained through Library-Loan at the University of Arkansas. When I wrote my books on Jesus: *Jesus and the Essenes* and *They Walked With Jesus*, I read every book ever written on the Dead Sea Scrolls. When I wrote my book about the origin of the American Indian race: *Legend of Starcrash*, I spent three years doing research into all the old Indian legends and history that I could find. All of this research has paid off because when I give lectures I have all this information in my mind and I am confident about what I am talking about. My earliest magazine publisher once said, "Research is very important. It is obvious that you have done your homework. And it would be just as obvious if you had *not* done it." I think it is a shame now that young people don't know how to do *real* research. They spend a short amount of time on the Internet compiling a few facts, without knowing the glory and wonder of combing through dusty piles of books in a library, and finding some forgotten or lost text. This is why I call myself, "the reporter, the investigator, the researcher of lost knowledge."

So I suppose it should not have come as too great of a surprise when I returned to a past life at the great and grand Library at Alexandria before its destruction in the fifth century. In that lifetime I was a man who worked in the library. I could not read the precious scrolls on the shelves, but I knew which ones were the oldest and most important. Many learned scholars came to the library, and I would find the scrolls they wanted to see. I watched in envy as they sat at tables opening the scrolls and reading them. I knew the most important scrolls were kept up high on the top shelves. There was one man in particular, dressed in a black robe, who came in often. I always knew in advance which scrolls he would want. I enjoyed this work even though I couldn't read. I was like a caretaker of the books.

Then came the fateful day of the destruction of the great library. I was there among the books when a great horde of men stormed into the library destroying as they went. In horror I watched as they grabbed scrolls from the shelves and piled them in the middle of the room. I screamed in terror as I saw them reach for the scrolls that were kept on the top shelves. Tears ran down my face as they tore at them with no respect for the knowledge they contained, and threw them into the growing pile. I knew I could not stop them, so I grabbed what scrolls I could and ran out of the building, just as they set fire to the stacks. My arms were full of scrolls and my eyes were so tear-filled that I couldn't see where I was going as I stumbled into the street. Just in time to be run over by a passing chariot. As I rose out of my body I looked back and saw it lying crumbled on the street among my armload of scrolls. The library fire was spreading and consuming the building.

I saw that this lifetime explained my love of books, why I can't stand to see a book mistreated and my desire to get the lost knowledge back. When I told this story at a conference panel when I was asked the question about my past lives, one of the others on the panel quipped, "Yeah, but did you have to try and rewrite the *entire* library?" The audience roared in laughter because we knew she was referring to my many books. Yes, this was probably the explanation, and it put my mind at ease. But that was not the end of the story. There was more that came to light in the 1990s.

I was invited to go to Bulgaria because my books on Nostadamus had been accepted for translation by Zar Publishers, Ltd., a publisher in Sophia. Drago had discovered my books and made arrangements with the publishers to translate into their language, and they wanted me to come and lecture there. I had been traveling all over the world, but had never been to Bulgaria or any of the Soviet countries at that time. The war in Yugoslavia had just broken out. My son was worried, "Mom, you can't go over there. Look at the map! Sophia is just over the border from Yugoslavia." I have never felt in danger anywhere I have gone. I have always felt it was an honor to be asked to go and speak. Somehow I knew everything was going to be all right. And I was correct, it turned out to be one of the most wonderful experiences of my life.

From the moment I got off the plane I was treated like some kind of rock star or celebrity. There was a huge crowd of reporters waiting at the gate when we entered the terminal. I was totally shocked. I had never had such a reception anywhere else in the world. I remember one reporter shoving a microphone into my face, and asking in broken English, "What do you think of Bulgaria?" I really couldn't reply because I had just gotten there. My books on Nostradamus had created a sensation that I was totally unprepared for. Reporters came to my hotel and set up interviews and TV appearances everywhere I went. There was even a press conference that would have equaled one by the President. I was subjected to an hour of questioning that was back and forth through my translator, Drago. Then I attended a meeting where I was questioned for two hours by doctors and scientists. They all wanted to know about hypnosis being used for past life regression and therapy. They had never heard about it before. They said that when they were under Russian domination nothing was allowed to be taught that did not originate in the universities. It was against the law. I asked if I would get into trouble discussing this. They said, no because I was a foreigner. But their interest was sincere and I felt like I had opened up a Pandora's box.

During my week long stay there I was kept busy with many appearances, interviews and lectures. When I gave a lecture the auditorium was totally full, and the crowd was so great that once I was pushed against a wall. Their enthusiasm was so great that it frightened me. Drago pulled me into an elevator and took me to another floor to wait until the crowd calmed down. He said, "I forgot to warn you. The Bulgarians are a very passionate people." When he felt it was safe we went down for the lecture. Afterwards when I tried to leave, there were people approaching me crying and pointing to others near them. That was when I saw a man in a wheelchair, and another woman who was obviously experiencing chemotherapy for cancer. They were respectfully grasping at me with tears in their eyes. I asked Drago what was going on. He said they had brought these people out of the hospital to see me. They were hoping for a cure or healing. I wanted to know why they thought that. Was this what was reported in the newspapers after the interviews? Had they completely misunderstood what I did? He said it didn't matter, they were desperate for help, and they thought that I was some kind of healer. All I could do was look at them with compassion and try to explain that I could not help them. (It was about five years later that I discovered how to use my technique to heal.)

My whole time spent there was full of these types of occurrences. Toward the end of our stay Drago came to our hotel and said that a Russian film maker wanted to do a documentary about me and my work. She wanted to film me doing a past life regression. It didn't matter that she did not understand English, the translation would be dubbed in later. I told him I would try, but who would be the subject that I would use for the demonstration? He said he was volunteering to do it. He felt it would go well because he understood English and we knew each other, so we would be comfortable. I agreed, even though I wondered what would happen. What if it wouldn't work, and he wouldn't go into a past life? These were certainly unusual circumstances, and there are no guarantees that *anything* would happen. Even if we were successful, ninety percent of regressions are dull and boring, mundane simple lives. So I didn't know if we would get anything that would be useful to them. Yet I felt I had no choice but to try it.

Drago took me and my daughter Nancy to the hotel where the filming and interview would be held. When we walked into the room the technicians were busy setting up lights and equipment all around the bed they wanted me to use. Then the Russian woman brought out a young pretty blond girl dressed in a sexy blouse and shorts, and announced that she would be the one I would regress for the show. I told her that it had to be someone that spoke English, and the girl replied in a high-pitched naive voice, "Me speak English!" And flashed a cute smile. I knew this would never work, but I also knew the woman thought it would make good television to show a young sexy girl lying on the bed. I then announced that we had decided to use Drago because he was comfortable with me and could speak English. Drago was a good looking man with dark hair and a beard, but definitely not sexy. She had no choice but to accept our decision. Since I had no idea what was going to happen, I wanted to put as many odds in my favor as I could. Later after the session I thought they might have thought we cooked the whole thing up, and had planned it in advance. But we had no idea what was going to come out, if anything. We certainly had had no time to rehearse or invent anything.

Drago settled on the bed with all the cameras, microphones and equipment gathered around us. If he was nervous he gave no sign of it as he relaxed and I began the session. My daughter, Nancy, was sitting behind me out of the camera's range. Then the unexpected happened, and I could only listen and conduct the session in amazement. He went back to a lifetime where he was a scholar and teacher who focused on astrology and numerology. He was constantly studying and spent a great deal of time at – (Are you ready??) – the Library at Alexandria. I couldn't believe it and I asked him many questions about the library to see if it sounded like the same place. It did indeed. He was reporting the same scenes that I had seen. While I was busy asking questions to verify it, I glanced behind me at Nancy. I knew that she had heard my story, and by the expression on her face I knew she realized what was happening and the importance of it.

As the teacher he wore black robes and usually asked to see the most important scrolls, and then sat at a table studying them. Then we came to the momentous day when the library was attacked and burned. He was also inside the library as the horde came through and started destroying the scrolls by fire.

He said later he was swept with emotion, and wanted to cry, but he held it back because he knew there were others in the room and the cameras watching. Otherwise, he would have burst into tears. In his desperation he grabbed as many scrolls as he could and tried to save them by carrying them out of the building. But the library was now on fire, and as he ran toward the entrance, part of the roof began to collapse and he was struck across the shoulders by a falling rafter. Thus he also died clutching the precious scrolls.

When we were finished I didn't say anything. I waited until we were walking back to the hotel. Then I said, "Boy, do I have a story to tell you!" The next morning when he came to our hotel he confided, "I didn't want to say anything until I was sure. But all of my life I have always had pain across my shoulders. I never knew what caused it. It disappeared immediately after the session." Then I told him about *my* experience in the library. We assumed that we were there at the same time, however, we probably didn't know each other, as he was a scholar and I was merely the keeper of the scrolls. We could only wonder at the similarities.

The rest of my stay in Bulgaria was equally eventful, but I will not go into it here. Except to say that before I left, the organization (Association of Phenomena) that brought me over there presented me with the Orpheus Award on a TV program. It was given for the highest advancement in the research of psychic phenomenon. Until that day it had only been given to Bulgarians. I was the first foreigner and the first American to ever receive the award: a large and heavy metal statue shaped like a stylized flame.

When Drago took me to the airport I said to him, "Isn't it amazing that we had to go half way around the world to meet again after fifteen hundred years." He smiled and said we were both trying to bring back the lost knowledge. Me through my regression work and my writing, and him through bringing in people to speak and have their books published in his country.

After the documentary aired Drago called and said that it had created such a sensation that the station was inundated by calls wanting to know more about past life regression and reincarnation. A few years later he told me that past life therapy was now being used and taught in Bulgaria. I suppose they used the technique that was shown in the film. A strange story of the reuniting of two souls across time and space. And I wonder if I was responsible for introducing a whole new way of thinking into a country half way around the world. Such are the strange ways of fate.

Another of my past lives was also verified, although not in such a dramatic way. That past life occurred in Athens at the Parthenon. Although during the regression I wasn't sure where it was, except that it had a Grecian feel. I was a woman living in a large house with a patio in the center, husband and children, and with enough money to have servants. I have since seen pictures of ancient living quarters in Greece that were exactly as I remembered. It felt so familiar looking at the photos. But that was not the main point of the regression. I went to a scene where I was running through the streets at night, and I had the overwhelming feeling of absolute terror. As I ran I kept looking behind me because I knew someone was chasing me. I ran up a hill to a large temple. There I paused for a minute to catch my breath, and when I did I saw a panoramic scene in front of me. I could see a bay far beneath me and could make out ships with sails on the water. It was very dark, and the moon reflected on the dark water. Then I turned around toward the temple. I ran up the steps leading inside, and saw there were no doors, only enormous pillars. Running through these there was an open feel to the building, as though there was lots of space. There on a platform was an enormous statue of a seated woman. She had one arm outstretched and was holding a huge lantern that provided light to the building. I flung myself down on the steps in front of the statue and lay face down. I was crying hysterically as I begged and beseeched her for protection. Then I heard a noise and turned over just in time to see a soldier standing over me. Death came instantly as he plunged a sword into me.

Bits of information came slowly after the session. I knew that my husband in that life was a proud domineering man that thought of me as a possession. I apparently had been speaking out and expressing my opinions too much for his liking, and he ordered my assassination. Also I have a dissatisfaction with religion in this lifetime. I think it came from that life because I apparently was a follower of the goddess of that temple. And yet here in the time of my greatest need she did not help me. I felt she had deserted me. This upset me more than the manner of death.

It was just an interesting regression, and I occasionally said that I knew I had lived in Greece during those ancient times. But it meant nothing more than that ... until ... in the 1990s during my constant traveling all over the world I was invited to go to Athens in Greece. My books were being translated into so many languages that I felt it was a necessity to go where the books were. I had always wanted to see Greece, so I accepted to go and do some lectures and book-signings. I stayed with a wonderful lady who arranged everything. Eleni lived on the outskirts of Athens in an old three-story mansion with only herself and her dog "Droopy." She wanted to show me Athens and the surrounding countryside. So one day we went by train into the main part of Athens and she took us to see the Acropolis, the Parthenon. This was the highlight of the trip because I always wanted to see it. We climbed up a dirt street that led to the ruins. They were being repaired and rebuilt so there was scaffolding and piles of stone blocks all around the building. Yet when I walked up the steps leading to the interior it all felt so familiar. I have heard people talk about deja vu, the feeling of having been in a place before, but I had never experienced it. Now I was. The platform was there, but there was no statue. In the museum located beneath the Parthenon it was explained that much of the building and its statues had been destroyed over the years. This was the temple of Athena, the patron goddess of Athens, and her statue was in the temple in those ancient times. There were no pictures left, but only verbal and written descriptions. It was supposedly a huge statue that almost touched the roof of the building. They said the statue was standing and holding a smaller goddess in one hand and a shield in the other. This did not match the vivid memory that I had of the statue, but I do not think that is a contradiction or a mistake. Because no one knows exactly how the statue looked. I saw it seated with an outstretched arm and a hand holding a huge lantern. Yet everything else was correct. When I walked out of the front of the temple I looked around from the high vantage point. I said to Eleni, "If this is the right place, then I should be able to see some kind of bay from here." She nodded, and pointed. Below were many houses and streets that blocked some of the view, but there was visible a part of the Mediterranean, and there were boats visible on the water. I was so excited. I recounted how I had run up the street and thrown myself down in front of the statue. It didn't seem to matter that I had died violently in that place. I was exhilarated about my discovery that my memories were real and had been verified.

* * *

So in the beginning my work was mostly the research of history through the information I discovered using the deepest possible level of trance, the somnambulistic level. I wrote several books in the 1980s and early 1990s before something unexpected began to happen. Another element came in (slowly at first) that had more knowledge and was able to facilitate healing. At first this was unexpected, but it seemed to have so much power and knowledge that I allowed it to help. When I look back at my early books I can now see that it was there all the time, I just didn't recognize it. I started calling it the Subconscious because I didn't know what else to call it. But it is not the subconscious referred to by psychiatrists. I have discovered that is a childish part of the mind, the part that can be used in the lighter levels of trance to help with habits. I saw that this part was far more powerful. I called it the Subconscious, and "they" said they did not care what I called it since it did not have a name anyway. It would respond and work with me. For the purpose of this book I will call it simply the SC. I now know it is the greatest power that there is. It contains all knowledge of everything that has ever been, and everything that ever will be. So it can answer all the client's questions and give wonderful advice. Advice that I would never be able to come up with. I found that it knows everything about everybody. There are no secrets, so naturally it can help because it sees the bigger picture. Then I began to see its wonderful and awe-inspiring ability to heal instantly. This has now become the most important emphasis of my work and what I am teaching all over the world. "They" used to say that this is the therapy of the future. Now they are saying it is the therapy of *Now*. I have found the SC has the answers to everything. It is so huge and so big, and is total love. Why not work with something like that? It takes all the burden off of me, the therapist. I just have to ask the correct questions and then sit back and watch the magic. And I do see miracles happen every day in my office. My students all over the world are also reporting similar miracles. So I feel we have found something of great importance. This is also where the information comes from that I write about in these books. Remember, I am only the reporter, the investigator, the researcher of "lost" knowledge. I have to put all the pieces together to form the bigger picture. Which is no easy task, yet it is one that I love.

So let us continue the journey into the unknown, and discover what new surprises the SC has for us!

Chapter 2

THE EVOLUTION OF CONSCIOUSNESS

During all my over 40 years of working in this field of hypnosis, I have been challenged by new theories, concepts and information. My one main characteristic has always been *curiosity*. This has spurred me on to travel down hidden corridors. I always want to know more. To know the "whys and wherefores" of everything I am exposed to. In the beginning I thought I had it all figured out. I thought I had discovered the intricacies of reincarnation. But I soon discovered that I was sadly mistaken. "They" began to give me new theories and concepts that seriously challenged my belief systems. The first was the *imprint* theory which caused me to rethink all the ideas I had about this work. I didn't want anything to shake my belief system now that I had it all figured out. But then I realized that if I didn't at least look at the new theory and examine it, I was no better than the religious system which says, "Do as we say and don't ask any questions!" That was my first challenge, and as I examined it, I began to receive more information. They were very wise in the way they did it. They know they cannot dump everything on you at once, it would be too overwhelming. So in their wisdom, they give you a small spoonful. When you digest that, then they give you another small tidbit. I know that if I had received the information I am receiving now, thirty years ago, it would have been too overwhelming. I would have completely rejected it, thrown it against the wall, said "I don't understand it! It doesn't make any sense!" and my adventure and quest of knowledge would have stopped. I would never have advanced to the state that I am now. Through one of my clients they said, "You don't give a baby a steak. You give a baby milk, cereal and mashed vegetables. You don't give it a three-course meal." So I had to take my baby steps in this magical field of knowledge. I had to digest my spoonfuls that I was being fed. At the end of *Convoluted Universe, Book Three* I said, "I think you have told me everything there is to know. I don't think there could possibly be anything more." And they answered, "Oh, no! There is more! There is much more!" And true to their word they have provided *more*. Enough for several new books. *Three Waves* was the latest of these. People have been asking to read my books in the order that I wrote them in, in order to see how I evolved. Some have told me, "But you said this in one book, and this in another book." That reflects my thinking at the time of the writing of that particular book. Then as I grew and absorbed more information, my way of thinking changed. And it is still changing.

As the New Earth approaches, our way of thinking is being challenged more and more. The Veil is thinning and lifting as our consciousness expands. This is a requirement for entering the new dimension with the raising of our vibrations and frequencies. The old paradigms and archaic belief systems must fall to the wayside to make room for the new. What made sense and was valuable in the Old Earth no longer applies as our consciousness changes and we move forward. In the last few months as I was preparing this book, I began to uncover new information that I believe has great importance. It caused a major shift in my belief system and consciousness, and I think it has great importance for the world as we go through this remarkable and amazing time. My greatest challenge will be whether I can convey it effectively to others. All I can do is try, and with "their" help maybe others will understand. Of course, everything always depends upon the evolution and evolvement of the reader. Here we go!!

A ll throughout my 16 books bits and pieces of these ideas have been presented. Now it is time to organize them to the best of my ability. These concepts have been repeated through countless clients so I know they have validity.

We all began with God (or the Source) and were sent out to learn and have experiences. This would not be a short journey because we eventually signed up to experience the very difficult Earth school. Once we signed on for this education, there was no turning back until we graduate. Many other planets have easier courses of learning, but Earth is the most difficult. It has been called the most challenging planet in our universe, and only the bravest of souls sign on for assignment. The souls that choose the Earth school are greatly admired because the ones on the spirit side (and our helpers) know these souls have chosen the most difficult course of lessons. Because it is a school, we have to go through a whole series of classes, each with its own series of lessons, gradually increasing in their difficulty and complexity. You can't proceed to the next "grade" until you complete the present one. If you fail the class or grade and don't learn the lesson, then you have to repeat that grade. It is that simple. You can't jump from kindergarten to college. The universe doesn't care how long it takes you (as an individual soul) to complete a lesson. You have all of eternity to work it out. But why would you want to take that long to progress, to learn one lesson? I would think you would want to graduate as soon as possible in order to return to God. Why get bogged down in the sticky glue of Earth, and be stuck in the same grade while others around you are progressing rapidly?

I will present this in linear fashion, even though I now know there is no such thing as time, and everything is occurring simultaneously. But for the sake of simplicity and to make it easier for our human minds to understand, I will explain in linearly.

In order to complete the Earth school we have to experience *everything!* We have to know what it is like to *be* everything! How can we understand life if we don't know what it is like to be other forms? This may be a shock to some, but we don't start out as humans. That is much later in this school.

First, you experience life as the simplest forms imaginable: air, gases, water, even simple cells, dirt, rocks. Everything has consciousness! Everything is alive! Everything is energy! In my work I have had many people experience these basic lifeforms, and there were valuable lessons to be learned. Lessons that are accumulated and understood and can be applied to the complex human. Just like we have to learn to print and write and read in a certain slow progression in order to get the basic building blocks of education. You must always start at the beginning in any type of school.

Then you experience the plant and animal kingdom. There are valuable lessons to be learnt from being a flower or an ear of corn, or from running like a wolf or flying like an eagle. I have explored many of these types of lives in my other books. I think these are valuable lessons to be learned because we can understand that we must take better care of our natural environment and ecology. We can understand this because we are all One, and we have all been these different forms of life in our early grades in Earth school. There are also the Nature Spirits: fairies, gnomes, leprechauns, dryads, etc. These have the job (or assignment) of taking care of nature. These beings are all very real, and we have all had lifetimes in these forms of existence. I believe we would treat nature better if we realized we are all part of the One consciousness.

Nature is a different sort of spirit because it is considered a "group" spirit. You can witness this very easily when you watch a flock of birds, a herd of cattle, a hive of bees or a colony of ants. They seem to work and think as a group mentality. So in order to begin progressing upward to the human part of the school (compare it to moving through kindergarten, grade school, junior high, high school, college, etc.), you have to separate the soul from the group. This is done through love. I have been told many, many times that love is the only thing that is real; it is the most important thing of all. If you take an animal into your home, or give it love and attention, you give it an individuality and personality, and help it separate from the group soul so it can begin progression through the human part of the school.

Then you begin the human stage and this also takes a long time. Nothing valuable is ever learned instantly. It has to be a gradual process. When you become human you also have to be *everything*. Progressing from the most primitive human form upward to the most intelligent, you have to know what it is like to *be* everything. You have to be male and female many times. When I say that at my lectures some of the men become defensive. One shouted out, "What do you mean? I have always been a man!" Think about it! What would you learn if you had only been one sex throughout eternity? You wouldn't learn very much. You have to be balanced, and this can only be accomplished by experiencing both. This is one of the explanations I have found for homosexuality. The person was one sex through many lifetimes and it was decided (by the powers that be) that they now learn what it is like to be the opposite sex. The first time they attempt it, they may feel uncomfortable in the body. Some of my clients have said they feel like a woman trapped in a man's body. There is nothing unnatural about this if you understand it in this way. They have to learn balance and adjust to the new and different emotions and feelings. Anything is different the first time you attempt it. Some adjust easier than others, just like learning to ride a bike or ski or skate. Some take to it naturally and others have to really work at it.

Then as you progress through the human lessons, you have to experience everything before you can graduate. You have to be rich and poor. Remember, sometimes being rich can be a curse rather than being a blessing. It all depends upon the lesson involved. You have to live on every continent in the world, be every race and every religion before you complete the school. You have to experience both sides of every possible situation. You have to understand all of these ways of living, existing and thinking. The main concept behind reincarnation is learning not to judge or have prejudice. We are all here in the same school at different stages of development. We are all aiming for the same goal: learn our lessons, complete the school and graduate so we can return to God. If you are carrying prejudice towards any certain religion or race, guess what? If it is not resolved by the time you leave this life, you will have to return as the very thing you are prejudiced against! This is the way the law of karma works. What goes around comes around! I have seen it time and time again in my therapy work.

When I make these statements at my lectures, I usually see some people looking depressed. "You mean I have to do all of that?" Don't worry! I have come to the conclusion that when people start asking questions and want to learn more about these things, they have probably already gone through most of these lessons and are on their way to graduation. Remember many of these lessons can be worked out in one lifetime. I have found this in my work. Yet there are others who are caught in a rut, a pattern, repeating the same mistakes with the same people over and over again, and not progressing. At that rate it will be a while before they graduate: a slow learner!

Then, as explained in my last book and some of this book, it was necessary to ask for volunteers to come and help the Earth because the souls who had been here for so long were caught on the wheel of karma. They would never be able to help create the necessary changes for this dramatic time in our history. So the Three Waves were brought in and they were able to bypass the regular Earth school because they have never accumulated karma and were not stuck. They also have no intention of being stuck. It is rather like when a school brings in a guest teacher or a person specializing in a certain area of expertise to help the struggling students. That person does not have to remain and participate in the continuing courses and education of the group. They do their job and then can get out and go back to their real home. So they are only here on special assignment. A great number of these do not like it here and desire to return home. But, even though they are protected from accumulating "normal" karma, if they leave before their job is completed, then they may get caught on the "wheel" and have to return.

I have received and accumulated a great deal of information about these volunteers and their missions, but I was greatly surprised at during a recent session to discover another brave group. It seems there are many more types who have come here on special assignments that are also not recognized by the general public. They have given great contributions to Earth. Remember, everything seems to be about the raising of the consciousness of the people of Earth. We are entering a whole new world and our vibrations and frequencies must be raised in order to exist there. The old ways of violence, hate and fear are no longer useful in this new world. So it had to be dealt with. It has been a slow process that I now know has been taking place over many years (perhaps centuries). Something had to happen in order to change mankind's way of thinking. Because of the gift of free will and noninterference, "they" cannot just step in and take over (although I am sure they would like to). We have to make the changes in our ways of thinking by ourselves. And because we are so entrenched in negativity, prejudice and judgment, we had to be given examples.

These were special souls that had completed all of their lessons in the Earth school, but chose to come back to help the others who were struggling. Some souls come, not to learn, but to *teach*. Of course, most of the great thinkers immediately come to mind: Jesus, Buddha, Mohammed. They came at times when mankind was truly stuck on the wheel. Their assignments were to present new ways of thinking so we could progress. Of course, the answer always has been love, and that was what they were mainly teaching. But because their ideas were radical, they were often met with violence. It is a slow process to change mankind's thinking, and often violence and tragedy is the only way to get their attention. You have to "go for the jugular" to get noticed. The same has been true of any great thinker who has presented radical or revolutionary ideas.

Anytime the world was ready for a giant step forward in the raising of consciousness, many brave souls have taken on difficult assignments and entered into the game called "Earth." I have found these to be souls who have already completed the easy phases of the school and have become accomplished at handling some of the difficult ones. They have enough experience that they now want to be handed the hard assignments. Just like certain students who have become bored may be given a special assignment because they have proven they are ready for it. So down through time they have come in, in droves to try to raise the consciousness and help change people's thinking. To try and drive home the concept that there should be no prejudice because we are all One.

The Civil War brought attention to the unfairness of slavery. World War II and Hitler brought attention to what happens when prejudice goes so far as to try and extinguish an entire of race of people. The Women's Liberation Movement called attention to the plight of women. The Civil Rights Movement did the same for the black population. In each of these cases there was often violence as volunteers played out their roles as attackers, defenders and martyrs. Remember they agreed to these things before entering this life. The agreement was to call attention to the different issues, and if it meant that their life would be cut short, then that was part of the agreement. They had to change the mindset of the people, and that often has to be done slowly.

If we look back in history, we can see that in many cases this has worked. Much of the discrimination against women, blacks, Jews, etc. has been lessened. Most of the young people alive today do not know how different it was for these groups just a few decades ago.

THE ROLE OF HIV/AIDS IN
THE RAISING OF THE CONSCIOUSNESS

In addition to prejudice against races and religions, there have also been prejudices against people with certain types of diseases or illnesses or handicaps. Here again many of these people volunteered to take on these roles for the purpose of teaching. I have been told in my work that there are more souls in line for the handicapped bodies than the normal ones. When you really look at it, it makes perfect sense. It was said that the soul can pay back as much karma in one handicapped lifetime that would normally take ten lifetimes. Look at what they are learning by being in such a body. Look at what they are teaching their parents or caretakers. Look at what they are teaching everyone who sees them or comes in contact with them. How do you react when you see someone in a wheelchair or a mentally handicapped child? Everyone learns something from them. The depth of the lesson depends upon the growth and development of the soul. When I see someone like that, I think, "You really took on a hard one this time, didn't you?"

There have been many diseases down through history that have created a tremendous amount of fear and stigma. In many cases the victims have been treated as outcasts and shunned by society. The disease, leprosy, in the Bible is a perfect example. Even into modern times, people with this disease were isolated from others because of fear of contamination. This was also true of TB (Tuberculosis) in the early days before modern medicines were discovered to control it. These victims were shut away in sanitariums for the rest of their lives in order to isolate them from others. In all of these illnesses, fear has been the main motivator. Then in our own modern times we have the stigma of HIV and AIDS. When the disease first broke out in the 1980s, it was shrouded in fear. Much of this also goes back to the fear of the unknown. Fear is a very powerful

25

emotion that can paralyze a person's reasoning and judgment. With modern medicines the stigma is not as bad as it once was when the person was shunned and ostracized (especially by the Church). In my work I see many sufferers of these diseases, and my job is to help them the best that I can. When you understand the laws of reincarnation, you know you cannot judge or be prejudiced. If only the Church would teach this, we wouldn't have so many problems.

Of course, down through history there were valid reasons for isolation and shunning because of the very real fear of contagious diseases that killed many thousands of people. But conditions are not the same in modern times as they were in the past.

This brings me to the session that brought about this new way of thinking, and a different way of looking at these diseases.

Michael was the young man who volunteered to help me when I was conducting a class in Palm Springs, CA. in July, 2011. He had been very helpful driving us and making sure we had everything we needed while we were there. He told us he had been diagnosed with HIV and was on heavy medication. The medication was barely controlling it, and without it, he could die.

Michael said that his T-cell count was very low, and blood testing was the way the doctors were monitoring his progress. I knew about AIDS, but I didn't know about T-cells. After the session I thought I should do some research in order to clarify it for the readers. I hope any physicians out there will forgive me if I don't have it exactly correct. T-cells are produced by the thymus gland and are an important part of our immune system and the fighting of infections. In a healthy person the T-cell count is 500-1300. In an HIV infected person the thymus is under attack and decreases production of the T-cells. If the count drops below 200 they virtually have no immunity and are susceptible to any infectious disease. They have nothing left to fight it with. This is when it develops into AIDS because disease can overwhelm the body. It has no effective defense system left. I find it interesting that the thymus gland is located in the lower neck. In my work any symptom occurring in the mouth, teeth, jaw or throat (especially the thyroid) means the person is not speaking their truth. They are holding back for some reason, and are unable to really express their feelings.

When it came time to pick someone for the demonstration on the last day of the class, I asked Michael if he would be willing to do it. He wanted to have a session and knew there was no time for a private one. This would be the only way he could get one, but he was hesitant. He is a gentle, kind, young man, but also very private. He was worried about talking in front of the class and telling his story. This is always a problem with a demonstration. I say it is like being in a gold fish bowl, having all these strangers looking at you. He was most worried about criticism and judgment if he told about being gay and having HIV. I told him I didn't think it would be a problem because there is not as much stigma attached to the disease as there once was. Besides, all the people in the class were dealing with their own "stuff." He finally agreed because he really wanted to have a session. He need not have worried because when he began to tell about his life and problems, the class was very open and kind toward him. They were very sympathetic and truly wanted him to have help.

Even though he was nervous, he dropped immediately into a very deep trance when the session began. At first, he went into a small pond of water and saw himself as merely a consciousness that was part of the water. There were no creatures, and the water was still and quiet. He didn't have to do anything except just *be*. When I asked him why he chose to just be part of the water, he said, "For the 'aloneness.' For the

27

solitude. For the quiet. Just to be away from everything. I chose to do it." When I asked if something happened that made him want to be alone, he said it was to get away from all the chaos in the world he had been in. There was too much turmoil. He liked the solitude, but was becoming bored. "It's quiet. There's no activity, so you can't have both."

D: *Do you think you want to experience something else?*
M: I'm probably ready.
D: *Do you think you've learned everything you can by being in solitude?*
M: Not everything, but enough.

When I determined he was ready, I had him leave the water and move through time and space to something that was appropriate for him to see. He found himself in a shack out in the middle of a field. It had the feeling of being in the Old West. He was a young female dressed in an old dress and he knew she was desperately poor. There were hardly any material possessions in the shack, and it was also very hot. (Michael had said that in his present life he doesn't like the heat.) He said in a depressed voice, "You do what you can. It's a hard life. Sweat, suffer, anger ... I feel pregnant."

D: *Why did you come there?*
M: Sentence is the word. I think it was too much expectation.
D: *What do you mean?*
M: It's common place at times to not have very much, so accept what you have. More and more acceptance.

She lived there with her husband, who was also unhappy because he did field work, and there was no work to be had. He didn't know anything else. He couldn't farm the land. "Too dry. Too much heat ... too much sunshine ... not enough rain or water."

D: *Can't you leave and go somewhere else?*
M: There's no way to get there.
D: *You have no transportation. How do you get supplies?*
M: Walk. It's two hours to walk to town.
D: *How do you get supplies? Do you have money?*
M: No, no money.—I trade myself.—That's all I have.

The husband didn't know she was doing this. During the session I kept wondering about the husband. Didn't he wonder where the food was coming from if they didn't have any money? Apparently, he had decided to turn a blind eye as long as they had something to eat. Then she announced, "The baby's not his." She felt ashamed about what she was doing, but it was the only way they could survive. Then she got to the point that she was unable to walk so far to town to trade herself for food, and they were starving.

I moved her ahead to an important day to get away from the upsetting scene, but we found one even more upsetting. When we got there Michael began to sob, but he wisely chose to observe the scene rather than participate in it. Under the circumstances, this was the best way to report it. He emotionally told what was happening, "I'm watching. He found out. He's beating her up. He found out! He knows it's not his. He found out. He kept beating her, beating her, and beating her. It was all his 'self-pity.'"

D: *How did he find out the baby wasn't his?*
M: They told him. The men that she was with told him. She wouldn't be with them anymore. She got to a point where she had to stop. The other men took it out on her.—The baby's not his and he's beating her ... trying to beat the baby out of her. Too much blood loss.—She dies and the baby dies. They both die.
D: *What did the husband do when he found out he killed her?*
M: There was much emotion to start with. He dragged her out of the house. He didn't care enough to bury the body. He just left it out there to rot.

D: *What happened to him?*

M: There's nothing left ... nothing left for him. He didn't do anything. He's hungry. She provided for him. She couldn't provide for him anymore. He doesn't live much longer after that. He passed shortly after.

D: *How does she feel about all this, after she has died and left the body?*

M: She did what she could. She took all that anger and guilt with her. She feels nothing for her husband. She was already dead before he killed her ... inside. He destroyed her emotions and at a certain point, she gave up.

D: *She did everything she could in the circumstances. She had to survive. There was a reason for everything she did.*

I then had him float away from the terrible scene and leave the woman to find her own journey to the other side, and hopefully find peace. Because this was a class demonstration, there was not time to explore what happened on the spirit side. I called forth the SC so we could find some answers. Michael's conscious mind tried to interfere and keep it from happening because, I suspect, he was worried about what the answers would be. However, I am persistent and I was able to push the conscious mind out of the way. We had found a huge piece of the puzzle, now we wanted the rest. When the SC finally came through, I asked why it chose that life for Michael to see?

M: Acceptance ... acceptance. No shame ... no shame ... acceptance. No shame and acceptance of what he had to do in that life.

D: *That's a big lesson. How does that relate to his life now?*

M: As she was dying, the husband kept shouting and calling her a whore. No more shame ... not to shame. He was carrying it forward. It belongs there.

I talked a lot with the SC about leaving all of it in the past because it was not needed in the present life. That Michael was a good person and didn't need to carry any of that forward into his life now. This had caused back problems that had led to surgery, but had not alleviated the pain. This was part of the load he had carried from that life, and identified as shame in his present life. The SC took care of that.

Then it was time to bring up the subject of why he had created HIV in his life. "Why did that happen?"

M: It was part of the agreement ... participates. The agreement is part of the acceptance. Experience ... everybody's experience. The ones that have agreed to it.

D: *What experience?*

M: Of the disease.

D: *You mean he made an agreement to experience it?*

M: Yes. Also move the consciousness ... outside of it.

D: *How do you move consciousness by having AIDS?*

M: By the consciousness of the people around him. Accept it before it happens. Such a bigger concept. He agreed.

D: *Can you help us understand what this bigger concept is?*

M: Yes ... three more days.

D: *What do you mean?*

M: The concept ... the understanding ... it would take three days to explain the concept. There are so many aspects to it. Part of the agreement. He's already accepted this. He has to trust. Trust that that's part of it.

This was difficult to understand, but I was able to get the SC to agree to work on the HIV. The doctors were keeping count of the T-cells in his body. That was their measurement of the advancement of the disease. Michael's had reached an incredibly low count and he could die. The medication was to help raise the count of the cells. The SC said he had learned his lesson, so they would be able to work on raising the T-cell counts. He could still be part of this experiment or agreement, but they said his suffering was over. "No more shame. No more suffering. He has another road to follow." The healing would be gradual because the T-cells had to be increased, but it would definitely occur.

I wanted to know if there was anyone in that life that he knew now in his present life. The SC's answer was a surprise. The husband that killed him was his father in this lifetime. Michael's father had abandoned him and his mother right after he was born. He had lately come back into his life, but there was no closeness there. I thought that was a strange agreement because the father didn't stay around to raise him.

M: No. His job was to give him life again.

That made perfect sense. He had killed him, so he had to pay the karma back by giving him life, helping him to enter the world again. Then his job was over. This was very important that Michael know this. "Very good. Acceptance."

I had one more question. I wanted to know what that was all about at the beginning of the session where he was under the water as a consciousness. The SC surprised me again. "He was a rock." He had wanted the solitude, and I guess a rock is certainly quiet.

An interesting thing happened when I brought Michael back and he opened his eyes. He looked around at the class and said, "Where did all the people come from?" He seemed puzzled and I thought he was referring to the students sitting in their chairs. But he said later that as he was coming back to consciousness, he saw many people, beings, all around the bed. They were standing in the open space between the bed and the class. He knew they were definitely not members of the class. I guess spirits and guides of those present had assembled to watch, and he was able to see them before he became fully conscious.

When we discussed the session afterwards, the students were very kind to Michael. They are the ones that came to the conclusion of the purpose of this experiment. The one that the SC said would take three days to explain. It had to do with judgment. The people who volunteered to come back and experience (and possibly die from) AIDS, had agreed to come as a group to teach *judgment*. The class was stunned by the revelation. You could feel the energy move through the group as the entire room shifted. Of course! These people who contracted this disease were *not* victims. They were some of the advanced souls who had experienced most of the other life lessons, and had volunteered to come en masse to teach tolerance and lack of prejudice and judgment at this time in our world. It was an absolutely phenomenal revelation, and I thought how wonderful it would be if people could understand their sacrifice. Maybe this will teach us to look at other groups out there that are creating changes, and see what else they have to teach us.

A month or so later I received an email from Michael. "I got my blood work back from the doctor (I waited about 3 weeks after the session to have it taken). My T-cells went from 293 to 429 in the four months since my last test. The interesting thing is that when someone's T-cells tank like mine did 3 years ago, a jump of 100 points per year is considered good progress. I had almost a 140 point jump in four months."

So it appeared that the reason for the lesson was learned, and Michael was now on the road to healing.

Chapter 3

THE SPIRIT SIDE

I have been receiving information about the spirit side (where we go when we die) since 1968 when I first stumbled into reincarnation. In those days everything was new and startling, and it definitely challenged my belief system. By the 1980s I had received enough information from hundreds of clients that I wrote the book *Between Death and Life*. The amazing thing is that nothing has been contradicted. I am still receiving information and it continues to broaden my knowledge and view of this fascinating subject. No matter where I go in the world I receive the same information from my clients and the same pattern emerges. I will briefly try to summarize it here for those who have not read that book.

When a person dies (or exits the body), it is so easy. They say it is just like getting up from one chair and sitting down in another. The feeling of release is exhilarating. They look back at the body and say things like, "I'm so glad to be out of there. I'm not trapped anymore. Now I am free to go wherever I want." Normally there is always someone who comes to take the person where they are supposed to go. I call this person the "greeter." It may be a deceased relative or friend. Or it may be their guide or guardian angel. The important thing to know is that you are never alone when you cross over. There is always someone to show you where to go. You are also never alone during your life, but people don't understand that. When you are born there is always a guide (or guardian angel) assigned to you. They are with you your entire life and will be there at the end. There are several different places that you can go after you die. These are described in *Between Death and Life*, and will appear in the regressions included in this section.

You can only go to the level that your vibrations and frequencies are compatible with. Hopefully it will be a higher level, and you have not slipped backward to a lower level. It all depends on what you learned during that class in the Earth school.

Sometimes the soul is taken directly to the "resting place," especially if the death has been traumatic. This is a place of complete quiet with no colors or sounds. You will stay there as long as necessary before rejoining the wheel of karma. Eventually every soul goes before the board (or council) of elders and masters to have their life they just left evaluated. This is called a "life review." They go over all the things that you did and thought during that life, and you are graded on what was accomplished and what needs more work. There is no God sitting on a throne waiting to judge you and punish you. *You judge yourself.* And there is no harsher judge than you yourself. You decide what mistakes you made and what needs to be done to rectify them. It must be remembered that there is no pain associated with death. There is just the feeling of remorse. "I shouldn't have done that! I should have done something more with my life!"

Then the preparation to return begins. No matter how beautiful it is over there, how much you would love to stay there, you cannot as long as there are unpaid debts or karma. You have discussions with the souls you were involved with during the last life and make your plan. "We didn't do such a good job last time. Let's go back and do it again. This time you be the husband, I'll be the wife. Or, you be the mother, I'll be the child." You can switch roles around any way you want. Remember life is just a play, a game, an illusion. When we're involved in it it seems so real, but we are only wearing a costume, a suit of clothes, to play that certain part. You are the producer, director, actor and script writer of your own drama. And because the script is being written as the play proceeds it can be rewritten and changed at any time. You have complete control of what happens in your life, once you realize this.

So you make your plan of what you *hope* to accomplish when you return to the Earth school. You make your contracts with other people as to which roles they will play so you can get rid of any leftover karma. It seems so easy when you are on the spirit side and conferring with the masters, but when you get back on the wheel of karma because this is a planet of "free will," everyone else has their own plan and agenda, and often these will conflict. Plus to make it doubly hard, when you come back, the veil comes down and you forget. You forget your plan. You forget your contracts. You forget it is only a school. You forget it is only a game. Because it wouldn't be a test if you knew the answers. You have to stumble your way back on your own. You have to regain all the knowledge and information you forgot before you can graduate from this school. You can't jump from kindergarten to college. You have to take it grade by difficult grade until you finish and return to God (or the Source) and download all your experiences and lessons into the gigantic computer of His information. There is much, much more about all of this to be found in the other *Convoluted Universe* books. I am just condensing and paraphrasing so the reader will have a guideline to understand the sessions contained in this section. It will be noted though that there is no contradiction, only more information added to what I have already discovered.

<hr />

SO-CALLED "BAD" LIVES

In my work I have heard horror stories of the way people were raised (as I am sure many other therapists have). Their childhood was so bad I wondered how the person managed to become a functioning adult. It is to their credit that they did. It underscores the inhumanity that man is capable of doing to his fellow man. Of course, I know that the perpetrating party is accumulating heavy doses of karma that will take a long time to repay. But the client always asks, "Why did this happen to me?" They wonder whether they did something horrible in a past life that justified them being treated in that way.

I explain that in my work I have found that they agreed to it before coming into a life. This is always met with incredulity. "That doesn't make any sense! Why would I want to agree to live a life like that?" Remember everything is a lesson. It is arranged to see what we will learn from the situation. If we don't pass the test, learn the lesson, there is always the next time. It doesn't matter how long it takes to complete that grade, that lesson. You have all of eternity. But wouldn't you rather learn it quicker, than take forever? When you learn what you're supposed to learn you move on to the next lesson, which may or may not be easier. It may be more difficult, but at least it will be different.

Which brings us back to the original question: Why did we decide to choose such a horrible experience? I had two cases close together where the person had a horrible childhood. In one the parents were involved in Satanic rituals that included the children. The client eventually left home as soon as she could and wanted nothing to do with her mother ever again. The other children in the family were not so fortunate. The girls turned into drug addicts and prostitutes, and the boy turned to crime and ended up in prison. My client said that at an early age she knew she didn't want to be involved in all of this. For a young child she had a remarkable amount of sense, and instinctively knew how to combat what was happening. She psychically put a brick wall around herself so she would be separated from the insanity that raged around her. She moved away and made a life for herself with no help from her family, and she didn't want any contact with them. During the session I asked why she had such a childhood, and the SC said that she chose it (which I knew). And she learned a great lesson, how to survive and succeed without any help from anybody. So although she was lonely and felt deserted, she had chosen that lesson, and she had passed with flying colors, so it was now time to move on.

Another woman was raised in a terrible abusive family where her stepmother beat her every day. Naturally in these situations they get out of the home as soon as they can. The SC said this was needed to teach her how to survive, how to grow, how to be on her own. It had served a great purpose, even though she didn't understand it growing up. As a child she only knew that she was not happy.

Another woman had the same abusive pattern and we wanted to know if there was any karma with these people that was being paid back. I was surprised when it said there was not. There was also no past lives with the main characters. The SC said that it was agreed before coming in that certain people would be placed in the life along the way to test her. Some of these might have been their dearest friends while on the spirit side, and in other lifetimes. But they had agreed to play the part of the villain in this play. And we must agree that sometimes they play their parts very, very well.

I always ask people who have had bad experiences (and everyone has some negative things that happen in life. That's what life is all about), what did they learn from it? They will usually find something if they really look at it and see the effect on their life. If they say they did not learn anything from the experience, that it was just not fair. Then they will have to repeat it again (take the class over) and next time it may even be harder, until they understand what the lesson was that they chose to experience.

Of course, all of this has to be looked at with all emotions removed, as an observer.

Chapter 4

LIFE AS OTHER CREATURES

THE SEA CREATURE

This idea of living a past lifetime as another type of creature besides human may seem strange or improbable to those who have not pursued my work. But I have found numerous examples of this. These are reported in my other *Convoluted Universe* books. Before we complete the Earth school, we have to know what it is like to be everything. This means we have to experience life in every possible form. Humans are later in the class itinerary if we think in a linear progression.

This session was conducted as a class demonstration in San Diego in 2010. It was very confusing because from the beginning Carrie had no idea what she was or where she was. It took quite a while for us to establish that she was some type of sea creature living in the ocean. One thing that confused her was that from the beginning she kept feeling heavy as though she was full of water. This made her insist on going to the bathroom. We had barely begun so I didn't want that to disrupt the session so early, but my suggestions that she felt fine did not have any effect on her. So I had some members of the class guide her to the bathroom with her eyes closed. Upon her return she said she still felt heavy, as though she was full of water; she felt like a bubble. When I tried to have her distinguish a body, she was more confused. She felt light and could see gray muted colors. "It's cool ... I can feel, but I don't see a body. I don't see feet. I don't have arms. I don't have them! I don't see body."

Since this sometimes occurs when the person is a spirit, I tried to pursue that line of thinking. "Are you aware of anybody else around you?"

C: No ... no ... I'm here by myself ... just me. In this ... I don't know shape, but I know it's within something, but I don't know what it is. Like ... a bubble. I feel like I'm in a bubble. I feel like I'm inside something. Where ... where? What am I doing? I'm just ... I don't even know what I am. I'm just here.

D: *That's why you can't see outside?* (Yes) *You can't see through the bubble?*

C: No. It's muted. It's this gray color ... I'm not even aware of an end or something that would put me somewhere else outside.

She was so confused that I knew she could not understand it from that perspective. So I had her move outside of the bubble and look at it so she could better understand what was enclosing her. Then she suddenly exclaimed, "I'm in an egg. I'm in an egg!!" She was very shocked by this revelation. "It's that color. It's that gray. When you're in the inside you can't see, but when I'm on the outside I can see that I'm in an egg!"

D: *So that's why you don't have a body?*

C: Yes.—It looks like a bird egg.

D: *Let's see where the egg is. We can expand our viewpoint. Where is the egg sitting?*

C: Oh ... like in a cave. It's not like a bird nest or anything, but it's an egg ... I'm in an egg in a cave. (Baffled.) I don't know what I'm doing.

D: *All right. We can expand our perception and see more that way. Do you want to see what laid the egg?* (Yes) *Where did the egg come from?*

C: It's a bird. I don't know what kind of a bird, but I see blue.

D: *Do your best to describe it.*
C: Not feathers. They're more like very slick ... no feathers ... it's like webbed wings.
D: *Do you mean more like skin instead of feathers?* (Yes) *Can you tell how big it is?*
C: Big. Because it's a big egg.—The bird is black in the face but a very pretty blue. A kind of pointy face.

Only after the session did an idea occur to me. It was a sea creature, so maybe a manta ray? When I did research, they are black colored and definitely resemble a bird with large wings.

D: *At least you're in a safe place. Nothing can hurt the egg if you're in a cave.* (She began making strange sounds.) *What?*
C: (Whispering) Heavy ... heavy.
D: *All right. Let's move until it's time to come out of the egg. How do you get out of the egg? See yourself doing it.*
C: (She was making motions.) Got to get through to the outside ... to the outside. (She was making butting motions with her head.) Get out... takes a long time. I want out. Now I want out!

I condensed time to where she had finally gotten out of the shell. I said, "It was hard to get out. It made you work. What does your body look like now that you're out of the shell?"

C: Not much. Hmmm ... don't look like the other birds! I'm not blue. I'm kind of gray.—I've got a lot of work to do. I feel like I have to do something. I'm just laying here. I'm not doing nothing!—I'm hungry!

She said she was feeling heavy again, and as though she was full of water. I didn't want this to distract her, so I tried to keep her mind off it. "How do you get food?"

43

C: My mom ... my mom brings it to me, but I don't know what it is ... (I laughed.) I don't know what it is. Ugh ... mushy. (The students laughed.)

She became upset as she realized she had to go to the bathroom again. She said she felt full of water again. I tried suggestions, but the only solution was to allow the others to take her to the bathroom again in trance. Each time this happened I motioned to the students to keep quiet and let her pass between them. Then she would be led back to the bed with her eyes closed and we would continue. This was unusual that she had to go so many times, but it may have had to do with the newborn creature she was experiencing. "Okay. Let's move to where you are no longer that little creature that needs the food from the mama. We're going to move to where it is grown. When you're bigger, you don't stay in that cave, do you?

C: No. Water ... water ... I see water. I'm in water. I'm a bird underwater. There are others! There are others here now.
D: *Do they look like you?*
C: Some do. Some don't, but there are other creatures. Some have lots of arms. Some are really big. We're all kids. We're playing. We're in the water. That's why I feel water so much.
D: *Was the cave also in water?*
C: Yes. It was deep under something.
D: *But you play with the other ones?* (Yes) *Even though everybody looks different.*
C: That's okay.
D: *Do you like it there?* (Yes)

I moved her forward to an important day, even though I couldn't imagine what an important day would be for such an unusual creature. When she got to the important day, she began to cry. "My friend ... my friend. She was eaten. She is gone. Something ate her. Something took her. She's not here. They're all crying."

D: *So that's why you're sad. Was your friend a creature like you?*
C: No. She was what you call a "fish." She was real pretty.

I reassured her and sympathized with her. Then I moved her forward to another important day. She was laughing now instead of crying. "We're learning to go to the surface. A lot of us are doing this. Lots of us like me. There's a lot of us."

D: *Are you bigger now?*
C: Yes. I can go out of the water and go back in. You can see outside on top now. It's beautiful above the water. There are skies, sun. We've never seen this. This is all new for us. We've never seen sky. It's beautiful, and we keep diving. We go back in. We keep going in and out. Yep, some of us get it. Some of us don't.
D: *Some can't figure it out?* (Laugh)
C: Nope, but we've got to help each other. That's why we do it together. We have to help each other. That's very important. We don't leave anybody behind. And it's beautiful up there.
D: *That's very good. You're learning lessons.* (Yes)

I had her leave that scene and move forward again to another important day. "What's happening now or what do you see?"

C: Something on the water. Something not good. Everybody under the water is very upset ... very upset because something up there is not good. They're trying to move away from that.
D: *What does it look like?* (Pause) *Do your best to describe it.*

C: They're trying to catch the creatures under the water, but *they're* not under the water. They're on top of the water. They catch, but not like me ... I don't serve. They want the food. They're looking for food, and they're hurting the creatures. They're throwing some back over, hurting them. I'm trying to help them get away from the catch.

D: *How are you helping them?*

C: Just scooping ... scooping with my big ... I don't know if it's a wing ... my arm ... my wing ... I don't know. I'm just scooping, and steering them away from harm. I can't get everybody! But everybody's here trying to help ... everybody. Oh, go away! This isn't your home! This is *my* home. This is *our* home. There are creatures here.

I couldn't continue with this scene because I knew I had to watch the time. When I am doing a demonstration for a class I don't have as much time as I would in a normal session. So I had her leave it and move forward to the last day of her life and find out what happened to her. "I'm old. I'm just old. I'm not blue no more. (The students laughed.) Not blue ... about the color I was when I was born. Kind of gray."

D: *Are you still in the water or on top?*

C: I'm still under the water. I'm old. I don't move like I used to, but I have many, many friends. They're all here.

D: *You've all been together and always helped each other, didn't you?*

C: Yes, we did ... time for me to go. I'm old.

D: *You had a good life, didn't you?*

C: Yes, we did. They came. We had a good life.

I then moved her to when it was all over and she was out of the body and on the other side of it. She gave a deep breath of release. You could tell she was glad to be free of that body. I asked what she learned from that lifetime because every life has a lesson.

C: To help. To help each other. To be there. That was very important. Yes, I learned. I did help.

I knew that she would now move to the spirit side in her spirit body. I did not want to pursue that for the class. I knew I had to show them how to do the therapy. So I moved her away from it and called forth the SC. I asked why it picked that strange life for Carrie to see.

C: She needs to remember this. She needs to remember to help. Sometimes she forgets. She needs to remember.
D: *She does help people in her life now, doesn't she?*
C: Yes, she's done a lot of work, but sometimes she forgets that not everybody is where she is. And she needs to help them where they are. Not where *she* is, but where *they* are. Sometimes she forgets that they're not where she is. That's why we do what we do. She needs to relate to them at their level. This is important. She has to acclimate herself to where they are.
D: *That was a rather strange life. What kind of a being was she in that lifetime?*
C: Sea creatures ... her lesson was to learn to help there.
D: *It was a rather strange one. I wasn't expecting that.*
C: I don't think she was either. (We both laughed.) She knows she's been many things. She didn't know that one.—She saw that not everybody may look the same, but everybody needs help no matter where they are. And that's what we have to do, is help.

The SC proceeded to tell her about her purpose and what she was to do with her life. She had to go to the bathroom yet again, and this time the SC was chastising her also. It said it was trying to keep her comfortable, but she was nervous, so there was no choice but to let her get up again and be led to the bathroom. At least I thought the class was seeing how to do it if this were to arise during one of their sessions. "Oh, yes, we talk to her. She does this to herself. This is what she does. She gets nervous and you see she pees." The students laughed.

D: *And you'll be here when she comes back, so we can continue?*
C: We're not going anywhere. We're always here.
D: *It's a hassle, but it's just the physical body.*
C: Yes, it is a hassle.

After she returned and laid back down, "We did wait because we've got lots to tell ya. (Laugh) We told her! That's why she didn't drink her coffee this morning because she knew she was going to have to pee because she does this. When she gets nervous she pees. Now she feels good. No more distractions."

They continued and answered her questions and gave advice about Carrie's husband and his problems. Then on to the physical concerns. Before the session Carrie had a rather strange request. It was one I had never heard before and certainly one that I would never have thought to ask the SC, but I thought, "How am I to know what the SC is capable of, if I don't ask?" I have seen it do miraculous things, so who am I to judge? I have found that this technique is a growing, evolving thing that has a life of its own. So I am constantly learning new things that the SC can do. It appears there are no limitations.

Carrie said she had had breast cancer and the doctors had wanted to do a mastectomy. She did not want to do something so radical, so she found a doctor that was willing to go in and do a lumpectomy (the removal of just the tumor without removing the entire breast). It worked and she was considered cured. However, it left her with one breast smaller than the other one, and she found this embarrassing. She wore loose, flowing clothes to hide it. She had already done much soul searching and discovered the reason why she had developed the cancer, so she felt that was resolved. So her request was not for healing, but to see if the SC could somehow enlarge the small breast to make it comparable to the other one. I considered it an unusual request, but thought it would do no harm to try. During the interview part before the session this was all explained to the class, so everyone was eager to find out what would happen, if anything. If the SC didn't think it could be done, then I knew it would tell me.

So now I brought up the subject of the breast cancer, and asked if she was correct in what she thought was the cause of it. "Yes, she was very hurt by several people when she was little, but she was also very loved. And sometimes she thought about those that didn't love her, and manifested the tumor in the breast." This goes along with what I have found, that the breast represents nurturing. And the left side of the body means it related to something coming from her past. "She thought she wasn't loved, when in fact, she was very much loved."

D: *And she ended up having surgery?*
C: Yes. We steered her to that doctor. She had other opinions. They wanted to invade her body. Of course, you know, we don't like invasion of the body. That doctor was chosen because he would do the *least* invasion. She did what she did from the fear. She's all right now. She's past the big stuff. Now we just have to bonk her on the head. We have to stub her toes. We have to prick her finger or something. When we do that it's to get her to pay attention.
D: *But she's still having problems in that left breast area.*
C: She knows it's better. She knows it's healed.—It looks good. It appears good. There's still soreness there but it's healed. She doesn't need to take the pain medication any more. We think she just does it because it's a habit. She can go off it easily. We will make sure she does. She knows she'll be fine.
D: *Good. Well, she had another question. You might think it's a little strange, but she wants to ask you. When they did the surgery it reduced the size of the left breast, didn't*

it? (Yes) *She wanted to know, is there any way you can bring that back to where it is balanced with the other side? Is it possible for you to do that?*

C: (Pause) Hmmm. We can. Where she had the surgery, there is space there. We can put something in that space ... put tissue in that space.

D: *To build it up?* (Yes) *Okay, where are you going to get tissue from?*

C: She has plenty on her body. (The students all laughed. Carrie is a little overweight.) That won't be a problem. (Everyone thought this was amusing.)

D: *So you'll just move the tissue around?*

C: We will.

D: *You do wonderful things ... things the doctors can't do.*

C: Yes. She thought about the reconstructive stuff and said, no. We can do this for her because we're very happy she didn't do that.

Then the SC went about working on the breast. "I'm looking at the area. She has enough space there. We could put something there. Not a big deal to her."

D: *You know how humans are.* (Yes) *She is concerned with her body appearance.* (Yes) *And you're pulling the tissue from the other parts of the body and putting it into that space?* (Yes) *And then it will be even with the other side?* (Yes) *Will this take very long?*

C: No, it won't.

D: *Will she notice it?*

C: Yes ... yes, she will. She'll laugh. She'll notice ... she'll notice. (Everyone was laughing.)

I decided this was a good time to ask another question that had been bothering me. I knew the SC could talk to me and answer questions while it continued its work. I referred to another case that was also a demonstration for a class in Chicago. The woman was scheduled to have knee replacement surgery on both knees because the cartilage was completely eroded away and she was in extreme pain. "They" replaced cartilage where there was none and her knees were fine. Everyone at that class thought they had witnessed me performing a miracle, but I knew *I* didn't have anything to do with it. I am only the facilitator. The SC is the one that does the work. After that class I started using that tape as an example in my other classes. There has been much debate about where the SC got the cartilage. Since there is cartilage present in the body, did it transfer some from another part of the body? This would be similar to what was occurring to Carrie in this session. The SC remembered the case I was referring to. "Where did you get the new cartilage from?"

C: We can put things back from tissue that is already there. We can use tissue that is already in the area to work to replace that which is broken. However, it is never easy to replace something that is no longer there.
D: *But it can be done?* (Yes ... yes.) *I think it's important for the students to know this, isn't it?* (Yes ... yes.) *But it takes faith and trust and belief.* (Yes)

Because we didn't have as much time as usual to work on Carrie, the SC said it would continue during the night while she was sleeping. It said the breasts would be balanced and everything would be fine.

Parting message: Remain in the state of connection with us and we are always here. We hear you loudly and we hear you clearly. We are always here for you, and this you know. Never doubt. Never doubt. There are times you do and it's not necessary. We are always here ... always. We love you.

D: *And you'll always help anyone who needs help?*
C: Yes, that's all we want to do is help.—And you, Dolores. We love to talk to you. You do good work.

Naturally when Carrie awakened and stood up all eyes were directed toward her breasts, and there was much laughter among the students. Carrie seemed embarrassed, but when she looked down at them she had to admit that something had changed; they appeared to be more balanced again. So it was a lesson for me, too. Never underestimate what the SC is capable of.

¢— ... •◆≽≡)—•✕•— —•✕•—◆≼≼◆•• • •— ⌐

LIFE AS AN ANT

When John first went into the scene, he couldn't figure out where he was. He was very confused, and his descriptions were confusing me, also. All he could see was thick brown fluid. "It's everywhere. It's like being under the ocean ... an ocean of brown. There's nothing else." I wondered if he was in the ocean. This has happened before, but it has not been described as being thick and brown. "It's like liquid chocolate. Earth came to mind ... rocks. It's very big ... very expansive. It's all that I can see." When something like this happens, all I can do is keep asking questions until we figure out what is going on. "Now it's like I'm in an air bubble. Like an air pocket bubble. I'm surrounded by it. That's what it looks like. This brown fluid is going around me, and I'm inside an air pocket."

I asked how he perceived himself, his body. He was surprised when he saw that he was some type of insect. "Strange ... like a bug ... like a grasshopper ... a bug. I have long feet, maybe four and two upper feet or arms that are like balls."

This did not bother me because I have had many clients go to past lives where they were insects, plants, animals, and even rocks. This is explored in my other books. It doesn't matter because everything has consciousness and contains a bit of the divine spark of life. I always explore it the same way I explore so-called "normal" past lives because the SC chose it for a reason. There must be information that the client needs to know to relate to the present lifetime. I never try to judge what "they" will do. They can see the bigger picture and always provide the scenes for a reason.

D: *Like appendages?*
J: Yes. I would say I am brown or black. Maybe an ant ... ant, that feels right.—Maybe it's brown water.—Yes, now I'm on a rock and it's going over me. Maybe there's a leaf above me, and the water is going above the leaf.
D: *So you don't feel like you're in the water?*
J: No. No drowning ... no. I'm waiting for it to pass, and then move on. I think I'm on my way back home. And I got caught in the rain.
D: *It came on unexpected?*
J: I guess. It just happens.

I condensed time till he had arrived at his home and asked him to describe it. "It's a nest ... maybe in an old tree. My friends, family or whoever are happy to see I'm back."

D: *Do you all live together in this nest?*
J: Yes. We work together.
D: *Like a colony?* (Yes) *Is it a big nest?*
J: No, it's fairly small. It is inside of a log that is lying flat on the ground, and it's rotten through the center. And you just walk up in it. It was a good place for a nest. We found it and then we built. We used wood fibers in the log, and anything that we could find outside in the forest; trees, leaves.
D: *Do you have a part that is just yours, or do you all live together?*
J: I think we share. There's not a place for each one of us. It's all ours together.
D: *A while ago you said "family." Do you have families?*

J: I feel like I'm one and don't have a family. I am one individual. I feel male.
D: *But you all work together and that's good, isn't it?* (Yes)

I wanted to know what his job was, what he did with most of his time. "Search, forage, search, forage, food."

D: *Do you do it alone or with others?*
J: I see just myself right now.
D: *Where are you looking for food?*
J: Under leaves, in the dark, sometimes up in the trees.
D: *What do you eat?*
J: It's just vegetables, plants. I don't see animals or other insects. Maybe leaves.
D: *Do you bring that back to the nest?*
J: Yes, and share with others.
D: *Do you like it there?*
J: I feel like I belong, and I am contributing and doing something that is needed. So, yes, I feel good about that.

I then moved him forward to an important day. It would be interesting to see what would be important to an ant. "It looks like the log has gotten washed off, and I'm all alone. I guess the water came up, and it took the nest and everything. It floated off.—And I'm all alone. I'm standing a few feet from where the log used to be ... the home. I know it was washed off. And I'm just wondering, what am I going to do now?"

D: *Maybe the others were all inside the log, in the nest?*
J: Yes. They may be okay.—I don't know what to do.—I can try to look for them. I just don't know what to do. I can try to start over.
D: *Is this your first time to be alone?* (Yes) *You have always been a part of a group?*
J: Yes, and that felt good.—I think I'll try and find them.
D: *Rather than start over?*

J: Yes. I'm going to look for them. I'll head in the direction the log washed off.—I'm going over leaves and dirt, and I think I see the log. It looks like it. Hmm, I don't see anybody there.

D: *Is it still in the water or what?*

J: No, it's up on the ground ... it's dry. It got washed up ... and it got set down.—There's one over there and I don't recognize him. Maybe the group was bigger than I thought. I just don't know him. Others are out foraging. I don't know if they are lost or not.

D: *Maybe some of them died when it was in the water?*

J: It looks dry inside. I think the others might have been out when the log floated off. So they don't have a home to go back to, unless they can find it.—So I'm going to go back from where I came. See if I can find the others.

D: *So you can guide them?*

J: Yes. I go back to where I was. They're starting to gather, and I take them back to where the log was and show them where it's gone to. I was relieved to find them. They had wondered what had happened to their home and why. They came out of the woods and there was no home to go to.

D: *Yes, the same way you felt.*

J: And so now they are relieved to be able to find their home, but it's in a different place. This has happened before.—And we're happy to come home, and I feel important that I was able to help people to find their way back home.

D: *So you had an important part to play.* (Yes)

When I moved him forward again to another important day all he could see was dark. He could not continue the story. "You're not in the nest anymore?"

J: No, I don't think so. I feel separated from the rest.

When this happens I know that the subject has died, and there is nothing more to see. This is always my answer to skeptics who think the person is inventing these lives. If they were making it up, he had a good story going, why didn't he continue it? The answer is that they never do. If the life is over, there is nothing more to see. I have seen this happen many times. They can't fantasize. When this happens I always return them to the last scene that was solid. In this case it was when they had found the log nest again. When that was established, then I moved him forward to the last day of his life, so we could find out what happened to him. "What do you see?"

J: I'm out foraging and I just ... no energy ... not a lot to give.

D: *Something happened to you?*

J: No. Just kind of stop working.

D: *When you stop working, what happens?*

J: It's like I go to sleep. Just lay down.—I will miss my friends, but they will carry on without me.

D: *So what happens after you lay down?*

J: It looks like a dark waterfall or something. I'm supposed to go up.

D: *Are you out of the body now?*

J: I would have to be, yes. The body is ... not needed.

D: *Can you see your body?*

J: Yes. It looks like an ant.

D: *Just lying there?* (Yes) *So now you see something like a vertical waterfall?*

J: Yes ... a waterfall or ... lines of something ... falling down. I'm supposed to go up in that general direction. I don't have to go up the waterfall, but I can go up next to it in the air.

D: *Does that feel good to be out of the body?*

J: It doesn't matter. It really doesn't make any difference.— Now I see a cloud. And some of the others are before me, and we're happy to see each other. Still look like an ant. They all look like ants.

D: *But they're happy that you got up there?* (Yes, yes, yes.) *Is there any place you have to go now?*

J: I guess we're waiting to be called. We wait there together. Then we're going to go up further. It's kind of a stopping area ... a waiting area.—Someone calls. We know when to go.

D: *Then what happens?*

J: It's like a judgment or a review ... a life review or something.

I have conducted enough of these regressions to know that when the person dies they have to go before a board or council to have a life review. It apparently doesn't matter what shape or form that life took. But I found this amusing. What would the life review of an ant be like?

D: *Is somebody there asking you questions?*

J: More like a guide. Somebody there to answer questions or help you.

D: *What does he look like?*

J: I see human. Gray hair, gray bearded man. We're supposed to discuss what I've learned. How did you do? What did you do?—I'm saying I don't understand what I'm supposed to have learned. Hmm, family, togetherness, being a part of something bigger, sacrifice. He said I did well.

D: *Those are good things. You learned those lessons?* (Yes) *What's going to happen now?*

J: I am going to rest for a while, maybe play. Yes, I have some time off. Rest, play. Hmm ... to go explore. Go out in space and just kind of fly around. You're free until you're called. It looks like I'm out in space right now. Mostly it's dark. Some stars ... some planets.—I am wondering where I'm going to go next. If I don't choose to do something, then I'm going to become bored. I'm

looking to see if there's somebody else out there I can
have fun with.—I see someone. I think it's someone I've
known before.

D: *So you're just going to float around out there together and
explore things?*

J: That sounds boring.—I think we're going to catch up on
what he's been doing and what I've been doing. And I tell
him what I've been doing, and he is listening. He's been
out exploring the planets.—I think we're going to come
back to a lifetime together. Yes, let's do something in this
lifetime together.—They're not ready for us yet.

D: *But you're making plans.*

J: Yes. Let's get together in this life.

D: *Do you think the people who call you will agree to that?
(Yes) So you have something to say about where you go
and what you do? (Yes) And who you do it with? (Yes)
All right. Let's move ahead to when they call you.—Have
they called you?*

J: Yes. I see a baby. I'm guessing that I'm being birthed.

D: *Before that, where did you go when they called you?*

J: There was a group or a council, and we talked about being
together in this lifetime. And they said okay, and talked
about what we're going to work on.

D: *Did they say it was okay to be a human now? (Yes) You
can jump from one species to the next?*

J: I had to learn something in the last one, so that's why I
had to do that.

D: *So it doesn't make any difference? There's no order you
have to go in?*

J: Not if there's a lesson to be learned.

D: *Did they give you any advice? Is there anything you are
supposed to be doing or looking for in the next life?*

J: I'm supposed to take care of him ... look out for him. I'm
supposed to learn something from him ... love, getting
freedom. I have to learn patience.

D: *Do they help you with your plan?*

J: I feel like we know where each other has areas to work on and so we come to an agreement to meet up later in life.

I decided to leave that and call forth the SC. "Why did you choose that lifetime where he was the insect, the ant, for John to see?"

J: The feeling of being a part of a group and making important contributions. This is what he needs *this* time. To feel like he's making important contributions and being a part of a family. That's what he's missing. He's going to have to find a group or interest and get involved with that, whether it be with gardening or meditation. Feeling togetherness. He will see that he is more of a family.

John was suffering from depression and was on medication. The SC did not like this. "It's not good for the body or the mind, either one. It was caused by a lack of belief in oneself in the most difficult situations. Didn't quite pull through on that ... not much we could do."

D: *You couldn't help him from the other side?*
J: No, he wouldn't take the help ... too stubborn.
D: *We want to get him out of this depression, don't we?*
J: He just has to ask.
D: *Go ahead and ask him and see if he has your permission to help him.*
J: Yes, that would be nice. Yes, he agrees.
D: *What are you going to do to help him?*
J: It's going to be a process. He will have to ask for help when he needs it and a process for him to get out of it.
D: *I know sometimes you can do instant healing, but this is different?*
J: The process would be better for him. The learning process he can use later on. He will feel lighter, laugh

more, easier going, relax. He will see changes over time if he looks at himself.

D: *What do you think about the medication? Is it helping or not?*

J: It could be a crutch right now ... a crutch. Over time he won't need it, but he needs the crutch right now to feel confident. The process will build confidence. He's got to work through the process. If only he'll start meditating again.

D: *How did he allow himself to get into that depression in the first place?*

J: Isolated ... nobody to balance his thoughts with ... nobody to stop his negative thinking, so it just fed upon itself.

D: *He didn't have anyone he could confide in?*

J: No ... didn't want to.

There were several personal questions. The next one is the eternal one: Purpose.

J: To help. To help others and not to be judgmental, and accept people for how they are. If he sees somebody that needs help, ask and that's it. See a need ... fill it.

D: *And this will help with the depression.*

J: And the confidence, yes.

The SC then checked out the body for physical problems. There was some damage done to the lungs because of his smoking. However, he did not want to stop, so there was nothing we could do about that because we cannot go against anyone's free will. "They" did agree to work on some moles that John had on his chest that could be precancerous. John was afraid that his life was going to end very soon. (But part of this was due to the depression.) The SC said it could. It was possible. But I knew if he got out of it before fulfilling his mission that he would only have to start all over again. The SC said, "That is not ideal."

Parting message: Start meditation. Very important ... get back on it. Then we can communicate, and he will evolve, and yes, it raises vibrations. And exercise. This will build up his heart and improve his mood.

THE BIG BIRD

I had another client (Rachel) go to a past life as a large bird. The life was mundane as the bird went through various adventures, including one where he was attacked by another bird for venturing into its territory. When it died lying on the forest floor looking up at the sky, it saw a large glowing white bird coming to assist it to the spirit side. So it seems the "greeter" can take many forms according to the life experienced. It will be something that the departing spirit can identify with and feel comfortable with. When she looked back to see her body, she saw a dark bird lying on the ground. Now that she was out of the body I knew she could see the entire life from a different perspective. "Every life has a purpose. Every life has a lesson. What do you think you learned from that life?"

R: It is okay to enjoy being alone and doing things with nature. It was a peaceful life.
D: *What do you think the purpose of that life was?*
R: Not to be afraid to be alone. It was nice to help others that needed help. That love is always there wherever you're at. And life isn't painful, whether you get hurt or die; there's no pain. Love is always there because that bird is somehow a form of love. It's like he's kind of peeking through space and time and the sky, and he's born of the light.
D: *What are you going to do now that you're out of the body?*

R: I think I'm just resting.

I then had her float away from the bird and called forth the SC. The first question I always ask is why it showed her that particular lifetime.

R: She needs to spread her wings. (That was a very good metaphor for representing that.) Be yourself and not be afraid to be who she is. She's a child of God and she's here to represent *Him* in her own special way, in her own little spark that she carries. And only she can do that. And if she doesn't spread her wings and be herself, she's not expressing God. And He put her here for her purpose.

This, of course, brought up the eternal question, "What is her purpose?"

R: Love. She does give everyone love and she does love everyone. She has a lot of love, and she receives a lot of love. But she doesn't trust herself. She's like "on hold." She's holding herself back. That's not good for her health. She needs to be able to verbalize. She has to express.—She's tried many things and failed and she has that fear of failure. She has to "try again." She is waiting for something to happen, but she needs to realize that *she* has to make it happen.

The procrastination had affected her health. I focused on that. She had a growth on her spine and, of course, the doctors were wanting to operate. Her problems with her back and neck were because she felt like she was carrying more than her weight. The SC removed it instantly. "Its time has passed. There's no need for it." She had also had breast cancer, and had surgery. The SC told us the cause, "She missed her children. They've all moved out and gone. She had nothing to nurture. She never wanted children, but when she had, them she just loved them so much." It was a shame that Rachel couldn't have known this before having the surgery, but, of course, we never know what our bodies are trying to tell us. There would now be no more problems with cancer.

Her next physical question was about sex. She had pain and discomfort in that part of her body during intercourse. The SC gave an unusual answer. It was caused by the excessive treatments the doctors had given Rachel after the breast surgery. They had given her chemotherapy which brought on early menopause, which was hard for her system to adapt to. She was still taking some in pill form. They were also giving her regular MRIs which were not needed. Their overcautiousness had caused damage to that part of her body. The SC said, "She still goes for some treatments. It's not chemo but it is a chemical on her bones. She doesn't need to have them. She was afraid that it would come back if she didn't let the doctors do these things."

D: *There's the fear again.* (Yes) *That's what is causing the problems.*

R: She can stop with that so her body can flush and heal on its own, and not fight those pills and injections that she's been getting. She should stop all of these medications. The cancer will never come back. There was never anything to be afraid of.

It was suggested that she take a job that would be working with children, then she would not miss her own so much.

Parting message: Be kind to yourself ... not so hard and judgmental on yourself. Be patient. Get going. I will always be here to help her. Her fear is gone and just to enjoy life.

AN ELEMENTAL SPIRIT

I was in Santa Fe to teach my class at the College of Northwest New Mexico. Before the class began, I stayed with Paula at her guest house in the hills outside of Santa Fe, where I was seeing clients. Very secluded and quiet. Bobbie had many physical problems, but mostly was suffering from depression. She had no energy, seemed tired and unhappy, and really wanted to die. She was only in her 40s, but looked and acted much older. She was totally worn out.

I usually use a method in which I have my client descend from a cloud into a past life.

When Bobbie came off the cloud, she was in the country and saw men in metal armor, chain link suits, holding spears. She saw one battalion riding on horses going to war, helmets, and eagle crests on their uniforms. She was in a clearing in the woods, between trees, watching the army go by.

This went from the normal to the strange when I asked about her body. "I'm shimmering, like a fairy being. I'm made of golden light. I'm giggly and sweet. There are sparkles of light on my neck and my wrists. I'm not part of the human world. I have no connection to the army people. It's all kind of funny to me. They don't see me. They're very focused. They have somewhere to go.—I'm very happy here in the woods, and I connect with the spirits. I live in the spirit world in the woods, but it's only one part of me. There's another part of me that belongs up there in the clouds. There are many invisible spirit beings that come and go. I feel them everywhere. People see them as fireflies, but they're not. They're spirit beings with a very orderly existence. I'm more visible than they are. You can see me as a shimmering kind of human."

D: *Is this your normal way of appearing?*
B: No, it's just a disguise.
D: *Why did you take on this form at this time?*
B: Because they sent me.
D: *Who sent you?*
B: The place beyond the clouds. There's a white world there and they asked me to go.
D: *Is that your home?*
B: I think I was sent on a mission and I'm not allowed to go back, so I'm not sure where home is. It feels like home is higher up, but now I can't feel that because I'm down here and I have to do something.
D: *Who were the ones who sent you?*
B: They look like fire beings that emerge from the cloud. There's some kind of council or trinity. Every now and then, faces appear out of the fire.
D: *So it's not physical then. Why did they send you? You said it was some kind of a mission.*
B: The image I get is as though one of those spirit beings put me out in a basket as a baby. She's a kind, loving person, who couldn't keep me there. The lady of the white place had to create an offspring that would connect with Earth. I'm a part of that lady and I'm doing exploration. I'm linking up with these fairy beings as a way to be invisible and to move around in this human world. I feel better being only part human, where I can be half light and half human—but more light because then I stay connected to the light place.
D: *You said you weren't allowed to go back?*
B: Not now. I have to do something. I've just started. It's kind of new. I'm playing. I just discovered the woods filled with cute animals who get along with spirits, and we're having fun. It's also a way to get closer to the humans.
D: *It's all right to play and experiment. We're allowed to do that before we become solid. Or do you want to become solid?*

B: I don't think so.
D: *What's your mission about?*
B: I know I have to go further into the village where the people are.
D: *But you don't know what the work is?*
B: Do you want me to ask?
D: *If you want to. Maybe they'll tell you before you get too separated from them.*
B: There's a lot of trouble going on—war. The place I'm from doesn't understand war, and I'm supposed to hang out for a while to help uplift the energy. The people in the villages are really despondent and they don't have any hope. Wherever I go, the golden light follows me and I'm supposed to spread it around so that the depressed people can remember how to connect with it. It will spark their minds so they'll be able to group together and think of ways to solve their problems. Right now, they feel defeated and they're not solving anything. I'm a type of hope bearer.
D: *Will they be able to see you?*
B: No. They'll feel the difference. It's like being around fairy dust. It raises their frequency and then the white group can lend their support. It's easy. I just have to be myself. I stay playful. That is my work. Just being myself and spreading energy around.
D: *Have you done this before?*
B: It looks really new because everybody seems inexperienced at this. It looks like a first try.
D: *Have you ever been physical?*
B: I lived in Egypt as a female, but I was not just human. I was part star being and part human. I was definitely more human than this fairy type life. I was in a kind of priestess world. I definitely was a full human being, but my energy doesn't feel fleshy. It feels really tall. That mission was much more serious. That was a really important time. The star energy had descended and mixed with humans

for a long time leading up to that life. It was how things were. I was part of many beings who were like that.

D: *They were evolving, experimenting and playing.*

B: No, it didn't feel like that. It felt as though Earth and the Star Galaxy were doing serious stuff. It was an important life. The fate of the world was going to change. There were a lot of dark clouds, a lot of big decisions, a lot of higher mind. It was really important to say and do the right thing because the consequences could be huge.

D: *It was important for you to be there at that time.*

B: Yes, but not because I was something special; it's because it was important for everyone.

D: *Did you do your job at that time?*

B: I don't look very happy. I think I was really stressed because the consequences were so huge. Those of us who were part of the star beings—not everyone had become part star being—had a responsibility as to how we were going to lead everyone else.

D: *It sounds very serious.*

B: It also didn't feel as though there was a lot of love present. It didn't feel bad, but it definitely felt more like a mental society.

D: *As you are remembering that life, do you think you accomplished what you were supposed to do?*

B: It's saying that we dissolved. It didn't move forward, but it wasn't painful. It was a lot of hard work, and it lasted a long time, and involved a lot of dedication, but it didn't continue. We dissolved in a good way.—But now I'm in the mischievous life. I'm in the woods and smelling the big huge flowers. I'm having so much fun. I'm mesmerized and looking inside the flower. Everything talks. It's filled with golden light coming out of it. Everything seems so funny to me.

D: *In your mission, you said you were supposed to go talk to the people or something.*

B: Oh, I guess I'm not in a hurry to go. Do you want me to go?

She was having so much fun that she was hesitant to move on with her mission. But then she did go into the village and reported what she was seeing.

B: A very plain life with many plain people. A lot of rats. I move around in the night and go through the streets, looking like a ghost, even though I'm not one. There's a lot of fear in the air all day, which is created by people's negative thoughts. It forms in dark pockets, which I clear up at night so that people can think more clearly the next day.

D: *And they won't feel the fear as strongly the next day.*

B: Right. It won't even be there because I will have removed it. The death around them creates a lot of fear. I am an elemental being and I have this job.

D: *Let's move ahead and see if anything important happens.*

B: There is a bloody battle scene in the countryside near the woods where I first emerged. The thing that's so new for me is seeing blood because I don't really understand that. I have never seen it before. At first I think I'm seeing pretty red flowers, and then I realize that it's people's stomachs opening up. From a distance it doesn't bother me, but as I get closer it's all pretty ugly.

D: *Do you have to do anything there during the battle?*

B: Not really. I'm more of an observer. I'm allowed to go home now. I'm feeling nauseous and I don't want to stick around. I don't have to.

D: *Is home the white world?* (Yes) *What's it like?*

B: The lady takes me back. It's like a very ordered society. There are many hallways. It's very silent. People speak with their minds. It seems as though everybody works and moves about effortlessly. Some work in cubicles, others at tables. Everyone is very free and clocks in and out as they please. There are some extraterrestrials sitting at a table working. We're all researchers of sort.

D: *What is your job?*

B: I am connected with those who are part of the council, but I am one of the younger people. I'm not part of the big decisions. I'm a bit on the fringe. But still, I'm allowed in the council chambers. I have more freedom than those who work at a table. I seem to be a sort of child to the council members. I'm still learning, but I understand the energy of it all. I'm very comfortable. It's all familiar— it's definitely home. Nothing requires explanations. I know where everything is. I'm not an elder, but I'm very intelligent.

D: *Are you still shimmering?*

B: No. I'm now one of the light people. I have a lot of spare time, and I spend a lot of time talking to the stars. This is some kind of galaxy, I guess. While everybody is busy and I haven't been given my full assignment yet, I sit around and wonder what else there is. I don't know that I want to leave. What we do is very orderly—not that I have a problem with that. But I'm aware that there's something else, and I'm asking the heavens if I should participate in something else. It's almost like you can be in your regular world and go to sleep one night and wake up somewhere else? It's a bit like that—changing realities.

D: *Are you talking about being in two places at once?*

B: I don't like this feeling of being in between. I feel weird and split. I don't know if it was right for me to think outside my group because they're so good and they're so loving, and we all trained for so many years and we do good work. I don't know if it's wrong to want something else.

D: *I think it's just curiosity.*

B: But I don't know if curiosity is wrong.

D: *What do they say?*

B: They don't really know about it. It's just happening between me and the heavens.

D: *So you're not being told by the council?*

B: No. This is just what I do in my spare time. I have thoughts about what else goes on in other realities.

D: *Are you aware of a physical body that you will have in the future called "Bobbie"?*

B: That same person is connected to the white world.

D: *It's so beautiful over there—why would you want to leave?*

B: It's more like I was up at night and wondering and then it's as though the wondering made me go to sleep and wake up somewhere else. As if by wondering about something, you start living it. But there's a part of me that doesn't want to get in trouble, that doesn't want complications, that doesn't want to do things outside of the intelligence of our society.—So I don't know how it happened.

D: *Isn't there someone you can ask about it? They know everything, don't they? They probably know what you're doing even if you don't tell them.*

B: That's true. I never thought about that. I'm going to the lady who is some kind of elder.—She's saying that in our society everyone has free will, but with free will there's a lot of responsibility. I shouldn't think in right or wrong terms because that doesn't work. And she's saying that part of me was aware of responsibility at an earlier age than what would have been appropriate. That created a longing because it's as if I was ready for responsibility before the time that was right in my society to take it on. She's saying that I needed the experience to fulfill the place inside of me that became aware of responsibility.

D: *So in that way, it's all right to enter a physical body?*

B: Well, I haven't seen it as that yet. There's a part of me that doesn't know what it's getting into. I'm still asking for permission, but she says it's not about permission. It's about what we create, and that I've already created this and so, it's just what is.

D: *So once you create it and decide to do it, you have to go through with it?*

B: Yes, and you have to fulfill your creation.

D: *Did you enter the physical body known as Bobbie as a baby?*

B: It seems like I had other human lives before.

D: *I don't think there's anything wrong with that. You're always curious and wanting to learn. What do you think about being in the body of Bobbie?*

B: I like her. She feels like she stayed connected to the purposes here—to the elders, to the light and to the work. And she's still orderly. So that's easy.

D: *But why did Bobbie have so many problems as a young child in her physical body? Is that anything connected with you?*

B: Well, in some sense, I think it's connected to part of the fear that I felt at first about questioning if I had done the right thing about opening up to unknown worlds. I think I've carried that fear. The lady reassured me that it wasn't wrong, but for some reason there was a fearful and queasy feeling about the unknown.

D: *About being disobedient.*

B: No, it's not about being disobedient. It was just fear of what can happen or what can go wrong in the unknown, and if you can get back home safely and if you lose what you had. Because that society doesn't go by right and wrong, so it's not disobedient.

D: But once you've created this and you've entered the physical body, you're more or less assigned or obligated, aren't you?

B: Well, I think I created it half-heartedly. It was more like the desire sprang out of me, but it's not that my full heart was in it. There was a lot of curiosity.

D: *But you hadn't had a lot of experience to know what could happen.*

B: That's it. I was still quite innocent. I hadn't, for example, formed bonds with any council member yet. And there's not really any family there, so you're just kind of on your own. In that society it's fine to grow up on your own, but you only really become mature once you've started taking on roles in the councils.

D: *You hadn't gotten that far.*

B: That's it. I knew the energy of it because my parents were there and I was next in line for it.

D: *But you decided to bypass that.*

B: Well, I guess. It's more like it happened. It wasn't like a rebelliousness. It was like the opening was there. So it's a weird thing.

D: *But now that you're in the body of Bobbie you're going to go through it. Why was there all that fear and all those physical problems when she was young?*

B: It looks connected to the incarnations before. They started out okay, but then they began to get hard, and by the time we got to Bobbie, it got really hard. It's like I ran out of steam. The part of me that had that slight hesitation or fear at the beginning caught up with me. I had about three and a half really good, solid lives as a human because I was completely carrying the energy of the white place. This one is the really bad one, but the one before was half bad. It started good and then it went bad at the end. So this one didn't have a chance. I don't know why I didn't go back. I don't know why I stayed this long.

D: *Well, you're still learning something.*

B: But there's free will in the other place. You're allowed to come and go.

D: *Was that why she had all those nightmares all the time? Is that still your insecurity?*

B: It's connected to the life before. It all started going bad when I ran out of energy. I stopped being the light being and then, it's like I had no skin. I didn't have what it took to be a human. I was already halfway through that one. But I keep wondering why I didn't go back.

D: *Maybe we can find out. But did the uncertainty and insecurity cause physical problems in the body of Bobbie?*

B: It's all linked to the past life. It didn't stand a chance in this one because it all happened in the other.

I encouraged her to explain about the other lifetime.

B: It's connected with what I saw on that battlefield: blood and guts in the stomach. For some reason, that image is coming up.

D: *Is it a continuation?*

B: Something similar. Yes, it's a continuation, the lesson just continues. I can only describe it as an image of light, which equals health, safety and wholeness. And then the light just ran out. As soon as the light petered out, there was just blood and guts without skin. It all turned into a disease, eaten by vermin. It looks like a disgusting dead piece of flesh.

I gave suggestions that she would not continue to carry that image. They said that all of that was still there with Bobbie as a child. I thought maybe she came back into the body too quickly because I know that often the spirit is sent to a resting place to erase things like that so it will not affect the next lifetime. Apparently she came back too quickly, before the memories had been erased.

B: Maybe because there was no light left to come in with.

D: *You should have gone back to get recharged.*

B: I know. I know! Why didn't I do that?

She had chosen her present family because they were connected to that other life. I gave suggestions about releasing all of this.

B: Shall we change it? Can we bring some light now into Bobbie's body? Do you want me to go talk to the society?

D: *Go and talk to them and tell them you made some mistakes along the way and ask them how you can fix things. As long as you're living in the body of Bobbie we want this body to be happy, with no problems.*

73

B: Well, the lady is really happy to see me. She's saying, "What took you so long?" I got stuck in adventures. She's like a mother to me. She knew things were getting bad and she wondered why I didn't come back sooner. They're all so loving. Now the council is out of their chambers and they're all here to talk to me. The lady is giving me a lot of comfort. She can tell I'm burnt out. She's holding me and giving me a recharge. She has great energy. I hadn't gotten so far out that I had forgotten what it was like to feel normal again. – It's as though all of my cells are dropping what doesn't work. It feels so normal. It starts at the feet.

Bobbie was really feeling the recharging and how it was affecting her body.

B: It's mostly emotional. I became so afraid, like a kid that gets lost in the mall. She's putting me inside her, and as I'm being recharged, the council is talking. They're so great. I love them so much. They're so wise. They've grown ever since I left. I should have been part of them. They say I never left or stopped being part of them. They don't consider that there's been any separation. There were 15 when I left, now there are about 45.—I created a long tentacle. They're saying that when I set out, it's as though I had to create my own umbilical cord. They're saying that now that they know what's going on, they can feed me through the umbilical cord. They can send light through it because it was looking like a tattered old thing.

D: *Where are they attaching the cord?*

B: It's attached to the front of my being like a suction cup. They're saying that they're very happy for what I did. There are no mistakes. It offers them an opportunity to try something new. They support me. So I jump back into the umbilical cord, like a big slide. What they're saying now is that the council is at the doorway in constant communication. They can send light because before, they couldn't due to the fact that it all happened in the night.

D: *That's why there was so much confusion in Bobbie's life. No plan.*

B: No. Just sort of wandering in the dark. Now I'm made of light like them. I'm remembering something from that other life too, about the fact that I'm now part light and part butterfly. When it's in the white place, it's just white light. But every time it comes to Earth—like the time I went out on the mission—I started out like a butterfly in order to become the next thing. Now they're telling me that I have the butterfly form, whereas when I first entered, I didn't have this because I had gone without their full support. It's these wings that seem to be the whole missing piece—meaning there's something about how the wings move that fans the light. It keeps things working. Before, the light ran out because it wasn't being fanned. Whereas in that other life, all was fine and I was able to go back because I entered with the wings. In fact, I kept them throughout really because I used to fly through the village at night.—It's saying that wherever there's full light, that's all there is. As long as I understand the wings. The wings represent the joy. There hasn't been joy in a long time. They're saying that was the biggest missing ingredient. It's like the bottom of my back is where the wings attach. So there's a lot that seems to want to get stronger in that place. The body is already filled with light. The light is just—whole. The wings give energy.

I kept trying to accomplish the healing, but the being kept contradicting with its own logic. "It's hard for me to answer any body questions because I'm in a butterfly of light, not really a body. So now is the first time that I'm trying to connect to this body here.—They're saying because I experienced myself as separate for a while, I need to spend some time feeling safe and connected, and remembering what that feels like. The memory is still having to come in. There are still tremors from being separated.—It's like getting more energy. Right now, the lower back is hurting, so a lot is going on. It's like having to fill the tank up again. So even though the light is all here, there's a process of what it takes for all that light to completely fill the body. It's not just the body, it's one's life. To have the light running through my home, my marriage, my bed at night. To be completely whole again. I have to reach that point again. I have to fill up so much because it's really important to be connected to their wisdom, and to be whole, and to be functioning correctly. It's not so much about bodies. It's about all my inner workings. Because that's how it works there—it's about inner working.—There's no time here. She'll know because then she's going to get that longing again. It's going to be that longing of 'what next?' She doesn't have a plan because that's not how the light works. The light has its own intelligence. It always moves in the right place at the right time and it does the right thing. It's all orderly. It takes care of everything. It's not important to know details. The real necessary thing is the heart—to remember the elders in my heart because that's where the fear started. The fear started when I felt I had left them, even though they didn't have a problem with it. I felt fear at leaving. There, everybody is independent, but everybody lives like a group. So it's the group feeling that gives the full strength. The only thing causing disease is fear. It's the only thing that can hinder the light. As long as the light is there, there's no problem. Part of my light had disappeared over time because fear had entered from the very beginning. So the fear caught up with me over time.—They don't think of it as bodies. It's organisms and being re-connected."

Parting message: The most important thing is that the gravity here on Earth really hooks into time and that's not my way. There's no point in relating to myself through experiences in time because it's just something that I borrowed in order to journey. They're saying to not assume that I'm made up of time because then I start to connect in with fear.

And in this other vibration, there's no fear because there's no time. Nothing bad can happen when there's no time.

Chapter 5

MANY CHOICES

Patti had just died after two simple, mundane lifetimes and was on the spirit side. One of the lives was easy and one was difficult. When I asked her what she learned from the lives, she replied: "The easy one was like a lifetime vacation, a chance to rest from other more challenging lives I had lived. The hard life was just one big difficulty after another. A lot of confrontation and friction. I learned there has to be a better way. I still had to go through it, but as I was going through it I knew there had to be a better way. But there were so many other different people involved. They were not quite cooperating, but I was in the middle of this and I couldn't get out of it."

D: *Because you had to interact with them. But then you went to an easy life. A lifelong vacation, you said.*
P: Yes, it was great.
D: *What are you going to do now that you're out of the body?*
P: It feels almost like I have too many choices to make. It's overwhelming.
D: *Do you have to go somewhere to make the choices?*
P: No, but I can go somewhere and get advice for which way I should go. I want all the advice I can get. My world doesn't work too well all by myself.
D: *Let's see where you go to get the advice. What's that like?*
P: (Pause) It's an old building. It feels old. I don't know if it's because of the individuals there. They're very old. Not old old, but wisdom old.

D: *What are they doing?*

P: They're waiting for me. They know me. I go through a door, and let the person there know why I'm there and who I want to see. And she is waiting for me. And so without delay she takes me to this room where I can talk to these people.

D: *But you said you had a lot of choices?*

P: Yes, there's a lot to be done. So what do I do next? Not that any one decision is better than the other, but any time you walk a path, when you get there you could make it really hard on yourself or have a good life.

D: *It's up to you what you choose then.*

P: Right. So I want to make an informed decision as to where I go.

D: *Do they show you the possibilities?*

P: Yes, they do. I just want to make sure that whatever path I take has the appropriate experience. Even though it may be a rough trail, that I have all the tools and experiences necessary to get through it. And learn whatever it is that I'm supposed to learn.

D: *But you said some will be harder than others.* (Right) *What are some of the alternatives they are showing you?*

P: (Pause) One would be in the military.

D: *What other ones are available?*

P: (Pause) The academic road.

D: *But you've done that.* (The past life.)

P: Yeah, did that. But it's more of a school ... not a training program, but more of a lifetime program, but then teaching it.

D: *Longer than the one you just left.* (Right) *Are there any others that are possibilities?*

P: (Pause) Some kind of work ... pretty difficult labor. Kind of remote.—There are many possibilities, and I know I'm going to have to do them all eventually. I'm not ready for the military one, so I'm going to go with the labor. I don't feel like I'm ready for the academic one. That sounds really boring.

D: *The teaching?*

P: Well, it's not so much about the teaching, but me being in school. At first it would be really interesting because you're learning so much, but there's no end. I don't get to apply it. It just keeps going and going and no end in sight, and it's really tedious.

D: *Is that a good idea?*

P: It was not my idea. They're giving me advice and it's good to know that I'm going to have to do them all anyway. I just want to do it in the best order.

D: *At least they give you a choice.*

P: Yes, I'm grateful for that.

D: *Then do you decide when you're going to come back and where and everything?*

P: Right, and what it is I'll be doing. I'm aware of the circumstances. What my job is, and the people involved.

D: *So you make contracts with these people?*

P: Not so much a contract, but an awareness. The awareness is more that they have to do what they need to do, and I don't know what their purpose is. In a way it's a relief. Everybody has their own path. It's their choice. They can ask me for input and I'll be happy to give it to them, but I need to let them go. In the end it's their decision, and I must respect that.

I then called forth the SC, and asked why it chose the rather simple life for her to see.

P: To show her that it really is possible to live a life that has actually minimum ... not challenges, but maybe difficult times. And that she doesn't have to make it bigger than it is and give that energy to those conflicts. In doing that her consciousness will shift and she will keep the focus on things she wants and desires.

D: *Do you think she makes it bigger than it should be at times?*

81

P: She doesn't mean to. She's much better at it. She does that at the input of some good people who want to help and just run it by them, and make sure her perspective is what it should be. She's getting there.

D: *That other lifetime sounded very similar to the lifetime she is living now.*

P: Actually it's a combination of the two. One was difficult and one was everything she wanted it to be. And so she needs to understand that she can choose how she wants to go. She can either give those conflicts energy, or focus on what she wants and everything else will take care of itself. Her life now is very similar, except it is bigger, and things happen much faster in this lifetime. Results are very clear.

D: *What would be the point of repeating certain circumstances?*

P: The really easy lifetime was set up specifically that way. There weren't difficult people that were put into her life like she has now, or in that previous difficult life. It's kind of a combination of the two. So how do you deal with that adversity and those difficult people, and still have at the end of the day what that first lifetime was like ... the easy one? A combination, so she knows how to work through adversity, but not be too much a part of it. In the difficult life she had work she had to do and even though it was necessary and important work, she had a lot of friction from the people around her. She was able to finish her work but everything was a battle ... a lot of friction and not fist fighting, but fighting. She was absolutely exhausted and couldn't wait to get out of there. The easy life was to show her it could be done. It didn't have to be a battle. And so it was set up so she didn't have the friction that she had before. And so now, how do you live that life by working through more difficult situations? So we still have that enjoyment, the easy going life, the ability to leave things where they belong, which is not always with her. To care but not to be so intimately involved with the process and the outcome because the outcome will take care of itself.

Much advice was given about the company where she worked and her involvement with the authority figures there. She knew the top people were corrupt and she felt she had to bring them to justice. But the SC said it would all be taken care of soon, and she did not have to instigate it. But to not be afraid to speak up when the time came. The next most important thing to cover was her physical problems, mostly the arthritis in her hands. I asked what was causing it.

P: It's coming from the fear and making the decision. She didn't trust her instincts. She didn't trust her intuition, so that lack of movement is what caused her joints to be diseased. Getting that movement and working it out and going forward and having faith. She knew what she was supposed to do, but the fear held her back.

D: *Maybe this will help if she knows everything is going to be fine.*

P: That's very important. Some people are able to work through their fear and they have this tremendous faith, but she has the kind of faith that has to be justified. It's faith based on past experience not just blind faith. So just understand that there's nothing to fear.

D: *Can we take away the arthritis?*

P: Yes. It's already served her purpose. And just having this information really puts an end to it all. Just go along and do her job that she's perfectly willing to do.

D: *But she's on some pain medication.* (Even intravenous.)

P: She doesn't need that anymore. She can stop that now. In fact, she has an appointment on Tuesday. She can just call in and cancel it when she gets back to town.

I asked how it was going to heal the arthritis. I am always curious and I like the SC to explain the process to me. "I have this really cool new tool that emits a white light, but it's not visible. She can feel the energy. Everything is light and energy. So I go into all the joints and just flood the entire joint with this white light, and it destroys the pathogens that are there and the toxins and the diseased tissue. And what grows back is brand new, perfect tissue. It functions perfectly without any effort of hers. She has a responsibility to take care of her body, but beyond that it'll take care of itself. The body is fantastic.—And it's fixing the DNA while I'm doing this. She's had this condition for a while now ... a long time. So it's embedded in her DNA and made her susceptible to the pathogens and the toxins. So the DNA is being affected by this tool that's emitting the light, and based on that it restores it to a perfect vibration. It restores all lost and inactive DNA strands, so anywhere there were holes in the DNA strands that were missing, those are regenerating."

D: *Good. That's going to make almost a whole new body, isn't it?*
P: Yes. It will. She will notice the difference and she just needs to accept it. It's been done. Be grateful for it and accept it and not hold onto the part where she did some things in the past. She would think it was going to hurt and sure enough ... it would hurt.
D: *Because she was expecting it to?*
P: Right. That's been her past, so she just needs to do these activities and think it is so great to be pain free. She needs to focus on what she wants.—These bodies, miraculous as they are, there are situations where there are points of no return.
D: *I always thought you could fix anything.*
P: Yes, but sometimes it's starting over with a new body. Everything has a life cycle.—The rest of her body is in pretty good shape. She's done a good job. Her diet could be better, but it's worse for her to stress out about her diet. It's better for her to just continue on and let the stress go. The stress is more harmful than a bad diet. She doesn't

have to deny herself anything now and then. A doughnut is okay. It's just not a food group.

She had a question about her partner: Jean. Did she have a contract or past lives with her.

P: Her past experience with her was in the inbetween life before this one. It was when she was deciding and setting up the circumstances for this life and she was feeling very overwhelmed. Like, "Oh, I can't get through it." And we told her, "You can." And so we offered this option of having Jean be there for her and to teach her how to look at things differently. And Jean will understand and help her walk through it and think through it and act through it. And they will help each other. Jean has worked through a lot of issues too, that Patti doesn't know about. It's not for her to know about.

It was very important that Patti had been given so much information about her future and the involvement and implications of what was going to happen to the company she worked for.

P: That'll be a big relief for her. That's going to give her the strength because she's not out of the woods yet. And it's going to be a much easier walk knowing that the shells are exploring ahead, but she's completely protected.—We don't like to tell people the future, but sometimes it gives them the reassurance that they are protected and this is exactly the way it should proceed and that they are safe. It helps them tremendously, so it's that sense of ease and comfort that gives them poise. Gives them a deep sense that it's not about them. That they're there for a reason, and it's going to be better than ever on the other side. That's how they find their strength. They have that sense of protection and safety.

The SC always gives the client a parting message: You're exactly where you need to be. You are on the right track. You are doing what you are exactly supposed to be doing. So just be who you are and know that you're not responsible for anybody else. You're only responsible for you. Take care of your people. Have fun.

THE HEALING WORK

As much as I desire to help every client that comes to see me, there are times when it just simply doesn't work. They are able to get into the deep level of trance, and the cause of their problems (usually physical) is discovered, and the SC works with great love to heal them and gives them wonderful sound advice. Yet afterwards they will insist that nothing happened, that they were not helped. In fact, some say they are worse than they were before coming. Sometimes (and these are rare cases) it works for a short while and then returns. It may be months later before I hear of this, and of course, they blame me. That is much easier than admitting that they are the cause of their own problems, including physical. It is always easier to put the blame outside of themselves, rather than acknowledging that they have created their own reality. And even though their reality is not pleasant, it is what they have manifested. This is the power of the human mind. This is why this power should be used to heal rather than be destructive. They come to see me with such out of proportion expectations. They are looking for someone else to heal them. I try to make it clear that *I* don't do the healing, *they* do. I am only the facilitator to allow the SC to come through and do the work. I teach this in my classes, that the minute the student thinks that *they* are doing the work, then it is their own ego. This will hinder the whole process. I am only a willing servant to aid the process.

These cases are rare, but they do happen. We all have free will, and no one can override that. The SC may say the person is healed and should be able to pursue a normal life, but if the clients themselves won't accept it, believe it and trust it, there is nothing anyone can do. The free will is foremost. After one session the client said, "I do feel better. There is no more pain. *But* I know it is too good to be true. It will return." Another one said afterward, "I can't be healed! I have been sick all my life. I will never be well." All self-fulfilling prophecies. If the client wishes to continue in that reality (even though they stubbornly say they don't want it) there is nothing I can do about it. There is also the possibility of self-punishing over some perceived guilt. People are complicated creatures. I have found that out after working with them for over forty years. Sometimes the thing they are punishing themselves for was long forgotten and buried in the unconscious memories. Yet they have turned themselves into the victim.

I just got off the phone with a client I saw a few months ago, and she spent almost an hour screaming at me. "I came to you because you said you could heal me. And I'm not healed! I'm worse than I was before." In the first place, I would never, ever say I could heal them because I know that is not possible. I do not have that type of power. In the second place, the final result lies with them and their belief system. There was so much *anger* in that person's voice. I could sense why she didn't want to release the illness (or why she thought she was unable to). Anger at what she perceived was the cause of her predicament, anger at her parents for the way they had treated her, anger at the doctors who had not been able to help her, anger at me for not being able to take it all away. The cause of their problem always has to be something outside of themselves. It hurts too much, it takes too much responsibility to admit that the cause might lie within themselves. It is easier to play the victim role, "Poor me! You don't understand how horrible I have been treated! Etc. Etc." We know in metaphysics and especially in my type of work that we made a plan and contracts before coming into this life. We agreed to the type of situation we would live in, even though sometimes we have been warned by our guides that our decisions would be difficult. Yet we insist and hope for the best. Because we forget our plan once we enter the physical body, we forget that we arranged the things that happen to us in order to learn from them. If we don't learn, then we have to take the lesson over again. This is the law of karma, and the way this Earth school is run. You have to come back again and do it all over with the same people and same circumstances until you have passed that grade in school. It is complicated, but then I don't make the rules. I just try to help people understand what they are doing to themselves.

There are other people who really don't want to be healed because they secretly enjoy what the illness does for them. They would never admit this consciously, but we all know people who are always sick and complaining about the newest pain, symptom, or medicine the doctor has put them on. They secretly enjoy the attention it gives them. Usually these types of people have nothing else in their lives, and they enjoy the attention. If you were to heal them, take it away, you would really be taking away their identity. And they would feel they had nothing. It is the only thing that makes them feel special and different. If the person is benefitting from the illness, they will be most reluctant to release it. In my work on the life of Jesus (*Jesus and the Essenes,* and *They Walked With Jesus*) I found that not even Jesus could heal everyone, no matter what the Church leads you to believe. He could look at a person and see why they had the illness. And if it was because of karma, then he could not take it away. He could relieve pain, but he was forbidden to interfere with their path, their plan. So if He couldn't do it, why do I think I have the power to override the person's free will?

After one trying day when I had spent four or five hours with a client, I left my office depressed and wondering if I was really helping anybody. I am sure any therapist, healer, doctor or psychiatrist has occasionally felt the same way. Then as I got in my car I heard as plain as day in my head, "Your responsibility ends when the client walks out that door. If you truly believe that you have done everything you could do, to the best of your ability, then the rest is up to them." That made all the difference, and lifted a load off my shoulders. As much as I truly want to help everyone, in the end, *it is not my responsibility!* They have to be ready to accept it, want it, believe it and allow it to happen. No one else can do that for them. I love working with the SC, but in the end it can only do so much. It is forbidden to override the free will.

So for the client that I just spoke to who was so upset, I can only send her love and hope she wakes up to the power she has within her, and allow herself to be healed. Maybe that is her lesson in all of this, to learn to trust herself and not depend on others to do what she is able to do herself. That would be a wonderful and important lesson.

Also to all of my thousands of students who have taken my classes, I say, "Do the best you can. Have compassion for the client and try all of your skills to help them. Then after that it is *their* responsibility."

Chapter 6

THE PLANNING STAGE

Amber came off the cloud directly into a scene. From the first words she was emotional, so I knew she had dropped into something important.

A: I'm up against the rocks and I see the men. They're not from our village. They are the Spaniards and they're questioning us. They're looking for something. I'm a young boy. I'm up against the rocks ... we're all up against the rocks.

D: *There are others with you?*

A: Yes, from our village and they're trying to get something from us. I don't know what they want, but the man that seems angry has a pointed beard. (Laughing) And this is so silly. They're wearing garments—no wonder they're so angry. They have to be miserable in those things.— (Sober again.) I don't know what they want. They're looking for something. I don't know what to give them.

D: *Can you understand them?*

A: No, no, I don't know what they want. I keep looking down, and they keep making me look up. They think I know something.

D: *Do you have any idea what it is they're looking for?*

A: The gold? (Laugh) I don't know the gold. Something about something goldish ... something that's shiny? I don't know what that is. I don't know why they think I do.

D: *What about the others with you?*

A: They're scared. They're hiding. They're trying to get behind the rocks. I think they've killed some of our people. They're so insistent. They're trying to scare us, but I don't know what it is they're looking for. I don't know what that is.

D: *Do you have a leader of your village?*

A: They're not there. They're gone. There're primarily older men and the women and the kids. Some of us young boys had been playing down in an area that's sort of in the side of a canyon in the rocks. My friends and I saw them and we alerted the village. And no one knew what to do, and they were coming. And they found us and got us all together.

D: *Have you seen these kind of people before?*

A: I've heard about them. I hadn't seen them. We were hoping they wouldn't come. But they did.—I think I'm going to have to take them. I think it's the only way. I don't know where to take them, but I have to take them someplace away from my people. Maybe I can trick them. Maybe I can get away, but I have to take them away before they kill more people. I have to. It's the only chance ... the only chance.

D: *So what do you decide to do?*

A: I decide to act like I know where it is, where they want to go, and what they're looking for. There are several men and they're on horses.

D: *What about your friends? Do they want to go with you?*

A: No, no, they don't want to go with me. They are very afraid. The mothers are calling to them and they're scared.

D: *Is your mother there anywhere?*

A: Yes, but I can see with her eyes that she's giving me strength to go. She knows what I am going to do.

D: *I think you're very brave to do this.*

A: Our people are suffering. There's not much food, and the men have been gone hunting for a long time. Our people are dying.

D: *Do you think they're going to believe you?*
A: Yes because they want to believe so badly. (Laugh)
D: *They don't think you would trick them, I guess.*
A: No, I'm just a young boy.

I condensed time and moved him ahead to see what happened.

A: I take them into a box canyon, but I make them go a long ways ... a long ways. It's a day's walk away from my village, and I make sure I go in and out of other places. Go back and backtrack and try to get them confused as to where we might be, so they couldn't go back. And in the meantime I am hoping my village will escape. We have an escape place at the top where they can be safe. I'm trying to give them time. Maybe the hunting party will come back.
D: *These people won't know how to get back?*
A: No, but they're becoming leery of me. I took them into the box canyon because I know a way out of it if I can get there in time.
D: *Are you walking, or are you on a horse too?*
A: No, I'm walking. I'm walking. They're following me. (Laugh) Their horses are so slow. They're asking for water for their horses. I take them so they can let their horses drink water, and then it's time to take them back into the canyon. I haven't been there in a very long time. I hope I remember it. There's a cave. I'm gonna tell them it's in the cave, and then I plan to escape. There's a path sort of in the stones that I can climb out of to have some protection from some outcropping brush, if I can get away.
D: *Then they'll go in the cave and you can escape.*
A: That's what I thought, but that's not what happened. I didn't think that they'd want me to go into the cave with them. I thought they'd be too excited and they'd forget about me, but they're making me go. We go inside the

cave and of course, there's nothing there. There are some drawings on the wall that they look at, but they're angry with me. And they decide they're going to kill me. They're tired. We've been gone all day, and there's nothing to show for it. I try desperately to point in another direction, but the cave ... we don't go very far and there's no way for me to escape. There's no way to get out and they're tired and they're upset. I shouldn't have gone in the cave.

D: *But you didn't have a choice. So what happens now?*

A: They kill me. A knife across my throat.

D: *Are you out of the body now?*

A: Yes, I'm watching. I'm watching them move, and they're leaving the boy's body—my body—in the dirt inside the cave. My family will want to find me.

D: *They won't know where to look, will they?* (No) *How do you feel about all of that?*

A: Disappointed. I was so stupid that I thought I could trick them.

D: *I think you were very brave to even try.*

A: I may not have been able to do anything for my family. After all that, they may go back. They may kill all of them. I feel so disappointed. I was so certain.

D: *But you were just a child really. You were doing more than some men would have done. Do you have any way to see what happened to your family, or any of the other people?*

A: Some were able to make it, but it's a long journey up the canyon walls. And those that were old were not able to make it ... not able to escape. (She sounded distressed.) The men went back and took their revenge and killed them.

D: *But I think you did the best you could.*

A: I didn't know what else to do, but some of my family got away. My mother got away.

D: *What are you going to do now?*

A: I try to help them even though I'm not there anymore. I try to help them as much as I can.

D: *How do you do that?*

A: Giving them signals. Telling them not to go in a particular direction, but it feels so hopeless. And it can help them for some period of time, but I don't know if I can prevent it all.

D: *Maybe you're not supposed to. Maybe it's too much for one person.*

A: I don't know.

D: *But you stay there for a while and try to help them?*

A: Yes, but now I can see it's getting further and further away. I'm drifting away from there.—Now I'm being pulled up. Drifting further and further away. I'm beyond that now. I'm by myself. I'm floating in darkness, and now I'm not so worried about my family anymore. Now I see a really bright light. It seems to be coming from nowhere and everywhere. Oh, my gosh, it's nice and warm. I'm just floating in it.

D: *It's a good feeling. Feels very nice, comfortable and safe. (Yes) What do you plan to do? Are you going to stay there?*

A: There's someplace else I have to go, but I'm supposed to just stay in this light right now.

D: *Is there anybody around that tells you what to do?*

A: Hmm ... I don't see anyone. I'm just lost in this light.— Now I see there's somebody waiting for me. Just what I need right now. Looks very wise ... fatherly or grandfatherly, with white hair. He greets me and puts his arm around me, and tells me that I did the best that I could, and he is proud of me.—He pulled me into a place that's filled with light.

D: *Do you mind leaving the other place?*

A: No. This place is even better. It's amazing! Everything seems to be filled with light. There are buildings ... oh, he says "temples," sorry. They're light buildings. They're temples. They are places of learning, but I'm not sure what I'm doing here. He says not to worry; he will explain.—Now I'm inside the building. It has a very tall, vaulted ceiling. Everything is white, but there's light coming in, but it's hard to see if there are windows. It's as though it's translucent and the light comes from the outside, and it lights up the building. It comes all the way through like something that can be lit from the outside ... beautiful. And long tables, but I don't see anybody there. Just these long tables. He's walking with me. There is a passageway to go through, but it feels nice in here. I don't know why the tables are there. There are no chairs, just these tables.

D: *No people?*

A: No. I feel they're in other rooms off to the side. He's going to take me to one.—I've been here before.

D: *It feels familiar?*

A: Yes, and there are books ... lots of books. He smiles at me and says, "Every book there ever was is here." Oh, my gosh! I've been here before, yes. I don't know when, but I've been there. I see it, the shelves with all the books. And there are people there that are looking, pulling books, putting them back. No one's talking though.—I'm so happy to be back here with the books! (Happy) Oh! Oh! Every book there ever was is here ... *every* book. Oh, my gosh! It's like running your hands across a piano as you play those chords. As you play those books, it's like each book as you touch it, you know that book. He says not to be so silly and play so much, but it's such a wonderful feeling.

D: *So, as you touch it, you don't have to read it?* (No) *You just know what's inside of it?*

A: It's like the Reader's Digest version. It's the executive summary of it as you touch it. Do you understand that? You still want to take it down and absorb everything, but you can run your fingers across it and get the notes and play it ... feel each book ... feel it. Oh! Oh, how wonderful! (She was ecstatic.) He laughs at me and tells me there will be time for that later. (Laugh) Everything I needed to know would be in there. He's laughing at me and says, "That's true, but there are different sections, and it takes time to go to the different sections."

It was obvious that she had been taken to the Library on the spirit side. This is my favorite place. I love libraries anyway, and can spend an entire day in one when I am doing my research. Yet this one is very special because it contains everything that has ever been known, and everything that ever will be known. A treasure trove for someone like me who loves research. It also contains what have been called the Akaskic Records, which have been described in many different ways. Each time I have taken a client there I have had access to all information. Much of this has been used in my books.

A: He's taking me further inside to the center. He said that there will be a special room for me with *my* books.

D: *So this is like a library.*

A: Yes. People come here to do their research and to plan their lives and to gather knowledge about certain things, but there are also many rooms. I can't even count how many rooms there are. But he's taking me to a room that will be my room that has my books. It will have my life, and the lives of others I was close to there.

D: *So it's just special for you?* (Yes) *So when people go there, they go to their own room?*

A: Yes. Different people do it differently, but he knows this is the way I like to do it. He knows I love books. This room is just mine.

D: *What is that room like?*

A: Nice ... there is one wall that is just a solid window with light, and there are shelves and rows of books. There's a table in the center and he takes me to this table. There is a chair for me that I will sit in. And he looks at me and says, "You know what to do next." And I say, "Well, I'm

97

not sure!" He said, "You do know ... now call the book to you."

D: *Call it to me?*

A: Call it to you. You don't get up and go get it. You call it to you, and then it's there in front of you. Whatever book you need, but the book he wants for me now, that I have to look at, is the book of *my life* that I was just in.

D: *The one you just left?*

A: Yes, but he knows how eager I am to go on, so he will allow me to stack another couple of books over to the side. But he teases me, telling me I can't look at them yet.— When I open up the book, it is like looking through a telescope, only it's more like a magnifying glass that the book becomes. And I am able to move it so that I can see where I lived. I can see the mesa. I can see the rocks. I'm seeing where I'm small and playing with my friends, my father, my mother.

D: *Of course, you didn't live very long in that life.*

A: No, but that was all right. I had certain things I learned, and I learned that my father was right. He told me when I was little that the friends that I had may not always be around to help me. And it was important to have friends that would help you, and that you had to help your friends too.

D: *What else do you think you learned from that lifetime?*

A: That family was important ... very important. But I couldn't help them. I couldn't save them, but I did do the best that I could do. And had I not gone, everyone would have been slaughtered.

D: *So you did save some?*

A: I did. I did.

D: *So that was the purpose of that life?*

A: Yes. My mother needed to live. I also learned that I had been a little foolish because the hunting party was gone and we boys were the ones who were supposed to be watching the village. Watching and looking out, and we'd been busy playing and we didn't sound the alarm loud enough.

D: *When the other men were coming?* (Yes) *Everyone is entitled to make mistakes, aren't they?*

A: Yes, but irresponsibility kills people. We didn't do it intentionally, but we understand why it was so important for us to do what we were told.

D: *Is this man telling you these things?*

A: No, when I looked through the book I see it. I just know it. He's very comforting next to me. He's not judging me. He's very warm and kind.

D: *Is there something you are supposed to take with you as you move on from that life?*

A: You can't save everyone. You can be smart. You can be tricky. And try to do all the things to protect the people you love, but in the end ... you can't save all of them ... not all of the time, but you do the best you can.

D: *Because everyone had their own life. They all have their own lessons to learn, don't they?* (Yes) *Do you think you've gotten everything out of that book that you can use?*

A: No, there will be more sessions where I can come back and look at it. But I got the main part, and he was proud of me for getting the main part. And we'll go back and look at it again. But he also tells me I need to rest, and he'll come back to us.

D: *He doesn't want you to look at those other books on the table yet?*

A: He's tempting me with them, but he won't let me have them yet. (Kidding) Because I'm not finished with this one. I have to finish what I started first before I go on. And he knows that's my weakness. He knows that's what I have to work on, is finishing things. But he's making it a temptation for me because he knows how eager I am to get into the next thing. I know they're there and they look wonderful, so I must continue on this. But he wants me to rest first.—He takes me to another place and it's open.

There are birds singing. There's a fountain, and I can just relax and wait there. I hear somebody singing.

D: *Are you by yourself?*

A: Yes. I can hear people. I can hear women's voices singing something, but I don't see anybody. It looks like an outdoor area with benches in a semi-circle. And they're carved and white stone, and in the center is a white fountain. And there are trees in the forest in the background. And I can hear the birds singing, but I am there by myself. He has left me there for now.

D: *It sounds like a beautiful place!* (Yes) *But he didn't go over any other lives you have lived?*

A: No. The others are in the books and I can go back and look at them when I need to because sometimes we have to remind ourselves so that we don't forget those things we learned in those other lives.—I'm too eager sometimes.—He'll come back for me later, but right now I am just to relax. Just to wait and to listen ... and to see nature. The nature part is a reminder, to absorb everything now, and to connect with that. To be feeling the wind and the direction that it goes. And listening to the birds and to not always be so eager to do the next thing. Just *be* right now, right here. There will be time for the others later. There will be time.

This could take a while as he would probably spend quite a bit of time just relaxing in this beautiful place in order to recover from the way he died in that lifetime. And to reflect on the meaning of that life. So I decided to move him ahead to where the man came back to get him, when he thought he had rested long enough. I assumed he would be taken back to the library where the precious books awaited him.

A: He doesn't take me back to the library. (Laughing) He takes me to my group. He knows that's who I was waiting for, but he made me wait. (Laughing and giggling) He made me wait.

D: (Laugh) *I thought you liked the books?*

A: Oh, I did (Laugh), but it was the *people* I was waiting to see. Oh, my gosh! It's my group ... the ones that we have worked together. It's our group. We come back in many lives together, and we are not in body. Even when we're not in body or when we are in body, there's a part of us that is still there. That's interesting. It's not quite the same, but we're all here.

I felt that was a very important statement, that even when we are on Earth in a body a part of us (an aspect) never leaves the spirit side.

D: *Do you like to be together?*

A: Oh, yes! We work well together.

D: *So when you go back into lives, you sometimes come together?* (Yes) *That way you are never alone.* (No) *What's happening with the group?*

A: They're asking me, "What took me so long?" They knew that I had to wait outside. I can't believe I forgot about them. We walked to the books and outside to rest, and I forgot that's what would happen next. How could I forget about them? Oh, my gosh! They're wonderful. It just feels so nice to be back with them ... so nice.—They're sitting at a table and they've been talking. The table is interesting because it is an interactive table. It looks like a translucent map, but then when you touch it, it zooms in to a particular place. You touch it again and you can see the people in that place. It's like a Google Earth, but when you touch it, you can *go* to that spot.—They're busy planning. Oh, this group can never agree. Everyone always wants to be somewhere different. They're planning. They were waiting for me. They think *this* place is the most important, that we need to be where we can do the most work. And the others over here .... Someone just said, (in a funny tone of voice) "Oh, we can be all over at the same time. What difference does it

101

make?" But we like each other so much, we want to be in the same place. We want to start in the same place.

D: *So they're looking at the map, trying to figure it out?*

A: Trying to figure out where to go next. They're serious for a moment. I don't know if we're ready for the next step.

D: *But you want to go together. You don't want to go by yourself?*

A: No, we will go.—There are several that feel very strongly that we need to be in the Middle East. Our group is to go where we are to go, and do what we are called to do. We know that and sometimes, what we have to do may mean that our lives together will be very short.

D: *Is there a reason for that?*

A: It's all a part of it and we're shown some pieces of it, and some things we just have to trust. I am so happy to see them, and I am so happy to be able to go back again with my friends, my group. But I am a little sad thinking we are picking such a hard life for the next one.

D: *But in your last life, you didn't live very long.*

A: No, but the next one will be harder. It will be short for all of us. In the last life, there were many who lived long. And even though I was killed, we had a good life together. In this next one, some of us will have to play some pretty tough roles.

D: *You're being shown what the scenario will be?*

A: When we touch the map and it goes forward we see the possible scenarios. I see Jews. I see Palestine. And I see lots of blood and I see that we will be on opposite sides.

D: *Is there a reason for that?*

A: It's because we have to be able to join to come together. There will be opportunities for us to come together, but there will be equal opportunities for us to destroy each other in that life. I will get a chance again to help my family.

D: *I see. I was wondering what the purpose would be. Because when there's conflict, you think, what is the purpose? What is the sense of it?*

A: It doesn't look like much sense, but we have to try to make the connection to show that people are more similar than unalike. Our group has already decided to go. It was just who was playing which part, and they were waiting for me. And it's pretty clear as to what part mine is. I just don't know what side of the fence I'm going to be on. (Laugh)

D: *Are you able to look at any other lives you'll be going into? Are you shown that far ahead?*

I, of course, was thinking of her present life as Amber.

A: They are, but again, they start teasing me about jumping around and doing other things. And so I have to stick with one thing at a time. And I know that after this next short life in the Middle East there will be a completely different life following that. But I can't get sidetracked right now or I won't have the courage to do the things I need to do.

D: *They can't let you know too much at one time?* (No, no.) *That makes sense. But each time you come back to this place?*

A: Yes, and I get to see my group and we get to talk and we get to be with one another's energies. And we all sit with these energies and I recognize some of them. Some of them that are sort of in the edges I don't see. My father's there. My friend, Rob, is there. And there are others, but I'm not sure who they are in my life now. (Her present life.)

D: *So you have to live the short life first before you come into the body of Amber?* (Yes) *That's important to do that first.* (Yes)

I didn't want to take the time to go through that lifetime, so I had her move to where it was finished and she had done what she was supposed to do, and the group had come back together again on the spirit side. I wanted to get her to when she would decide to enter the body of Amber. "You come back together at the same place. What about the life in the Middle East? Did you do a good job?"

A: I think I did. In that life in the Middle East we shared music. And he saw I was not evil, and I saw he was not evil, and we carried that with us.

D: *What happened if it was a short life?*

A: There was an explosion, gunfire, and I'm dead. (Matter of factly.)

D: *But you learned things, didn't you?*

A: Yes because some part of me knew during that short life to continue to look in the eyes of the others and see what was behind them. And they weren't all evil. They were just people.

D: *All living their own lives.—But now you came back to this place. Does the group always gather together, or do some go on different assignments?*

A: Well, it's interesting because as they gather around the table, those who are closest sitting at the table are the ones that are not currently in body. But towards the outer portions are the rest of the people of the group, but they are of a *dimmer light*. And that lets us know that they are incarnated. So a portion of them is in that room to participate, but not in the same way that they would if they were not embodied. Does that make sense?

D: *Yes, I can see that. I can understand. They're there so they can still plan.*

A: Yes, and they can still participate because they may be incarnated already and we may come join them at some point. So part of them is still participating. They're just a *dimmer light* in the room.

Maybe this is occurring when the person is sleeping, and therefore they are not aware of it. This would explain how plans and contracts could be made with those souls who had already incarnated, and would play the roles of mothers or father, grandparents, etc. I had assumed these contracts were made before any of the souls incarnated, while they were all in the spirit world. However, we apparently still have contact even while living our present lives. And the plans and preparations are ongoing. It also shows how the plan can be changed.

D: *Are they discussing the lifetime you'll come into as Amber?*
A: Yes. They tell me I'll get to go back to New Mexico. (Laugh)
D: *Were you there before?*
A: Yes, as a boy ... the Indian boy.
D: *So that's where that was.* (Yes) *Was there any gold there?* (No) (Laugh) *So it's important to go back because of what happened?*
A: We're still working on my issue of trying to save the world. (Laugh) So they think that maybe if I go back to the same location, I can remember that I can't save the world. But I can save my own little piece, which is me. And they told me that it's going to be a very different life than I had before, and to be sort of humorous about it. They reminded me of when I was trying to be tricky and going in and out of the box canyon, and how I was setting a trail. That's kind of what they're doing in this life. I have a lot of places I'm going to have to fall. And there may be false directions to go and come back, but I have to find my way. So they are laughing.
D: *They think it's funny because of all these probabilities and possibilities?*
A: Yes, and they know we're getting closer, and so as it gets closer it becomes more complicated.
D: *What do you mean by closer?*
A: We're closer to finishing up this stage and we're getting towards the end. And so it becomes a very complicated, complex arrangement. There are more choices, more elements for free will to be exercised. More opportunities, and you have to come through, being able to show you can

go past certain temptations that may be easier. And you have to get past things that might be distracting. It's very complicated.

D: *What do they mean about the last stages?*

A: I don't know where we go next, but we won't come back to this room. We'll go to another building. We're, I guess, graduating from this place and we go to the next.

D: *Does that mean you won't return to Earth again or what?*

A: We return differently, and only if we so choose. That's why we have to get it right.

D: *There won't be any more opportunities to come back and correct it?*

A: There will be, but I want to stay with my group.

D: *Because people do make mistakes.*

A: Yes, they do. And it's not about perfection. It's about knowing that the learning is important. That you're open and willing to learn.

D: *Can they show you what's going to happen in this life as Amber?*

A: Very tricky.

D: *But some of these people are coming back with you to play their own part?*

A: Yes. And by being there, they are their own reminder of where we should be and that we are together, and we can help one another.

D: *But when you get into the body, you don't remember, do you?*

A: No, but there's this sync knowing and we all know it. But we're here to encourage each other. Not to take the easy way out. Not to go the short road.

D: *What would be the short road?*

A: The short road is to stay away from challenges.

D: *That's the easy way, but you don't learn much, do you?*

A: No. You wouldn't get to go to the next step, and they're all excited about going to the next step. That's why we agreed to help each other. So we won't get stranded behind. We'll all progress together.

D: *What is the next step? Can they tell you anything about it?*

A: There's a group that we will appear in front of, and they will talk to us. But it's in a different location. It's up in the top of a dome. Floating in the top like golden light.

D: *You've never been there before?*

A: No. My group really wants to go there badly. We know where it is. We know we haven't been there and that's where we will go next.

D: *Like a graduation, you said.* (Yes) *First you have to get through the challenges of this lifetime.* (Yes) *And most of the people you meet in the lifetime of Amber will be from the group?*

A: Not most. Just a select few, and they will be there as reminders that I am in the right place doing the right things and going in the right direction.

D: *Are you going to have children in this lifetime? Can you see that?*

This was one of Amber's questions.

A: Yes. I have chosen that and they're laughing at me at the things I'm choosing. I am selecting everything. I don't want to be on the short path. I'm putting everything on my list. And they're laughing at me because they're saying there's no possible way I can handle all of these things. But I'm so determined that we are going to make it to this next step, the next stage, that I'm loading up as much as I can.

D: *That can be challenging.*

A: It's as though we take a marble out of a box, and we put it in a bowl. And each marble represents a challenge. And usually people will pick one or two. The people from the group will pick one or two marbles and put it in a bowl. I'm filling the bowl up to the top. They're not really happy with me. (Amused.)

D: *Are you really sure you want to do that?*

A: It looks easy, you know.

D: *Oh, it always looks easy there.*

A: I know if we do this, we will graduate. We will go on. They're looking at me. They're saying, "You realize when you put the marble in the bowl, it is *your* marble. Others are there, and they may deal with it sort of on the side, but it is your marble." And I say, "I know. I know."

D: *All right. But do you know anything about the children you might have?*

A: I do see a little girl. She's wonderful and she has so much to teach me, if I let her. It will be hard. She will be different from me and those around me. She's not part of this group, but I have agreed to bring her because she has so much to give. But it is a special situation. She can teach me if I let her, but she's also a marble in my bowl. She's a different vibration. She has trouble staying on the Earth. Her body is very light and she needs to learn ways to ground herself. It's very important to teach her that. Teach her how to play. Teach her how to be on the Earth and walk around on the Earth. The more time she can spend outside and next to the earth, the more grounded she will become. Nature. She will flourish. There will be a lot of the fear because it's a strange environment. She is not used to being in a body. And the body won't always cooperate with her.

This description matched Amber's daughter Adriana. She has always seemed like she didn't belong here and has needed special attention and love.

D: *Can you see who your mate will be in this lifetime?*

A: Hmm. You said "mate," and they said, "More marbles."

She said the mates would also not be from the group. They would have different lessons for Amber to learn. I did not want to spoil the fun she was having with her group and their planning, but I thought it was time to get to her questions.

I asked if I would be allowed to ask questions, and they agreed, "You may ask." They knew what we were doing and it was permissible.

D: *I don't want to spoil the fun they're having or ask for things she's not supposed to know.*
A: No, we will let you know.
D: *They know that you are in the body now, and you are here trying to get information.*
A: Yes, of course. That's what she would do. She has already learned a lot from what she's been told.

One of her questions dealt with her present job. She was not happy with it, and felt like she was at a crossroads, trying to decide on making a career change.

A: It's those marbles. (Laugh) She knows what she needs to do. She does need to change and she will find a time that is right, and she will know that just because she had the marbles in the bowl doesn't mean that all of them have to represent something that is a burden. A challenge is not always a burden.—She needs to recognize that in a human body, there is only so much that one person can do, and there are limitations. Otherwise, she would not be in a human body. And she has to learn to be able to work with her human body to allow her to do the things she needs to do. When she goes against this, her body will shut down, and it has proven this.
D: *It will rebel so she has to take time to herself and time to rest?*
A: Yes. She cannot heal others until she heals herself.

She had had an interesting connection with her husband over many, many lifetimes. They were not of the same group, but were of the same vibration. They had agreed to help one another, and most lifetimes they were helpful friends. Her father was one of the group. "He agreed to be here first for her so she would know where the path was. (So she wouldn't get lost.) He has done his job and more, and he has done a wonderful job in helping people. He's had many occasions when he could have left, and each time he chose to stay and help, and we thank him for his work."

Parting message: She will know that she can access me anytime she needs to. She simply needs to become quiet and listen and she knows the places she can go to hear better and the people she can be with so she can listen better, but we will always be there for her. We will continue to be there for her. And just remember about the marbles. (We laughed.)

Chapter 7

A SHORT LIFE

K im was a retired airline attendant in her 60s. She went into trance easily, but went into a life that seemed to be the one just before her present one. It appeared to be in a small town near the ocean. She was a fifteen year old girl living in a three story building that had a feed store on the first floor. She lived there with her mother and father and three brothers. The description of the kitchen suggested the late 1880s or early 1900s: a water pump and a potbellied stove. The feed store was the family business and they all helped out when they weren't in school. Her job was to take care of writing the orders. It seemed to be a simple, tranquil life until I moved her forward to an important day. She was walking down the stairs that led from their upstairs living quarters into the back of the store when she tripped and fell down the stairs. She was badly hurt, but she couldn't cry out. She could hear people in the store, but she couldn't cry for help. She had to lay there until someone found her and carried her back upstairs. When the doctor arrived he discovered that she had broken her neck.

"He's putting a sheet over my head. I don't think I made it. My dad's with me. I'm watching from across the room. I wish I hadn't fallen, but I can't do anything about it." So she died tragically and suddenly at sixteen. I, of course, wanted to know what happened next, now that she was out of her body. "There's a light. I'm going up there."

D: *Tell me what happens as you go up to the light.*
K: It happened so fast! But I wish it didn't happen.

D: *But you can't go back now, can you?* (No) *So what happens? What are you experiencing?*

K: Just this peace. It feels good.

D: *Are you by yourself or are there other people with you?*

K: I don't see people. There's a presence ... "Can I go back?"

D: *Is that what you're asking?* (Yes) *What does it say?*

K: "No. Your body is broken." Why did that have to happen? "It's what you wanted." Why would I want that? They say, "You needed to ... it was your time. You were done."

D: *But it wasn't a very long life.*

K: Yes, and I don't think that's fair. They say, "It's what you wanted."

D: *Ask them to explain it to you because you have forgotten.*

K: "It's what your soul intended. To be there for a short time. To learn."

D: *To learn what?*

K: Just lessons. And what did I learn? I learned what I learned. About being young ... about the best part for your body. Your body never gets old, but your soul doesn't progress. When your body breaks and you're young, your soul doesn't get to progress. It couldn't keep the soul.

D: *It might have been crippled.* (Yes) *Then maybe you wouldn't be able to do what you were supposed to do?*

K: I wasn't supposed to do anything else, I guess. Just to learn what it's like to be young. So then you'll go back and get old. And then you'll want to be old and have your soul grow. Because now you know that your soul doesn't get to grow if your body breaks when you're young. Then you'll appreciate growing older. And taking care of the body, and being more careful. Don't fall if you can help it.

D: *After they talk to you, do you go somewhere else?*

K: There's sort of a burst ... warmth ... just like you're in a cocoon or something.

D: *Did somebody tell you to do that?*

K: Yes. I have to go on and be a part of that universe there. Be a part of that for a while.—Into that burst of light ... just to think about that.

D: *To think about the life you just left?*

K: To get ready again for another one.

D: *Do you have to do another one?* (Yes) *How do you feel about that?*

K: (Joyful) I think that's okay. I want to live longer, and I don't want to go upstairs. (Loud laugh.)

D: *You don't want to take a chance on that happening again. (Laugh) Are you talking to somebody about your plans?*

K: Yes. We're talking about it. About if you came back, be what you want to be, how long you would live and all of that stuff.

D: *Making a plan?*

K: Yes. So I have to think about that and it takes a long time to figure that out. They talk about the different possibilities. They ask, "Well, do you want to live around the snow?" No, no ... I like snow, and sometimes I'll be around snow, but I wouldn't want to live there.—But I think I planned this life that I'm in right now.

D: *Is that what they're showing you?* (Yes) *How are you making the plans?*

K: I just have a big piece of paper, a pencil and a writing pen. And we're figuring it all out. And they go, "Well, you didn't have much more to learn, but you needed to learn to take care of your body. You've learned a lot."

D: *Are you making plans with other people or what?*

K: Yes. You know ... where you decide to live ... family ... and all of that stuff. I guess I've decided about this life right now, and I tried to keep myself off the stairs. That was bad. (We both laughed.)

D: *You're talking about the life as Kim?* (Yes) *Was there anyone in that life that Kim knows now?*

K: David (her present husband) ... I think he was the doctor.

D: *Why did you make an agreement to come back with him?*

K: Because I was gone, and I didn't get a chance to know him. And he seemed really nice and caring. He cried.

D: *So he agreed to come back into the life of Kim to help?* (Yes, yes.)

Kim had asked about her adopted daughter, Robin. "She was my mother in that life. She was really upset because I went."

D: *She wanted to be with you again?* (Yes) *But she couldn't come as Kim's natural child?* (No) *Did she know beforehand that she would be adopted?*

K: Yes, that was part of her plan. I almost did it. I almost broke the body. (Kim had a car accident.) But she had to get to me.

D: *And she chose you over the birth parents?* (Yes) *Was there a reason for that?*

K: Oh! They were sixteen! When she was my mother I was sixteen and I broke my body. Then she had to leave her birth parents because they were sixteen and too young to keep her. And come be with me again.

D: *So this was the agreement beforehand that they were going to give her up. She already knew that Kim was to be her adopted mother.* (Yes.) *That's interesting because it shows that it all falls together.*

K: Yes. I hope those parents are okay.

D: *We can find out. You're doing a wonderful job answering the questions, but I think we'll call in somebody else who has more answers. Is that all right?* (Yes)

I then called the SC forth. I always ask it the same first question, "Why did you pick that life for Kim to see?"

K: So she would see that she needed to take care of her body.

D: *She did have some accidents, didn't she?* (Yes) *She really messed up the body, didn't she?* (Yes) *The subconscious couldn't stop it from happening?*

K: No, we didn't. We thought she needed to be reminded. She was starting to forget.

D: *She told us about how her daughter made a decision to come and be adopted. What about Robin's birth parents? They were very young when they had Robin. Can you see if they're alright?*

This was a question that Kim had asked to find out.

K: The birth mother was her brother in that lifetime. Her mother was really busy with the store, and she had to take care of that little brother.

D: *So there were agreements made between everybody? (Yes) Well, Kim expressed a concern. The parents that had Robin were very young, sixteen. She was wondering what happened to them in this present life. I know you can see these things if it's appropriate. What happened to them after Robin was born?*

K: She went to school and has other children.

D: *That will make Kim feel better if she knows that. So it all turned out well.*

One of Kim's physical issues was concern about her throat. (Thyroid) I asked what was causing her problem. "She wanted to call for help. When she fell down the stairs and broke her neck, she lay there for a long time and tried to call out, but couldn't."

D: *Why is it affecting her throat now?*

K: She's still trying to call for help. This started when her mom got sick. As long as her mother was there, she was okay. But when her mother started to get sick and die, then she wanted to cry out again.

I then proceeded with the therapy to leave the throat symptoms in the past with the other girl, and to reassure Kim that she couldn't do anything to help her mother anyway when she was dying. She was simply punishing herself. Since it was only a reminder left over from another lifetime, the SC agreed to heal the throat and return everything to the past. It healed it by sending energy to the glands in her neck and relaxing them. The SC said, "You don't have to cry out. You just have to relax."

After that was completed I went on to her next questions. She was concerned about ringing in her ears. It would switch from one side to the other. In other cases I have been told it had to do with adjusting frequencies. I suspected the answer would be the same in this case. "What's causing that?"

K: The Earth. The vibrations are changing and it's just going to happen. She will have to adjust to the frequencies. We can help by raising her vibrations.

The accidents had caused serious problems in her body and surgery was required. The SC was having a more difficult time trying to adjust her body to the vibrations because: "Sure a lot of wires in there! That's why it's so hard to adjust to the frequency. Let's see what we can do."

D: *That happened when she broke the body again. (Yes) Can you help with the vibration frequency so it won't bother her?*
K: Just trying to adjust it.
D: *Do all those wires create a grounding effect or what?*
K: It increases frequencies ... interference. It interferes with the natural process. She's pretty good though with all that going on. Considering.—We told her to take care of that body. (Laugh)

Wilma was going through a simple, mundane, primitive life when I asked her to move ahead to an important day when something was happening. When she did, it was obvious that she had leap-frogged into a different lifetime.

W: (Frantically) There's water. I can't breathe.
D: *What do you mean?*
W: I'm in the water. I can't breathe.

I took away any uncomfortable physical sensations, so she would be able to talk to me objectively, if necessary.

D: *How did you get in the water? You can move backwards and find out what happened. You can see it. It won't bother you at all to look at it.*
W: There's a car and it went off the bridge.

That was a surprise. Now it was obvious that she had leap-frogged. I had no choice but to follow it.

D: *Were you in the car?*

Her voice was shaking with fear as she answered, "Yes."

D: *It's all right. You can look at it. Were you driving or what?*
W: No ... I was in the front seat.
D: *Who was driving the car?*
W: My mom.
D: *Who else is in the car?*
W: My sister.
D: *How old are you?*

W: Seven.

D: *Were you going somewhere?*

W: I guess so.

D: *Did you live around there somewhere?*

W: Uh-huh ... not real close, but around there.

D: *Where's your father?*

W: I don't know.

D: *What happened? You can look at it. You don't have to experience it.*

W: She hit something or.... We're on the bridge. The front of the car just went up over the side of the bridge and flipped over and it hit the water, and water started coming in the windows, and I can't breathe.

I again took away any unpleasant physical sensations. "Do you know if your mother and your sister are around anywhere?"

W: No. None of us got out. We all died.

D: *You're all in the car?*

W: Yeah.—I'm going under.

D: *You won't feel it. You won't feel any discomfort whatsoever.—It was a shock, wasn't it?*

W: Yeah, I didn't see it coming.

D: *Your mother didn't either, did she?* (No) *She didn't know what was going to happen.*

I moved her ahead to where it was over with and she was on the other side of it. It is easier to get information after the person has left the body. I don't need them to go through the actual death. I asked Wilma (the child) if she could see the car.

W: It's under the water. It sank with everybody in it.

D: *Did anybody know you went into the water?*

W: No, there was nobody around.

D: *What are you going to do now?*

W: Well, I died in there, so I guess I'm just kind of floating off.

D: *Are your mother and your sister around?*

W: They're in the water. They died also, but I don't see them anymore.—I don't really want to go.

D: *Why not?*

W: Because I don't want to die.

D: *You were young.* (Yeah) *But it was an accident.* (Yeah) *Did you have a good life?*

W: I wanted it to last longer.

D: *It was a surprise. It wasn't supposed to end that quick.* (No) *Do you see anybody?*

W: Yeah, there's some people up here waiting. They know I'm coming.

D: *Are you going to talk to them?*

W: Uh-huh, there's my dad right now.

D: *You can ask them why it happened. Why did you die so young?*

W: He just said I didn't need to be down there longer.—I wanted to stay.—I'll forget really fast what it's like being down there, and then I'll know why it's better to be up here.

D: *But you were down there for a short time.*

W: He said that's all I needed. He said I learned what I needed.

D: *How do you feel about it?*

W: Well, like I said, I'd have liked to have stayed there, but maybe it's better up here. It's not as constricted.—There are some other people here. There's my aunt. She *was* my aunt.

D: *So there are people that you know. Where do you have to go now? Did anybody say?*

W: No, we're just kinda standing here ... floating here, I should say. They say we have to go up, but there's no rush. He said it's not like it is down there. I can do it in my own time.

D: *What do you want to do now?*

W: I'm ready to go up, I guess.—I can't go back.
D: *Might as well go up and see what's there.*
W: Yeah. He likes it there. He just took my hand, and we're going up. My aunt's coming.—I can't see very much right now. It's just kinda cloudy. There's stuff in the air.

I moved her ahead faster to when she got to where she was supposed to go.

W: I don't know where this is. I still can't see very much. There's stuff in the way.—Okay. There's somebody up there. Now I know I should know them, but I don't know who it is. He's kinda "filmy," but I just know it's somebody I've been in contact with up here before.
D: *So you feel you've been here before?*
W: Yeah, lots of times.
D: *So it's familiar to you now that you're there?*
W: Yeah, I think so. (Whispering) I wish I knew who that guy was. I don't know what he does right now. I can't describe. He sort of welcomes me when I come back there.—My dad's leaving. He has to go somewhere else.
D: *He has a job to do?*
W: I think he just did it ... just to be sure I got there.—So now I'm just kind of standing here with this person.
D: *Is he going to take you somewhere?*
W: We're gonna go over here for now, so that's what we did.—There's such fog. I can't see.—(Laugh) Oh, I wish I could do that!
D: *What?*
W: He just changed the way he looked ... just like that. He's changing himself so fast.—Oh, he's just being funny. He doesn't always do it.
D: *Let's see where he takes you. It'll become clearer.*
W: I'm going to school.—I see white colored stone and some steps and pillars and it's pretty big ... like the steps run a long way. There's probably only about six steps, but they run a long distance across.—So we're going to school.

And I was out, now I'm in and I didn't even get to see the door. How do you like that?

D: *What's the school like?*

W: There's lots of stuff going on in here, but this is where I figure out what I'm doing next.

D: *What are they going to teach you at that school?*

W: Just how to handle things down on Earth ... such a hassle being down there.

D: *Do you mean how to handle things when you're back in the body?*

W: Yeah, because up here, we can see how to handle stuff down there. It's easier to see it from up here. But down there, you can't see anything. It's just ridiculous. That's why we all have to get it straight up here.

D: *When you're down there, it doesn't always go the right way, does it?*

W: No, because we can't remember what we're doing. We're pitiful.

D: *Do they say why you can't remember?*

W: Well, let's see. He just says it would be too confusing. I think it would be easier if I could remember, but he says it wouldn't be.—I want to remember, but he says that's just not the way it is.

D: *He thinks it would be more confusing if you knew?*

W: Yeah, that's what he said. He said we're just programmed to stay on track and somehow internally programmed. He said that up here we'll get to do everything with you. And because we've done that, when you get down there you'll know, even though you don't actually remember. Because he says it's all recorded up there, so you don't have to worry about it. When people are up here, we go over what the plan is with them. So even when people go back down to Earth, they know what the plan is, even if they don't actually, quote, unquote, "remember." They know. They just don't know that they know.

D: *But many times when they get down here, things don't always go by the plans, do they?*

W: No, but we have fixes for that, too.

D: *What do you mean?*

W: Well, you know, we try to influence a little bit if we need to, just to kind of keep people on track, or get people back on track or whatever we can manage from where we are, without breaking any rules.

D: *How do you do that? When they're on Earth, people can't see you up there.*

W: No, they can't see me, which is good. Because if they could see me, I might not be able to do the things I do.— Sometimes you have to kind of encourage people to go a direction that they do not think about or want to go.

D: *That's not interfering?*

W: No, we do it within the rules. We know the rules and we don't ever break the rules.

D: *What are the rules?*

W: Just that you can't interfere, and you can't go down and take somebody by the hand and lead them around. But sometimes you can set up road blocks; block off a certain avenue that might change things for many people. We try not to do any more than we have to.

D: *They have free will when they go back into a body, don't they?*

W: Yes, yes. They can do a lot of things if they want to.

D: *Are you going to make a plan?*

W: Well, I'm going to work with her, and we're going to figure out what she needs to do next. But I think she's going to school for a while.

D: *The little girl?* (Yes) *She needs to go to school to be trained?*

W: Well, we don't really call it training, but there's just stuff she'll need to know before this next time around. So she'll do that while we're working on the plan.

D: *Does she have anything to say about the plan?*

W: Oh, yes. If she didn't want to do it, we'd work out another one. We don't want anybody doing something they don't want to do. That's no fun.

D: *They have to agree to it then?* (Oh, yes, yes.) *But then the plan can be changed when they come back to Earth?*

W: It depends. There have been times when the plans have been changed, but we try not to do that. I mean, we try to make sure the plan is solid before we send anybody down.

D: *Because you have all these other people with their plans.*

W: Right, and as you know, they all interweave together.

D: *Sometimes they don't work out the way the person wanted them to.*

W: Well, no, and they do have free will. So there are things that happen so it's not as if they chose that.

D: *It's all the other influences, too.*

W: Right. She'll be in some sort of general classes until we get the plan. And once we get the plan, then we'll know better what she needs to do the next round. We go over the plan first with her, and if she likes it, we send her to various areas where she can learn stuff, but we'll be helpful to her in that life.

D: *Why did she die so young in the car wreck?*

W: We just didn't need her there anymore. She agreed to a short run that time.

D: *She learned everything she was supposed to learn?*

W: Yes, and she was helping some other people, too, I believe, if I remember correctly.

D: *When she died, she didn't want to go right then.*

W: No, most people don't, usually. Not all the time. Some people are willing, but ... they're still attached to the body. And they don't know where they're going. They don't remember being up here before. They think they're going somewhere they don't know, so they're scared. And she was little so she was probably more scared than someone who was an adult, maybe, it just depends.—We wanted her back up here. We had some things going on that she likes.

I moved her ahead to see what the plan was, what she was supposed to do.

W: It's not set in stone yet, but we're thinking about a male. I see a business suit and ... I don't know if she's gonna want to do this.

D: *You mean to come back as a man?*

W: Well, not that. Her life is going to be really complicated. I don't know if she needs anything that complicated right now.—(Talking to someone else.) Oh! Yes, we need to ... I don't think this is right for her. Was it someone else's? I think they got the plans mixed up. (Laughs and whispers.) Okay, you go get it.

D: *That happens sometimes? They get them mixed up?*

W: Well, it's not supposed to.—(Laughing) We want to be sure that everybody gets the right plan. Yes, kind of got that confused there ... sorry.

D: *Do you have a lot of people you're taking care of there?*

W: Yes, and that actual plan was for the person ahead of her.

D: *Okay. Let that person have the complicated one.* (Laugh)—*Okay, what do you see for* her *plan? What looks right?*

I knew from the beginning that we were speaking about Wilma in her present life because if the other little girl died in a car accident it couldn't have been too far in the past. Wilma was born in 1963 so it was probably the life just prior to her present one.

W: I pulled some stuff out here, and it looks like she's going to be a mother next time. That's all I can see.

D: *Does that look like a good plan?*

W: Well, I wouldn't want to do it, but ... now she's shaking her head. She doesn't want to do that. She doesn't want to be a mother. (Laugh)

In this life, Wilma has never married and has no children.

D: *She has the final say, doesn't she?*

W: Yes. We never make anybody do anything they don't want to.—Usually people figure it out if they think they don't want to do it. Usually if they think about it long enough, they can see how they'll get ahead that way, so they'll do it.

D: *I was thinking that some people just can't be trusted to make up their own minds.*

W: Well, there are those, but I don't do anything with those. Somebody else deals with that.

D: *Did you show her another plan?*

W: We're gonna have to work one out. It's gonna take a little time to study it to make sure we get everything in place properly.—I want to give her a good one ... not so traumatic as the last one.

D: *It will be longer than the last one?*

W: I think so, yes. Yes, it'll be smoother sailing. She'll like something that's not as tedious.

D: *Sometimes is a short one like that a lesson for other people?*

W: Sometimes they are, and there were some lessons for others involved in that situation.

I moved her to where the plan was solid and asked if she agreed to it.

W: She's gonna have a career or a job. She likes that. She lives past the age of seven, so she really likes that. It's good if you want to be down there that long. I wouldn't want to be, but she thinks that's a great idea.

D: *What kind of a career?*

W: I can't tell. She liked it, whatever it was. She liked the idea of it.

D: *Is she going to agree to it?*

W: I think so. She's got to see the rest of it, but I think she likes it. It's gonna be a while.

D: *Not going to go right away?*

W: Oh, no. Now that she likes this, there are certain things we are gonna have her acclimated to.

Even though the entity I was speaking to had no concept of time, I had to tell it that we were working with time here. I asked if it was aware that it was speaking through a physical body. It said it was definitely aware.

D: *This is the physical body we call Wilma.* (Yes) *Is this the body, the life that the little girl goes into, or was there one in between?*

W: I think this is the next one.

D: *The one she was making the plan about?*

W: I think so, yes. She didn't want the other that was gonna be a mother, so we got rid of that.

D: *She didn't want the responsibility?*

W: She just doesn't need it. I don't know if she's ever done it before, but she doesn't need to do it. She's on a scouting mission this time.

I needed to ask her questions, and I wanted to be sure that the entity we were speaking to would be able to answer them, or if we would have to call forth the SC. It said, "I can't see everything, but I can see a lot." There was always the eternal question, "What is her purpose? What is she supposed to be doing with her life?" She has a career, but she was not satisfied. They said she was going to change that. They gave her a lot of information about the new career she would have by next year. I reminded it that we needed money in this world so we could live. "I know. That's why I'm glad I don't have to come back there anymore."

I asked the SC why it wanted Wilma to know about the short life of the child. What was it trying to tell her?

W: That's why she doesn't feel good.

D: *Is that what's causing her physical problems?*

W: Yes, she was at the bottom of the river for a while.

Wilma had a problem with her lungs: fluid retention, the feeling that she was drowning in her own fat and fluid.

W: She's not drowning anymore. She died there. The little girl is dead now, so Wilma doesn't need those physical feelings.

D: *But it seems as though she's carried them over to the body of Wilma.*

W: Oh really? God, we don't want that. That's not what we want.

D: *She said she has had this feeling all her life, and so she's drowning in fluids like she's having fluid retention in her body.*

W: Well, she was down there for a long time. I don't see any reason why she should carry that over to this body. That was the last life of that little girl. It doesn't belong anywhere else. It should not be a part of her present life.

I gave the suggestions that it be left in the past where it belonged, so it wouldn't bother Wilma any more in this life.

W: I've never seen it, but there's a lot of stuff I haven't seen yet. I could probably ask around and someone would certainly have heard or know of it.

D: *In my work I do find people bring forward things associated with the way they died. And we don't like that because it causes problems.*

I went through the steps to take it away. They said there was nothing else wrong with the body, only the aftereffects from the drowning incident.

W: Wilma was never going to get that problem worked out here; that was easier from up there. We just dissolve it. We focus on what the body should be and how it should function. And then we separate that stuff and get it back into the proper area as far as the other life. It does not belong here.—We got that one out so we're just

127

visualizing what the body should be in the healthy state it's in, and a much more comfortable state of being for her, and consider it done! We're all done. (They also stabilized her metabolism. Her hair falling out was also caused by the slow metabolism.) It only happened because she was getting lives mixed up.—I'm not an expert on that part of it, but sometimes that can happen and as careful as we try to be, sometimes things sneak by us.

Parting message: I just want to tell her to carry the torch and she knows what she's carrying it for. Just to remember that she's here for a reason and reasons aren't always clear. But all of you have to carry the torch and we just want her to remember to carry the torch.

D: *What do you mean by carrying the torch?*
W: Jobs to do and you can. Just keep her eye on the ball; to not lose sight of what she wants to do.

Chapter 8

A DIFFICULT ASSIGNMENT

Mary came off the cloud into a beautiful country scene with trees and fields and many animals playing among the trees. She was a little girl of six who was enjoying being outside by herself. She did not like to be in the house where she lived, but preferred to stay in nature. She said there was a lot of stress in the house because everybody was scared. They were afraid of making their father angry, so it was tense in the family. I asked who else was in the family. She answered in a childish voice, "I think of tomato worms as my family—but my brother and my sisters, and I have a great-uncle and a grand-dad. Also my mom. She's tired a lot. She works real hard. It's a big farm. There's other people coming to help with the crops and she cooks for everybody. Dad's not happy. He doesn't want to be there.—There's turtles in the ponds and the tomato worms are big and green and fat. They feel good. They are better than family." They lived in separate houses but all on the large farm. "I stay pretty much by myself, but we have cats with kittens. I like the plants and the animals. I climb trees to see the baby birds in the nests."

D: *What do you want to do when you grow up? Have you ever thought about that?*

M: I don't know that I'll last that long. It seems too far away. I don't think grown-ups are happy, and I don't want to be like that.—I'd like to be taller.

D: (Laugh) *You will. Believe me ... you will. You'll grow. Everybody grows.*

M: I just want to stay on the farm. The animals, the plants ... we have a big garden ... catch turtles in the pond. Feel the dirt between my toes.

It was obvious from what Mary had told me during our interview that she had gone to a time in her present lifetime. She was reliving her unhappy childhood on a farm with unloving parents. I moved her backward to when she was a little baby. This way I would be able to move her out of this life and into the past. She saw herself as a baby in a crib. All her brothers and sisters were gathered around staring at her. They seemed so much bigger than her.

D: *What do you think about being in this family now that you're in a baby's body?*
M: I don't know. I'm not sure about this. (Pause) Doesn't seem very happy. Doesn't seem like they know I'm one of them. I'm so much smaller and there's curiosity about me.
D: *That's because you're the new one in the family. It will work out okay.*

I then moved Mary further back to when she was first making the decision to be a baby again, and asked what she saw.

M: It's a table with charts on it, or maps or scrolls. I'm at one end of it. The table is an oval shape, but with funny corners. It may be marble ... something cold when you touch it. It seems like the table has a light inside it, but I don't see how it can do that. There are maps and papers. Something's spread out and it seems to glow from underneath.
D: *Is there anybody else around the table or are you by yourself?*
M: It feels like there are a couple of people that are older. (She suddenly started to cry and said with a dreadful

sound to her voice:) I don't want to go!—They say I have to go back. (Crying) I don't want to go back. (Crying)

D: *Is that what they're deciding?*

M: They said I have to go back.

D: *Why do you have to go back?*

M: I guess there's more learning.—I like where I am now though. It has great beauty and clear water ... beautiful green hedges, landscapes and fountains. Calm and peaceful.—I don't want to go. They said it would be better in the long run.

D: *Can they tell you what you have to learn?*

M: Relationships are one thing. Thought processes and staying clear of negativity.—Everybody has to go through the lessons. I guess I didn't get it right last time.

D: *What happens if you don't get it right?*

M: There are lots of different options, but they're telling me this is the one I have to take.

D: *Did they show you some of the other options?*

M: No because they said this is the one I had to take.—The goal is perfection.

D: *But you don't think you got it right last time?*

M: I guess not. I didn't think I did that bad of a job. (Depressed) They said it would be different this time. Different characters ... different play casting ... different parts. (Frustrated) You can't fly down there.

D: *Did they show you anything about what it would be like?*

M: They said it would be healing for the family.

D: *For your family you're going into?*

M: That we all agreed on.

D: *The others in your family agreed to come together too?*

M: Yes. Some of us have been together before, but not all of us ... to try to get it right this time. I know that some of those people have tried before, but I guess they didn't get it right. And there are new ones. Everyone has different parts ... they're not the same.

D: *Different characters are brought in for the play. Is that what you mean?*

M: (Disappointed.) Yes ... I guess. They said for my healing and all our healing, I had to go and do this.

D: *Did they tell you how you're supposed to do that?*

M: There are just a lot of different options.—Do no harm.

D: *That's important, isn't it?*

M: I guess if they're gonna make me go back and "do it," it is. (Annoyed) I think there are other ways I could do it.—They said something about a time table that we could get it done the quickest.

D: *It has to be at a certain time period?*

M: I don't know if I have to get *it* done in a certain time period or everything I have to do. This is faster than some other ways of taking care of it.

D: *So all the people that are going to be in your family have all agreed to come together?*

M: Yes, I guess. Others will come along as they are needed.

D: *I've heard that you make contracts. Is that true?*

M: Well, we all have our assignments, if that's what you mean. My assignment is to go, and *do no harm.* (Emphasizing.)

D: *And the goal is perfection, which is difficult, isn't it?* (Yes) *Of course, it looks different when you're up there. What do you think? Are you going to be able to do the assignment?*

M: (A heavy sigh.) I just think there ought to be another way to do it. But they said this way would take care of things faster.

D: *What happens if you don't get it right?*

M: Doesn't sound like I have an option this time, for some reason.

D: *So you have to get it right?*

M: That's what the expectation is.

D: *I'm just curious. What happens if you don't do it right?*

M: Got to come back again.—But it can be in different places.

D: *Different settings, different countries, and different situations?*

M: Different planets.

D: *Oh, so you can do that too. Have you had many different lifetimes and different experiences?*

M: I've had some.

D: *I just wondered if you've been doing this a long time.*

M: (Upset) Sure feels like it.—Seems like there are levels, and they change levels and this is on different levels, and this will eventually end on a higher level. (She sounded very distressed.)

D: *So you go to different levels. You have to learn things and finish that level first before you go on to the next level?*

M: Yes, I guess so.—I just think it's stupid ... just stupid! Because the place they want me to go you don't remember anything after you get there. It's just stupid! It's like you sign up for a certain grade in college; then when you get there, there's no books and no clothes. You don't know where your class is. You don't know who your teachers are, and it's just stupid! It's the only place they do it that way. Earth! (Disgruntled) Other places ... other energy systems ... other galaxies. They know what's going on.

D: *You don't go in just totally blind. So, Earth is different.*

M: Yes. Get it done! Thing is, go to it and get it done. It's so frustrating.

D: *But you didn't make the rules.*

M: No, but they make me play by them.

D: *Did you tell them you didn't think it was a good idea?*

M: Oh, I think I've made myself clear.—They see *big* events, but not just for me. We're all interconnected, so it's like a quantum leap forward, they say. There are a whole lot of us coming in at the same time, kind of the same mission. Orientation to new ways of doing things that haven't been ... well, they're the way things have always supposed to have been, but it's got all screwed up down there. So it's reorientation to the way things should have always been, but it's changing back over again. The human brain, not all of it's been hooked up, so it's just been in its infancy. Like it doesn't know everything it can do, but the brain can do a whole lot more. So it's like there are a whole fleet or batch of us that are having to go back and reorient people.

D: *Have you been to Earth before?* (Yes) *So you know what it's like down there.*

M: Yes, but it's always a surprise.

D: *Did they tell you how you could remember your assignment once you get down there?*

M: They said, don't worry about it. It's going to have just a minimum flow, but that hasn't been my experience.

D: *Is there any way they can help you once you get there, if you run into problems?*

M: Yes. We're never really disconnected, but it feels like we are. Everybody's kind of in the same soup, so they have to help each other out. I'm told that I would get helpers as I went along.

D: *Probably wouldn't even recognize them, I guess?*

M: They probably won't even recognize *me*. (Emphatically) —I just don't want to go. It's so pretty here ... waterfalls and clear water.

D: *Do they have any idea how long it will be before you can come back there?*

M: They say, when I'm finished. I know no matter what, it's going to feel like forever because it always does down there. (Very childish)

D: *You can't argue with them, can you?*

M: I have been, but it doesn't get me anywhere.

D: *And you will return eventually. I've heard that when you go back it's like a blink of an eye. You won't even realize how long you've been gone.*

M: Yes, that's the song they have been singing.—But I've been there. It's heavy and you don't have any wings. I like to fly. (Wistful.) I like the freedom.—At the stage I'm going in, I have to do the whole birth thing and childhood thing and their schools.

D: *From the very beginning.*

M: We just have to teach and it doesn't have to be like that.—It's going to be different in the future. Once we get everybody back to the way it's always been, then you can recreate. You don't have to be stuck in gravity and 3-D.—Is that the right word ... 3-D ... dimensions?—It won't be like that. It'll be different. They've forgot. They'll be different when the energies are changed. We're all going to help change the energy, and the brain will be all wired up, so you can take care of that. And be in one spot and concentrate and think and be in another spot. They can do it now. They just forgot.

D: *Do you mean that in the future, they won't have to start out as a baby and go through all of the childhood stuff?*

M: Right because the whole thing's changing, and it's not going to have the boundaries—no, not boundaries—constraints.

D: *You mean they will just have an adult body and keep that?*

M: Yes, or not even have a body. You don't *have* to have a body. It's just all these different steps and they're lumbering around in these big physical suits and they don't have to be doing that. There are a whole lot of us that are going to help them remember. But in order to get there, we have to forget. See what I'm saying? It's just stupid.

D: *But in the future, if they have a physical body, they'll just keep it or what?*

M: Yes. The energy is the only thing that changes, and it gets lighter and people can come out of different dimensions and show up there. They don't have to start as babies. There will be energy facilitators for it at the beginning to help.

D: *So in the future there won't be babies or little children?*

M: There will be if you want to come in that way, but it will just be an option you can choose.

D: *I have heard there are some beings that are just energy.* (Yes) *They don't have a body at all.*

M: Kind of a consciousness that never dies. It's just consciousness that remains.

D: *Is everyone on Earth going to move up to this way of doing it?*

M: The people that stay in the physical will shift, but there are going to be many people that don't stay. That wasn't their thing this time, so there will be people that leave. But then the people that stay will be able to remember how to use the brain. All will be wired up correctly.

D: *But is everyone who is alive now on the Earth going to be able to do this?*

M: All the people that stay will. Some quicker than others, but you're gonna pretty much have to because the whole framework will change. It's like the computer won't recognize the software if you stay. You know what I'm saying? Accept the old programs. You'll have to upgrade or it just won't work.

D: *I was thinking about the people that are so much into karma and negativity.*

M: They will eventually shift. Oh, God, they're negative! They're so negative. This is judgment ... black, white ... right, wrong ... yes, no. There are many other ways of being.

D: *You said earlier that you're supposed to change negativity, didn't you?*

M: Yes, we're all supposed to work together to lighten. Change the way the vibrations are on the planet to bring the full integration of the human mechanism to the way it's supposed to be. The way it has been before. I suspect the way it is everywhere else other than that planet.

D: *But it sounds like some of them are going to be moving at different speeds, different vibrations. They won't be doing it all at the same time?*

M: Yes, they won't all get the realization or whatever.

D: *I find it interesting that you're supposed to be there, but you're not really happy about going. (Laugh) Sounds like you have a big job to do.*

M: Yes. It's a big job all right.

D: *They wouldn't ask you to do it if they didn't think you could.*

M: (Quietly) Yes, I'm going ....

D: *They have confidence in you that you're going to be able to do it. Stupid rules ... but I think you're able to do it and you will do it just fine.*

I had her drift away from the scene and called forth the SC. At first there was resistance from Mary's conscious mind as it tried to gain control. The SC said she was fighting allowing it to come in because of fear. I couldn't see what she could be afraid of after all the things we had already uncovered and had been discussing. So Mary finally relaxed and let go of trying to control the session, and then the SC was able to come in.

D: *We thought we were going to past lives, instead she was a little girl in this life. Was there a reason why you took her there?*

M: She's done with the past.

D: *You've told me many times that we don't need to focus on the past anymore.*

M: Not any longer.

D: *Things are changing, but Mary sounded like she came down to do a very important mission. And things haven't turned out the way she thought, have they?*

M: It's not over yet.

D: *That's true. She said she was supposed to adjust to it, and help the negativity?*

M: That's true. That's what she and everyone is supposed to do.

There was a lot of discussion about Mary's personal questions and circumstances, especially with her family. They had influenced her negatively for many years, and she was still having difficulty releasing the ties they had on her. We worked on all of this. Then we got to her physical problems (of which there were many, mostly caused by her work environment [chemicals]).

D: *She had a lot of damage done when she was working there, didn't she?*

M: Yes, she came very close to transitioning.

D: *Oh, it was that bad?* (Oh, yes.) *Why did it have to develop that far?*

M: She didn't follow the cues and she was used to having such abundant energy and going from dawn to dusk. She took it for granted and then she began spending so much time in that environment; it wasn't just a six or an eight hour shift. It was much, much overtime and she was saturated in these chemicals, and it was also an exit point she could have chosen. It was an open door for her. She could have left, and she chose not to. She realized since then that it was an open door and she wishes she had darted through it, and so it has been a source of depression for her.

"They" proceeded to work on her very complicated physical symptoms. One was interesting that dealt with her brain. "She knows that it has received some rewiring, and some of this has been because of the changes on the planet. She knew if she went with western medicine that she would be in more trouble. And she knew intuitively if she could just get away from what was causing it, that eventually the body would turn itself around."

D: *You said the brain had been rewired already?*

Many times the SC will rewire the brain if it thinks it is necessary.

M: Yes. It had to go through. If someone would do the right scan, they would see it and she knows that if somebody took the right pictures, they would be able to read it and see it. And she's right about that.

D: *You mean after the damage (chemicals), you went in there and rewired it?*

M: That's exactly right. The way it works now is not the same.

D: *But she thinks she has lost some of her functions.*

M: Well, she is different than she was. She was pretty dialed in before. She was doing her meditation and her exercises. She's very sharp and notices little inconsistencies and she is right. She's not the way she was, but we would offer to her assistance and we would say that by following the paths of healing and art the brain would have changed anyway ... in other ways. So she's saying, "I'm not the way I was before I started working at the plant." Our response to her would be, "You wouldn't be the same no matter what you did, and your functioning is getting closer to 100% even if it's somewhat different than it was." She has to get used to it and not see it as something negative.

Her stomach and elimination system also took a heavy hit from the chemicals and she was carrying a lot of heavy metals in her system. "We would also say she had started a beginning cleanse with herbs. In the last couple of days she got fouled up on that. And we would tell her that we will continue to offer assistance intuitively as to know what herbs to go on in the future to keep things righted. She has this sense about her, 'Nobody's helped me. I'm gonna have to do something about it myself.'"

D: *She didn't ask for your help, did she? (Laugh)*

M: But she's taken a leap of faith by coming here to see you.

D: *Are you able to flush all of those toxins out of her body?*

M: Yes, she may notice "not pleasant" things in the toilet over the next while, but it's all of good reason and no harm. We'll get rid of all of that. She may want to increase her fluid intake and make sure it is all spring water. And she knows that she should be eating more fruits and vegetables. She has noticed she doesn't require as much meat as she once did. And this is a very positive thing as she continues to heal. She's also put out that prayer that she would like to get to the point where she doesn't eat food at all. And we just wanted to say, "One step at a time." She's not there yet, and she may not be there in six months. But that's her goal and we would say that it is an attainable goal.

D: *You said she'd notice things in the toilet. Do you mean like diarrhea?*

M: She may see darkened stools and the color of her urine may change, but that's part of getting rid of all of this.

Note: The whole time that Mary had been in my office she had not drank anything, even though I kept offering her water. After the session, before we had said anything about the session, she went to the bathroom. When she came out she said, "I think I'll take you up on that offer of water. My urine is a funny color." So it had already begun to take effect immediately.

M: We would ask that she stay away from meat; probably two times a year would be enough.—She will get back to 100%. It will take some time in rebalancing diet and figuring out what she needs now to live on, and it will be different than it was in the past.

Message from the SC: Calm down about money. We hear her and understand her concerns. She's not going to starve to death and die, though she would like the "die" part.—She just doesn't realize how big the advances are that she has already made. And she thinks it's far more complicated. She's frightened she won't make it to the new Earth but, in a way, she already has.

D: *Yes, it's already here. It's already happening.*

M: Her association with you is very positive. (She had taken one of my classes.) She can do the work you teach. We will assist in the self-esteem areas and bring her clients that she has positive outcomes with to build her self-confidence. So she can practice, and she will be a "huge" service to people because she has had such a rocky road. She feels alone, but she is never alone ... no one ever is.

Chapter 9

BALANCE IN LIFE

Chelsea had some confusion at first when she came off the cloud. She found herself in a strange unearthly environment. She saw an orange sky, orange ground and a forest of purple trees with no leaves. Instead of bark they had a leathery texture, smooth but with an imprinting in it like the cells on skin. The deep, dark orange atmosphere was heavy, an almost gaseous environment. As she moved through the forest of strange trees she sensed that she did not have a body. That did not bother her, but the lifeless quietness of the scene did. "I feel mostly disappointed because there's not much else there. It's kind of empty." After wandering around for a while she decided that she wanted to find something else.

So I had her pull away from the scene and move to another appropriate time and place. When she stopped this time it was a green environment of regular trees and forests. A normal Earth type scene. She saw that she was a little Indian boy who was hunting rabbits to help feed his family. He described his life with his family in a large settlement of tepees. As we moved his life forward he grew to an age where he was allowed to join the other men as they rode their horses in a hunting party. In addition to hunting deer for the village, he announced that they were also going to kill people. "They're settlers who are in our area. They're where they don't belong, and we're getting rid of them. They have built a structure there. This is the first time I knew they were there. I think the others knew. I am surprised that we are going to kill them. I feel a little confused. There are women and children there, too. But the men say they have to go. We have to get rid of them or more will come, so we have to kill them all."

When the killing began he really didn't want to be a part of it, but he would be considered a coward if he didn't help. So they killed a family and he participated even though he didn't feel good about it. The men decided not to tell the others in the village about the intruders. They were afraid they would get worried and panic. So they decided to keep it a secret, and did not tell anyone what had happened when they returned to the village.

But it had accomplished nothing. When I moved him forward to another important day he said more strangers had come. The men felt they had no choice but to kill them, as many as they could. "What other choices do you have? Are you going to leave? Why should you have to leave your home?" There was no keeping it a secret now. The entire village was involved. So I moved her forward again and he announced that he had been shot and was dying (a young man in his twenties). The family they attacked this time had guns, and he was shot in the chest. "The others are fighting. I'm dead by the time they realize I'm dead."

Now that he was free from the body he felt weightless as he floated upward through stars in space. It was a very peaceful feeling. I asked him about the life he had just left. "It was sad that I had to do something I didn't want to do. I think we all could have learned how to live together, but there was not any trust at all.—Killing children is not a good thing!—Sometimes you have to do things you don't want to do for the betterment of everyone around you, even if you don't like it. It's a lesson, but I'm not sure it's the right lesson. There didn't seem to be the option of not doing what was required ... not if you want to be a part of that group."

I then condensed time to where he arrived somewhere instead of just floating. "It's a white, white area, just bright white. There's an energy, a presence, but it's like many energy cells that are one now. It's a part of one big mass.—Now you have to look over your lifetime. It's like a review. You go through the whole thing."

D: *What do you think as they show it to you?*
C: Oh, I was a good person. I didn't live very long, but I was a good person, for the time I was there. The killing part wasn't a very good part. Even though I didn't want to do it, I did it anyway.
D: *You were part of the culture, though. Sometimes you can't get out of situations.*
C: No, but I could have been an influence. If he would have spoken up, maybe he could have changed the outcome. Instead of doing what everyone else expected, being part of a group mentality.
D: *Following what everybody else thinks?*
C: Right, and taking responsibility for that reason.
D: *After you finish the life review, what happens then?*
C: Well, I have to go back down. I guess I'll go into a situation where I'll use my judgment for a different outcome. A situation that will go against a group mentality.
D: *Do you have to make any agreements with other people, or is that part of your review?*
C: I just sense there is someone I killed. That maybe I shouldn't have killed them. Even though I thought it was right at the time, it really wasn't.—I think I made an agreement with this person that I did kill. It was a child ... was a girl that I killed. I have to come back and do something positive to replace the negative. I have to make it up to this other individual somehow.—It's being discussed on what we'll do. They're figuring out where I should go. I am a part of it. I have to go into situations where I'm able to make a choice to do something that's wrong, or to be different from everyone else and do what's right. (Chelsea was moaning.) I'm going to be a soldier. I don't think it is my decision. I'm going to go

back and be a soldier because maybe in the same situation I can do something different.

D: *Soldiers kill too, don't they?*

C: Yes, they do. It wasn't a good choice, but that's what I did.

D: *Tell me about that one. You can see it in a condensed form. What happened in that lifetime?*

C: They are saying it's German WW II. Or is it WW I?—I have a nice uniform. I'm a young man.

D: *Did you want to go into the army?* (Yes) *Did you want to fight?*

C: I'm proud about it. Because it makes me important to my family.

D: *You weren't important before?*

C: I think it's just a direction right now. I'm grown-up. That I've picked something to do.

D: *And the war is going on?*

C: I'm not in the full swing of it. I'm just in uniform.

I had him condense it to find out what happened. He got into the fighting, the war part, but he was injured before he had a chance to kill people. "The battle was just starting out. I didn't know what I was doing. I got hurt and was released." He was shot in his chest and arm, and it became infected, so he didn't have to return to the war. Instead of being happy, it made him feel like a loser. "Because I didn't get to do much of anything before I had to leave." He went home and his mother was taking care of him. "My mom is okay with it. I'm not happy, though. It would have been one thing if I had gotten further along than I did."

D: *It wouldn't bother you to kill people?*

C: That's what I went into the army for.

As we moved him further ahead in his life his chest still caused him pain. There were tiny pieces of shrapnel in there. He got a job in a factory. "I don't have a choice. That's what I

146

have to do now. It's not what I like doing but I have to do it anyway. To live." He now had a family so he had to have something.

I then took him forward to the last day of his life and he saw that he had a heart attack. "I'm old."

D: *You've lived a long time?*
C: Relatively speaking. I'm going to say I'm in my sixties. My health was swept downhill and I couldn't work anymore. I was just worn out from breathing and smoking ... pains in my chest. It just hurt and there were too many pieces of shrapnel to remove.—I'm in bed and it's hard to breathe and there are pains in my chest. I'm having a heart attack.—My wife is there.

I moved him to where the death was over and he was out of the body. I asked him if he learned anything from that lifetime. "I let myself get all depressed. And I just had blinders on. I chose to feel sorry for myself after the war ... after I got injured. And I let that ruin the rest of my life. I chose to be upset over it and I was never really into anything. All that was in my own head. I could have done much better. I could have had a much better life."

D: *But you let it drag you down?*
C: Yes, and you can't do that. I threw that life away. And you should not do that.
D: *You can't really see what you're doing when you're in the middle of it.*
C: No ... until it's too late.
D: *If you had a chance to do it again, what do you think you would do?*
C: I think I would have had a different attitude. Maybe not going into the service to start with. And even if I did and I had to leave, I'd just make the best of it and do something else. You don't mope over what went wrong. You can't obsess on the past. You just drag down everyone else

around you, too. You can't let things get you down. You can control a lot of it with your own head.

I then had her move away from the death scene and called forth the SC. The first question I always ask is why these lives were shown. "You picked three different lives for her to see. I can see the continuity in two of them. Let's go back to the beginning. The first thing you chose was the place that had purple trees and the orange environment. Why did you pick that for her to see?"

C: There's life in other forms than just what you expect. She needed to know it's not just the human life. There are all spectrums of life. It's not always about a human being.

D: *A human being is just one part of evolution, isn't it? (Yes) Then you showed her the lifetime as an Indian who had to kill.*

C: Because sometimes you have to do things that are not popular if it means sustaining the entire community.

D: *Sometimes it's the only way you can exist in those communities?*

C: That's right. So sometimes you have to put your own personal feelings behind for the better good. Sometimes she doesn't always realize that. It's not just about what she wants to do. It's about what makes sense for the better good.

D: *I can see how that one connected to the next life where she was a soldier. In the life as an Indian she was killing and didn't want to, but in the life as a soldier she was hurt before she had a chance to kill.*

C: She shouldn't have let the circumstance ruin the way she perceived the rest of the lifetime. She should have gotten past that. It should have been about making what was left of the life better, and dealing with whatever circumstances.

D: *Instead she let it pull her down.*

C: Right. She wasted the whole life. The lesson is to take adverse situations and not let them dictate the rest of your life, but to turn it to something different. You can choose to be a victim and let something you don't want to happen, happen and not do anything about it, or you can take it, overcome it, and do something else that's positive.

Chelsea was experiencing many serious physical problems and was on medication for depression. She did not like her job as an accountant and felt overworked. Her husband was drinking and she felt neglected. So she had created a similar situation where she had turned it into a negative one instead of focusing on the positive side. The SC said the main cause of her problems was wanting to escape from life. When she came home every night from work she would shut herself up in her room and spend all her time on the computer, especially e-bay where she was buying and selling constantly. She said it was merely an innocent hobby, but the SC said it had gotten out of hand, and she was shutting out everything that was important in her life. A repeat of the last lifetime. The SC suggested getting rid of the computer all together so she could rejoin life. But I think that will be very difficult for her to do. She was told that if she spent more time with her husband, their marriage would be better and he wouldn't feel the need to drink. Chelsea definitely had a lot of work to do. The SC will offer good and valid suggestions, but it is always up to the individual whether or not they will accept them. Because we have free will they can never interfere. But if we are smart we will listen to them because they can see the bigger picture.

C: You have to have a balance in everything. She can do volunteer work. She can do less compulsive activities. Be more of a wife to her husband. She can help him with his situation. He has suggested more walks and doing things that would help him with his health. And if she weren't so glued to the computer every night, then maybe she'd spend time doing that and helping him too.

Parting message: You have to take everything in perspective and balance. The job's okay, but you're not responsible for the outcome. And you need to cut back on all the hobbies. It's become too big a distraction to avoid real life. You can help your husband. She just needs to balance everything out.

Chapter 10

TRAVELING

Linda was chosen to be the demonstration in my class in London in 2008. During the interview Linda cried as she described the events in her life. She had had every horrible thing that it is possible for one human to do to another happen to her. It is to her credit that she was able to survive. It would surely have destroyed a lesser soul. A horrible childhood, an equally horrible marriage, and then having her children taken away from her by the husband who she knew was involved with incest with his daughters. She ended up losing everything, and felt she had nothing to live for. She was seriously contemplating suicide. She said whenever she drove home after work, she dreaded the trip because she knew there was nothing for her in her house. I was not surprised when she said she had been diagnosed with a cancerous growth in the female organs. It was obvious she was suppressing great anger. It was very moving for the class to hear her story, and many of them had a hard time listening to it. But they had to learn that this is what therapy is all about: listening without judging or prejudice so that you can help the client. I did not know anything about her life before I chose her for the class demonstration, but it was obvious that she desperately needed help.

When Linda came off the cloud she found herself in a landscape of brownish sand. Nothing else was visible. It was hot, and to her surprise she saw that she was a barefooted old man. His legs were bare and hairy, old and brown, and he was dressed in some kind of fabric that was just draped on him. "My arms are old and my body feels strong, but old and worn,

151

tired. My hair is black and gray mixed, and comes to my shoulders. Hair everywhere, my face is hairy and rough. Even my arms, hairy and black and gray ... (Bewildered.) I'm old!" He was holding something in his hand. "I'm holding onto it tight. It's a stone."

D: *Why are you holding onto it so tight?*
L: It's my life line. It keeps me connected to remember who I am. Keeps me connected to the others. So I will always know that I'm a part of the others.
D: *What does the stone look like?*
L: It's gray and it has a symbol on it. Engraved within.
D: *What is the symbol?*
L: It has three points, but ... it curls like that and there are three points. (Motioning. It was difficult to describe.)
D: *Like a pyramid?*
L: No. It curls at the top. It's like one continuous motion. It's three. The inside is solid and the tips curve.
D: *What does the symbol represent?*
L: My belonging. My connection. My remembrance. I keep it with me. I look at the symbol. Because I'm away from the others and it connects me to them. I can remember and I can communicate. It's my life line, and I have it in my hands. Sometimes I wear it within my breast. It's like a radar ... a way of finding my way.
D: *Where did you get the stone?*
L: From the others.
D: *Tell me about the others. I'm interested. You can trust me. It's okay, isn't it?*
L: Yes. The others say, yes. The others are my source ... my group ... I'm one of the others.
D: *Where are the others?*
L: They are everywhere scattered like seeds, and we are in many different places, and we're connected. And the symbol is to remind me of my connection. I'm going to places, and sometimes there is the possibility of forgetting that I am not the place. I am *with* them, but not *of* them.

D: *And you've been on Earth a long time?*

L: Yes, I come and I go. I've been a part of the making of the darkness of the Earth, and I'm a part of the lifting of the darkness.

D: *Is that what you're doing now in this place with the sand?*

L: I'm in the sand because it's where I find the others, in the aloneness of the sand.

D: *Do you mean you have to be away from the other people?*

L: Yes, and the others connect with me and I have my symbol in my hand because I'm reaching out to the others. And when I'm amongst the people, I wear it in my breast. Yes, to my heart, there it is.

D: *So that's part of the reason for the stone, so you won't forget where you came from? Do you remember why you came?*

L: The stone is to open the channels for me to send back to the others my occurrences ... what occurs within my life.

D: *You said you were sent to erase the darkness?*

L: Yes, to alleviate, yes. To show the way out of the heavy density, yes. I walk with them and I lead them out, so I am *of* them but I am *not* them. I see the way out, so I go in and I feel and have the life .... (Wondering if that's the correct wording.) I have the life they have, and then I show them the way out.

D: *How do you show them the way out?*

L: By knowing how they feel, how they think. How they react and showing the other way of being through that.

D: *That's difficult, isn't it?* (Yes) *How do you keep from being trapped in it yourself?*

L: With great difficulty, but then I have my symbol as it rejuvenates my spirits and it feeds to me impulses from the others. And the others lift me up above the occurrences so that although my body is in it, my essence is above it.

D: *It's hard to keep separated at times, isn't it?* (Yes) *That's why you must have that so you won't forget and become trapped. Is that a good word?*

L: Yes because sometimes we do. It takes tremendous love.

D: *And the others are doing the same thing?*

L: Yes, and different, but all the same purpose.

D: *You're all mixing with the people?*

L: Yes. Live in the reality of the people.

D: *And they all come into physical bodies?*

L: No. Some stay in spirit form because they elevate those of us who venture into the physical. Without them it would be impossible because we would get lost. That's why we have to hold the symbol.

D: *You said you help the people by just being among them and sharing in their experience?*

L: Yes, as one way. First you gather the feelings they have by having the experiences, to create those feelings and that way of being. And then through that path of the others, we show them the way out, so it's very purposeful as far as dipping into the murk. First dipping into the murk and showing them out to fluff it off.

D: *Do you do this by talking to them?*

L: No. Sometimes language is important, but it's more a vibration. Just by being with them, and feeling the impulse of what to do, and when to do.

D: *Just your presence is enough then?*

L: Yes because through the presence, the other things occur as need be, through the openness of being with the presence. So with some it could be language or speech. With others it could be a look. With others it could just be the love in them, but with all they feel the vibration and it soothes.

D: *Are you going to remain on the Earth a long time doing this?*

L: Whatever is needed.

D: *Will you know when it is time to leave?*

L: Yes because we get called back.

D: *You know where to go?*

L: Just traveling from place to place, as need be. We're directed where to go. Whatever place or time.

D: *How do you get your food and things you need?*

L: We are always taken care of. All is provided and this is what we teach others, on trusting that we are connected and all will come as need be, and so there's never a worry about provisions. And sometimes we lack provisions, as that is an occurrence within the planet that we need to experience how others feel with the lack.

D: *Have you always done this, or have you lived normal lives?*

L: Always done this.

D: *You've never lived a life like the other ones you're helping?*

L: Have lived them but with the purpose of the helping. It's the learning. The understanding, the taking on of the Earth vibration. Because we formed life within the planet, and we nurture and guide the life and live the life and move it.

D: *Don't you accumulate karma?*

L: Yes, and that is a must so that we have complete understanding, and sometimes we are sent to rescue one of our own. And sometimes we have to allow them to move as they feel directed.

D: *I thought maybe you would be kept from karma so that you wouldn't get involved.*

L: Without karma we do not fully understand what the Earth is about. Karma is purposeful with the planet.

D: *But you don't want to hold onto it.* (No*) But sometimes you are sent to rescue one of your own?* (Yes) *Why would that happen?*

L: Because sometimes we forget why we're here, and fall deeper into the murk, and so my stone is my visual remembrance.

D: *What happens if somebody does forget and you're afraid they're going to be lost?*

L: With the universe there is no lost, and so if they spend a longer time, so be it. Because within each of us information is always being sent back, and so even if one is here many, many, many times in many capacities, that information is always fed back.

D: *You said sometimes you come to help one of your own.*

L: Many times we will shake them to wake them up. Sometimes those of us within the physical realm are sent to trigger another's remembrance, and sometimes we are successful and sometimes we're not. It's very difficult when you experience the density to sometimes remember the connection.

It was obvious that the old man's life was spent doing this, so I didn't think it would do any good to move him to an important day. Besides, this was a class demonstration, so I knew I wouldn't have as much time to spend on it as I would in a private session. So I moved him ahead to the last day of his life and asked what was happening. He saw himself lying on a stone, a slab, surrounded by many people looking down at him. The body was dying because it was very old. "My beard is very gray now and white. Everything's white."

D: *Did you just decide it was time to leave?*

L: I'm called back.

D: *How do you feel about that?*

L: Joy ... I'm happy. I'm looking forward to the freedom.— The others come for me. I feel they're holding me ... lifting me and I just rise up from my body ... a peaceful death. It's a good departure. It is freedom. I'm no longer confined to the trapped restrictions of the body. I feel lighter. I'm going back.

Her voice was filled with complete joy. She was delighted to be leaving the physical and returning home. "They're greeting me. I feel the love."

D: *Let's move ahead to when it comes time to return. Does anyone help you with the decision?*

L: Yes. I'm being shown different bodies and I pick a male, and they tell me no ... no, no, no ... a female.

D: *They want you to be female next time?* (Yes) *Do they show you what the life is going to be like?*

L: I laugh because I think it's easy. (Nonchalantly) After being a man, being a woman is easy. They laugh with me. They say, "We'll see!"

D: *Do they tell you anything about what it's going to be like?*

L: Yes. They sound a little arrogant.

D: *What do you mean?*

L: I'm full of my capabilities. I'm confident.—They say to me that because of my arrogance and my confidence, if I choose a male body within this time frame, I will have a hard edge and I will be too willful. So they say, no, a female because as a female, I will have more inner empowerment ... inner power capabilities, inner abilities to keep connected with them.

D: *They don't want you to get lost, do they?*

L: No because then I will defeat the purpose.

D: *Are you aware that you're speaking through a human body as you're talking to me?* (Yes) *Is this the body that you chose, that we call Linda?*

L: Yes, but there's a disconnection with the body. There's a split within the body. There's the body—the physical Linda—and there's the essence of the others throughout the whole Linda lifetime, so there has not been a complete physical. There's been an in and out of the body, but that was preplanned to allow the body to survive the existence. If I was allowed to only be the physical body, I could not have survived intact.

There have been similar cases reported in the other *Convoluted Universe* books. Sometimes the spirit takes on too much and the circumstances in the life are more than the person can handle. In these cases another aspect is allowed to come in and take over the responsibilities (especially the karmic connections with others). Sometimes the original aspect and the new one trade places back and forth throughout the traumatic episodes of the life. (See the other *Convoluted Universe* books for explanations of the splinters and facets of the original soul.)

D: *Is it all right if you answer questions, or do we need to call in the subconscious? What do you think? Can you continue to tell me what's going on?*
L: Yes, I can do that.
D: *I thought so. But she chose this life, didn't she?*
L: Absolutely.
D: *Was it supposed to be so difficult?*
L: Yes, and it could have evolved worse.
D: *It could have?* (Yes) *It sounded pretty bad from the things she was telling me.*
L: Yes. She decided to experience it all so she wouldn't have to keep coming back.

It sounded to me like she had really piled her plate full, and the heavy load would have broken an ordinary person. So Linda was far from ordinary. She was an exceptional human being to be able to handle all that had happened to her. We discussed some of her family relations, and she was told many of the karmic situations that she had been working out. "In every lifetime with the planet, the purposes are the same. That is why she survived this, and that is how she survived it where others wouldn't. It is now time to release the guilt of what she brought within the Earth plane in the early stages because that was preordained. That was a part of the plan. And we are encouraging her determination in building the resources for the work ahead so all has not been lost."

D: *What is her purpose? What do you want her to do next?*
L: Her purpose is to assist the planet in lightening the heavy load it bears. Her purpose is to shift the vibrations within others and within the planet. And her purpose is to see why she's had these experiences because her body, as you

know, is the same as the Earth. Her body is like a transformer and so she takes in negativity, to use that term, and she transforms it into a purity. She has to take on the Earth to be able to shift the Earth. Now she can do it without thought. She needs to accept that she needs to stop wearing the "hair shirts."

That's a Biblical reference. It was a garment of rough cloth made from goat's hair. It was very uncomfortable and worn as a form of penitence or self-punishment.

D: *What do you want her to do to help people?*
L: To breathe ... to allow the breath to flow because, as you know—and we know that you know this—the breath is the connection to Source. And so she needs to stop holding the breath and to assist others because, as you know, the holding of the breath is the trapping of fear. And so she is to assist with the release of trauma, fear and pain. She is here to help the planet breathe. And because people think with consciousness, she has to enter liaison with them through consciousness and shift that. Do you understand?
D: *Is there anything in particular you want her to focus on?*
L: We want her to focus on herself. We want her to focus on who she is within. She spends too much time looking out. She sees herself of no importance and so she focuses on importance out there. And we would like to tell her that it begins within. And from the within nothing needs to be done because as within so without. So she need not seek actively because when she goes into this active way of thinking, she gets stuck within the conscious, and then she falls back into the body.
D: *She gets trapped in the karma, the family and all of that.*
L: And so when she arises from this bed, she will have left behind the need to do anything. She just needs to *be*. And she has noticed this expansion happening within herself and this heat rising, and she is trying to hold it back in.

And it is bursting to come forth. She's pregnant with the new, the possibility, and she needs to give birth to that. Otherwise, she'll discover that pocket will start erupting there, as she has this growth there. (The cancerous growth the doctors had discovered.) Do you understand?

D: *Yes. It's wanting to let out the energy. It wants to go out and create. That makes perfect sense.*

L: And she's to bless her children and her ex-husband because they've been a part of her creating her purpose to be.

D: *Even though it was painful.*

L: An illusion. It is a game, yes?

D: *We live in an illusion. We're trapped in an illusion, and it seems very, very real.*

L: When one comes into the physical body, they forget. And in the lifetime where she had this symbol (the stone), it was to visually and deeply remind her of the purpose. It's very easy, when you come into this dense energy, to forget.

D: *Now she can realize that all the pain she's suffered had a purpose, and she doesn't need to hold onto it anymore. (Right) She can use those experiences to help other people. Is that a good idea?*

L: Absolutely! How else would she have learnt why people are the way they are? And we say to you that many within the planet come through abuse. You'll find that in this time and place, most of those who are purposeful to the planet, choose dysfunctional backgrounds because they formulate what they need to experience. And once they find the way out or see the way out, it's very easy to lift others. And this is why she said when she was at the mountaintop trying to pull others, "You cannot bring others up. You just accept and be with them, and the vibration of the unsaid is what elevates and gives, and creates for them a safe environment to actually be moved." And with her just being in that place of being, we work through that to access others.

D: *Do you think that she forgot her purpose when she came in?*

L: Yes and no. She has throughout her life been having inner teachings and remembrances, but within the physical she has had a lot to contend with, and she knows that. But the only times she is actually physically in the body is when she's feeling physical activity or physical pain, so her pain was heightened to keep her in her body. Because when she feels the pain, she is then physically conscious.

D: *One thing you want her to do is to release these people in her life. (Yes) She can't do anything about her husband and her children. That's not her job anymore, is it?*

L: (Joyfully) And she communes with them daily on the other side.

D: *So she has not lost them. They are just communicating in a different way.*

L: We're going to do some work with the rewiring of the brain to adjust that for her. Rewire differently and reconnect some things that have been disconnected for a purpose.

D: *Will she notice a difference?*

L: Oh! *You* will notice a difference. (Laugh) You will see within her eyes and feel her as she rises.

D: *The main thing, and I know you will agree with me ... no harm ever to the person ... always with love.*

L: That is the oath she mentioned writing, was to bring into the physical remembrance: never any harm. You see, with the circumstances of her life, she could have harmed, but she knew ... no harm. She just took it all in, but she transformed it into the proper places.

D: *Can you tell us how you are rewiring the brain? I'm always interested.*

L: If you think of roadways that have put up blocks, for example, on some streets. They block it off and make it go one way. We're releasing those blocks to make two ways. And we're also rethreading areas that are frayed. We're repairing. And we're releasing all the one ways, and opening to full capability. And we're working in, especially, the back of the neck. The pain she feels within the back of the neck and the shoulder blades. She thinks it has to do with flexibility, but we would say it's been closed off to allow the experiences to occur. And so it's like a buildup of energy, and so we are opening those pathways. And within the connection at the back of the neck, we're wiring to the center to reopen the crown and to reopen her forehead.

D: *The third eye?*

L: Yes, and so she no longer has to doubt herself and look outwards, but she'll be free to look everywhere.—We are stretching out between the shoulder blades as everything has been compacted. And this is where she finds distortion in the back because everything has been compacted and so everything that should be expressing out has been blocked inwards.

D: *What about the growths under her breast?*

L: That's a buildup of energy, saying, "Pay attention!" See, she has been disconnected from her body. She has disowned her body and so we are remaking her body safe. A loving place to be.

The SC then described how it was going to remove the growth. "We are going to melt it. And allow it to flatten back out to normal health, and the energy she has been building up is being released." They have told me many times when working on similar cases that they dissolve or absorb tumors or growths, and allow them to be passed safely from the body. They affirmed that this was what they were doing. "As it melts, it moves back into where it came from. And absorb is a good word.—We suggest that she does a fast to allow the detoxing of the break-up to flow."

D: *By fasting, do you mean you don't want her to eat anything for a while?*

L: No. Fruit juices ... fruit ... lots of water.

D: *For how long?*

L: Five days.

D: *Five days of a fruit fast, I guess you would call it.*

L: Yes. It will shift out what we have broken up, and a part of the sweating she feels is heat through every pore as the body is trying to release. There's been a resistance with her and her body. She will notice a difference right away.

D: *What about the abdomen area? She had a swelling there.*

L: Yes. She uses the word "pregnant." (She said it felt and looked like it did when she was pregnant.) You might say she was pregnant with the energy. And this is her body being used to get her attention to be giving outward instead of not thinking she is capable.—She has been locked in a battle with her children and herself. And she will see that within her actual release, she will free up her children to be able to come to her. Because within every occurrence there is a gift given in return. We never work with anyone to say, "Okay, you're to suffer for the sake of suffering." No. It is like the diamond being formed through fire. There's a gift within it, so she has actually delayed the process by creating the energy for them to stay away. Now they are free to return, and she's free to be released.—This cradle of the womb she has carried and felt deeply, but this is prior to this lifetime. This is eons and eons of carrying the guilt. We want this being to realize that in being a part of the formation of the planet, and seeing whatever has been occurring, that it is preordained. There is no guilt she needs to carry for anything she has done because, as you know, it's a game.

D: *That's what I tell people, it's a game.—I've spoken to people who said they were there for the formation of the Earth. Is she one of them also?* (Yes) *She's been here a long time.*

L: Yes. She's from the beings with the Cyclops ... one eye.

D: *In the very beginning of the Earth?* (Yes) *So they were real and not legend?*

L: Yes. They were very real, and she carries that thread of guilt that gets propounded when in the physical body.

D: *Why was there guilt associated with the Cyclops?*

L: Look at the planet. Look at the disease. Look at the pains of Mother. Yes, but it's purposeful.—And so she's caught in this duality of feeling her greatness and feeling her humbleness.

D: *We've always thought the Cyclops were fairy tales.*

L: Yeah?

D: *But I've been told that every legend has a basis of truth.*

L: The body is feeling the heat and the heat was to get her attention ... to pay attention to the body we are speaking to ... listen, listen, listen.

D: *Well, she had one other question. Will she find a partner?*

L: Yes. She first needs to partner herself. Get the balance of the left and the right. (Laugh) Because now she feels she's looking for someone else to do it for her. Otherwise, she will get caught back into ... You have to see for yourself ... merge. (Very strong.) Look within! Do you understand?—We are saying to her to look within ... intertwine that DNA ... meld that left and right. Find your wholeness within yourself. Then attract the being because then you will attract someone you are not having to fix.— It's time. We have work for her. And the longer she hid herself away ... no work could be done. She's going to see herself shift in leaps and bounds. You understand the leaps and bounds, so they will be the freedom of movement she has been holding back. We thank you with much joy and bless you.

D: *So have you finished working on the body?*

L: Yes, and we will continue over the next days within the sleep state. We first did the brain so that she would not defeat her own purpose through her consciousness. We have shifted the consciousness.

D: *And you do want her to do the fruit fast to flush all this out of her system?*

L: Absolutely. And see, she knew something was coming, so last night she ate many things she was not allowed to eat. (Class laughed loudly at this.)

D: *But you will take care of her body from now on?*

L: Absolutely. This is a body we love; we work through. She's been holding back the work.

I explained that I recognized from the voice that I was speaking to the part that I was familiar with. I also explained that I was trying to show others how to contact "them."

L: They come to you, but we say to them, "You already have within what Dolores has. It's just accepting that." And those that are worried about the advanced course. Hmmm. (Class laughed.) We will advance you! We will help them!

Parting message: The love you are seeking is within you, and we shower you continuously with love. Open your heart to feel it. Do not think the love has to come through beings and little ones. True love comes from Source, and true love is showered down through you. Look no further. Feel within yourself and know that we are always with you. Never are you alone ... ever. We bow to your greatness. We bow to your dedication. We uplift you, so do not take any sorrow forward. There is no such thing. (Very tenderly) We love you.

D: *Is that all you want to say?*

L: Oh? Do we have more time? (Laugh) We will say that we love all and that all that is within this space and time is destined ... yes ... you are all called forward this moment because all is for you as well. So walk away knowing that as you arise from your seat, you have left behind what you have set down with, and don't even puzzle it out. Just accept that it is so and we will see you in your sleep.

Linda's life changed dramatically as soon as the session was over. Even on the way home, she felt happy. Before, she had dreaded going to an empty house. Then she thought, "Oh, yes, my brain was rewired!"

Chapter 11

ACCUMULATOR OF INFORMATION

Cathy came into the scene and tried to describe a strange environment. "I see smooth formations on the ground. They're almost like rocks, but they're not rocks. I don't know what to call them. I don't have a name for them. It's like a big, round rock. I can sense it is slippery or shiny. It's not sharp or rough. It's very smooth and it has many layers, and it's not one piece. There are many pieces. They are formed together. —I haven't gone to see the rest of the place yet. I sense there's a lot more to it than I see." Then she saw a building, a city in the distance. "It has sharp roofs like ice cubicles, but they're pointed up and they go in all directions, too. Some of them are flat and they look like ice."

D: That color?
C: No, it's transparent. They look gray and white, but they look like ice from a distance. It's a big cluster of tall buildings. They are strange because they go sideways and then in the middle they extend upwards, too. Points up and points sideways, irregular. Strange buildings. From a distance it's strange because it's in the middle of nowhere, in this empty space, and there's nothing else. It looks like it's leaning on a hill on the side of a bigger, bigger hill.

The whole thing about these buildings is there's no pattern. It's so irregular. Like a step can be here or there. When somebody built it, that's the way they built the buildings. It's not organized. Maybe that's the way they organize. I don't know. You don't know what to expect when you look at one side of the building because it will not be something that you can expect in a building.

She wasn't sure if she lived in that city or not. It was very strange and unfamiliar. Yet she agreed to go inside and explore it. "I have to go into the entrance to the whole city first because there is a certain entranceway that you have to go through to enter. When you go inside, it's a city, but it's empty. It has streets and they are made out of the same kind of ice material.—I feel I need to go up at one tower. I call it a tower because there's a round spiral staircase, and you go up and up and up the stairs. I guess everyone has their own tower they go up to.—The top is open, and I can see very, very far away. At the top of the tower, it's not a room. It's open. It's an observation place where the purpose of that place is to observe places far away."

D: *So it's not a place to live? It's a place to observe?* (Yes) *What do you see as you look?*
C: I don't see anything yet. I know the purpose of this observation deck because you can see whatever you want to see. There's another thing that you can control or command so you can see. It's not like a place that you randomly see. You have to tune it to see someplace.
D: *Is it done with machinery?*
C: I don't see any mechanical thing. I think they've done it with different technology or mind or something that I cannot describe, or they don't have it in here. When I say machines, I don't have a word to describe it. In our world people will call it a machine, but it is really not a machine. It's some kind of method or technology that you can use.
D: *With the mind?*
C: Yes. You just decide. You just think about it. But for some reason you have to be there to go to see things. You don't go physically, but you can see everything, and know everything that is going on. It sends a part of you ... your mind goes there. Or your whole awareness is there and

you can sense everything there. Then you can come back. (Something like a portal or probably a window)—You gather information and you store it. Everything is recorded. Everything is stored in the tower where they gather information. They store it there where they first receive it. And I think they might put it somewhere else after they gather all the towers and all the other information. Then they put it all together in some other location. Everything is stored.

D: *Do all the people in the city do this?*

C: I don't know yet. Let's see.—There are other people doing it, too.—I go away from this place. I don't stay all the time. I haven't been to this city for a long, long time, so I don't remember many things about it.

D: *Do you have to eat? To consume food?*

C: No, I don't consume food.

D: *What do you do to keep yourself alive?*

C: I don't do anything. It's the air. It's all in the atmosphere. I'm supported there. I don't even think about eating.

D: *So it's an easy existence, isn't it?* (Yes) *What do you do with most of your time?*

C: I like to go to the tower to observe. That's one of my favorite things to do, and if I don't do that, I go off to other places to play. I can go anywhere. I can go to different planets far away.

D: *How do you travel to the other planets?*

C: I just go. I just think I want to go somewhere and I'm there.

D: *You don't have to go in anything like a ship?* (No, no.) *But your body is physical, isn't it?*

C: No, when I do that I'm not physical. When I travel I don't have this body.

D: *What do you look like when you travel?*

C: It looks like energy, but I can't explain it. It is like a current. Like you have electricity in the water, and you feel the electricity but you don't see it. So it travels like that. I just go.

D: *Then what happens when you get to the place you want to go? Do you need a physical body in those places?*

C: If I want to. If I want to stay. It depends on what I want to do. If I want to just stay and watch, I don't have to have a body. If I decide to stay then I can have a body if I want to.

D: *If you want to stay for a while and participate?*

C: Yes, if I choose to.

D: *Then how do you get a body if you decide to have one? How do you change from one form to the other?*

C: It takes a long time to stay in one place to have a body because you have to go through many, many life forms. Then you go through many, many bodies. You choose a body, but that is not the only body that you have. What I mean is, if you choose to stay in one place, it's a long, long, long time that you stay in that place. You could be there for many thousands of years.

D: *So you don't just go in, then come back out?*

C: You can do that, but once you make a decision to stay, you stay for a long time. Or you can choose not to stay, and you can just zoom right out and go to another place.

D: *That's just observing, isn't it?* (Yes, yes.) *But if you decide to stay, you're committed. You have to stay longer?* (Yes) *Is there anyone who tells you that you have to stay there longer?*

C: I don't see anybody telling me.

D: *Or giving you instructions?*

C: Instructions? I'm trying to find out if there's anybody instructing me.—Well, the decision is if I decide, it is my choice. If I decide I have to follow the laws or the rules of that place, I have to go by the rules. And once you go by the rules you have to stay there until the whole cycle is finished.

D: *Otherwise, you just like to go and watch?*

C: Yes, but I have a feeling that I don't. I either stay or go. Because it will be very interesting to me or not interesting to me, and then I'll be gone to another place.

D: *Is that what was happening when you were looking at that city made out of ice?*

C: No, the city of ice is my home base.

D: *Then when you decide to go, you turn into this electrical current body.* (Yes) *Then if you decide to stay somewhere you'll be away from your home base for a long time?*

C: Yes, I like that. It's a different way of gathering information. Then when I return I put it in some kind of storage device, and everything is stored. And someone else will come in and gather all the devices, and they put it into another place to do something with them.

D: *So accumulating information is very important, isn't it?* (Yes, yes.) *You never know what someone is going to do with it.*

C: You don't know.

D: *Well, do you know you're speaking through a physical body?*

C: Now?

D: *Yes. That's how you're communicating. Did you just decide to come live on Earth?*

C: I'm here to do something. There are more dangers to observe. It has some kind of a purpose to it. I'm going to observe Earth and I'm also going to experience it myself, instead of watching it. That's one of the jobs. It's for my own purpose so that I know how it feels to have all the experiences.

D: *Once you make a commitment to go, you have to stay for a long time?* (Yes) *So you've already gone through other life forms?*

C: Yes. For some reason the rocks came to my mind. I don't know why. The life form of a rock. It's like I stayed there for a long time. Stayed being a rock ... but I've gone through that. I've done that.

D: *What did you learn from being a rock?*

C: That it's nice to be stable, to stay in one place. Then butterfly came to my mind.

D: *What was that like to be a butterfly?*

C: I see it as being very beautiful, almost the opposite of the rock. So I had to go to the opposite. I go from one end to the other end and learn from it. Opposite ... everything is opposite, but if I move around all the time ... rocks don't move ... and a butterfly is prettier. A rock is just one color. And also a butterfly will change from a caterpillar to a butterfly. And the lesson is about transforming because you think it is one thing, but then you change to another thing. Rocks stay the same all the time.

D: *So everything has a lesson.* (Yes) *But you had to go through many forms before you became human?*

C: Yes. That's what I thought, but I wasn't sure. I didn't want to say it because it sounds so strange.

D: (I laughed.) *Nothing sounds strange to me.—But you had to go through a progression before you decided to be the human?*

C: Yes, yes. It's a necessity. It's like a natural cycle. If you are going to learn, you have to do that.

D: *To be everything?*

C: Yes, and that's why the Earth is so important because it gives you the opportunity to go through so many life forms. Other places are dark, and they have only a few colors. Not as colorful, and not this kind of weather atmosphere.

D: *They don't have as many life forms?*

C: Yes, I can sense it. They are darker and colder. It's different.

D: *But each place has something to learn?* (Yes) *But then you went through other human bodies, too?*

C: Yes, I went through human bodies. I don't think I went through many other bodies, but several important ones to help me learn lessons. Covering a whole long period of time.

D: *Then you eventually decided to enter the body of Cathy, the one you're speaking through now.* (Yes) *Why did you choose this body?*

C: (A deep breath) I chose this body because this body is strong. This body has always been strong and healthy. I didn't have a problem with this body in my childhood. The genes are good. The genes are strong in the body.

D: *Does anyone tell you what to do in this progression from form to form?*

C: I think there is some guidance. Somebody is giving wise advice.

D: *Is there a purpose for coming into this body?*

C: The purpose of this body is to see how the female body is growing in a culture that doesn't have a lot of freedom. And move through it and back to normal, and be able to see away from it. (Cathy was born in China, and later came to America.) The whole purpose of the body is ... breaking every system that I see. I will be in something and then I will have to break it apart ... deconstruct the whole thing. See through the whole thing and then come out and see the real picture. It's to not conform to everything, and see if I can make it through in one piece. I would have to break through the parents, the culture, what everybody expects of me, what I expect of myself. I expected myself to be a pianist and everything that I expected fell apart. Everything my parents expected fell apart. Everything I expected ... my marriage ... even my son sometimes and my daughter. It's like I'm going against a current all my life, and I run into obstacles. That's the story of her life.

D: *What is she learning by going against the current?*

C: I'm learning that many belief systems are hurtful to people.

D: *She is interested in working with crystals in her life now.*

C: Yes, she trusts the crystals because the crystals will always help her.

D: *Has she a history of working with crystals in other human bodies?*

C: I am hearing that I have worked with them before, but I am not supposed to know that because they won't tell me.

There was a lot going on in other lifetimes, and I know the technology. I know how it works and I was good at that, and I can do it, but I'm not supposed to do it that way. (Confusion.) I'm just to know that I cannot do it that way. I need to be okay with that.—When she dreams the dream ... that's when she travels. That's when she goes to council. They make all decisions together and sometimes she makes decisions, too. Her main job has always been to travel and accumulate information and to observe people. And she will help when it is needed. She will give her input, too as she's in the body. She's already doing what she's supposed to. I don't think she needs to really be concerned about that.

It seems as though when the part of the soul decides to commit to a lifetime on a specific planet they have to be there for many, many lifetimes in order to complete the cycle, the order of progression. This means they must experience every form of life from the simplest to the more complex. And as Cathy said, once you have made that commitment, you are bound by the rules that have been set up on that planet or system. This is why the law of karma prevails on Earth. You must play by the rules of the place you have chosen to experience. But because of the required amnesia, you make mistakes and cannot progress further until the karma you have accumulated is repaid. This has been the problem of Earth, too many souls are caught on the wheel of karma and are not progressing, but are just spinning round and round.

This is a valid reason why a soul would choose to be an observer in order to help without being caught in the cycle. They come to watch and to help and then go on to something else. I have been told that these pure, gentle souls come into this life with a sheath or covering around them to prevent the accumulation of karma. This is to keep them from being trapped here. Because once the cycle of karma is begun they will have to keep returning to repay it. They don't want to be caught, just do their job and get out of here. Many of these gentle souls decided, as long as they are coming here, why not experience everything possible about the human condition? This was a big mistake, but in their innocence they did not realize it. In my books there are some cases reported where the soul said, in essence, "Bring it on! Dump it on! I want to experience it all!" And they have lived a horrible life where they have had to experience every terrible thing that man can do to man. It had nothing to do with karma, they just asked to experience it to know what it was like, so they would have the information to report back. Another type chose not the horrible physical experiences, but the emotional ones. They wanted to experience every type of emotion in its extreme state, so they would know what it felt like. Many of these gentle souls take on way more than they can handle, and the knowledge provided by these sessions can help them find a way out of the mess they have created in their life.

Thus the majority of souls on Earth are trapped in the cycle until they complete it. The volunteers, or observers, are not trapped (unless they take a wrong turn and accumulate karma). They are here on a one time mission, and are free to go to other places to observe when their job here is finished. There is more detailed information about these in my book, *The Three Waves of Volunteers and the New Earth.*

Chapter 12

CARRYING GUILT

Amanda talked about her life with a controlling, demanding mother. She left home at an early age and was happily married. She arrived at my office in a wheelchair although she was able to walk with some support. I knew we would have several things to cover in the session.

***

Amanda had just died as a little boy from a contagious disease that swept through the village he was living in.

D: *What do you feel you're going to do now that you're out of the body?*

A: I see that I'm shooting through this tunnel and I'm going to go back to the school that I left before.

D: *Before you came into the body of that little boy?*

A: Yes, I'm going back to school.

D: *What's that school like?*

A: I know everybody that's there, and I also know people I knew from other schools. Some of them are joining me in this school, which I am welcoming. And then there are people I don't know that I'm meeting. And the school is expanding, which was a surprise to me. It has gotten bigger than before and so it's a happy thing. It's always a happy time to go back to school.

D: *What do they teach you at that school?*

A: Lots of different things. You know how if something's coming to you and you swat it away? You don't have to swat it away because you are the one that brought it, and you learn that you caused it, and you don't have to be afraid of anything, nor do you have to fight it. You don't have to respond in kind. And that was a big lesson to me. And you don't have to defend yourself, and if somebody is planning to cause you harm, you could just let it go through your body and it won't touch you. You don't have to fight it. If there's aggression coming to you, you can just let them do it. It will go through you like energy going through a wall that isn't there, and so you don't have to swat it away. You don't have to respond because it really doesn't touch you because you're vibrating at a higher level of understanding.

D: *What else are they teaching you?*

A: Following sounds of music and current, and floating on the sound current, and letting it come in. Breaking the sound current inside of you, and you *become* the sound current. And there are no boundaries and no barriers except the barriers that you have made. I'm learning that there is no barrier because I made it, and so I choose not to have that barrier. It isn't there and it really never was there. It was just that I thought it was there.

D: *So sound currents are important?*

A: Oh, yes, sound and light, and the light current, of course.

D: *Are those things you would encounter on Earth?*

A: Oh, yes ... everywhere.

D: *I am curious as to what they mean by the sound currents and the light currents.*

A: It's everything, basically.   It's the all-ness.   It's everything. It's the current.

D: *So you'll be able to identify them when you are in a physical body?* (Yes) *What do you do with the sound currents and the light currents when you become aware of them in a physical body?*

A: You enjoy. You ride the sound currents and enjoy the sound currents. You enjoy the light. You are taught by the sound current. You learn everything by the sound current and the vibrating rate. You learn and you are nurtured. You actually can live on the light and that can be your food. Your nourishment where you don't need to eat anything, but the sound current and light ray. You don't need to eat anything else unless you choose to.

D: *That's remarkable.*

A: Really you don't need to.

D: *You can exist on that?*

A: Yes because that is the full true nourishment. That is it. That's the all-ness.

D: *So when they are teaching you at the school, how do you know when it's time to return to the physical?*

A: You get a feeling of being pulled back by floating back.

D: *You can learn so much there, why don't you just stay there?*

A: If you are asked to become a teacher, then you stay there. If you can impart the teaching and you are needed to stay, then you stay because you wouldn't leave where you are needed. But I fall back many times because I needed to learn more.

D: *So, when you're ready you go back to a physical body?*

A: Yes, and I have.

D: *You said you feel pulled back?*

A: It's not really a pull. You feel this attraction. It's like smelling a rose. You know the scent, and you just follow it. You have this need to follow that scent. You know you can choose not to, and stay where you are, but you just know that is a good thing you need to do. Nobody yanks you somewhere. There's no force ever. It is, "Would you like this now?" That's kind of how it is. I think you are invited. Messengers come and invite you if you would like to come or you stay if you choose not to.

D: *Do you think you learn faster by going to the school, or by going to the physical?*

A: I think that this life I went to, I chose to because I knew that I would learn more if I went. And I did learn more and when I came back, when I got home, I saw that I understood more. My awareness was expanded. I did more and I found more people when I went back to school here.

D: *So you can learn in both places. You were allowed to go into the physical at different times.* (Yes)—*Are you aware that you're speaking through a physical body right now?*

A: Part of me is speaking through the physical body.

D: *Do you know why you chose to come into this physical body that is called Amanda?*

A: Oh, yes, yes. Mainly she is going to be working on spirituality again. There's a tapestry that Amanda is understanding now and she is excited about. And that's one of the big messages that she will be bringing in this lifetime to people is: how do you notice the tapestry? And she will be discussing it in ways that maybe people will understand it. But there's a lot that people will not understand. She understands just a little bit of what that tapestry really is. It's vibrating energy and it's alive and it's all knowing, of course, and it's very aware of everything. We are the tapestry. There is no separation. It's just that we think we are separate. So that's really the big awareness, to understand first that there is a tapestry, and number two, that you are not separate from the tapestry. And then the third thing is becoming aware fully of the tapestry. Be aware of it. It's the all awareness. It's the all beingness.

There is a lot of information about the tapestry room in *Between Death and Life*. This has been seen as a huge tapestry located in the Temple of Wisdom complex on the spirit side. Within this temple are located the great library, the healing room and many other places of learning. The tapestry is representative of all life. Every single living human being is represented as a thread in this tapestry, and it has been described as appearing to be breathing and undulating. Because all the threads are interwoven it shows that although we are one, we are also part of the whole, the All. There is no separation.

D: *Why did she choose to come into this lifetime? Did she make a plan?*

A: Yes. Actually she had to finish some mistakes, some karma, and she's been working on that and she's pretty much gone past all of that.

They explained the karma between Amanda and her mother and how it had been worked out.

D: *Why has her physical body been having problems?*

A: Guilt. She felt guilt. Her sister that's ill. She felt badly that she was allowing herself to be free and her sister accepted the burden of what the mother wanted. And when her sister got sick, Amanda wasn't living in the family. She was having a wonderful life and then she felt horrible. Guilty of the fact that she got away and her sister didn't.

Her sister developed MS (Multiple Sclerosis). When Amanda first began having trouble with her legs and hand, the doctors suspected MS, but the tests did not confirm that. So Amanda, through guilt, was mimicking her sister's illness all too realistically.

A: It really wasn't her fault—but the guilt is not real. Guilt is not real at all.

D: *Because her sister made her own plans ... her own decisions.*

A: Right ... right. So she should let go of that because that's not real anyway. In the past life she was shown the boy doubted his ability. He is the one that held himself back. And that's the problem in this lifetime, that she is again holding herself back with the guilt of her sister. She took on empathy in this lifetime, and so she feels the empathy of other people and she takes on that, and then she feels this with her sister. She felt the guilt of, "Why am I so lucky when she is not?" And so she took that on. She needs to just get past all of that. Don't do that empathy. I mean, you can be empathetic, but you don't have to feel guilty.

I then wanted the SC to work on Amanda's legs. The SC said she needed to stop the medications she was on. It said she was forgetting to take them most of the time anyway. "They" were helping her forget to take them. She would be walking again.

D: *What about giving up the wheelchair?*
A: We are working with her, and don't worry. She'll know, and like a kid starts to walk, and all of a sudden they sit down and they don't think they can do it again? She's all of a sudden say, "I can do this!" We showed her. She was driving a car without any problem and she stopped totally. We surprised her and now she has no problems. She can drive. By Christmas she will be using the cane and not be using the wheelchair at all. This will happen if she releases the guilt.
D: *They say there's a retina detaching in her left eye. Can you fix that?*
A: I think we can. We're pretty good at everything. (Laugh) She didn't want to see what was happening in her life. Right now it's locked because she thinks it's locked.
D: *I've seen you do miracles. Can you fix the retina?*
A: I believe I'll work on it right now. We're going to be pulling the light rays and we'll be stitching. Let's get on to the stitch job.—That's really all we work with is light energy and sound.—She was very healthy before. It will happen again. She also has such guilt, you know because she's had other lifetimes where she's done some bad things ... we all do. And she really doesn't want that karma anymore. And we like the fact that she's very careful now because some of her old incarnations are actually memorable.

Message: There's going to be a big moment coming up before the end of the year, and don't be afraid if you get a real pull to go out-of-your-body. Go with it because we're going to bring you to a big place and you'll really enjoy it. Just go. Actually it's not a go. It's a come. No one ever goes anywhere, remember? They just come back.

Chapter 13

CHANGING THE PAST

Monica saw that she was an older man (about 50) standing on sand in a barren environment, wearing simple, nondescript clothes with brown unkempt hair and beard. Carrying a satchel on his back that contained food, he said he was just walking, on a pilgrimage. He announced sadly, "And I don't expect to survive." He began to cry, "I feel I failed. I feel I let everyone down. It feels like a self-imposed exile. That I took myself out because I wasn't good enough. I failed and so I left.—I'm going on a pilgrimage to absolve my sins."

D: *Did other people think you failed?*
M: That doesn't matter. I know I failed.—I can't live with myself.
D: *We all make mistakes, don't we?*
M: Yes, but I'm not supposed to. I'm the one people come to for wisdom, and I've failed.
D: *Did you live around there somewhere?*
M: I wasn't from there. I came there. I was sent there.
D: *Was it a city or what?*
M: It wasn't a city. It was a place that people would come that was not too far from the city. There were a few others there who helped me.
D: *What kind of wisdom did you give people?*
M: How to plant the crops, how to have a better life, how to get along, how to see things differently, and how to be more in their heart. It was simple.

D: *Those are all good things.* *Did anyone train you to do those things?*

M: Yes. I was sent from far away. I want to say "above."— I'm trying to see where I came from and I ... I just feel like I was sent there, but I do not have a clear picture of who trained me.

Of course, my curiosity was not going to allow that to be the only answer. I had him move backwards to see the place where he came from with the wisdom.

M: White temples and blue water. (He became emotional.)

D: *Tell me about the place.* *It sounds beautiful.* *Did someone train you there?*

M: That's all they do is train. They train you for whatever you need to do. And so I was trained for this. It was like a university.

D: *Have you been there for a long time?*

M: It feels like a really good place to be, and I don't know how long I've been here.

D: *Then whenever you were trained and you learned everything you needed to know ....*

M: Then they just drop me off at the site.

D: *How do they drop you off?*

M: In a space ship or a merkabah or vehicle. There was a pilot and he conveyed me to this place. It was like a sphere of gold ... small ship. Just big enough for the pilot and myself. He took me to this place on this planet, and it's like they were expecting me and no one's afraid of me. I walked to this place. It's almost like I was the replacement. Like there had been someone there before, and then I was to fill the other one's shoes.

The people knew he was coming, so they welcomed him. "They look for guidance.—I did healing too."

D: *How did you do that?*

M: By holding them. Just held them and the energies healed them.

D: *It seems as though you were full of love for these people.* (Yes)

He really liked helping the people and was happy there. But then something happened that changed everything. I had him move forward so he could look at it again and tell me about it. "A man came ... a big, angry man."

D: *What was he angry about?*

M: I don't know. All I see is this black. It's almost like a black energy came into the abode where I was. And I couldn't calm it or control it.—He wanted to kill me.

D: *Why would he want to kill you? You were doing good things.*

M: He hated that.

D: *How did he know about you?*

M: Everyone knew. It wasn't a secret.

D: *So he decided he wanted to kill you?* (Yes) *What happened then?*

M: I told him he couldn't.

D: *You knew he wouldn't be able to?* (Yes) *Because you have protection, don't you?*

M: Yes, but my people didn't have protection and he killed them. They didn't know I didn't need protection and they sacrificed themselves to save me. Many, many people.

D: *Did you try to tell them?*

M: It happened too fast. It was like a tornado coming through. He had a weapon and they stepped in front of me to stop him, and they were all killed.

D: *Then what happened?*

M: I killed him! I just sent the energy and stopped his life force.

He was making hand motions as though pulling energy from above with one hand and directing it with the other.

187

M: I sent the energy through me and I used it to kill instead of to heal.—That was why I left.—My people were already dead. There was no reason to kill this man, and I did it anyway because I was angry. It is against protocol. I was not supposed to hurt another human being, or other beings of any kind. It's against protocol. (Sobbing) It's against protocol.

D: *But it was an emotion.*

M: I don't have emotions. It is not allowed ... not allowed. I am love. I am not emotion.

D: *That's the only emotion you were supposed to have was love?* (Yes) *You had never experienced that kind of emotion before?* (No) *That would be a total opposite of love. But you know love is a powerful emotion, and this other emotion would be equally as strong.*

M: Yes, and that's why I did it.

D: *You couldn't control it?*

M: I could. I did it deliberately. I killed that person deliberately. It was an emotion, but it wasn't. I couldn't stop myself.—I am not allowed to be any emotion. I am love. I must pay. I must redeem myself. I don't know if this is possible. It's not supposed to happen. It's against all my training and against everything I stand for.

D: *When you went into that body, were you like a human?* (Yes) *So you did take on some of the human characteristics.*

M: I'll have to check that out. I don't know if I did that or not.

D: *I was thinking if you took on some of the human characteristics, those basic human emotions would be there.*

M: I was supposed to overcome that. That was my job.—I couldn't live with myself. I went against protocol. I went against all my training. I failed. So I decided to leave to redeem myself.

D: *Did anyone try to keep you from leaving?*

M: No, everyone was shocked and in mourning. It happened too fast.—I think I walked a long ways and eventually ended up in the desert. So I'm walking across the desert and I don't feel I will survive much longer.

D: *So you are punishing yourself?*

M: Yes, I am. I am. I don't know what else to do.

D: *Isn't there anyone you could get advice from?*

M: With that act I severed my connection. The force ... it's severed. I am nothing. I am dirt.

D: *So they couldn't come and help you in any way?*

M: No, it was severed. It was severed.

D: *So there's no way for you to go back to the place you came from.*

M: Until I can redeem myself and reconnect myself to Source ... to the force. I could not do the work as I did before because of this severing of force. I cannot go back until I redeem myself.

D: *How do you think you can redeem yourself?*

M: I have no clue ... through self-punishment, through suffering.

D: *That's kind of drastic, isn't it?*

M: I went against protocol. I did the unthinkable, the undoable. Severed my connection to the force.

D: *But everyone makes mistakes.*

M: I'm not allowed to make mistakes.

I decided to move him forward in time. He said he was wandering through the desert. "What eventually happened?"

M: I found an oasis and I prayed there. I prayed for redemption. Forgiveness.—It didn't come.—I didn't walk away from the oasis. I just stayed there. There was enough water and food for existence. I feel like the body got old and died.

I moved him to where it was all over and he was on the other side. "What do you think was the purpose of that lifetime?"

M: I feel like I took whatever anger the man that came there had ... that man's anger, and it's still with me as I look at the lifetime. Inside I feel this anger that isn't mine and I cannot connect to myself. ... Let me see ... I'm just noticing that there's this anger energy on me even though I'm in spirit ... anger that I held onto and embraced to punish myself.

D: *What are you supposed to do now?*

M: I want to ask the anger, "What is your purpose? Who are you and what is your purpose?"—**I am death and you did my bidding.**—"Do you belong with the man that I killed?" **Yes, it was his time.**

D: *You were just the instrument then?*

M: Yes. And I'm asking for the man and the man's council to come and explain if this is true.—And man and his council are there, and they say, "We are grateful to you." And I ask, "For what?" And they say, "For providing him a timely death." And I say, "It was against my protocol, against my training, against everything that I believe." They say, "It came from love." (He became emotional.) And I ask, "How can that be ... how can that be?" I don't understand. I feel that I made a failure in judgment of protocol.

D: *Ask them to explain to you what they mean. This is very important for you to understand.*

M: They say I freed him from the energy that was ... I freed him from himself. He, at an unconscious level, did not want to continue hurting people and did not want to continue accumulating karma. So it was as if he came and wanted me to kill him and stop him, but it wasn't conscious. It was what his soul wanted. And my soul recognized that and I did not blame him for the deaths of my people. I didn't berate him or touch him. I simply killed him, and I assumed that it was out of anger. I did what I was supposed to do even though it was against protocol. And I don't understand how it can happen. (Sorrowful.)

D: *I know you said you had been trained and that this should not have been allowed to happen. But when you enter the human body, you get caught up in human emotions because those emotions cause people to react in unpredictable ways that you could not have been prepared for. And you were being affected by those emotions even though you were trained not to be. So you can't blame yourself.*

M: Yes, they are saying that this was a built-in possibility, so they knew it *could* happen. (As though that was an unexpected revelation.) I had never thought of that! Why wasn't it explained to me while I was in my training? I thought I was prepared for anything. "You didn't need to know everything. It would have influenced your learning, your mission. Besides, it was only a remote possibility, a loophole, that was built into the program, but not expected to be used. You were supposed to learn from the experience. Not carry it to the extreme of punishing yourself through many lifetimes. That serves no purpose and only holds you back in your progress."

Monica had told me during the interview that she had had regressions performed by other hypnotists, and they were always lives of suffering and self-punishment. Of course, the other hypnotists did not know how to carry this further and find the reason for the pattern. So they did not probe to discover why she had to experience these. She had even carried it into her present life and was still experiencing much suffering that seemed to defy explanation. This was why she was desperate to find the answer.

D: *Sometimes there are higher forces that take over.*
M: Yes, there are higher forces.

D: *And you were used as an instrument.* (Yes) *They don't condemn you, do they?*

M: No, I condemned myself.

D: *So are you going to stay over there for a while or what?*

M: No need to now. I can reconnect myself now. I couldn't live with the pain of what I'd done.

D: *There's no need to carry anger or any kind of guilt, is there?*

M: Not now, and I understand. And the redemption isn't necessary. No one else punished me ... only myself punishing me.

D: *And the man apparently forgave you.*

M: The man was grateful. He understood.—Now I can go on with what I'm supposed to do. Otherwise, I would have spent *more* lifetimes punishing myself.

D: *That's not any good.*

M: It was against protocol. It was against everything I lived for. Now I don't have to live all those lifetimes of pain and suffering. I can go in a different direction.

D: *We can now leave it in the past. Now that you realize that, there's no reason to follow that pattern, is there?* (No) *A whole new life can open up now, can't it?* (Yes)

I considered this a gigantic breakthrough and I had received excellent answers, but I still felt the need to call in the SC. It was probably part of what I was conversing with anyway. It came through instantly, "We are willing." I then asked it why it chose that lifetime for Monica to see.

M: It went directly to the heart of the matter. She punishes herself.

D: *I could see that, but I wanted to hear you say it. It's totally unnecessary for her to punish herself, isn't it?* (Yes) *She's a good person. She has many talents. She can help many people, can't she?*

M: If she will allow herself to.

D: *She's been holding onto that memory.*

M: And others. The man was punishing himself by going through many lifetimes of punishment. Self-sacrifice is done. It's complete. She was to fully embrace self-sacrifice and she has successfully done so. And now it is time to move on.

The SC explained this was why she chose such a bad childhood in this lifetime, and why she went into a bad marriage. It was more self-punishment. Now she was finished with it, and it was important that she not stay cooped up in her house isolated from people. It was time for her to fulfill her purpose of helping people. She was now to bring joy to others as well as herself. She was to teach. "Teach being in divine connection, and just joy of being. She is to just allow it to come, to flow."

D: *You will give her the words, won't you?*

M: That is what she has known, that we will always provide the next step for her, so that she can provide it for her clients, and so it goes.

D: *You've always been there, but she just wasn't quite hearing you, was she?*

M: She did ... she has followed all the steps ... all the obstacle courses that we have set up. She has done well. It was not to be an easy lifetime. It was to be a pivotal lifetime and the energy needed to be a magnitude to pull through the other that she is moving into now. She needed to understand the other first. She cannot teach if she does not understand that because these people she is teaching need to know that she understands them.

D: *She says she doesn't feel comfortable around crowds.*

M: Every person who looked at her reminded her that she had failed. That will change in time. She will go out more ... not initially.—She loves working with the animals. They are beautiful. They reflect her and she needs to know that their beauty is her beauty. Like a mirror that she was refusing to see. There was too much pain.

When I asked the SC to look into Monica's body for healing, it said, "Body will survive. It is going to take time to heal." But I knew it could heal faster than that. "She does not expect that." I knew "they" would only do what is appropriate, but I asked it to go through the body and see what was the most important thing to focus on. "A lot of dark energy at the top of the head that needs to go."

D: *Is that hanging on from the other life?*
M: Many lives ... many lives.
D: *She doesn't need to be living in a shadow. We want her living in the sun ... the bright light. We can leave that in the past. Can you take that away?*
M: We did. Just poof, gone!
D: *What else do you want to focus on in the body?*
M: There are many sets of pains throttling her. Sets of pains trying to kill her. That's what she wanted.—But not anymore, so we will just remove them pound by pound. Her whole body is filled with pain. It's mostly self-inflicted. She has done a good job of clearing others' pain, and hiding her own pain. We are removing the self-punishment and the self-hatred. So now we will remove the rest. She is complete with that peace. We believe she has suffered enough for her lessons. We believe she can move beyond this now. We would like to see her smile.

They went through her body healing and explaining the causes of the problems as it went. She had experienced excess menstrual bleeding and they said, "She thought if she created more pain she could redeem herself. She was to go through those lifetimes without understanding to reach this lifetime. She is to understand that she was to go through all of that. It served a purpose. It will help her to bring forth the joy now. She needs to embrace herself. It is time to reconnect and embrace her wholeness. She is done with that lesson." She would also now be able to go off the medications she was on.

Her entire body had been affected in some way. She had not missed any part in her desire to punish herself. Now it was time to stop, and this was the important thing she was to teach others, not to punish their bodies.

Parting message: We have long awaited this time and we are happy. We realize that this has been a challenging series of lifetimes and we are grateful that you are willing to complete it. You did not understand the purpose and it was not time for you to understand the purpose. Just know that it is complete and now it's time to move on, and we are grateful to you. We love you and we embrace you and look forward to our path together in more and more connections in love and life.

There were some things in this regression that made me think in a different direction. Others have asked if it were possible to go into a past life and change the circumstances in that life. That would definitely affect the person's present life. I always thought it would not be possible, and would it be advisable? The person in the other life experienced the events and learned from them. So I didn't know if it would be possible to alter events. Of course, in this case we did not alter the events *during* the life. We were not able to stop the killing. We were able to change the man's outlook after death. Is it the same thing?

Monica had lived many, many lives of terrible suffering, and it had continued into her present one. It was all caused by the man's misunderstanding of his training. He felt he had failed, had gone against his mission, so the only solution would be to have many lives of punishment, knowing that he would never find redemption because his crime had been so horrible. He was unwilling to go to the other side for advice because he was too afraid of condemnation. Yet when we found that the killing had a purpose, one that he could not possibly have known, and that he had not failed, then he realized he didn't need to experience all those hopeless lives. He then was free to go in another direction.

In my work we are always talking about time lines and endless possibilities and probabilities. Does this mean that those lives now cease to exist? What about the other characters in those lives? What about karma that had been incurred in those lives? By uncovering the cause and changing the man's viewpoint, does that wipe the slate clean, dissolve all of that? It has been said that it all depends upon our focus anyway, to discover our own reality. However, no matter how this can be debated, at least it had a profound effect upon Monica's present life. She no longer has to carry the burden of suffering and self-punishment and self-hatred. If those on the other side do not condemn, then why do we feel we have to judge and punish ourselves? Life is all about lessons and experiences, and what we learn from them.

There is much to ponder here.

Murders

and

Suicides

Chapter 14

MURDER AND THE RESTING PLACE

When Carol came off the cloud she found herself in a typical Old Western town: wooden buildings, board sidewalks and dusty streets. She was a woman dressed in the typical style of that time. She found herself in front of a general store, and when she went in her attention was immediately drawn to the piles of cloth material and sewing needs. She was a seamstress, but was disappointed by the drab selection. She was not happy in the town, and felt she was stuck there. She didn't really want to be there, but there was nowhere else to go. Any cities were far away. She lived alone with her little girl. Her husband had been killed in an explosion while they were building a railroad to go further west. She couldn't leave so she took in sewing to make a living for herself and her little girl. Her home was simple but adequate for their needs. She loved her daughter, but it was hard to lose the one other person that she loved, her husband.

Then when I had her move to an important day I discovered she leap-frogged. In other words, she jumped into a different lifetime. She began describing a totally different environment. When this happens it usually means there was not much of importance happening in the other life. In most lives one day is just like the next. When this happens I have to make a decision: do I continue to explore the new one, or return to the one we left to find out what happened to her? I decided to explore the one she had jumped into because I knew the SC had a reason for showing it to her.

This time she saw herself in a city with cobblestone streets and street lanterns. It was a rainy, drizzly evening and she

199

went into a pub. She knew it was England or Ireland. She was a young girl in her twenties with red hair dressed in a velveteen dress that laced up the front with a blouse at the top. Quite different from the simple woman in the Western town. That was how I knew we had leap-frogged. There was music in the pub and people were drinking and laughing and telling jokes, and just generally having a good time. "It's like everybody's kicking back after a hard day's work. And everybody's just having fun laughing, and it's loud in there." She described the pub in minute detail, and it sounded like maybe 1880s. I asked if she had a job, since she mentioned a hard day's work. "I socialize. That's what I do. I do favors for men, and they like me. They like me a lot. I mostly hang out in that place. I just am what I am." She was happy there with no responsibilities and no worries. She lived nearby, "Upstairs. I've got my place. I have to go up and it's not very big. It has a bedroom and a chair in there. I don't spend a whole lot of time in there because I'm mainly downstairs. Dancing with the men and .... They have lots of music going on ... lots of joking ... lots of kidding and everybody knows everybody. There's a bar down there and there's food that's served and you have all the socializing, eating and drinking ... it all goes on down there. I'm on my own. I can take care of myself. Men like me and I like them. And they do me favors and I do them favors. They give me money. They make sure I'm okay. They care about me a lot, not just because I'm a plaything, but they genuinely care about me.—It's not like I'm just loose. I am, but it's not like you're dirty. You serve a purpose and they respect that and they're good to me because I'm good to them. I have a lot of friends and they don't expect much. I'm just happy the way I am."

When I moved her to an important day, she went to the day of her death. "I was killed. I wasn't very old." I told her she would be able to watch it as an observer if she wanted to, so she could explain what happened. It occurred in that upstairs room where she slept. A man strangled her. "He was jealous over somebody seen with me and he killed me. We had been together before and he knew what I was and who I was. But he killed me because he couldn't stand what I did for a living. He was very angry. He wanted to take me away from all that. I didn't want to settle down and be with one person. I had a good life. I was happy. I didn't want to leave my life, and I didn't want to leave my other friends there."

I had her move to when it was all over and she was out of her body. She watched the scene. "He's very ashamed. He's sorry, but it's too late. He's already killed me. It's over with. He can't bring me back. Nobody can. I'm just there on the floor. And I see him bent over me crying and sobbing. He's so sorry. He just made a mistake." I then had her look at the entire lifetime and tell me what she thought she learned from that lifetime. "To be more responsible with my affections. I was enjoying myself, but look what it led to. People being jealous, tempers flaring ... angry, and I end up dead. And I was young and beautiful and vibrant, and now I'm dead. I wasn't ashamed of what I did. It's just who I was."

D: *What are you going to do now? Are you going to go somewhere?*

C: I just want some peace and quiet. I just want to rest. I want to be away from everything and everybody for a while. I just want to heal.

D: *Do you go somewhere so you can heal?*

C: I go to a quiet place. It's blue ... and it's like a cocoon. It's like I'm being held in a cocoon. And I'm being nurtured. It's not like I sleep and I wake up. It's not like that. I'm just there and I'm healing and there are people tending to me. They take care of me. They take care of everything. I don't have to worry about anything. I don't have to worry about making a living. I'm just suspended in this nice warm cocoon. I'm getting my strength back. And I can stay there as long as I want until I'm whole again. There's nothing but love.

I knew she was in the resting place on the spirit side. She could spend a long time there if she was recuperating from the violent way she died, so I had to speed time up to where she was ready to leave that resting place. "What happens when you decide it's time to leave?"

C: I kind of sit up and I open that pod thing and then light starts coming in. It doesn't hurt my eyes or anything. And I can go out and do anything I want. I see light all around me. There are pillars of light. There's magnificent light. There's a brilliance all around me. It's like I was in a deep, dark, smooth velvet place of comfort. It was like being in a room practically. And then I open up that chamber thing that I'm in and I walk out, and there's this brilliant light. Beautiful, beautiful mansions upon mansions of crystal light. All these structures and they go on forever. And the light reflects off of all these buildings. All the colors of the spectrum and it is so brilliant, but it doesn't hurt my eyes at all. I can see it all.

D: *Is there anybody else there?*

C: There are tons of people there. Tons of people and they're looking at books. They have videos they're playing, but they're *not* people. They're not people, but they're there and they're doing all this stuff and they're so nice. And they're trying to guide me through and saying, "This is this room, and this is this room. And you can do this and you can do that, and you can cook. You can eat. You can do everything. And they can't show me fast enough.

I laughed because of the excitement in her voice.

D: *If they don't look like people, what do they look like?*

C: They change. Some are blue lights, pink lights, white lights, yellow lights. Sometimes they're balls of light and then sometimes they pop out arms and legs and take a form of what a person looks like. And yet you can see through them.

D: *That sounds like a beautiful place.*

C: Oh, it's nice. And it goes on forever. These big old long hallways, and as big as it is, it doesn't seem like an institution. I can't believe all the records and stuff they have. You want to look up anything, every answer is there. It's just trying to navigate my way through it. I don't know where to start. I don't even know where to go. I want to learn. I want to know what it's all about. I want to know everything.

D: *Would it be hard to learn everything?*

C: You would think so. There's so much to know. There's so much to learn. I want to find out if all the people are dead that I know. I'm trying to listen to everything. They're trying to tell me about all the different aspects of this wonderful place, and all the records and all the media and all the gadgets ... all the gadgets of information! And yet while trying to learn all this stuff, I'm trying to connect with the people that I know.

D: *Do you mean in other lives or what?*

C: I don't know. It's just like I know everybody. It's not like they're strangers because they're so nice. And I feel really welcome here, and it's like you've been away for a long time. It's like homecoming.

D: *Is there any one main person that can talk to you ... somebody in charge?*

C: I have one person that's kind of my "buddy" that finds me. They help me get out of that special place of healing. And they're going to help me to know the lay of the land, so that I can start digging in and figuring things out. It's like my assignment "buddy," or the person I report to. The person that's been assigned responsibility to get me up and running again because I was very broken. I was very injured ... very injured. I was so happy in that life and to have it taken from me ... I don't want to be murdered again.—They want me to get acclimated. Get used to everything that's there. Take my time. Don't rush anything. Move around. See everything there is to see.

This could have taken a long time since they were in no hurry to send her to her next assignment. So I had her condense time and move ahead until she had done those things, and see what she had to do next. "I have to give a report."

D: *Like in school?* (Yes) *What kind of report?*

C: I have to report in and tell them if I'm doing okay. Tell them if I'm getting well and if I'm ready to look at everything I did, and help me to figure it out. Why I was killed and what I did with my life.

D: *What did you find out?*

C: Well, they don't think I was bad. They saw I had a lot of fun doing what I was doing, but it worked to my disfavor to play with people's emotions like that. Even though everything was on a superficial level, sometimes people take it much deeper than that. And I didn't realize how I might have been hurting somebody by not recognizing their affections. Like that man who killed me. It was hurting him.—I need to work on that.

D: *But there's no judging is there?*

C: No, they don't think I'm bad, but if I want to do better, I have to look at that. I can't go on and keep doing that. I mean, you have to be aware of what you're doing. You can't just go through life and have fun and not think of other people. You have to think of other people and how you affect them. Because that's a responsibility you have.

D: *So have they given you any advice?*

C: Think less of myself and more of other people, and that will help me not to hurt them.

D: *Do you have to go somewhere to do this, or what do they say?*

C: I have to stay there a while and study. There's so much. There are big volumes of stuff I have to take. I can look at what I did, and anytime I can go backwards. I can go forwards. I can look at everything. I can talk to other people. It's a place where I'm supposed to learn.

D: Did they tell you what's going to happen after you feel you've learned it?

C: Then I can try it again.

D: Do you want to?

C: Oh, yes. It's really nice to do that. But I don't want to get killed again.—I've been strategizing on where I want to go. I think next time I might settle down and try to have a family.

D: So you're making plans?

C: I'm sure trying to.

This would explain the life in the Old West. If we think in linear time it apparently would have been after the one where she was murdered. She had a family, yet one of the loved ones (her husband) had been killed. She definitely had to think about other people and put herself second in that life. It was dull and simple, but it served the purpose.

I then thought it was time to call forth the SC and find some answers. I always ask why the person was shown the lives that the SC picked for them to see.

D: The first one where she was in the western town and her husband was killed working on the railroad. Why did you pick that lifetime for Carol to see?

C: Because of my little girl. She was everything to me.

D: Why did the SC show Carol the little girl? How does that relate to Carol in the present lifetime?

C: I know that little girl.

I instructed Carol to allow the SC to answer the questions and not try to interfere. "I was to show unconditional love." Carol is a lesbian in her present life, and the SC explained about the people in her life now. She was currently with a partner, but a new one (the little girl in the Western life) had come into her life. It was creating a problem. They stated that she had been with Michelle (her current partner) too long, and it was time to move on, and allow someone new to enter her life. I asked if Carol had had any past lives with Michelle. "They were in Europe. Carol was a young male student, beautiful violinist ... very gifted, very talented. Michelle was a teacher. There was trouble. Michelle, as a teacher, was very, very hard on Carol. And yet, Michelle would tell the other instructors how gifted Carol was. She would never say that to Carol. She pushed harder and criticized more and more and more, and it cut into Carol's self-confidence. It was almost like Michelle did it on purpose because she was jealous of the talent that Carol had."

D: *Then why did they choose to come together in this lifetime?*

C: Carol has to regain her confidence. There was karma between the teacher and the student. Michelle owed Carol. The contract is now over. They have been together for a long time, but it is now time to separate. It's going to be difficult, but it has to be done. She has to go. Deb (the little girl) will now be free to enter Carol's life. There is great love there (because of the past life as mother and child).

D: *Maybe this will help if she knows these things and can understand them.* (Yes) *Then you showed her the lifetime when she was in the pub and she was murdered. Why did you choose that lifetime for her to see?*

C: To show how you can hurt people by your actions.

There was no one in that lifetime that she knew now in her current life. I was surprised because I would have thought the man who murdered her would be a current character. She had asked about her short marriage, and although it was related to a different past life, the SC refused to give details. It was better if Carol did not know.

D: *What did she learn from that short marriage?*

C: To learn to love unconditionally ... to be honest and when you really, really love, don't hold back anything. It was a short contract, but very significant, very strong. To be totally yourself to the person you love. To be able to talk about anything and everything, but to be honest and open because that's the only way that true love can endure.— She didn't have these same feelings with Michelle. That was a different relationship. She has tried everything to maintain a loving, kind friendship with Michelle, but it's going to be up to Michelle to accept it. Carol can't control that. Carol can't clear her head when she's with Michelle. She can't create when she is wrapped in a net. Michelle wants too much from her.

Another question that I already knew the answer to, but I wanted the SC to tell her. "She wants to know where she came from?"

C: She came from the Source. All it is ... everything that is. We are from the Source and we always return to the Source because we are all one.

Message: Never lose faith. We're always there to help you. You're never alone.

Chapter 15

FEAR IS CARRIED OVER

Dionne entered the scene standing on brown soil, hot and dry like a desert. She became aware of an ancient Persian style archway off to the side. Just seeing it filled her with an unexplainable amount of fear. The fear was so strong she wanted to cry. I knew that whenever this happened, we were about to discover something important and significant for the client. You can't fake emotions, they come from the very core of the issue, even if they don't make any sense at the time. I thought if I could get her mind off of it then we could proceed, so I asked her to focus on her body. She was an older bearded man dressed very simply in a loose garment and a turban. His body felt tired and weary. "I'm anguishing over something on the other side of the arch ... something going on inside there. I am feeling afraid of what's happening inside, on the other side of the wall. There are lots of people, loud voices. I feel as though someone I know is in there and I'm worried about them." I asked if he wanted to go inside of the arch and see what was happening, but he was feeling extreme fear. "I'm afraid to go inside and I'm afraid of what's happening inside, too. I think I need to go in, but I'm feeling a fear of it."

D: *Who do you think is in there that you're concerned about?*
DI: I feel like it might be my daughter. Almost like, she might be accused of being a sorceress or something, and the crowd is screaming for her destruction.
D: *Do you think she is a sorceress?* (No) *Why do you think the people would think that?*

209

DI: Because they're ignorant. She has a gift that most people don't have, and they don't understand it. She confided to someone and they didn't understand and were frightened and incited the rest of the people to fear. And trustingly, she gave this part of herself to this young man and he turned and used it against her.

D: *You said she had a gift they didn't understand. What kind of a gift was it?*

DI: The gift of prophecy. She told the young man her gift and gave him a prophecy which came true. And he turned and accused her of bewitching him and creating the situation instead of just seeing it. He believed that she created it.

After much procrastination he decided to overcome his extreme fear and go inside. "They're going to kill her if I don't, and when I go in, they're probably going to kill me, too, so .... I don't know how to do it because if I just go barging in and try to take her, I know they'll just subdue me. So I don't know if I should go in posing as one of them and somehow figure out how to get her free. I just don't know what to do because if I just rush in, that won't work either." He decided to go in. "She's in the back of a wagon, and they're screaming for her to be executed. The young man is saying that she's a witch and he's proved it by what has happened. And the crowd is just a herd of cows really catching the fever.—I don't want to lose her, and I don't want to be killed and then have her be alone." To speed this up, I condensed time and moved him ahead to see what he decided to do.

DI: They end up killing us both. The crowd. They string us up and hang us both. They throw ropes around something and they hang us. They considered me guilty by association. I went in and tried to reason with them, but they were unreasonable because they had caught the fever. I tried to free her, to grab her and pull her, but I was restrained and by association, I was condemned as was she.

D: *There were just too many people.* (Yes.) *Well, how do you feel about the people who did this?*
DI: I hate them! I'm angry at the crowd for their ignorance. The young man was one of them. I don't think I've ever trusted people since. It was unnecessary because nothing changed. She wasn't a witch. She didn't do anything. Nothing changed. They just felt relief. They thought they were safe now that she was gone.

This is never a good idea to carry anger against the people who cause your death. It is certain to create karma that will be brought forward into other subsequent lifetimes.

D: *They were governed by fear.* (Yes) *I think you were very brave to try and save her. But it didn't solve anything, did it?*
DI: It didn't work ... no.
D: *Now it's over with and you're out of the body, so you can look back at it and see it all from a different perspective. Can you see your body?*
DI: Yes, they're just two lifeless bodies. Actually, I feel like they also stabbed us in the stomach. But anyway, they're just two bodies heaped on the ground. The crowd is cheering and now they are dissipating. Nothing has changed. They believe they're safe, but nothing has changed really.

His daughter was with him in spirit as they both looked back at the gruesome scene. I explained that every life has a lesson. "What do you think you learned from a life like that?"

DI: I loved my daughter, and I learned tolerance because she was different. I had to learn tolerance because otherwise, I would have had to push her away. And I also had to learn tolerance for people's differences. I didn't understand it, but it was not evil because she was not evil.

So I learned tolerance and yet, I also took away with me intolerance of what the people did.

I asked what he was planning on doing now that he was out of the body. If there was any place he felt he had to go, or anything he had to do. After a pause he said, "I guess we could go find the wife that I had that died." His wife had died earlier, that was why there were only the two of them to care for each other.

D: *How would you do that?*
DI: Probably turn around and go in the opposite direction from where I'm looking.
D: *What's in the opposite direction?*
DI: I want to say the "Sun," but the scenery below has just become a smaller pinpoint.
D: *It's not something you really want to watch anyway.*
DI: No. I can't go back there ... can't go back. I still feel the weight of what I just experienced. It's not gone. It didn't disappear. I still feel the fear.
D: *Definitely. It was a traumatic situation.—Which direction do you want to go?*
DI: There's only one lighted area. There's one place to go really. It's just turning away from that scene and turning toward the other. It just seems bright and a little tentative. I don't know where I'm going. Seems like I should recognize it. I've been there a million times.—I feel I'm still that person.—I'm just sort of floating towards the light.

I condensed time and moved him ahead to when he arrived at the place where he needed to stop. "You'll know when we get there, and we can stop."

DI: I have a vague feeling that there are other people there. It's like I'm coming in from a traumatic experience and everyone wants to hear what just happened, and I am telling the story. It seemed like my wife is there, and she's probably my husband in this life. I feel like my mother and my father are there. The faces are sort of unrecognizable as the ring of people gets far away from me. The faces aren't real clear.

D: *Sometimes it's more of a feeling anyway, than it is recognition.*

DI: It's sort of a relief to be there. It's like a trauma still close to my heart in a way. I'm still upset about what happened, but I'm relieved that I'm okay. Yet I still feel sad about it. —I probably just have to go to sleep for a while.

D: *Does someone tell you that?*

DI: I think I'm just aware that I have to go through a period of time where—I don't know what the word is—just decompress.

D: *Just to rest. That sounds like a good idea. What about your daughter?*

DI: We're together. I think we're just going to take a nap next to each other now.

D: *What does that resting place look like?*

DI: It's sort of like a cloud in a way. I just feel troubled. I feel like something happened to me that shouldn't have happened, and it was senseless, and it's hard to let go of it.

D: *So you're going to stay there for a while and just not think about anything.* (Yes.)

When people go to the resting place they can stay there a considerable amount of time. It just depends on how long it will take before they feel able to get back on the wheel of life again. It may be a short time, or for some it could be as long as hundreds of years. So I condensed time again to when he had completed his resting, and it was time to leave that place and do something else.

D: *Do you feel better now that you've been able to rest?*

DI: I have this fear permeating my whole being.

D: *Even though you went through the resting, you still have the fear?* (Yes.) *What is it a fear of?*

DI: I guess it's just a fear of being destroyed.

D: *Well, they did destroy the body.*

DI: I know. I know.

D: *But they couldn't destroy you, could they?*

DI: No. I just feel the weight of it and the fear. I don't know how to get rid of it.

D: *Is there anybody there that you could ask questions and get answers from?*

DI: There might be somebody off to the right. He looks like one of those Ascended Masters. He's Asian.

D: *Do you want to ask him questions?*

DI: I could if you want me to.

D: *We could get some answers. Tell him you want to understand this fear. Fear is a strong emotion. Tell him you want to understand where it's coming from.*

DI: He says it's the opposite of the God Source.

D: *Ask him why you are still holding onto that fear?*

DI: Because it's become a crutch.

D: *Because the fear should have been left with the body once it was killed, shouldn't it?*

DI: Apparently I've been living with the fear for a long time and using it as a crutch.

D: *Not only that life, but other lives?* (Yes) *So it didn't go away in the resting place?* (No) *What does he mean, it has become a crutch?*

DI: A way to protect myself in a way. It would keep me from entering situations that would be harmful.

D: *From that respect it is good, isn't it?*

DI: Yes, but when I recognize situations like what was happening with the crowd, then my fear kicks in and I'm in a constant fight or flight mode. I perceive it around me all the time so I'm constantly wanting to run from something, but I have to force myself to be calm and not run.

D: *That's not a good mode to be in, is it?*

DI: No because it's stressful. And to always be suspect of people. To always suspect that at any moment they could turn.

D: *That's not a good way to live, is it?* (No) *What does he suggest? It sounds like he may be very wise. Maybe he has advice.*

DI: Earth is a good place to go. He says that the biggest thing we have to do on Earth is to overcome fear. And if I don't, then I would have to come back. If I do overcome it, then I won't have to. If I get it under control or overcome it, then I won't have to come back unless I want to.—However, I don't want to go back there again. I don't understand why everything has to be so horrible on the Earth.

D: *It doesn't have to be, does it?*

DI: It seems like it is. (Upset) Just cruelty. That's just "what it is." The Earth is that way. People are that way.

D: *Maybe they're not. Maybe they need help. Ask him, if you decide to come back to Earth, could you make a difference to change things?*

DI: To help other people or to help myself?

D: *Either way. What does he say? Do you have a choice?* (Dionne became emotional.) *It's okay to be emotional. That's good. But do you have a choice of whether to go or stay?*

DI: Sort of, but not really. I don't have to go, but I know that if I don't go, then I won't finish what I'm supposed to do. And so I *have* to.—I just don't want to go! I wish I didn't have to work anything out anymore. I wish I could just stay here.

D: *What does he say? Are there rules and regulations about this?*

DI: He said there's a lot left to do.

D: *What did you agree to do?*

DI: Go through it all until it is done. Just to go through whatever it was going to be until it was done. I didn't

215

count on it being this bad. I feel like if I go back, it's just going to be another horrible thing.

D: *Maybe it wouldn't be as bad as what you just went through. Does he know if it will be that bad or easier?*

DI: It can be whatever I make it.

D: *Then you're in control, aren't you?* (Yes) *You're more powerful than you think you are, aren't you?*

DI: I feel sort of like a victim in a way.

D: *I think it's time to turn that around. Is that when you make the decision to come back to Earth?*

DI: I know that I have to in order to fulfill my agreement and to finish, otherwise I'd just be putting it off. I'd have to do it eventually.

D: *And the agreement was to experience everything?*

DI: To go through it, yes. To go through the physical reality.

D: *All the good and the bad?*

DI: Yes, but I didn't have any idea how bad the bad was going to be. It's sort of like somebody that lives on the equator and you try to explain what snow is. And they have an image, but they don't really know what it is until they get there.

D: *You never really know until you experience it yourself.*

DI: I didn't think I was going to *feel* it as much as I have, I guess.

I thought we had learned as much as we could at this point. We knew he had made the decision to come back because procrastination would only delay the inevitable. So I asked if it was all right to call in someone else who would be able to supply more answers. The other entity was agreeable to doing that. So I thanked it and then called forth the SC. Of course, the first question was why it chose that lifetime for Dionne to see.

DI: It was the time when the sadness took hold. It was building up to that point, but it was that one time that the sadness took hold.

D: *So she had experienced other negative lives, but this one was the final straw?* (Yes) *Why did you want her to know about that?*

DI: She's an empath in this life and she needed to know.

D: *An empath takes on everybody else's feelings, don't they?*

DI: Yes. She needed to know that in order to be an empathy, she needed to experience all of the emotions that exist.

D: *That's big.*

DI: Yes. In order to be an empath, you have to have experienced all of the emotions in order to know what emotion you're experiencing. In other words, you have to experience fear to be able to know it's fear. And she can read people and feel what they're feeling before they even verbalize it.

D: *That's good, but what do you want her to do with that talent of being an empath? How do you want her to utilize it?*

DI: It's always been to help others. It gives her much compassion.

D: *But she tends to stay away from people, doesn't she?*

DI: Yes, she has developed a distrust of people.

D: *Does that come from that lifetime?*

DI: Yes, and others.

D: *People showed their violent side.* (Yes) *But in this life, no one's going to treat her like that, are they?*

DI: Oh, they do. Some of those same people from the crowd are in her life today.

D: *People she developed karma with?*

DI: Yes, there's karma. The people from the crowd were strangers to her, and they appear every now and then in this life. And they continue the same behavior, only it's tailored to what her life is now. So there are people in her life that subconsciously want to destroy her. Her close family, her immediate family, wants to protect her. The other ones that have come in and left were just acquaintances. They came and went. Just to keep playing out the same pattern that they have played for a long time.

There are people in her life that subconsciously recognize her from that other time. And they react subconsciously to her in the same way that they reacted at that other time. The agenda is not to destroy her in this life, but they have an immediate recognition of her, and an immediate negative reaction to her. There's a soul recognition and it manifests in them as a dislike of her. And they don't realize it and they don't understand their negative reaction to her.

D: So what is the purpose of that? What is she learning from that?

DI: She needs to learn detachment. She gets too personally involved.

D: Then she should learn to not take it personally.

DI: Yes. She felt betrayed and misunderstood and in her current life she has had experiences that, to her, confirmed that she's worthy of betrayal. No one in this life has tried to betray her, but she perceives it that way.

D: Was anyone in her family now, with her in that lifetime?

DI: Her husband now was her wife, and her daughter now was her daughter. Her mother now, was part of the crowd but not one of the crowd. She was a helpless bystander in the crowd. She was part of the crowd, but she didn't like what the crowd was doing. But there was nothing that she could do.

D: So there's no karma there.

DI: There's something going on with her mother. Her mother feels remorseful.

D: But her mother didn't have an active part in it.

DI: Her mother reacts to her at times the way other people react to her on a soul level. So she has a fear of her daughter the way the crowd had a fear of the young girl. But she also feels sadness toward her the way she did as a part of the crowd ... sadness for what was happening to these two people. Because she was helpless, in this lifetime she was critical of her daughter because she saw aspects of her daughter that she possessed and she wanted her daughter to be strong as she was. And so she used criticism in order to try to strengthen her, but it weakened her daughter instead. Her daughter saw this as confirmation that everyone was evil and negative and not trustworthy.

D: *But how can we get rid of this fear that Dionne is still carrying? Now we know where it comes from. She doesn't need it in this life, does she?*

DI: Not really. It's sort of an ingrained pattern with her. It has gained power over the centuries. It's fairly ingrained.

I asked the SC for suggestions on how to alleviate the fear and make it easier for Dionne to handle. We wanted her to get rid of it now so she wouldn't have to carry it any further. The SC said that one factor was that she was in a negative situation where she works. It created fear which she gave into. "The people are not on her level. She needs to be with people that are like she is. There are people out there, but they are few and far between."

D: *What is she supposed to be doing?*

DI: She's supposed to be creating. She has a lot of information and a lot of knowledge and a lot of wisdom, but it's scattered. She needs to pull it together so she can share it with other people. She could be talking to people and she could be writing about it.

D: *You have to be careful who you talk to because many people don't understand.*

DI: No, the world is in the left brain. (Laugh)

Dionne had started writing some novels, and the SC encouraged her to finish them. "She needs everything that she has experienced to click in her mind and for her to understand it. She's been in her left brain too long, and the left brain keeps people stuck in a cycle of thinking that goes nowhere. And she's forced by circumstances and also by nature to be in the left brain a lot.—She's in a dilemma needing to pay for certain things, but as long as she's in that job, she'll never create. She has certain talents that not everybody has that she could utilize to make money." Mostly her sense of humor which could be utilized in a unique way through her writing, and through acting. The main thing that was holding her back was her fear: the fear of the uncertainty of it, the fear of failure, the fear of not being good enough at it. It was her fear that was keeping the money at bay.

DI: There's a pattern on a cellular level almost of distrust; fear if she speaks, that she'll be shot down. That's why she's become somewhat reclusive in the past because of what she knows other people will do to her. They're always going to react to her. It's whether or not it crushes her when they do. She has a small group of people that care about her. Her husband cares very much for her and their daughter.

She was encouraged to begin the writing again because that was extremely important. And she had to quit her job because the conditions there were holding her back. They said that another, better job would come with all the ideal conditions that she needed. Her physical conditions of fatigue and depression were easily explained because she was not doing what she was supposed to be doing.

DI: She's not doing what she's meant to do and she knows that. She senses that and her body is not enlivened with what she's doing. When she starts doing what I tell her to do, then she won't have the depression anymore. She will be energized and excited about life.

The SC then went through the body and made corrections and improvements. It said now that she understood where the fear was coming from, she would be able to handle it, although it would take work on her part.

Parting message: I love her very much, and she was created different from other people on purpose. She's different because she's not supposed to be like the other people. She's special. All people are, but she was created to be special and she was created so that her light would shine bright for those other people to see. And she has gifts that she is supposed to be developing and using and giving back to the world. It's okay that people recognize her and have an immediate negative reaction. It's okay because it's more about who *they* are than who she is. If she listens to that little intuitive voice and acts on it every time, then she will find happiness and fulfillment.

Chapter 16

MURDER AND SUICIDE

One of Julie's main complaints dealt with her liver. She was scheduled to have an operation that was very dangerous and could possibly kill her. It had to do with a rear biliary duct scarring that caused bile to dump into her bowels. If the surgery didn't work, they had her on the list for a liver transplant. Julie had a long history of major surgeries, and many physical complaints, especially her back. She was on many different types of medication because she was in so much pain. She was also being treated for depression by her psychiatrist and was taking more medication for that.

Julie came off the cloud on a beach by the ocean. She was a fourteen year old native-type boy with black hair and chocolaty brown skin, walking along the beach holding the hand of a little boy that he knew was his brother. When I asked where he lived, he said it was no longer there. There had been a village up on the ridge, but it had been destroyed in a bad storm with heavy wind and water. He and his brother were not there when it happened because they had been out gathering berries in the woods. When the storm hit they hid underneath a fallen tree and a rock, and he tried to protect his little brother. "I hit my head on a big, big branch of the tree. I waited for everything to stop ... ate our berries." They didn't see what happened until they returned to the village. "I can't find anybody.—Where did everybody go? My mom ... mommy.—Everything was just flat and blown over. The storm was bad, but not so bad to do this!" He was very emotional and upset, and kept whispering "Mommy" over and over. "I don't know what to do or where to go. I don't know where the others are."

He became very emotional and was crying, so I decided to condense time and move ahead and see what happened. "The white men got us.—I knew white men were there but they're bringing their God. The white man's God is taught in the village, but other white men have come to take us.—I don't know where my mother is."

D: *Why would they want to take you and your brother?*
J: I don't know. (Bewildered) I'm frustrated. Nobody will tell me.
D: *Do they take you somewhere?*
J: Yes ... (Sarcastic) ... many of us. I found my father. My brother is not here anymore. They took him. They beat my father, and my father's ashamed.
D: *Why is he ashamed?*
J: They killed my mother ... not the storm ... not the storm. She fought. My father is ashamed that he could not protect. He won't look at me.

They were being held prisoner with many people in a place in a village with "white men's guards." He described the men wearing belts with swords and leather boots. They disgusted him, "They stink." As I moved him ahead to see what happened, his voice was filled with hatred and anger, "They starve us ... and they beat us ... and then they want us to kneel to their God." I asked how their God was represented. "This man, I hear them, that his name is Padre. He disgusts me. We have to bow before him and their wood cross." He said, like it was a bad taste in his mouth, "They say that the way to salvation is through the man on the cross, and that we are nothing more than animals." He had a distinct accent throughout this emotional recounting. "They think we are animals. They beat us like animals. They gather us like animals. They kill us like animals." He was extremely upset and was crying as he said, "I eat the root! I am going to kill myself. They will not!" He said a boat was coming to take them away somewhere. The idea frightened him, "I hear stories. They make us go ... and then we die. And they say they *own* us, and that they own our land. You cannot own land. It's God's. We are God's people." He was so frightened he thought it was better to kill himself by eating the root which he knew was poison. "And my stomach hurts!" I removed any physical sensations so he could explain what was happening. "I killed the Padre with the root. I tricked him to eat the root. He like me. He touch me. (Sobbing) I told him 'good yummy.' He is like a jackal. He is strong and stinks, but I can kill him." He was proud that he had tricked the priest into eating the root.

D: *You didn't like this man, did you?*
J: No ... he hurt me.—*He do to me what man not do to man!* (Very thick accent.) He was not a man of God ... not my God!

His voice was filled with so much disgust and hatred, it did not take much imagination to know what he was talking about. So I will not go into details for the readers.

J: I was sneaky like the lioness. I was telling him "good to eat" and I ate it first. I gave him the worst part of the root. And he ate it.

The boy's stomach was hurting and it didn't take long for him to die. He was out of his body and looking at himself. "I have been wasted by the white man ... and the white man's God." He saw they were trying to help the Padre, but he knew there was nothing they could do, and he would die. He smiled, "I have done right by my mother." I asked what he was going to do now that he was out of the body. "I will dance. I dance for those that cry and weep, and I will dance 'til they come home ... my family. I want these men to leave, but I will dance 'til they come home. They took them all, and left me with the Padre because he liked me.—But now I can go anywhere. I am free. I am free!"

D: *You're free from that, and even though you killed yourself and killed him, you feel it was for a good reason?*
J: Yes. I needed to stop him from hurting other people, and making us kneel to his cross. He was powerful. He was a God in his own mind, and those around him bent only to his words, his words. And now they do not have their disgusting God.

I then had Julie drift away from the scene, leaving the boy there to continue on his own journey. And I called forth the SC and asked why it had chosen that life for her to look at.

J: Out of love for community. Sacrifices are often made when least expected, even from the young.
D: *Because it was a rather violent life, wasn't it?*
J: Only that portion. The rest was good. There's much to be said about sacrifices and community and love. She has always had a depth of love. Love is that ultimate love she talks of.
D: *But even though in that life she killed. You think it was through love?*
J: No. He felt if he killed him, it would stop others from being gathered from other villages, once this powerful man was gone.
D: *Because this man of God would no longer be there?*
J: Yes, but it didn't stop it. Too many people. They just replaced the one that they lost.
D: *He did what he thought was the right thing to do.* (Yes) *He might have helped some people by doing that.* (Yes) *What does that have to do with Julie's life now?*
J: Sometimes she thinks she's always sacrificing to help others, and she does. Anyone who requires her attention and needs sacrifice, she'll give it. It's not healthy for her.

She needs to take time for herself and to heal her pain ... her self-inflicted pain. Just like taking the root.

D: *Does the way she killed herself have any significance in her life now?*

J: Only that it is poison now to take and ingest what she takes and ingests. Medical doctors think they are helping her. They try. They are not helping Julie.

D: *So you think the things they are giving her are not good for her?*

J: Yes, and by thinking that she is doing the right thing, she's killing herself.

D: *Again, you mean?* (Yes) *We don't want that because in this life it's not the lesson to be learned, is it?* (No) *She learned that lesson already.* (Yes) *In this life she has work to be done. She will help many people.*

J: Many.

D: *So we don't want her to poison herself again.*

J: No. She only helped a few in that life, but now she can help many. If she just doesn't take the poison.

D: *Which are the things you don't want her to take?*

J: The neuro pain medication they give her, and the regular pain medication with the Tylenol ... bad ... and the prescription medication with Tylenol. (Loudly) The Tylenol is killing this body!! It is affecting her liver and her kidneys. The Tylenol is killing her! She needs to stop! Even when she has a headache, use Reiki and it can make her headaches go away.

D: *Can you flush the medicines she's already taken from her body?*

J: Yes, I can.

D: *Is there any other medicine she's taking that you don't want her to take?*

J: Yes. What her psychiatrist gives her is not necessary.

D: *The anti-depressants?*

J: Yes. I want her to wean off of it; completely stop ... do not use.

D: *By weaning off, you want her to do it gradually?*

J: No, stop!
D: *Will this cause an effect on the body if she just stops taking it? We don't want to harm the body any more.*
J: She may feel extreme mood swings if she completely stops. She can choose either way. The best way would be to completely stop, but it may be too difficult emotionally to completely stop, but it will only take about a week.

I didn't think that would be very long to get all of this out of her system.

D: *So she may notice mood swings in that time period, but she'll know where it's coming from.*
J: Yes, and she will balance out.
D: *We want her to be balanced. Is there anything else you want her to stop taking?*
J: Her attention deficit medication. There's nothing wrong with her mind. She's very, very aware of herself.

I have found that many times when the client is taking several different types of medication that they interact with each other, and often produce unwanted effects. I mentioned that the doctors were talking about operating on her liver. This always upsets the SC because it doesn't like surgery. It said the liver would recover if she stopped the Tylenol and other pain medications. "No operation ... no operations necessary!" I asked the SC to go into the body to the liver area and make some repairs. Julie was scheduled to have an MRI when she returned home. I thought if the doctors did their tests and then saw there wasn't anything wrong, they wouldn't want to operate. "No, they will not."

D: *You know how doctors are with their machines.*
J: Yes. They're proof positive for them.

The SC said it was already working on the liver, and I asked what it was doing. I am always curious to know how it is done. When the SC works it gets quiet, so I like to keep it talking to me so I can know the progress. It has told me in the past that I can talk to it as it works.

J: Pressure on the inside of the liver is building and pushing. I am rotating around it with energy that heals. Her body has been building up the energy while we speak, so that I can do this.

D: *When she goes back to the doctor and he takes the pictures, will they notice that something is different?*

J: Oh, yes.

D: *Of course, they won't understand it, will they?* (Laugh)

J: No, but she will have a very keen, funny way of letting them know.—Her body is very hot from the amount of energy. I needed it to build up so that we can do this. It never ceases to amaze us.

D: *So it's healing the damage that the Tylenol did?* (Yes) *They were even talking about taking the liver out and putting another one in ... a transplant.*

J: And she said that made her liver quiver. (I laughed.)

This showed that the liver has an awareness and consciousness of its own. It reacted at the thought of being removed from the body.

D: *It didn't like the idea. That's the only solution they have, just to operate.*

J: Yes. To mutilate the body. This body has been through so much. It's been mutilated enough.

D: *We don't want to let them mutilate it any more, do we?*

J: No, she doesn't need it.—She's a stubborn one.

I asked if it could look at other parts of her body that she was having problems with, the lower back, in particular. It said, "Of course, I can." I asked for the cause of that problem.

J: Honestly? *(Yes)* Her past ... yet unfortunately, she slipped and fell in life and in spirit.

While it worked on the body I asked if there was anyone in that lifetime that she knew now in her present life. It said the little brother was James, a good friend in this lifetime. Of course, I wondered if the Padre was anyone she knew. It confirmed what I was thinking, that the Padre was her grandfather in this life. During our interview Julie confided in me that her grandfather had molested her as a child. Apparently they had made a contract to be together again (in different roles) so that he could repay what he had done to the young boy. But it seems as though he still had not learned that lesson and had carried that sexual problem forward. Instead of repaying, he had accumulated more debt. I asked the SC about karma.

J: She's completed hers in the past. This man has a lot of karma. And he repeated himself again. It's his problem, not hers.
D: *Julie doesn't need to have any part of that any more. You said she worked her part out.*
J: Very much so. She loved him.
D: *So in a case like that, murder and suicide are not considered negative?*
J: Not in a case like that. It seemed to be the only answer to a young fourteen year old boy.—Things were pivotal for *her* at fourteen also.
D: *Was it related in some way?*
J: In some ways she found love instead of hate ... grace instead of anger.
D: *She had a mastectomy at fourteen.*
J: Yes, she did.
D: *Is there a connection there?*
J: Not to that life in particular. Other than pain and suffering and mutilation of oneself. No matter how necessary you think it is, it's not always necessary. But this had to do

with her mother also. She wanted what was best for her daughter. She wanted to help her. Even though she knew that the mass was benign, she insisted. And this poor girl lost her breast, but she's not attached to this body at all. The asymmetrical deformity made them go in and rebuild the breast. Her mother told her that the tumor was cancerous, and it was not. Julie knew no difference. She never had cancer. Her mother asked for the breast to be rebuilt after the removal of the tumor. And the breast, itself, had a staph infection afterwards that was horrible ... it almost killed her. She has no memory of that. She just remembers being very sick and being in the hospital a lot.

I thought it was interesting that this occurred at the same age that the young boy had experienced his trauma in the past life. But now that she understood all this she should have no more physical problems. The SC insisted that she had had enough physical problems.

Next I asked the inevitable question, "What was her purpose?" She should be writing, even though this was something she thought was difficult. She had an interest in healing, but the SC did not think that was a good idea for Julie. "I think it will work for people sometimes, but she must be connected on a very deep level for it to work. She's too empathic. She takes on like a magnet people's illnesses and energy."

There was a surprise when I asked about her husband. They had been having problems, and he was considering either retiring or going to another military base in Washington. "I think retirement is still a ways off. Too soon."

D: *Can you see what's going to happen with him?*
J: Yes. He remarries. (This was a surprise.)
D: *You mean they are not going to stay together?*
J: No. In the end, even though she thinks this is what she wants, it still makes her very sad when it comes to

fruition. He will take the job in Washington, and she will stay in Virginia.

D: *How will Julie be able to support herself?*

J: She will begin by going back to school and taking some classes; nothing extensive. Education ... not in a university. It's going to open a door for her to meet new people ... connection. She's going to meet a gentleman that is older that will help her to gain the confidence to write.

I was running out of time, but she had another question. Many times while she was sleeping she would speak in other languages. Her husband had even tape recorded these. She wanted to know what was happening when this occurred.

J: She is channeling other lives. Memories... cellular memories. She speaks the language.

D: *I was thinking that when she took that poison, maybe that's what was affecting her in this lifetime. It caused pain in her stomach in that lifetime.*

J: No. There is a contrast between taking something that you think will help you and by death. He thought it would help him in the end but it only kills you in this life.

The final message before leaving: "Stop taking the medications. Know that you are open psychically for us. We always send you the loving information that you will write about.

I don't often hear back from my clients after the sessions, but in Julie's case she emailed to tell me what happened afterwards:

First off, on the way home that night (after the session) on our way out of town back to Virginia, I fell asleep as my best friend drove. He woke me later wanting to know if I was okay because I was dripping, no, soaking wet with sweat. It was as if my physical body shut down and was trying to detoxify all the medications the doctors were giving me out. I have never sweat like that before, nor do I imagine I will again. I could wring out my dress, Literally!

In May I had a 14mm scarred open bile duct that caused bile to dump into my bowels. Preventive surgery was in order and then on to the liver transplant list for a new liver with healthy size ducts. (Our session was done in June.).

In the past month (September), I finally had the second MRI done and the doctors were stunned at the results. In fact so much so, they say it is like looking at two different people's liver and duct system. I had a 14mm scarred bile duct that was unable to close down due to scars. Now I have a 9mm bile duct with NO signs of sclorosing or scarring anywhere. Needless to say, a liver transplant is no longer necessary. I am no longer terminally ill. The only other thing that changed was that I stopped all medications and Tylenol for pain. Just as my higher self instructed emphatically to do. NO TYLENOL! It was poison.

At the same time that we had this session, there were notices on CNN and in the newspapers warning people about taking these medications containing acetaminophen. Tylenol and other pain medications all contain this same harmful ingredient that damages the liver. Since this session, I have tried to warn people about the dangers of these drugs.

I have also had other clients experience purging reactions after sessions such as this. Some experience vomiting, diarrhea or sweating. Each client has different symptoms. The interesting thing is that the client is rarely concerned. They realize that the poisons are being released from the body, and the symptoms do not last very long. It is a purging.

Chapter 17

A SUICIDE

After coming off the cloud Evelyn found herself standing on a mountain looking down into a big valley below her. There were many trees, and the valley was very deep, so far down that the sun couldn't reach the bottom. It was a beautiful, pristine place. She was standing next to a Chinese style building with curved type roofs, which she perceived to be some type of monastery. Inside there were wooden floors and the impression of many shiny things, also a Buddha. This was one large room, with other rooms off to the sides adjoining it. Light was coming in from above, as though it might be open to the sky. There were bamboo rugs on the floor, and a small miniature garden in the middle with a bonsai tree.

There was confusion when she first looked at her body. She wasn't sure if she was male or female, but she saw she was wearing a long robe with an intricate purple and gold embroidery design like Chinese brocade. She was in her early twenties and had straight, coarse black hair. Her skin was a pale yellowy, not olive, but not white. Her sleeves were very wide and she could see she was wearing a jade bangle like a circle on her left hand. She was also surprised to see she had long fingernails. The place had the feel of a monastery because there were no families there. They each had their own, very plain, sleeping room. But when they ate there were large tables where people sat on the floor. She saw them eating bowls of soup.

I asked her to see if there was anything particular that she did with her time. She saw herself writing songs, and manuscripts on tall, rectangular white paper. "It looks like a tablet, but I'm not using a brush. It's a pen. I'm not writing across. I'm going up and down. I'm writing illuminated manuscripts." I asked what she meant by "illuminated." "With the pictures in the corner. It's so pretty. It's mostly about words, but there are borders that are pretty, or letters that are pretty. I think I did it all, the drawings as well as the writing. The drawings are the fun part. I don't know if it's religious or if we're students. Now everybody is together in that eating place, and they all look the same age. I might be a student, but I don't want to leave this place." She then became emotional. I couldn't understand why. She began to cry. "I don't want to leave it. I'm so afraid. I am so happy here." She had been living there for several years.

I then moved her forward to an important day. "We are all going into this meeting hall. I think they are going to tell us something.—There's a man doing the talking. I think he is a warrior. He has a sword on him. I think it's a military takeover. It's not going to be what it was." She suddenly spoke loudly as though she was agitated or afraid. "I don't like this man! I can only see *him* right now. But it's an army." She then, for the first time, became aware of what sex she was. "We're all girls, the people who live here. I thought it was a monastery because we live there, but we're all the same age and we're all the same gender."

D: *But now this army has come, the soldiers?*

E: Their boss is here and he's telling them to take over ... trying to tell us everything will be okay, but it's not going to be okay. Because he's a liar. You can see it on his face. We're not stupid.

D: *Because you're isolated, they think you don't know any different.*

E: Right. It's a school and a beautiful place on the top of a pass. It's hard to get there, and you don't see many people, but it doesn't mean we can't see the writing on the wall. You can tell. We are not stupid.—I feel this is a bad thing. I think he intends to bring in his lieutenants, and they're going to stay where we are. And their people, the main people, the army, is going to be out front.—I know they're going to force themselves on us. Why else would they come here? We have everything they could ever need, and then there are all these women. This isn't their end point. They're just on their way somewhere.—But now I think I'm going to kill myself!

I could sense the fear building in her. She had difficulty talking about it. I had to encourage her by telling her she could tell me anything because I would understand.

E: I think they're going to rape us, and it's not going to be very nice. They're animals. They might dress well and be neat, but they're not nice. It's fun for them.—(She was obviously watching this.) How long is it going to go on? What's going to happen? Maybe I should just go to the edge and just jump off!—I think I'm going to do that. I'm going to go do it.—It's awful. It's not going to get better. I think I'm just going to go out really quickly. There's a piece on the edge there that's really sharp and sticks out. That's why it goes down so far to the bottom. It's dark.— I think I'll just go and run at it real fast. I won't have time to think about it and then the momentum will take me over and then ... it'll be a long way down. Then I'll be fine.

D: *Is that a solution?*

E: That's what I'm going to do. I think I'll do it.—Okay, it's over!

D: *So what did you do?*

E: (Matter-of-factly) I jumped off! I didn't want to live like that.

D: *What was that like to fall like that?*

E: I think it was frightening. The air has to rush up real fast, doesn't it? And my legs are flapping me around, but I knew that when I reached the bottom I would be dead because it was a long way down.—I'm smashed on the ground beneath there. I see a body there. It's quiet and I'm alone there. There's nothing to disturb anything. It doesn't hurt now. It's all right.

D: *Now that you're out of the body, you can look at that entire lifetime from a different perspective. What do you think you learned from that life?*

E: Mostly it was beautiful.—But maybe I learned not to resist things. I mean, if you resist things, they just get harder.

D: *But you felt it was the only way out of the situation, didn't you?*

E: I could have lived and I could have helped the others, and I could have made a life after they left. But you never know. Maybe I wouldn't be alive after they left because maybe they would have killed everyone. But I didn't know. I wouldn't know what happened.—Well, they're only men and these bodies are only things.

D: *I wondered if you were angry at them.*

E: I was angry at them. I was horrified, but after I died it turned out I'm not. It's just a thing that happened. I don't suppose they could have done anything different. I mean, they were a product of their environment. (She started laughing.) I'm wondering if I made a mess out of that whole thing. I was pretty dramatic.

D: *Yes, but where are you going to go now? Do you know?*

E: I can turn around and there's something behind me ... some light thing ... fluffy thing, adoring. There's a feeling I can go into this place with people I know already. People I knew before I went there.—It's like going back to mother. I don't know how to put it. I know them. It's like school. It's like you go and say, "What do ya think of that?" Then you think, "*Well*, did you do what you wanted to do?"

D: *You mean, you discussed what you just experienced?* (Yes) *What are they saying about what you experienced?*

E: They don't make judgments. They let you talk. Kind of helps knowing that nothing is good or bad. It was beautiful, but there was this intense ugliness as well.—I don't know what we're going to do now. I think this is a place of waiting and soothing it over. I think I'm going to have another life. (She started crying.) And I don't know what it is yet.—I know those people and I went with them, and they said, "So, hey, how did that go?" They all knew about it. I think there is a place where you go to discuss those things.

D: *What is that place like?*

E: The people wear these white robed things. There's no differentiation, no status between anyone else. You can feel that someone is more mature by your feeling of them, not by the way they dress.

D: *And do you evaluate what you've done?*

E: I knew when I first went in there that was what we were going to do, but that was with joy. It was a strange thing to say after an experience like that.—Oh, it's good to be back. It feels like home. It's a good place. The other place was an experience. The people in the white ... that's home.

D: *You said you're going to discuss what you're going to do next?*

E: I don't know. I just had a flash that I was going to have another life. I can see it coming. It's like a circle is coming toward me.

D: *Are any of them going with you?*

E: I think some might, but I don't want to go just yet. I think it's my choice what it's all about. I think they give you advice.

D: *What are they telling you?*

E: I hear the word "limitations," like we have to know our limitations.

D: *What does that mean?*

E: Well, I killed myself. (Laugh) The discussion was of the life that ended. That was one option. I don't think it's considered to be optimal, but if you're going to choose difficult experiences, you have to be sure you can do them. It was about knowing your limitations. Because if you get into a situation that is very intense and you can't handle it, when you shut down then that's your limit. That means you've gone past what you can do. You can breeze through the thing and come out with a different attitude. I could have carried on or maybe I would have got to a different place. I wanted it to be over. I wanted to be out of it.

D: *So what about your next life. Are they telling you what that's going to be?*

E: It's going to be completely different. I'm not sure. It might be the one I'm in now. I think so. I just see glimpses. I don't know the whole story. I'm seeing this life I'm in now.

D: *What do they want you to learn in the next one you're going into?*

E: Some things are obvious. Not to be so hotheaded about things ... to go with things and not resist things.

Evelyn was getting some answers, even identifying some people in her life now that were in that life. But I thought we could get more answers by bringing in the SC. I asked why she was shown that lifetime. "So she would see the emptiness that caused her to kill herself is not real, and the emptiness that she feels now is not real either."

D: *Why does she feel emptiness now?* (Evelyn became emotional and began to cry.)

E: Because all the people that she came in with are gone. We arranged for them to come over together.

D: *In that lifetime Evelyn committed suicide. It was because she was in a situation she felt she could not get out of. (Yes) I know you don't condemn anyone ... there's never any right or wrong. But I'm always trying to understand the suicide part. I know that suicide is often condemned because it is considered breaking contracts.*

E: In this case it was an option. It wasn't a bad thing. It felt like it might have been, but it was not. My feeling is that it wasn't maybe the smartest thing to do, but she did it and so ....

D: *How does that apply to her present life? What was she supposed to learn from it?*

E: Endurance. Not to give up. She has given up many times in this life. She has to stop it. There's no point in this beautiful place called "Earth." Life is so beautiful. She needs to be happy ... just happy with everything ... every day.—You choose to come here. There are more dimensions than you know and you can feel joy. It's not over. You can feel joy.

Physical: Asthma all her life.

E: She doesn't want to breathe. She's resisting things now. She held her breath all the way down when she jumped. She doesn't have to do that anymore.—Sometimes I think she feels bad when she can't handle limitations. We can take it away. It's not really there. There's nothing wrong with the lungs. She creates this problem in the body. She's used to it, but she doesn't need it. She worries that things are going to hurt her all the time. She thinks it's going to hurt her, but nothing's going to hurt her. It's fear. She's waiting for it to happen. You don't need to feel fear. She has to understand that there's nothing to fear.

Overweight: "She wanted it. She did! (Laugh) Because she felt safe. She liked it. She shouldn't do that to herself. It's just gonna go away. She knows that we're very light on the inside and that we can lift off the ground if we want to.—I think her problem is that she didn't think her life was going to be this long, and she kind of gave up. And there's still a lot longer to go. She doesn't count her accomplishments.

Chapter 18

A HEARTBROKEN SUICIDE

When Helen came off the cloud I could tell by her facial expressions that something was bothering her. She whispered that she was standing all alone among many gravestones at night in a cemetery. There was fog rolling in and she felt cold. "I just don't like it here. It makes me want to cry." She sounded very sad and lonely. "I'm looking around, but I can't find what I'm looking for.—I just want to be sad ... like somebody died. Somebody died.—I'm trying to find something." She then became aware that she was a young female in her twenties dressed in black boots and a long dress which was covered by a cape. Her voice then took on an English accent, "I'm distraught. It's like I'm looking for someone and I can't find them.—It's a child ... I think I'm looking for my baby." She then began to cry, "A baby boy. I think I lost the baby. I lost the baby!" Even though she was sobbing I encouraged her to talk to me about it. "He was sick, but I was sick, too. A fever. I woke up and he was gone. I am trying to find him in the cemetery. He was under five. Very sad ... very sad.—I think I lost a baby, too."

She had lost two children at the same time because of the sickness. There was only a small amount of medicine, so nothing could be done. Her husband didn't get sick, only her and the children. "It happened really fast." She said they lived in a small town, sounded like Siking (?) in England. "A small town ... very wet and cold and dark." She then had a flash of recognition that her husband Rob in her present lifetime was her husband then. "I just see that graveyard and I'm looking around ... very lost without my babies. They took them. I

243

wasn't there (she was not conscious). I was sick. I didn't see it. They're in the graves ... in the graves."

D: *So it happened while you were sick? That's why you didn't know where they buried them?* (Yes) *Does your husband know?*

H: He's coming to me. He's showing me.—I'm just out of my mind ... just out of my mind. (Crying) I can't ... I just can't take it.

D: *It's a big shock.* (Yes) *So you got well and they told you?*

H: I just knew ... I just knew it. Yes.—Oh! I think I had a baby inside of me. It seems like it was a baby that had died inside of me.

D: *Is this the one they buried, or is this another one?*

H: It was a fetus and a boy ... a blonde-haired boy.

D: *So the fever killed the baby inside of you.*

H: Yes, that's why I was sick.

D: *They took them and buried them, and now they are showing you where they're buried?*

H: It's a mound of dirt. And a headstone ... a little cross.

D: *Does it say anything on the headstone?*

H: Maybe it does ... Thomas ... it says Thomas C. And a date: 1873.

D: *But there was nothing you could do, was there?*

H: I just feel really bad. I let him down. It's duty. It's duty to have children. It feels like I let my husband down.

I spent some time consoling her and telling her it wasn't her fault and there was nothing she could do about it. This is important because sometimes these situations carry over into the present lifetime and can be the cause of all types of problems (physical and otherwise).

D: *How is this affecting your husband?*

H: He's sad and disappointed, but he still loves me. He feels guilty because he thinks he could have done something more.

D: *There are times when nobody can do anything. You said there was very little medicine.* (Right)—*At least you know where they are. You found them, didn't you?*

H: Yes ... in Heaven.

D: *What does your husband do in that town?*

H: Clergy. He takes care of the church. Some sort of clergy. I see black and white clothes.

D: *Is he like a priest?*

H: Yes, he's holding a Bible and a Catholic cross thing ... yes ... very pious man. Pious, pious .... He's very respected and people look up to him.—I feel like I'm nothing.

D: *Is that how he treats you?*

H: No. He just treats me like a woman. He just treats me like a servant.

D: *Is that the way women are treated in that place?*

H: Yes ... and I failed. Because I didn't give him a child.

D: *But you did give him children.*

H: I know, but it's just me ... that's what happens ... children die. It's too cold here ... too wet. (Pause)—I think I just go out of my mind. (Sadly) I don't want to stay there anymore.—I just don't want to live after that.

D: *You don't think you can have more children?*

H: No. He just ignores me. He just leaves me alone. He's just closed.

D: *But he's supposed to be there helping people in the town.*

H: (Matter-of-factly.) Oh, he does. It's just a facade ... just his job.—Between us ... there's no contact.

D: *So it really wasn't a marriage of love.* (No) *Just to have children and take care of him?* (Yes) *So there wasn't anything to stay there for, is that what you mean?*

H: No, and I just die in my bed.

I took her forward to that day so we could see what happened. I always instruct the person that they can look at it as an observer if they want to. They don't have to physically experience anything. "What happened to you?"

H: Just anger ... (Pause) I ... I killed myself. (She became upset.)

D: *You can watch it as an observer. You don't have to participate.*

H: I just see myself stabbing myself.

D: *You said there was a lot of anger?*

H: Yes. Like I wasn't suited to be that person ... and with him, I knew I just didn't want to be there anymore. I was so angry at myself.—I see myself stabbing my stomach and my heart. I was screaming.—No one was there, but Robert came in and saw me dead like that right after.—I see him covering his eyes and being sad, but with no emotion ... no emotion. I think he's better that I left. I was useless to him.

D: *If you couldn't have children, you weren't of any value.*

H: Yes. I wasn't suited to that life. After I lost the baby, I just didn't want to be there. I didn't know how I got into that. I didn't understand about life.

D: *So you are out of the body now?*

H: Yes. I see a body ... but I am much happier out of that body. I was only about twenty.

She watched as they took the body to the same cemetery, dug a grave, put her in and covered it up with dirt. There was a white grey stone. "Becca. Rebecca."

D: *Is there a last name?*

H: Starts with a C.—It's just a body. Thank goodness I'm out of it.—When I went into that life I wanted to bring light into the darkness. That place was so dark.—It was all too hard ... too hard to do.

D: *So you planned to do one thing, and it didn't work out that way. Is that what you mean?*

H: Yes. It happens a lot. It's just not safe. My heart keeps getting hurt every time I come to this Earth. (She was upset.) I'm just supposed to be ... love ... helping.

D: *Those are good things. Did you have bad experiences in other lives too?* (Oh, yes!) *Tell me what you can see or what you can remember.*

H: Um ... so many. Lots of wars. We're so stupid.

D: *You were involved with wars?*

H: Yes ... but dishonor death.

D: *But when you came into those lives, had you intended to be in wars?* (Oh, yes.) *You made plans to do that?*

H: Yes. I kept thinking I could conquer it. That I could make a difference.

D: *Even in a situation like that, even in a war?*

H: Yes.—I just felt so alone and those times I couldn't connect to the people I wanted to.

D: *So you made plans that didn't turn out the way you wanted them to?*

H: Yes. Not like I wanted it to. ... I just see a lot of blood ... lot of dying.—That didn't happen every time I came to Earth. I had several good lives. That's why I thought I could do what I tried to do. Because I knew the light was good and it was needed.

D: *You had good intentions.*

H: Always.

D: *But that's what happens when you get down here in the body?*

H: It's like mud ... it's so heavy and people just don't understand me.

D: *When you get into the body, you forget your plan, don't you?*

H: Yes, and I just go hide. I hide.—I just saw Rob (her present husband). He was the man! He was that man!

I moved her ahead until she was making her plans to come into the body as Helen. "Can you look at that part, where you are making your plans?"

H: What do you want to know?

D: *What was your plan when you entered the body known as Helen? That's the body you are speaking through, isn't it?* (Yes) *Let's see what your plan was, what you wanted to accomplish. We don't want to make the same mistakes, again.*

H: Oh, she did it again anyway.—She's very sensitive. She holds an energy inside of her that is very strong. It's like it doesn't matter what she does particularly. She still has the energy to hold for this space ... for this new time ....

D: *What kind of energy?*

H: It's for the Earth.

D: *The Earth during the time that Helen's alive?*

H: Yes—The plan was really simple. All she has to do is to be herself. Just to enjoy life. That's all she has to do.

D: *That sounds simple.*

H: She makes it so complicated.

D: *So she's supposed to just come in and enjoy herself this time?*

H: Yes ... yes ... yes ... yes.

D: *Does she carry this energy you are talking about?* (Yes) *Is she supposed to do anything with the energy?*

H: She says she is a beacon of light and that is what she is.

D: *How can she share this beacon of light? What was the original plan?*

H: It's for the area that she lives in. The matrix ... near the grid ... now.

D: *So when she planned to come here, she knew she would be living in that area?*

H: She knew ahead of time, yes ... but not consciously.

D: *How is she supposed to spread the light if she is just enjoying herself?*

H: She loves to help people.

D: *Does she know she is limited here on Earth?*

H: She struggles with that. With knowing where she came from and knowing what she has to do here.

D: *Where did she come from? Maybe it would be good for her to understand.*

H: Many places. Sirius is her favorite. She's a traveler. She goes all over. She has the capability of just living where she is needed.

D: *And she's not supposed to do anything ... just be there ... be a beacon of light?*

H: It's important that she does it.—It's hard to share everything with her because we want her to stay the way she is. We know she is frustrated. It just has to be that way. Her personality is so strong that we need to keep the ego in check.—And she is very protected. She should not worry.

Helen sounded like one of the Second Wave who have come to spread their energy to help people. They usually don't have to *do* anything. They just have to *be*. And for many people that is hard to understand how they can influence people by just being.

D: *She wants to accomplish things in this lifetime, too.*

H: That doesn't really matter because it's all in motion. She should just enjoy her life. That's her purpose ... to enjoy it. She's had many lives that were not enjoyable.

D: *The one you showed us was not enjoyable, was it?*

H: No ... that's causing her pain now. It's stuck in her body. That's why we're working on her already.

They were referring to the heart (chest area) and the abdomen area, the places where she stabbed herself.

D: (I referred to one of her physical questions.) *She said there's a fibroid tumor in her uterus. Can you see it?*

H: This is not my area.

D: *That was where she stabbed herself, wasn't it?*

H: Yes. Very unfortunate for that. (Deep sigh.)

D: *People make mistakes when they think they can't take any more. Are the physical problems being caused by the trauma of the stabbing?*

H: Partially.

D: *(I referred to one of her physical questions.)* *She said there's a mass on the right side. What is that? Can you see it?*

H: This is not my area. It's not my area.

D: *What is your area?*

H: I don't know. (Small laugh.) It's not that though. I just feel it for her.—I'm not the subconscious.

I didn't think it was, but it was giving us some answers so I let it talk. Before I called forth the real subconscious I wanted to emphasize what this part had already told us. "You want her to have fun? That's what the plan was ... to enjoy herself?"

H: The way she knows how to spread joy is very good. And that is what we want her to create. It is very needed at this time.

I tried to get the answers to some of Helen's more specific questions, but they said again that was not their area and they couldn't answer. "Then is it all right if we call in the subconscious and let it answer more questions?"

H: Please do what you need to do.

D: *I really appreciate the information you've been giving her. I think she's going to listen to it, and maybe it'll make a difference.*

H: They are working on her.

D: *Who's working on her?*

H: Her guides.

When I first tried to call forth the subconscious they said that Helen was resisting. "There's fear lurking. It's hard for her to release. Her expectations are very high." I explained that she had already allowed most of the questions to be answered and that there were only a few left. "Her brain won't

250

stop thinking." I explained that it had already stopped for over an hour, and she didn't even know it. So all she had to do was stand over to the side and let us finish. She could watch if she wanted to. The logic was persuasive and apparently she realized that a lot had already been done without her knowledge. So it agreed to allow us to proceed. The first question I asked was why they chose that lifetime for Helen to see. "This one where the children died and she committed suicide."

H: To heal it ... to heal ... (louder) to heal!

D: *She's still carrying that with her?*

H: Yes. It was a release to relive it. It was releasing for her that memory.

D: *She didn't even know she was carrying it, did she?*

H: No. She had an idea though.

D: *Was there anyone in that lifetime that she knows now?*

H: Yes, her husband ... her husband now.

D: *Why did they come back together in this lifetime?*

H: To have love. To finish ... to have it be the way that she envisioned it ... with love.

D: *Because he was very indifferent in that lifetime, wasn't he?* (Yes) *So it was to have him come back and work out his karma?*

H: Hers! We don't like it when people take their lives. It was a real waste and then ... how she felt that she was a waste in that life.

D: *Of course she went through a lot. She felt that she couldn't handle any more.*

H: We understand.

D: *So she had to come back to this life with the same husband?*

H: Yes. He's a good man. Things are a lot better ... she still worries too much.

D: *What does she worry about?*

H: Being provided for.

251

D: *Yes, that was one of her questions. She's worried about money.*

H: Everyone is. It's a human thing. It's not going to be the worry that she thinks.

They then continued to answer the questions she had about her work and developing a center. They wanted her to relax and stop worrying because everything was getting ready to happen and her life was going to flourish.

H: We understand that she's in a place of challenge. She has to be there for now. She's learning to trust herself and be in divine guidance ... true knowing requires these tests. She must trust herself. (She began to cry.) We're just releasing energy for her. She is just so full of energy. She traveled over America and she has so much energy. She just puts it all over the Earth. The Earth needs it so much. It is a very good thing. We always want to be gentle with her. We want her to stay on this Earth. She has *much* work to do.

I then wanted to know about the fibroid tumor that she said she had in her uterus. This was the health question that the others could not answer. In my work I have found an interesting and unexpected answer to fibroid tumors that really surprised me when it began to come through my clients. Fibroid tumors are *unborn babies!* I have had several cases where the women had abortions. In some cases they felt it was justified: too many children and they couldn't take care of any more, or inconvenient pregnancies. They said it did not bother them; however, their bodies said differently. They were trying to replace the baby they had lost. Other cases were women who desperately wanted children and felt their biological clock was running down. They were getting older and knew they did not have many more chances. They also developed fibroid tumors. Their body was trying to produce a baby. I have been told that often when a fibroid tumor is cut open, the doctor found teeth and hair inside of it! Isn't it remarkable what the human body can do? At one of my recent classes I was given the information that a Chinese herbal doctor had discovered. He said that since China enacted the "one child only" law, the rate of fibroid tumors in Chinese women had jumped threefold. This showed they were trying to produce babies.

The majority of these cases that I have seen deal with events in their present lifetimes. However, Helen's seemed to be a carryover from the past life we had examined. She lost her children in that life and she was now symbolically trying to bring them back. In this case the problem belonged in the past with the other woman and had no place in this life, so we would be able to leave it in the past. I still wanted verification from the SC. I asked, "What caused the tumor?"

H: Many things. That one life was only one life where she had troubles. She was willing to experience painful things for love. (In other lifetimes also.) Some things got trapped.—I can absorb and dissolve it.

D: *That's what I've seen you do before ... dissolve it and absorb it and then it can be passed out of the body safely.*

H: It's like a little bomb.

D: *Are you going to dissolve it slowly or how are you going to do it?*

H: No, NOW!

D: *It's time to release it. And she is ready too.* (Yes) *So you're taking it away?*

H: Most of it. It's really messy. (She groaned in pain.)

D: *But it can be released from the body safely?*

H: Oh, yes ... oh, yes.

D: *Is that the most important thing to work on in her body?*

H: Her whole nervous system and her heart .... (She winced.)

D: *What's wrong with her heart?*

H: Nothing. It just needed to be activated, so to speak.

D: *Because that's where she stabbed herself. It left a traumatic mark there, so to speak?*

H: Not so much there. She just remembered that.—We started working on her a long time ago.

D: *When we first started this session?*

H: Before.

D: *That's wonderful! I am glad you're doing it for her.*

H: I'm just one person, one entity, not one energy. She holds many, many energies.

They said they would continue to work on her for the next few days, especially when she was asleep, so it could be done in a gentle fashion.

H: It's dreadfully dreadful.—She is learning at the same time so I need her to be asleep. She's so strong at times.

They answered some more of her questions, but they are not pertinent to this story, so I will not repeat them here.

Parting message: She needs to hang on. Continue on. She's greatly ... *greatly* loved, more than she can even contain. She cannot even contain how much love she has inside of her. And we are with her and we always will be.—I thank you for this time, and she is ready to end her session.

The question of suicide has always been a questionable one in my work. In my book *Between Death and Life* it was said that suicide is never justified. That it never has a positive effect, and that the person must always come back and relive the same circumstances with the same people. The sessions in this section and in some of my other books caused me to wonder if that was true. Is suicide ever justified? Does it always carry negative karma? Or are there extenuating circumstances? I have found many cases where the person in the other life was put into an unbearable situation where there was no way out. Where suicide was the only way to end the suffering. Is it justified in those circumstances? In these cases they have said that it was an option that was built into the projected plan for the lifetime.

In my research it seems as though the main circumstances where it would not be considered favorable is when contracts are broken. When we are doing our past life evaluations on the spirit side, and going over (with our counselors) what is needed to be worked out during the next life, we make contracts with participating souls. They agree to come back and help us work out past mistakes. These commitments and contracts are taken very seriously, and are part of our plan. There are many types of contracts. Some of these are long term, such as marriages, birth and the raising of children. Some are short term, friends and acquaintances who will be there to help us for a certain period of time. One example of a short contract would be a one night sexual encounter that results in the birth of a child. The father has agreed to be there only to provide a way for the child to enter the world, and then the contract is over. So we make different types of contracts of varying degrees. These contracts are taken seriously because the other souls have agreed to take time away from their own development to help you advance. Of course, maybe they have also agreed to advance with you.

When the person faces what they think are insurmountable obstacles in their life (and remember, these are only obstacles that they have agreed to put there to learn from) and they commit suicide as a means of escape, they are breaking contracts. This disrupts all these other people's plans. The suicide still has to return and take that grade or class over. They have failed the exam. They do not "escape." They have to play the part again, same circumstances, same characters. Only next time it is even more difficult. But because the person has broken all these commitments, all these contracts, are the participating souls going to be willing to help again? Maybe not. They say, "I stopped my progression in order to help you in your lessons, and you let me down. You backed out. Why should I do it again for you? You will just have to wait your turn now while I go on with my own evolution. I gave you a chance, now I don't know if I can trust you again to carry out your commitments." In this case the growth of the suicide is greatly impeded. What should have been worked out in one lifetime will now take many.

Chapter 19

A SUICIDE REPAYS KARMA

When Joan came into the scene she was standing, but not on the ground. She felt she was standing on a *bubble*. I asked her to describe it.

J: Sort of opaque. It's not really clear. It's holding me easily, but it feels like a blown-up surface, so that it has tension to it. Just looks like some stretched material.—I feel like I'm floating in space somewhere. I'm not really seeing anything, just the sky and the clouds. But I think it's taking me somewhere.—Now I somehow slid inside of it and I'm just gently floating down, inside of it.—I feel like I'm going down a shaft. Not seeing anything. Just gently dropping down somewhere.

D: *Become aware of yourself. What is your body like?*

J: (Pause) It's see-through. Almost like it's taking on a gray-white color of a cloud. There's not a lot of substance to it. I feel very much an observer just looking around.—I feel like I'm actually waiting for something to happen ... for it to show itself.—Another being just popped up. I guess you would say, just appeared in front of me. Like it's going to take me somewhere. Again just more of a shape. Gray and very white. I feel like the bottom of the bubble opened up. It's more of a void, but I think it's like a slide though. Another part, I guess, of the universe. It's opened up now, and it's like I'm in the sky. Floating.

D: *So are you out of the bubble now?* (Yes) *Maybe it was just a way of getting where you were supposed to go?*

J: That was the feeling I was getting, like it was a passage.

257

D: *And now this other amorphous being is taking you somewhere?* (Yes.) *What are you seeing as you travel?*

J: Just blue sky and clouds.

D: *Let it take you to where you're supposed to go. Can you communicate with it?*

J: (Long pause) Do you want me to communicate with it?

D: *If you can.*

J: I just feel like it has come to guide me somewhere. The message I'm getting is it wants to show me something.

D: *All right. Do you want to go with it?* (Yes.) *Then let it take you and show you whatever it is. And we can do this quite rapidly, too.—What does it want to show you?*

J: Lots of angels.

D: *Where are they?*

J: Like a city in the sky. A gathering of all these beings.

D: *What does their city look like?*

J: I haven't seen it. I get the sense it is. It's like sliding, floating. And I am more and more visible as I'm coming into this.

D: *How does that feel?*

J: Very loving and good. Very nice.—He's taking me through the groups, I guess you would say. I'm just moving through them now. (Pause) I see an image of a big book opened up. (She suddenly became emotional and started to cry. She couldn't understand why.) I feel very emotional.

D: *That's okay. Emotion is good. That means it's something that's important.*

J: (Crying) He's showing me something in the book. I don't know what it is.

D: *Ask him to tell you what it is.* (Pause) *What is it he wants you to know from the book?*

J: (Pause, still emotional) I'm only sensing this, but he's just showing me this lifetime, and the events, the pains I've gone through. And standing back and watching it again.

D: *What do you think of your life as you look at it that way?*

J: Like I've forgotten how painful it was, and seeing it again is bringing it back up.

D: *Is that important to bring it up again?*

J: Yes. Because it's over now.

D: *Ask him why you had to see it again?*

J: To acknowledge how far I've come. It was a passageway, it was a completion of all that preceded it.

D: *So it was something you had to go through to complete.* (Yes) *Ask him, all the pain and everything, did that have to do with karma?*

J: The pain was to find the balance. The balance wasn't there. The pain was because I wasn't in balance. And it was through that, that I kept seeking a balance. He keeps saying that's what Earth life is all about, getting that balance, and I've got it now.

D: (Chuckle*) It was difficult, wasn't it?* (Yes) *But was there karma involved while you were finding your balance?* (Yes) *Can he tell you where it came from, so you can understand?* (Long pause) *Maybe he can show it to you.*

J: Yes, he's showing it to me. He's showing *me*. It's more like an inner vision of times when I was horrible, dreadful, and made terrible decisions.

D: *In other lifetimes?* (Yes.) *What was it that you did?*

J: I get a sense of myself as being really evil, mean, and angry.

D: (Pause) *So in another lifetime you hurt other people?*

J: Yes. It's almost a template of who I was. It's weird. I'm seeing like a flat template. It's like a painting, you might say, but it's sketchy and the horror is ... It doesn't have much detail in it. It's like a slice, the way it's coming to me. It's almost like an overlay. The power and energy I was holding and just the sense of the horror it created. I don't have any details ... just the sense of the horror it created.

D: *Maybe that's better to not go into details anyway. (Yes) The details are not necessary, but you have done many things that were negative?* (Yes) *Was there anyone involved in that lifetime that you had to come back with in this lifetime, to repay any karma. Or can they see that?*

J: It's embodied through my father in this lifetime. He set up a lot of scenarios which caused me personal pain or anguish, so that I would become sensitive to the way other people feel.

D: *So that was his purpose?*

J: Yes, but he was so dark himself, and I never understood that. The challenge was that he stayed in that negativity to develop sensitivity myself, and move beyond it and not get caught up in it, which I did manage to do. There was no joy in him.

D: *But that was his job to do this so you could grow.*

J: Yes, like a piece of the slice was embodied, if I can put it that way. (She shuddered.) Amongst other things I tortured ... and in a lifetime where *I* was tortured. I couldn't endure it.

D: *You mean you also tortured?*

J: Yes, and that's why I was tortured in another lifetime.

D: *It always comes around, doesn't it?* (Yes) *But how does that relate to your life now? Wouldn't it have paid back the other lives when you were tortured also?*

J: That's what this was about. It was about payback and I couldn't endure it. That's when I suicided. I couldn't endure the torture that was inflicted on me.

D: *Who was the one doing the torturing? Was it anyone Joan knows in this lifetime?*

J: Yes. It was the being who was Richard in this lifetime.

Richard was her husband for thirty years before she divorced him.

D: *Does that mean she tortured him in another lifetime?*

J: I don't know that. It was something like the slice that represented all I've ever done that was negative or evil. It's like little things bubbling up out of that and incarnating in other lifetimes so I would get the experience of what I'd done. I don't know how far back it connects, but I don't need to know that. It's like a pattern, a "moving through."

D: *You mean in the other lifetimes Joan had done much torturing, and because she was very negative she had to be tortured and treated cruelly in another lifetime to be paid back?*

J: To know what it was like, what I had done.

D: *And it was too difficult for her and she committed suicide?* (Yes) *How did she kill herself in that lifetime?*

J: I sense a fire. I started some kind of fire. It's like a barn or some kind of building, and going into it. Burned up.

D: *Then it seems to me that she would have repaid it all. Why would she have to come back with the same entity, Richard, again?*

J: Because she killed herself.

D: *But she had a lot going on that was very difficult for her to take.*

J: But I didn't balance out the karma.

D: *Could she have overcome it if she'd stayed with it longer? Is that what you mean?* (Yes) *It was a lifetime to balance it all out?* (Yes) *But instead she committed suicide. Explain to her what happens then because it's as though she repeated the same thing.*

J: She hadn't transmuted it into an understanding of what it was really about, evolving. That's why she suicided because she couldn't ever understand the higher purpose of it all, evolving back to the Source.

D: *She didn't understand she was not supposed to commit suicide. Is that what you mean? That was not the contract?*

J: That's right. She was supposed to gain enlightenment through the experience.

D: *So when she came back to this life, she had to go through the same thing again?*

J: That way it gave me an opportunity to go past myself, as I was at that level ... to life?

261

D: *And with the same person ... the same entity?*

J: Yes. (Whispered.) And I was given a father who had a very similar energy field to Richard. It really echoed that, but it was the dominating, controlling father that I was able to escape by growing up and moving out. But I hadn't fully gotten the understanding and strength that comes from seeing it through, right to the end. Richard helped me to become more understanding of others who go through difficulty. I would have left that part of it behind. In the sensitive state that I was through my own childhood, move through something else and therefore, never feel it because I knew I had a mission.

D: *But you knew you had to get all of this out of the way first.*

J: Yes, but it was also vital to my own growth and strength for the bigger purpose of guiding others more quickly because I understood it in the end. And to give understanding to them and help them move through even faster than I was able to because they didn't have as much time as I did to work through.

D: *So Joan had to come back to this lifetime with the same entity to repeat the same circumstance.* (Yes) *Now it's her job to go on and help people.*

J: They don't have the same time that I had. Everything's speeding up. There are opportunities they must prepare for quickly.

D: *We can't take time working on all these things anymore?*

J: That's right. Not on Earth.

D: *We have to repay the karma quickly to get it out of the way?* (Right. Yes.) *What normally would have taken many lifetimes?*

J: Yes. There is the opportunity. She understands now. She can open many doors for people through understanding what they're in, what they're going through, that she wouldn't have been able to do otherwise.

D: *Unless you experience it yourself, you can't understand what other people are going through.*

J: Yes, and it's not even a same experience. It's a sensitivity feeling their anguish, though it may be different causes. Feeling their anguish and knowing you can come through it.

D: *Yes. So many people feel trapped, don't they?* (Yes) *They feel they can't get out of something.—Is this why you chose to show her that rather than taking her to past lives?*

J: Yes, it's a template. I think that's why it's like a slice. It's like a pizza, if that makes any sense, and it's not all covered with all that mix-up, yucky colors when you think about it. But it's like droplets, so the slice represents the essence and there's a lot of clarity in it. There's more clarity than anything. These drops are like pizza gunk and those represent the negative lives where there was kind of an imbalance. And this is like clearing up the last of it, the last of this life.

D: *Because there's not any time left to go over these things again and again?*

J: That's right, yes, and by my doing this, it clears that last little bit for me, but also, the way I chose to do it, instead of just me getting through it. It's me understanding what others are enduring. It helps speed them through it, so they don't have to be in anguish. If they could only understand how easy it is to step out of it. I can fast pace them through it.

D: *Did she start on a cycle of negative lives, and just get caught into it?*

J: No, it's like in the whole mix of all the lives. She's like a big slice and it's really clear and white, and there are these splotches like pizza with all these yucky colors. And you think pizza? With the red and the brown, orange and all splattered through it, and pulled up from that was this particular life where I because of the things I had done, it was my turn to feel what it's like to be tortured because I had done it. And I couldn't endure it.

D: *She was in a life where she was hurting other people, so it all had to come around.*

J: I had to experience it to know what it feels like, and to know and to realize it.

D: *That's why Joan spent so many years in that situation until she was sure that was enough. Is that what you mean?*

Joan had experienced an abusive childhood, then married an equally abusive husband. She finally discovered metaphysics after 25 years of marriage and then had the courage to divorce him.

J: Yes ... that she could get through it on her own. That was the important thing. That she had it inside to break through everything.

D: *It had to be her own decision?*

J: Yes. Not blaming, not relying, just to dig deep and find the inner strength and the inner understanding.

D: *Because with the blaming, that just creates more karma, doesn't it?*

J: Yes, like being reborn.

D: *Now she's reached a point where she's finished with that. It's over. It's in the past. We don't have to go through that again.—What about Richard? Is he still carrying karma for what he did to Joan? He's out of her life now.*

J: That was only a piece of him, like that pizza stuff. He's got his own stuff. That pizza stuff was like: Push me through or give me a chance to work through, come what may, but he's got his own stuff.

D: *Does that mean that Richard won't carry karma for what he did?*

J: No, he won't.

D: *Because he did it for a reason?*

J: Yes, but unfortunately, he has other issues that he hasn't dealt with. He could have dealt with, but he just wasn't ready. He's gotten trapped in them and couldn't let go of them.

D: *Do you think it's too late for him to change now in this lifetime?*

J: Yes because of the habits and attitudes. He closed too many doors instead of walking through them.

D: *So he's going to have to walk his own path, but it has nothing to do with Joan.*

J: That's right.

D: *He'll go on his own way.*

I realized that I was speaking to Joan's Subconscious. It had come in somewhere along the way. It is always obvious when it enters the conversation. I asked if I was speaking to it, and it acknowledged that I was. So I knew I didn't have to call it forth because it was already there. Then I knew I could go ahead and ask her questions.

D: *We always think we are going to go into past lives when we do this, and you didn't take her to one. You took her to the Book of Records. Why did you choose that instead of taking her to a past life?*

J: Because it's more than just one life. It's the essence of everything she is. She knew that most of her lives were very good ones, and that's why she was shown that ... the color, like splotches in the white.

The main purpose was to show her that she had been out of balance, and that going through the negative experiences in this lifetime had brought her back into balance. And Richard would have no part in her life anymore because that had all been resolved (from *her* part anyway). He had played his role and did what he was supposed to do. And now it was time for her to move on. Of course, the main question she wanted to know about was her purpose. She had many plans and wanted to know about her future. What did the SC want her to do now that she was free?

J: To help as many people move into the new Earth as possible. To touch them where they are, and move them forward with the understanding she's gained. So many people are still stumbling in the dark, but they are close to breaking through. They need people like Joan to help them. That's her role now.

D: *How do you want her to help other people?*

J: To be someone they can trust and step out into the unknown. And trusting the light that she shines and make that leap of faith, trusting that there's integrity that people respect and trust about her. And now, given the courage to break through what's holding them. They can have an opportunity to sense the peace that's waiting and the beauty to enable them to let go and move beyond where they were. It's like a bit of the new Earth there for them to experience and say, "This is what I want." All she has envisioned will occur, and even more. She will be able to manifest anything she wants. She's coming to understand how to do it.

D: *She thought she has fulfilled most of her contracts.* (Yes) *She thought she would be given a new contract. Is that true?*

J: Oh, yes. That's what she's doing now, drawing people up because the intent is so pure, uncontaminated with her own issues. She's gotten past all that.

D: *I know when we come into a life, we make contracts.* (Yes) *I didn't know you could make or create new contracts as you go along.*

J: She didn't know that either.

D: *So if you have done everything you're supposed to, and the contracts are finished, you can make a new one?*

J: Oh, yes. And new visions keep coming forward. She thought it was so limiting, but is coming to realize quite the opposite.

D: *Do you (the people on that side) help with the formation in the new contracts?* (Yes) *Because you can see what the person is supposed to be doing.* (Yes) *The most important thing is to get rid of the old contracts first, the old stuff. Then you can move forward?* (Yes)

I turned to her physical questions. The most important one dealt with problems with her spine. I asked the SC to look in that area. "It was shattered many times in her other lives. Oh, goodness, the price she paid. And it's pieced back together, but it took its toll. Now that she understands, they can all mend and be straight.—I'm pushing. The pieces are out of line. I'm bringing them back in alignment. They don't have enough strength on their own to keep it stable. She hasn't been in full alignment with everything, and then she twists and turns along the way."

I allowed it to work on the spine and then asked if it had finished. "Almost ... I need a little more time." I was quiet as it finished its work and then announced that the alignment was done. I gave suggestions that it would remain in stable condition. I knew that once the person found the cause, the work they were supposed to do, then the condition would be removed, and the cure would remain as long as the person stayed on the path they were supposed to be on.

J: This is the last alignment she wanted. It will facilitate everything else now, this alignment of purpose.—This is one of the things that is part of the breakthrough; part of the challenges, the betrayals, the shattering of her own esteem, but by her agreement to become sensitive, that was the only way. That's how it was set up, for it to happen in this lifetime.

Parting message: Become very strong in trusting and knowing that the mission you agreed to fulfill is a part of the whole universe, and you have many working with you on all realms.

The subject of murder is also an interesting concept when looked at with all emotions removed. In my book *Between Death and Life,* we talked about various ways of repaying a murder. It is never, "You killed me, so I'll kill you!" That just keeps the wheel of karma going. There is a way that is called the "Soft way." For instance: you may have to take care of your victim in the next life. You have to devote your entire life to them and you cannot focus on your own and what your desires are. These have to be put to the side while everything focuses on the other person. This can be a child, someone who is handicapped, a parent who needs care, maybe even a demanding boss. If you are in a situation like that, this may be a different way of looking at it. It never makes sense in the present life, but when you examine the past life, it is clear and justified. The following is a portion of a session I had with a woman who is a very good healer practitioner in this life, but one who has also had a great deal of difficulty with relationships and childhood parental abuse.

Monique went through two past lifetimes. In the first she was killed as a young preteen girl by an invading army. She was stabbed in the stomach by a sword. In the second life she was a Roman soldier doing the killing. He died as a warrior with a sword through the stomach again. This explained the current persistent stomach problems Monique had. He came into that life as the soldier to experience the other side. "It was part of the learning to remember how he was killed before, and how it felt this time to be doing the killing." He didn't want to live a life of violence, but that was what they did at that time. He learned the lesson that it was wrong to murder like that, and the people who were murdered learned a lesson, too. They knew they were going to experience that before they came. "More than a lesson. To experience what the other person felt and so you realize you don't want that." He accumulated karma because of what he did as the soldier. "He didn't listen to his inner voice that said he shouldn't do it. He could have put his pride aside and not done it. He could have gone somewhere else, but you see, at that time the parents thought it was an honor." Now he would have to work the karma off. I asked, "With the people he killed?"

M: No, not necessarily with the people he killed, but with the people who have been killed in that way. So perhaps he could be a doctor, a healer, to heal these people who have been hurt so horribly, or lost a leg or an eye. So he could help them in that way and see how this person has suffered.

D: *So it doesn't have to be the same person he killed.*

M: No, just someone.

D: *Once you learn a lesson, you can turn it into an advantage and go a different way. Does that make sense?*

M: It does. It's a long way from that war ripple he came from.

D: *What does he decide to do when he comes back? Is he going to be someone who helps?*

M: He's going to be someone who helps, but he's also going to be someone who has loved ones who get hurt and killed.

D: *What is the purpose of having loved ones who get hurt?*

M: Because he will experience what the loved ones experienced of the ones he killed.

D: *You always have to see both sides of everything, don't you?* (Yes)

This was an interesting concept that would naturally occur during wartime when many, many are killed. It would be difficult and take an extremely long time to repay the killing to each and every one of the victims. So the circumstances have to be repeated instead, and the repaying would be in helping others who had been in these situations as the victims. Also the turn-about of having loved ones be hurt or killed. This always seems so unjust when viewed from the perspective of just this present lifetime. "Why was God so unfair? Why was that person hurt or killed, who was such a good person?" Now maybe we can look at it from the perspective of the other people involved in the scenario. It doesn't matter if we remember the lives where these events occurred. What goes around comes around!

Of course, in my work I have found that you can get rid of any leftover karma by forgiving others for their misdeeds against you. But even more importantly, you must forgive yourself. It always takes two. There are always two sides to every story. Neither one of these things is easy to do, but if you want to stop the wheel of karma, they must be done.

PART TWO

THE CONVOLUTED UNIVERSE KEEPS EXPANDING

The Beginning of Earth

Chapter 20

BACK TO THE BEGINNING

Naomi found herself in a strange, alien environment when she came into the scene. The ground was black like coal or obsidian, and she was standing on the top shelf of a rock formation similar to the Grand Canyon, looking at shelves of rock going down into a chasm. When she looked above the deep abyss, there was no vegetation, only gray air like gray clouds. I asked if she wanted to go down. "No, I just need to stand against the rock and look out. The earth is not dirt, it's like obsidian ground up very fine, but I'm looking out at the gray clouds ... it's like a gray mist." When I asked her to describe herself she said she did not have a body.

This has happened so many times that it does not bother me.

"I think I'm more like the cloud. I'm up against the mountain. I'm up against the obsidian. I feel like I'm part of the mist. It feels like I keep things cool. I keep things cool."

D: *Is that your job?*
N: Yes. I keep it cool. There's heat over on the side away from me, so I just keep it cool.
D: *Where is the heat coming from?*
N: Coming from the center where this place is. It feels like a volcano type of heat. I'm not part of that. I'm simply part of the mist.

Those who are familiar with my books will understand that there is nothing extraordinary about her not having a body and being in an apparent gaseous form. I found that this is part of the cycle of reincarnation that we must go through before we enter a human body. These cases have been reported in many of my other books. To explain it in a linear sense (even though we are now learning that is not accurate because everything is really simultaneous), we are first in a gaseous form, then part of the dirt and rocks, then plants, animals and nature spirits before we are ready to attempt the more complicated human form. Of course, we are now discovering that the three waves of volunteers are bypassing these requirements, but they are a special group that are not bound by the commitment to the cycle of reincarnation on Earth.

D: *You're part of the mist that cools the ground, the air or what?*

N: That cools the whole region. I'm supposed to keep it all cool. It's a very big job, but it's easy.

D: *I thought it would be hard.*

N: No. There's something about it that makes me sad. Keeping it cool when there's too much heat. If there's too much heat, it destroys.

D: *So that could be dangerous if heat builds up too much?*

N: Yes. This is my job ... just the mist. Because if I don't keep it cool, then the planet will blow up.

D: *Are there any others helping you do this?*

N: Yes, it's all the mist people. It's a group.

D: *So you call yourselves the "Mist People," and you're keeping it cool so the planet won't blow up.*

N: Yes because the planet is new. It's newly formed. The core of the planet is hot, and our job is to keep the mist. And it cools down so that other life forms can come on it.

D: *They can't come if it's too hot?*

N: That is right.

D: *So your job is to keep it cool so eventually life will form?*

N: Yes, that is correct.

D: *Do you like what you're doing?*

N: It is what I choose to do. We all hold it together because it is our chosen way.

D: *You mean you could have chosen something else?*

N: Yes, but this is the one. This is harder to do. The mist people can do this. It's just that it's tedious to keep holding the heat.

D: *But this is a new planet?*

N: Yes, it's just forming.

D: *It doesn't have any plants or life on it at all?*

N: No. It only has the heat that's being cooled and the dark obsidian that's been cooled from the mist.

D: *Were you there when it was being formed?*

N: Yes, I agreed to be part of the original team.

D: *Did you watch the planet as it was being formed?* (Yes) *Can you tell me what that was like?*

N: The ball of light comes and then becomes hotter, and then the hotter becomes hotter. It becomes fire. Around the fire forms molecules of matter that go together and form the black obsidian. Black obsidian forms around the fire. The fire stays inside and continues building the planet, but it has to have the mist to cool the matter so the matter forms solid matter.

D: *If it just kept getting hotter it would burst forth?*

N: Yes, it wouldn't form. The light would not come to form the hot heat. The heat would not form the molecules to form the matter. It would have simply been light.

D: *Where did the ball of light originally come from?*

N: Source. Source sends out the ball of light.

D: *Then the ball of light generates the heat and the molecules on its own?*

N: Yes, and then the different people choose—they're not *people* in your terminology—the different ones with the different energies come to form around what is needed.

D: *Each one has their own special job?*

N: Yes, that is correct.

D: *What do some of the other ones choose to do?*

N: Some of them chose to come to be the original point of light. To be the points of heat around the light forming greater and greater vibrational intensity of trying to expand it into the heat. Into the fire out of the matter drawing the matter. The energy beings who came to be part of the matter. And the people, the energy beings, who came to be part of the solidity, of the black solidity. And the beings that came to be part of the mist. And there are other beings waiting to come to be part of the other formations that will occur.

D: *The ones that will come after it's cooled down?*

N: Correct.

D: *After the planet is formed and cooled down, do the other beings leave?*

N: Some do. Some don't. Some stay inside. Some become other forms of life. Each has choices of what they can become. Some need to become plant material. Some become other aspects of the air, other aspects of water, other aspects of minerals, other aspects of unknowns that this planet does not have.

D: *So some don't leave right away. They stay to help with the development?*

N: Yes, that is correct.

D: *And you stay there until it is cooled down enough?*

N: Yes, until there can be formation of water on the planet. Then I'm free to make another choice with my commitment.

D: *They must have water. Isn't that true?*

N: Some planets do. Some planets do not. This planet chooses to have water.

D: *So water is not always necessary for the formation of life?* (No) *Some places live on other things?*

N: Yes, that is correct. Many varieties.

D: *But you don't have anything to do with the formation of water?*

N: No, nor the formation of where the water will go. I will be able to choose to be part of the water that stays that will form other forms of life, if I so choose at that time.

D: *You have to wait until that time to decide then.*

N: Yes, that is correct.

D: *Have you always done this type of work?*

N: No. I've been heat. I have been light. I have come from Source many times in many different regions, many different forms.

D: *When you finish the work, do you go back to Source?*

N: Sometimes, yes. Sometimes I go to other places directly.

D: *Just keep progressing?* (Correct.) *This would all take great periods of time.* (Yes) *Although I've been told time really doesn't exist.*

N: It's just what one does. No measurement.

It was obvious this could have taken an unimaginable long time, eons, so I had her move ahead to when she had completed her job of being part of the mist and cooling down the planet. "What are you doing now?"

N: Now I'm becoming part of a water pool that is in a very small shaded part of rock. It is a beginning formation of the water pool. Those other beings can come with me and they can become part of this pool also. This pool will grow. Its collectives starts out as a drop. I was not the originating drop. I was part of the formation of water.

D: *I was wondering where the water comes from.*

N: It comes from the mist that forms into drops. Then it forms into a pool.

D: *It starts out as small pools at first?*

N: That is correct.

D: *Do you think it will grow larger?*

N: Yes, and mist beings are coming to form larger bodies of water. They are bringing other beings with them that will form parts of the water chain that will bring forth plant life and animal life on this planet.

D: *Then the water has to be there first so the plants and animals can develop?* (Yes) *Do you like being part of the water?*

N: Yes, I like the feel of the water. It is really no different than the mist. It all just is, but it is a nice feeling.

D: *None is more important than the other because they all have a part to play.*

N: That is correct.

D: *Does anyone tell you what to do?*

N: No. You know. You have been given your imprint when you come in.

D: *Your imprint tells you what your job will be?*

N: Yes. When I became the mist, then at the end of the mist period, I made a choice to become the drop. The drop went into the pool. Now I have a choice to become an animal form or a plant form, or an evaporative form of air.

D: *Let's move ahead. What do you decide to do next?*

N: I decide to become the air, the evaporative air. I want to be around the planet.

D: *At first you were creating the water; now you're evaporating it.* (Yes) *What is the purpose of evaporating?*

N: It is to form an atmosphere around the planet.

D: *So it has to have an atmosphere as well as water.*

N: This planet does, yes. Not all planets have to. There are many different variations. Each is suitable for that place.

D: *What do you do when you become part of the evaporation?*

N: I form a shield around this planet that expands outward for the planet's growth. So that it serves as a barrier to other air beings that could be coming in to affect the air on this planet. Other air beings ... different ... different ... you would say gases ... different gases.

D: *I see what you mean. These would be gases that would not be conducive to what you're trying to create here?*

N: That is correct. What this planet would need for its maximum operation. It has to be the right combination of the evaporative materials that come from the planet, and some come from off planet. So the mixture is formed for the planet atmosphere.

D: *And you are the ones that keep the wrong type of gas from entering?*

N: Yes, that is correct. On the outer barrier between this and other air types. To keep the outer barrier protected. Shielded is the more appropriate terminology from the language available.

D: *Language is always difficult.* (Yes) *These sound like very important jobs that you had at the very beginning.*

N: These are no different than others.

D: *What do you do after the atmosphere has been formed and your part in that is complete?*

N: This particular assignment is complete, so now I go back to a rest place.

D: *You don't have to continue in other forms?*

N: I can ... I can ... I have chosen to go to a rest place. The rest place is where the Light is.

D: *Can you tell me about the Light?*

N: The Light is just a light where nothing has to happen. We just simply are the Light. There is nothing else that you are required to do or be or to imprint or to bring forth from the Self. Simply you are one with All, so there is a sense of completion.

D: *Do you rest for a long time?* (Yes) *All right. Let's move ahead to when you decide to leave the resting place. What is your next assignment?*

N: I am on the currents that carry things from one place to another. I am a current. It is similar to a current of air, but not air. You don't have a word, but I would say it is like a current of combination of electricity and light and air and thought. It is a combination.

D: *I was thinking of currents like the wind.*

N: Yes, it operates in a similar fashion, but it is different. It is the helping of the moving of consciousness, of awareness. It is a current of evolution, for your term. It is to assist a galaxy to evolve, so the current has to flow into the galaxy and around all of the containment of the galaxy.

D: *I was thinking you were talking about the wind on the planet.*

279

N: No. This is the galaxy and the cosmos that requires assistance in moving. And the current assisted in moving it in the direction that it desires.

D: *But you said it is also to help in the movement in consciousness?* (Yes) *What is the consciousness that it moves?*

N: It is to move into a spiritual consciousness, for lack of a better word, a consciousness of harmony, a consciousness of awareness. It is love that is the vibration.

D: *So it's still dealing with galaxies and larger bodies at this point?*

N: Yes. It is to give a different level of experience; a broader level of experience to the galaxy.

D: *What do you mean by another level of experience?*

N: Within the galaxy all planets, all beings, all thought forms, all consciousness within the galaxy have a certain level so that when the galaxy is almost complete with that level, there is to be another brought in. Another current brought in so that movement can be made beyond the edge of where the other movement is.

D: *This is all part of creating other things?* (Yes) *What kind of things can be created in this way within the galaxy?*

N: Everything that the thought forms bring forth. Anything that matter wants to bring forth. Anything that there is a line ... it is a light line that can be formed. It's like a light that can be tapped into that can be formed. It can form anything the thought forms bring forth.

D: *So the other spirits like yourself are the ones that bring the thought forms?*

N: Yes, that is correct.

D: *So they can create anything they want?*

N: That is correct. All they have to do is tap into the light line.

D: *No one tells them what to do?*

N: No. They bring the consciousness of the galaxy up so that others can know to do this, but it has to be brought in at the higher level before they can have it available.

D: *What about the creation of life on these planets? Do you have anything to do with that?*

N: No. I only bring in the current. I am only the current.

D: *You like that better?*

N: Yes because I can see more. I can see how more fits into the All.

D: *Do you think that by entering the physical body of a plant or an animal you have restricted your view?*

N: It is a different view. It's not all encompassing as it is within the galaxy. To be able to see the galaxy view within the operation of the planets. To see how everything fits together within one galaxy and then how that galaxy connects with the cosmos is more interesting at the moment. The views are different.

D: *Eventually do you stop being the current?* (Yes) *What happens at that time?*

N: I can choose another place to be.

D: *There is so much to choose from, isn't there?*

N: Yes, there is.

D: *What is the next thing that you choose to do?*

N: I choose to go to a place of learning. It is a place that everyone goes ... all beings go to. Whoever chooses to, they can go there when they need to learn more ... do not have the other source.

D: *Tell me about that place.*

N: It has everything that we need to know *ever.*

D: *What kind of a form do you have when you go to a place of learning?*

N: Just consciousness.

D: *That's what it's all about? Learning and creating?*

N: Yes, evolving. You simply ask to learn and it is given to you. You just know it automatically.

D: *No teachers?*

N: No. It is given to you ... given to your consciousness.

D: *What do you prefer to learn in this place?*

N: I prefer to learn about the vastness of what the Source has created. I have learned parts and pieces of galaxies, of universes, and planets and life forms, but I want to learn the vastness of the entirety of the creation, so that I can be beyond what I see now. Because my present levels of the cosmos includes galaxies and planets, and minor—not minor—but what is minutia, and so I want the bigger vastness.

D: *Have you learned that there is something bigger?*

N: Yes, it is never stopping. All creation expands, so the vastness that I receive within my being at this time, there will be greater vastness to be acknowledged at another time.

D: *So is there ever a time that you can learn it all?*

N: You can go back to Source to rest.

D: *And when you're there you can know it all?* (Yes) *That is a vast amount of knowledge. Do you spend much time at the learning place?*

N: Yes. I want to know at this point in the All of time.

D: *And you're absorbing all of this information?*

N: That's correct.

This goes along with what the SC has said many times, that you have all knowledge and all the answers within you. You really don't need to search outside of yourself. You can learn to tap into this incredible font of information.

D: *What are you going to do with all this information after you've absorbed it?*

N: I'm going to be transmitting it to others where other parts of it are needed elsewhere. There must be willingness on their part. There must be openness. There also must be their level of receptor of availability.

D: *So you just broadcast it out?*

N: Yes, those beings that are at the receptor levels to enact or to receive or to transmit further, pick it up.

D: *It is like a beacon transmitting it everywhere.*

N: That is correct.

D: *So you have no desire to go into a physical body?* (No.) *That would be limiting, wouldn't it?*

N: It would not be limiting because I would not know of the limiting. But it would not be at the breadth that I have access to at this time.

D: *Are you aware that you are speaking through a human being, a physical body?* (Pause*) Are you aware that you're communicating with me?*

N: I'm sending out the beams to the being so the being can send it to you.

D: *You are not in this being that you're speaking through?*

N: No. It is more like your transmission towers for your phone systems or your radio systems ... your waves. It is directly to this being.

D: *I've found that the only way we can do this communication is when I put them into this state of consciousness. Then they're receptive.*

N: Yes, that is correct. A physicality cannot hold the level.

D: *Why did you choose to come through her today?*

N: She is willing to receive the information.

D: *Of course, with the volume of information that you have we don't want to overload her systems.*

N: That is correct. She has a tendency to overload. We do not want that.

D: *So you think it's time for her to know more and have more information?*

N: Yes, the vehicle is ready. The transmission lines have been connected. She is going to be a transmitter, a human transmitter. It will not matter what she does in what form. The transmission will be through her.

D: *So she can go about her normal life?*

N: That is correct. It comes through her as though it is a vehicle around the atmosphere. The vehicle is similar to the planet Earth in that there are vibrations and matrixes and atmospheres, and all kinds of things around the Earth that feed transmission.

D: *You want her to transmit just by* being *or what?*

N: Yes, that is correct. She transmits it through just the essence of the self, the essence of the physicality, the essence of the atmosphere around the physicality.

D: *So she doesn't have to write it or to speak about it?*

N: She doesn't have to. She can if she chooses, but it will be transmitted because the level of transmission is such that many could not understand this spoken word or the written word.—This is her chosen path, to be a beacon. She is like a tuning tower that refines the planet, those on it, in it, and around it.

D: *Are there other beings on Earth doing the same thing?* (Yes) *Are they aware of it?*

N: Some are. Few are. Most of them, no.

D: *That is one of the things she was wanting to know. What is her purpose? What is she here on Earth to do?*

N: She's a transmitting tuning device. She is doing this as the device. She refines the physicality, the atmosphere around the physicality. And the other bodies or the words that are used on this planet, the physical, the mental, the astral and the spiritual bodies. It was her choice. She continues to serve as a device as long as she is in the body. She has been at this device for her entire life. She was placed in various places so that the transmissions could be attuned, sent to various places so that the transmissions would be "amped."

She sounded like one of the Second Wave of volunteers. They are described as beacons, transmitters, generators and channels to broadcast positive energy to others. (Check my book *The Three Waves of Volunteers* for more information.)

D: *You've told me before that everywhere we go we leave some of our energy.*

N: Yes. It is not energy per se, in your terminology. It is a combination of things that ignite and bring forth more of what is to be brought forth. You call it "energy" in this planet's terminology. It could be called "energy," but it is more refined than that. It is a finer attunement, a finer transmission that assists in making everything around it finer and allows more light.

D: *What is the purpose of doing this at this time in Earth's history?*

N: So that the Earth can bring forth a higher level in its evolvement and eliminate the heavier, darker, denser, less light bodies or energies; whatever you want to call them, the essences that are holding the planet back.

D: *So those are the ones that are leaving?*

N: Yes, that is correct.

D: *So you can have more light, more knowledge and more information?*

N: Yes, that is correct. More of the transmissions that come in can refine it at a greater rate ... a faster rate.

D: *Are there more people coming in now who are doing this?*

N: Yes, that is correct, there are. They're doing it through their laughter, through their play, through their music, through the less structured methods of being.

D: *But they're doing it without realizing it.*

N: Yes. There are many who know, but there are many who cannot know because of where they are. Because if it were known, then the beings around them would make an attempt to close it off.

D: *Would it be advisable for her to not talk about this?*

N: She will know when and she will know when not to. Most of the beings she is around at the present time, she cannot speak of this. They would not understand. There are the darker, denser beings that would make significant attempts to stop the transmissions.

D: *This is why most of the people are doing it in secret?*

N: Yes, they are. They appear as though they are loners, in the terminology of this planet, and in fact, they are light. They are from Source in direct transmission and, in your terminology, would be "high voltage."

D: *But everyone is from the Source, aren't they?*

N: Yes. However, there are those that by free will have unwillingness within the Self to bring forth more light.

D: *So it's all up to the free will of the individual?*

N: Yes, on this planet.

D: *And some of them have declined.* (Yes) *I was surprised at going back to life at the creation of the world. We thought we'd go back into normal past lives.* (Laugh)

N: This is normal for this being.

D: *It's happening more and more when I work with people. They go back to the unexpected.* (Yes) *This is that time in the world right now, I guess.*

N: Yes, and it is part of *your* evolution.

D: My *evolution?*

N: Yes, that is accurate because you are a transmitter of Source.

D: *A different type than she is.*

N: Yes, that is accurate.

D: *I know the information I have been receiving is very, very different than when I first started out.*

N: Yes, that is accurate, and that will continue.

D: *I always say you won't give us more than we can handle, though.*

N: That is correct.

D: *And I am to continue giving it to the world?*

N: Yes, you have made much of the igniting, ignition, activation, evolution of souls as well as the planetary essence.

D: *Will the work continue to grow?*

N: Yes. So we leave you with a transmission for both of you for lighter beingness and the essence of grace.

Parting message: She is to maintain the Self so that the Self is to be aware of the Self at all times. And not allow the Self to be monitored, to be overtaken, to be manipulated or be any way used other than for a being who will walk beside her. And we are with her always.

D: *I call you the subconscious. You said you don't care what I call you.* (Laugh)

N: That is correct. We know the self needs the names to connect.

D: *But I didn't have to call you through today because you were already here.*

N: That's correct. We are always here.

Chapter 21

"TWEAKING"

Ella was so eager to get into the scene that she did not even wait until I finished the induction. She was immediately walking through extraordinary gardens filled with beautiful flowers. There were colorful birds in the trees. She then saw a Roman type building that she knew was a huge library. "Part of it is a library and, oh, you can do all kinds of things there." The place seemed very familiar and she knew she had been there before. She was eager to go up the steps and enter the building. "A friend of mine is opening the door. Someone I've known forever. He is very knowledgeable."

D: *Does he know why you've come?*
E: He always seems to know everything about me. He's very kind and gracious. I think he's been waiting for me.
D: *Is there something there that you've come to see?*
E: I come to discuss.—It seems as though the background is now changed. I am in the presence of "my twelve." My councils. There are three below, seven in the middle and two on the top. They sit and I'm in front of them. My friend is to my left and encouraging me to speak to the council.
D: *Are there twelve including your friend or is he separate?*
E: He's separate.
D: *He's encouraging you to talk to the council?* (Yes) *What do you want to talk about?*
E: Oh, there are so many things. So many things. Who do I have the opportunity to work with? I feel as though I will

be working with those who were not born here on this planet. I'm developing relationships and ties with different ones ... seeking more knowledge of that.—There are three below. There are seven in the middle and two above. As I'm looking at the council, the one to the left at the top just opened his mouth and a spark of light came out. Something's happening.

D: *But you're asking them who you are working with, or who you're supposed to be working with?*

E: I think it's who I have the opportunity to work with. I believe in my present life.—When they open their mouths, it's like stuff happens. Like a door is being opened.

D: *So you mean they don't have to communicate with you?*

E: The ones down below I can kind of understand. The ones in the middle, I can't really understand what they're saying. And the ones at the top communicate in different ways that I don't understand. The three below are with me most of the time. I stand before the council to ... it's like I seek permission to do different things. And they discuss and think about it or advise about it, but these are my council.

D: *You said the three on the bottom are with you most of the time. What do you mean, guides or what?*

E: I can't tell. I just know they are energy. I can't tell what they are, but the one in the middle in the bottom of the three communicates with me in ways that I can most understand. It's like electric.

D: *When does he communicate? While you're sleeping or what?*

E: I think anytime.

D: *You said you wanted to know about the ones you're going to be working with?*

E: Right. The ones that it's been opened up that I can work with.—I already have the permission. It's just that I don't realize and trust in myself to know this.

D: *Well, when you're in a human body you perceive things in a different way.*

E: Right. And I already know this and they smile. (Laugh) They are communicating love.—Now I'm being taken somewhere.

D: *Who is taking you?*

E: I don't know. It's like I'm being whooshed a little bit backwards and to the right.

D: *Let's see where he's taking you.*

E: I'm at a place but I don't know what I'm standing on. I don't even know if I *am* standing, but I am looking at where I will be working.—I'm seeing various planets. I'm seeing various star systems. It's quite vast.—I'm being shown this so that I can remember, but I already know this. It's a number of different planets. It's a two star system ... a binary star and planets around them. That's not the only place, but that's primarily what I'm focused on. Interesting. Oh, there are many different creatures. Some are just being hatched.

D: *Hatched? You mean just now forming or what?*

E: Right. Just beginning ... just starting. I'm seeing the different small, small life forms.

D: *Where are these life forms?*

E: On the various planets. Different planets have different life forms. There are many to keep track of. There are many to help. There are many to watch and then we introduce to different places. We do experiments. We look and see what may work, and then we introduce that to the atmosphere and introduce that into that particular planetary body ... with the permission of the body. The planetary body is a part of the process. It is a total dynamic.

D: *So you mean the planet itself has to give permission for the different life forms it accepts to live on it?*

E: Yes, and the sun systems are also a part of them.

D: *Do the sun systems have to give permission or just the planet?*

E: Everyone has to be in agreement.

D: *But you said there are many different life forms?*

E: Yes, and I'm working with many different kinds to do this work. There are some that look like very weird spiders, that are very good at mathematics. There are some that ... oh, it almost looks like the bar scene in *Star Wars*. (Laugh)

D: *But everything is alive. It doesn't have to have the same forms, does it?*

E: Oh, no, it doesn't.

D: *Whatever is adaptable to that atmosphere?*

E: Right. But the ones that are working on it were on a craft or many crafts. But there is one in particular where we go and we look and we calculate and we experiment with what would work on that planet. And what various forms can and will evolve based on our experiments on other planets. And all of us on the ship confer. We try different things. We have many different approaches because we have different backgrounds.

D: *This is all done on this space ship?*

E: Yes, we have many different space ships, but this one in particular we like. There's one in the middle and then there are seven around. This is a fairly good sized one. We can do almost everything in it, although sometimes when we go down to the planet we are in smaller craft. Or sometimes we just take a part of our understanding or our being down there ... just a part of our consciousness.

D: *So you don't have to take all of the consciousness?*

E: No, just a portion of the consciousness to go down to the planet and view it. You can travel that way just by your consciousness, or you can take everything with you. Your instruments or what you have onboard the craft. You can do it either way, or you can do it both ways. It really doesn't matter. Whatever is needed. There are many of us. It is a whole brigade of us. We have many different ones from many different backgrounds and we are here to expand light. That is what we are doing. We are expanding the light. We are going into parts of an unknown, but based on our background and our expertise

... all of us together help each other to add life of various and varying forms on these various planets.

D: *But you don't live on these planets? You live on the space ships?*

E: Right. That's not where I come from, but this is my job and what I enjoy doing. And I enjoy the camaraderie with all of them. There's one that looks like ... the closest would be a praying mantis. Just very majestic, very old, very knowledgeable. Just an incredible source of knowledge and information.

D: *These beings are all different and have different jobs?*

E: Yes, but we all confer. We all work together.

I asked her how she perceived *her* body. "I can be whatever I want."

D: *You have that ability to change forms?* (Yes) *Do some of the others?*

E: I don't know. Each one is different, but yes, *I* can be what I want. There is one thing that I particularly enjoy. I guess you would call it a long gown; it has many different sparkly colors in it, but those are energies. There's a reason and purpose behind that. It's different energies. You don't have to have a body. You can just be a consciousness if you want.

D: *How do you perceive yourself in your normal form if you don't change into something?*

E: I'm relatively tall, slender, nothing like my Earth body. I wanted to experience that and see the difference. Really tall.—You can be what you want to be.

D: *So this is not your home, but this is where your job is?*

E: Yes because it brings me joy. But I visit home. That is in a different dimension. It's quite different. You go through a portal to—oh, how would you say?—Different energy highways. You can do it that way or you can just think it and be here.

D: *I was wondering if it would take a long time to get to your home planet.*

E: Instantaneous. In fact, you can be at both places at the same time. You can be in multiple places. And you know yourself, and you go between your different selves, whatever brings you joy. But you can be called to different places by different ones. The energy calls you back. But you can still be where you're at and a portion of your energy goes back to address whatever, to communicate, to be a part of that life. There are so many possibilities, but that brings me joy. The camaraderie, there are many of us, but there are ones that are more adept, advanced. Older—not older—more experienced. There are ones that are more adventurous than others. Some have been doing this for eons. I'm relatively new to this.

D: *Even the ones that have been there for eons still enjoy what they are doing?*

E: Yes, they do. If not they would be somewhere else. They can go anywhere they want.

D: *Is this the main job that you are doing right now?*

E: Based on my background, based on the places that I've been. I bring experience, emotions, and then when the life forms get to a point where they can incorporate that, then I suppose that is my expertise, instilling emotions. Much as we have here on Earth. We are all combinations of very many different variations. And so, based on my background, I would take that knowledge and discuss it with my colleagues because they want to have lifeforms that experience more emotions than they have experienced. And they see it's a dualism. It can be very hard, but it can be very rewarding.

D: *So some of the beings on the craft do not experience emotions?*

E: Not to the same extent that we do ... not the full emotions, no.

D: *Why do you have that background, the feeling of emotions?*

E: Because I have been on Earth. I've experienced Earth.

D: *That's where emotions come from?*

E: Yes. Well, this part of my DNA strand ... that's a part of my understanding. That's a part of my coding and decoding. That's part of how I have changed. My coding has changed and we incorporate our different coding into different life forms. We take strands from the various groupings of my colleagues. We take strands of our ... the easiest way to explain it is coding. I understand it as more than DNA—a coding process. And we take a part of that and we mix variations and then instill those into life forms on various planets who have reached a certain stage.

D: *So you mean you didn't have emotions before you took on Earth bodies?*

E: I had emotions, but not nearly the range.—I see a fan. And you open up the whole fan, and in each little fold of the fan you have a different emotion. And on some planets the fan is open only a little bit, and on other planets the fan is open a quarter or halfway or three quarters. But here on Earth it's opened—not quite the full breadth of the fan, but quite open—and we have all different emotions that we, as we live here, overcome. We learn those energies and we learn how to harness those energies, and we learn how to control those energies. And it's not until we learn how to harness or control that we have more or less graduated to go on.

It has been said that the main things we come to the Earth school to learn are emotions and limitations. That's what makes this the most challenging planet in our universe.

D: *Because the emotions are very complex on Earth, aren't they?*

E: Oh, incredibly ... incredibly.—Where my colleagues come from there are places where they have some emotions, but not the full range ... not quite an understanding. There's bewilderment. They see everything that's happened here. They see everything that's happening everywhere. You just focus your attention and you can see it. You can feel it. You can know it.

D: *You said they don't have the full range of emotions, but what are the basic ones that most of the people would have?*

E: They would understand love and anger ... love for fellow beings, love for family, and anger in ... I'm thinking of a "reptilian" ... an understanding for love and very quick to anger. It can be both but doesn't have the degradations of higher forms of compassion, higher forms of multiple emotions at the same time. We on Earth can be angry, sad, happy, delighted, joyful and venomous all at the same time. And that's odd to them because they primarily are living in one emotion and not multiple ones simultaneously.

D: *Because humans are very complicated creatures.*

E: Yes, and it can be very hard, but it can be exhilarating, too ... absolutely exhilarating to be here.

D: *If those beings have those two basic emotions, those are very strong emotions.*

E: They have emotions like jealousy, although they look at that as a mental illness. They also have more of an understanding of unity in that we are all one, and they experience that oneness. Here on Earth we've gone through a long stage of feeling as though we're separate. And we have learned much during this time period by viewing life in that way.

D: *Does that mean that the being you are, there on that craft, is existing at the same time as this person on Earth that I am speaking to? Do you understand what I am talking about?* (Yes) *Because you know you are speaking through a human being.* (Yes) *Are you both existing at the same time or what?* (Yes) *So you're existing on the spacecraft at the same time that you are speaking through Ella?* (Yes) *Can you explain how that happens?*

E: Different parts of the consciousness.

D: *So this means that Ella has had other past lives on Earth?* (Yes, yes.) *The emotion that she experienced in those lives is transferred back to you?* (Yes) *So you don't actually have to live the life?* (Correct.) *That's what I am trying to understand. You are receiving the emotion from her by osmosis or something?*

E: Correct. That's one of the reasons she's onboard the craft. She is, as you say "tweaked," so her coding is downloaded and passed on simultaneously to others.

D: *This is all done in a laboratory or something?*

E: There are different ways of doing it.

D: *And more or less put into a data base or something? I'm trying to use our terms.*

E: Like a computer, if you were to think of a large computer bank that's accessible to everyone in the universe. If they want to have that information, they can have that information. It's all shared. It's all one.

D: *Then that emotional part is downloaded onto other beings on other planets?*

E: If they so choose, yes.

D: *Humans have free will, so these other ones have free will in that way?*

E: Yes, of course.

One of the questions on Ella's list had to do with an experience that occurred when she was a little girl. She was in a car that her mother was driving, and she saw a huge space ship. I asked if they could tell her about that experience.

E: Yes. (Amused.) Actually it was a smaller craft. She thinks it was big.

D: *She was a little girl, so maybe that's why things looked bigger to her.*

E: This is true.—It was small in comparison to others we have. There are others that would seem immense by human standards.

D: *I have heard that some are as big as a city.*

E: Oh, larger ... larger.

D: *Did she really see this when she was in the car with her mother?*

E: Yes, she did.

D: *Her mother saw it also.* (Yes.) *Did anything else happen that day?* (Yes.) *Can you tell her about it?*

E: I'm trying to show her what she wants to see.—Just a minute.—She has seen the interior of the craft. There are various compartments—rooms, you would say—different functions for different parts and varieties of scientists aboard. She knows these people.

D: *Because of you or because of herself?*

E: Because of herself. She knows. She was bewildered as a small child, and we did not want to hurt her. She has much to do in this lifetime.

D: *How did she get on that craft?*

E: It was just part of her conscious self.

D: *So she didn't have to be physically taken out of the car?*

E: You can do it either way. She's been both physically aboard and conscious self. You split a second, as you say because time is not what you think it is. You can in essence split a second, and as you split a second, you take it apart and you freeze where she's at. Then she's free to be in another dimension.

D: *So it happens very quickly?* (Oh, yes.) *Almost simultaneously really. Is that what you mean?*

E: Yes, but that was done later in life. This time she was allowed to see because it would spark a memory because it would help with her awakening. She needed to see that.

D: *Was her mother also taken?*

E: No. The mother is not necessary.

D: *This is not part of her mother's experience?* (No.) *But her mother saw it, though.*

E: Yes, in order to validate for Ella later in life that she was not making that up. She had the validation, and with that she put more credence into that thought and more understanding.

D: *You said this was not the only time that this happened to her?* (No.) *Did it happen before that or after?*

E: Before and after ... many times after.

D: *You said a while ago that she was taken and "tweaked"?*

E: Tweaked, as you would understand. It means that the consciousness is changed. It is not reformulated. It is added to so that she can deal with life here on Earth, so she can accomplish what she came here to do.

D: *You also said something about the DNA, too.*

E: As humans would understand, when they look to see the components of what they are, they look to see primarily their DNA. But they don't understand that also there is much more to that. It's as if it's a mathematical coding process. You have magnetics around you as well that interplay. There are Earth magnetics. There are human magnetics. In order for the spark of life to attach to the body to function, all of those things need to be in alignment. And at times the alignment needs to be altered and changed. "Tweaked," as many would say. To come into alignment because sometimes human bodies fall out of alignment. It is not as if it is better or worse. It just *is* the alignment, and to keep that entity, that person, that unit, in alignment, it is ... I suppose it would be like a checkup. You go to a doctor on Earth who checks you over and makes sure that you are functioning correctly. And if you are not, they try to get you into alignment with a functioning body, whether by things they do, things they suggest, medications. They have various forms. They have many medications here on Earth as opposed to herbs and the natural way of doing the same thing. But we don't do that. We realign so that it is a balanced entity most capable of undergoing what it needs to do.

D: *It sounds like you probably use energy, too.*

E: Yes, energies, crystals. Many different, as you say, modalities.

D: *Because if the body gets out of alignment, that's when illness comes in, isn't it?*

E: This one doesn't have to worry about illness.

D: *Yes, she seems to be pretty healthy. But when the average person gets out of alignment that's when ailments occur?*

E: Yes. But there are higher things going on as well that they may have—as they came into this life—chosen to overcome.

Ella wanted to know if she made a contract when she came into this life. They said, "It was an agreement." Yet when I asked what the agreement was, they said they couldn't tell her at this time.

D: *Okay. Is she fulfilling her agreement?*

E: Yes. Her life will change in ways she cannot even imagine. She wanted a lot of change.

D: *Positive changes?*

E: It is not a matter of positive or negative. These are changes she has agreed to. All things are good ... all things. She will be pleased.

D: *But you don't want to tell her any more at this time?* (No.) *That's fine. Let's save it for a surprise.*

E: She will understand as it unfolds. It is not time yet. She will know the enfoldment when the time is right.

Then we came to the "eternal" question, the one every client wants to know. "What is my purpose? Why am I here? What am I supposed to be doing?" The answer was the same that I have heard many times, "She's here to help." They never say we are here to party, have sex, drink and make a lot of money. Oh, darn! They always say we are here to help people, to help each other.

D: *You said when she has gone back to the craft, it was to adjust the DNA and to make improvements to the body. Is that correct?*

E: Adjust the coding. You would interpret it as DNA, but we think of it more as the coding. There are other things too that happen.

D: *I've been told that the DNA is changing in everyone right now.*

E: Yes, yes. It's because of the energies. The energies are changing.

D: *The vibrations and the frequencies are changing, aren't they?* (Yes.) *I've been told the DNA or coding has to be changed to go with it.* (Yes.) *Because the Earth itself is evolving.* (Yes.)

I was trying to go down Ella's extensive list of questions. Most of them dealt with possible association with ETs. She remembered consciously little bits and pieces of possible experiences. "Why would she have to go to different crafts?"

E: Different reasons ... different entities she interfaces with ... different purposes. She's expanded her purpose.

D: *She had the feeling that the people she meets on these craft she has known for a long time.* (Yes.) *Almost as if they're friends or family.*

E: They are.

D: *I'm trying to draw the difference between you and her. Has she had other lives on other planets?*

E: Oh, yes. Many lifeforms. Many different planets, yes. All lives are the same. It's not a linear. This is happening now.

D: *Why did she choose to come to Earth? The human body is quite different.*

E: To help to bring light to this planet to help her people ... to help.

D: *Many are coming, aren't they?*

E: Yes. They come to help ... each in a different way.

D: *And when Ella finishes her work here she will go back to the spirit side?*

E: It is beyond what you would consider the spirit side. It is more the light going to the light.

D: *Back to the Source?*

E: If she chooses, but this is almost as if beyond Source. You go through the Source to go to this other dimension.

D: *Is this the huge bright light that some people report seeing?*

E: Creator, yes. To go beyond that to expand.

D: *So there is more than we can understand, isn't there?*

E: Oh, yes, much more than the linear brain can centralize.

In my work I have been told that eventually we will have learned all of our lessons on the Earth school, and will graduate, so to speak. We graduate from all the schools (on Earth and elsewhere) and go back to Source. I thought that was the ultimate, the final destination.

E: Understand that there are various levels of Creator. There are Creators, and then there are, as you say, the mothers and fathers of those Creators. And there are mothers and fathers of *those* Creators. There are so many different levels that it is hard to conceptualize for the human brain. In the capacity that it chooses to use for the present, it is hard to conceptualize. There is beyond Creator, and this is to go beyond Creator for creation on the other side.

D: *This is one of the questions people have asked me when I talk about God or the Source. They ask, "Who created Him?" Is that what you're talking about?* (Yes.) *In that way it would go on into infinity, wouldn't it?* (Yes.) *So then there really was no "beginning" way back there.* (Laugh) *I'm trying to understand.*

E: Yes, but the beginning is also the ending which is also the middle. It is also right now.

This was beginning to muddle my mind. "I was told that all of our questions would never be answered because the human mind, not the brain, has no concepts to understand it."

E: The concepts on which to base that this is true, but also understand that in this human form you only use a minor, minor part consciously of what it is you carry with you. And you carry it with you in each and every cell of your body. You carry it all with you in each and every cell.

D: *I was told there are no concepts to really explain it for us to understand.*

E: Right, but you will understand at some point.

D: *I was told that some information is as poison instead of medicine because we wouldn't understand it, and we would come to the wrong conclusions.*

E: This is true.

D: *They also said they had to be very careful how they worded things because it could be misinterpreted.*

E: This is true. This is true.

Time to stop philosophizing and return to the topic of the session. "But if you're on the space craft, do you live as long as you want?" (Yes.) "You don't have limitations like the humans do?" (No.) "And you said you were like a consciousness that could create any form it wanted." (Yes.) "That way there wouldn't be any way you could die, so to speak."

E: None of us die.

D: *I know we don't. We just change. We go into a spirit form when we leave the body. So it's not really dying. It's just changing form in that way. But you don't have a physical body. A physical body does have its limitations.*

E: Correct. The box you put yourself, the consciousness into, has its limitations. And that's what we're working with, those limitations, to make it a better box so that it will last longer.

D: *We have to have a vehicle to live in.*

E: Actually, no. You can live without the vehicle if that's what you so choose to experience. That is your choice.

D: *I am thinking that on Earth we have to have a vehicle.*

E: There are many consciousnesses. Some are viewed as "orbs." Those are consciousnesses. Sometimes what you consider to be an individual orb, is also a whole civilization all within the same orb. The shape of a circle by a sphere is the perfect vehicle, the perfect shape, by which you can come into this atmosphere, come into this density and not get stuck. The shape is perfect for this particular density in being able to view, to look, to travel, to experience, without getting stuck. Because most do not want to be stuck in the heavy, lethargic atmosphere and energies that are existent on this planet. Only the stronger ones venture forth. Only the stronger ones are allowed to be here.

D: *Because when they get stuck they have to keep returning again and again, don't they?*

E: It is their choice. That's coming to an end, but it's their choice.

D: *That's what I'm finding, that not many people have karma anymore.*

E: Try to view a large shape, say a diamond shape, with many, many, many facets. Each life is akin to a different facet on that diamond, and once you have completed that facet, you no longer have to address that. But some surfaces, some facets, take you many lifetimes to accomplish that. You work on many facets at the same time. It's more expeditious to do it that way, and also souls are quite anxious to experience many different things simultaneously. But once you have completed what is on a facet, then you no longer have to address that. You can come back and help others with that same facet, but it is not something that you are bound to, or are karmically tied to. Think of it also as a circle and this is what many people on this planet think of in karmic terms as far as a karmic circle. And they see on one side of the circle trying experiences in life that are challenging. And then on the other side of the karmic circle they see experiences that are more rewarding or pleasing to them. As humans are learning, the way to get off of that circle is to go within. So if you have a circle going round and round perceived as good on one side and perceived as difficulties on another, go within where you are neutral. You are neither good nor bad. You take no judgment of anything that happens within your life. You are neutral. When you are neutral you understand that both good and bad perceptions will come to you in a neutral state. But continue to stay neutral in anything that comes to you in a lifetime, then you will move off of that karmic circle.

D: *I call it the "karmic wheel," but it's the same thing.*

E: Wheel, yes, however it could be a sphere. It could be a ball. You could see it two dimensionally, one dimensionally, three dimensionally. But as you go within, which is also symbolically going within yourself, as you are the *universe.* So go within yourself and be neutral. And as you are neutral, you are away from that karmic cycle, and only by being neutral you can go on.

D: *I have many clients that come to see me that are so bogged down in the karma of things they perceive people have done to them over the lifetimes, that they won't get out. They won't let it go. They're just stuck there.*

E: They can get unstuck within a matter of seconds, but it has to do with the change of perception that they are no longer victims. If they are perceiving themselves as victims of something they perceive of in the past, they are hanging onto it for a reason. They're learning from it. They are feeding on that energy. They are experiencing what they want to experience, and they will do that until they see that there is a different way, and then they will go and experience the other way. It's just a matter of perception and you can change the perception within a matter of seconds.

D: *That's my job to get them to see that they've made themselves sick by holding onto old things that have been done to them.*

E: And it takes so much of your energy. Why waste your energy in that fashion?

D: *I try to get them to see it and look at it, so they can release it.*

E: Right, but as they become aware, they will release it and they will take on a different perspective. We've all been there. We've all done it. We've all experienced.

Parting message: Much love. She is going to help a lot of people. We will speak with her later. We are always here. We communicate with her quite often when she is sleeping. She is in the process where her dream is the reality and the reality is the dream. It will switch over.

Chapter 22

THE CREATION OF HUMANS

Tim was a young construction worker who said he never felt safe, always the victim. He carried a lot of irrational fears and this naturally drew undesirable and negative events into his life. The explanation that the SC provided was something he could never have anticipated or imagined.

When Tim came off the cloud he seemed to be somewhere in space. "I see light ... the universe. It's like a cloud nebula. It's beautiful, many colors. I see many lights, stars and space. I can't tell if I'm actually in space or in a ship. Maybe I'm just a point in space.—There's a place here that I wish to go.— Now I came down to a place that's very green. I don't know exactly how I got here. I sure did like the lights.—I'm coming down through mist and clouds ... fog ... hard to actually see beyond. Now that I'm down it's hard to see much of anything. It's green with a thick fog."

D: *What does it feel like you're standing on?*
T: Soft and moist, kind of mossy. There are also pine needles, something crunchy in it too ... maybe branches.— There's something very peaceful about this place ... very familiar. It seems to be consistently foggy here.

When I asked him to look at his body, we were in for a surprise. His body was covered with fur, and was big and powerful. "It's big, gorilla like. I don't believe it's a gorilla, but it's not something I recognize actually. I would say gorilla-like ... maybe as big as a Sasquatch or a Bigfoot. But as

307

primitive as this being is, it's also highly attuned to its own environment much more so than other bodies. It has a oneness with this place. Other forms that I have known are nowhere near as in tune with its surroundings as this. It feels the vibration of the land. It is very enjoyable. It's very peaceful and very much in harmony with the vibration of this place."

D: *You can't really see much about your surroundings?*
T: No, this is a misty place. It's interesting. There's a lot of mystery here, but this shell, this body, seems to know these mysteries. And I'm not in touch enough to understand what it knows.
D: *What do you mean, there are mysteries there?*
T: I'm a rather visual person, but it's rather hard to see here. Sight isn't necessarily the best of the senses to use. And this body doesn't rely on vision as much. It relies on more intuitive aspects.
D: *Do you think it's always misty and foggy at this place?*
T: I, predominately, think it is. In this body in this place, they do interact very well, and yet I'm not able to make sense of what this body is sensing.—This land is alive. The vibration here is alive and this body knows what it means. *I'm* having trouble sorting out what these vibrations mean. I am so comfortable here, to the point that I don't pursue any of these mysteries. I'm comfortable and I don't need to delve into that.

His food mainly consisted of fruit that he found in the forest. "That's primarily what this place is. It's mountainous and dense forest, and mostly shrouded with odd fog. And there are in the forest things to eat that are fruit-like."

D: *And you're able to find these things by instinct more than by seeing?*
T: Yes. It's as if they call to me, and I just know they are there, but I don't see them per se. I mean I could, but that isn't the primary sense.

D: *Do you have a place where you live?*

T: There are actually several. One is like a rather natural tree house, if you will, and another is more like a cave. They both serve two purposes depending on the seasons or the weather. If it's more fair, I'll be in the tree. And if it's more inclement, I'll spend time in the cave.

D: *So you do have weather there?*

T: It seems that it's mostly rain or fog.

He did not have anyone that lived with him. He was mostly alone. There were others like him in this place. "They're rare, but they do exist. It's a large physical territory." So he didn't need anyone. "I find this place in the physical is very peaceful and allows me time to contemplate my inner being. My time spent in the light. This difficult body is very intuitive. It's very powerful and also very much in tune with the higher energy."

D: *You said you like being in tune with the light.* (Yes) *What do you mean by that?*

T: It's easy to just quiet down and go within and be in alignment with my highest self.

D: *I would think an animal wouldn't really think about things like that.*

T: That is a typical human response. Humans are animals, too, and not very enlightened ones most of the time. Oftentimes, too many conflicts to really be in tune to what they really are. And so this being is much more contemplative, and less of a need to nurture and shield itself or fend for itself physically in this place. It has all it needs.

D: *It sounds like there are other kinds of beings there too, aren't there?*

T: There are others in this place. There are other beings like me, but again, we're rather solitary and we don't often get together. Again, this being and the way it interacts with its environment is totally foreign to me, and I'm not used to it. It interacts on a total intuitive basis and not how we know it typically, so I'm having a difficult time describing this being. It knows where the other beings are and it knows how to interact with them if they so choose, but it generally chooses the light. It needs to be alone.

D: *What do the other type of beings look like, the ones that don't look like you?*

T: I don't really see them. I intuit them. I feel them but I don't know what they are. I don't have much to do with them at all. There are creatures that are bird-like maybe, but in terms of actually describing them, I don't work that way. I don't see them per se.

D: *Because sight isn't the primary sense.* (Yes) *I was just wondering if you needed a mate of any kind.*

T: That occurred, and again that is intuitive and that is something that when needed, takes care of itself.

D: *But you don't have to stay together?* (No)—*But this light you were talking about, how do you perceive that?*

T: It is everywhere. It's like my physical body knows what it needs and when it needs it, and it takes care of that, but this light is really what I am. It's my connection to the universe, if you will. I can see through everything. I don't have to focus on one thing. I can see everything.

D: *This happens whenever you're working with the light?* (Yes) *It opens up your intuitive ability, I guess you would say.*

T: Yes, and I'm studying it right now. I'm looking at it and it's beautiful! It's as if I'm in a physical body someplace, and I am also the universe.

D: *So whenever you think about the light, you become the universe?*

T: Yes. I can focus my attention anywhere and I'm there. I have this physical body, this quiet being in the shrouds, and yet I'm of the universe. Not just the physical universe, but the ones beyond the physical universe as well. It's just a matter of where I choose to direct my attention. I can focus it there, but yet that's what I was alluding to earlier. There are many mysteries here. There are many things I can focus my attention on, and yet I don't seem to be interested in much except the light itself. Absorbing and drinking it in and being one with it.

D: *Can you describe what the light looks like?*

T: It's all encompassing. It focuses and I guess for a lack of a better way to put it in my head. I guess to describe it to you, it would be like in your third eye, and yet it is everywhere. If you were looking out into deep space with a great telescope, there are many things you could focus on, and yet there is nothing you could focus on. It depends on how you want to look at it.

D: *You also said you could see beyond the physical universe. What did you mean by that?*

T: Physical universe, as vast as it might seem to those with physical bodies, it's actually rather small. There's not much to it at all. There are many that are much vaster than the physical. And we have essences from each of these universes within ourselves, as well. We have emotions and mental capacities and etheric capacity, which are all part of these other universes and those are part of our beings, too. In fact that's really the main part of our existence. We get so caught up in surviving mode and that's what's nice about here. Survival is just a given in this place.

D: *There's no need to do anything or be anything.* (Right) *That's rare, isn't it?*

T: It is. And this physical body virtually takes care of itself. It knows exactly how and where to get its sustenance without effort.

D: *And you are very close to the other senses.*

T: Correct, and that's very comforting to be one with these other parts, if you will.

This was an interesting creature, but I was wondering how to move the story forward. In a place like that one day would be very much like the next. Yet I still decided to move him forward to an important day. I didn't know if he would be able to find one where something different would be happening. But he surprised me when I asked him what he could see. "I am being transported. Seems to be not all together against my will, like I've agreed to being transported."

D: *What do you mean, transported?*
T: I don't know, on a ship destined for the Earth.
D: *Did the ship come to the place where you were living?*
T: It seemed to be part of the civilization that was there; part of the technology that was our race.
D: *But you were not involved with that in the area where you lived?*
T: Correct.
D: *So there were other parts of the planet that were more evolved?*
T: Yes, and somehow or other, I've agreed to be transported elsewhere.
D: *Do the ones that are taking you know how intelligent you are?*
T: We're all about the same in that regard. We're all highly intelligent. Highly in tune with the universe. And it's part of a mission. What I enjoyed about this body was how intuitive and free it was in its own place. But we have the ability to shape shift. The body can take on any physical form it wishes. In its own environment there is no need, but away from home, there's a need to become different forms. And we have the ability to do that, too.
D: *To survive and to adapt?* (Yes) *Did someone come and take you?*
T: Yes. It's part of the agreement that we had and it was more of a call. They didn't come to get me per se, as we mutually agreed to take up a mission, and we're heading someplace. This is part of what we do with our creators. We help to generate new places and new life forms sometimes as well.

D: *But you don't remember the agreement until you go with them?*

T: No because it's not necessarily linear time. It's just sort of a holistic facial—this is what we do—you had time to contemplate, and you now need to go manifest your contemplation and we help each other do that. But part of it, I think, was going back to the cave or the dwelling to get clear and get clarity. And so I had my time of clarity and now it's my time to go and perform my mission with the others.

D: *You were so happy there because it was so comfortable and perfect. Do you mind leaving it?*

T: Yes, I do. These missions are very enjoyable and very fruitful, but often they're fraught with peril as well.

D: *In what way?*

T: Just the fact that there are energy and lifeforms that are not as evolved, and are programmed to be afraid. And we do a lot of the programming. In fact, we program some of the physical shells that other essences take on. We program some of this in so that the other essences can get the experience with these other types of energies, but it's not always the most desirable things to do.

D: *Is this part of the creation process you are talking about?* (Yes) *But now that you are on the craft, do you have to shape shift or do you stay in the same form?*

T: You stay the same form, for the most part. The big furry form, for the lack of a better way to put it. I don't think it's actually gorilla furry, but that's my description of it.

D: *What do the other beings on the craft look like?*

T: They're much the same as me. We go into places and we'll change our physical appearance so as to not upset the programming of the other beings that we encounter. Most of the time that's how it's done.

D: *So they also look furry like you do?*

T: Furry is not exactly ... that's my description. It's now more like shimmering light, many bits of light. It's not fur.

D: *Do you know what your mission is on Earth?*

T: It's part of a collective. We all have things that we have worked out individually in our own vision class, if you will. Back home in our contemplation of what the universe needs next to unfold, and so we all have our own individual missions and destinies. But we also have a collective mission that has been decided, too.

D: *Do you know what you're going to do when you get to Earth?*

T: Yes, we're going to colonize it.

D: *This is the larger mission or the smaller part?*

T: This would be the larger part of this mission, but a smaller part of one, too.

I decided to move him ahead to when the craft arrived at the planet Earth, and asked him why he chose that planet.

T: Somebody else, another lifeform, put it together in such a way that it would be easier for us. So that we wouldn't have to do everything from the ground up. There is already a process that would support life forms: a planet and an atmosphere. We don't have to do that, although we're capable of that. We don't typically get into that.

This goes along with parts of my other books. One type of creator beings created the galaxies, the planets and eventually the other essential things needed on Earth in the beginning. There were other beings that came to a planet when it had cooled down enough to begin the process of seeding life (in whatever form). Some were to stabilize the atmosphere, and develop the seas. Then to begin the process of simple one-celled organisms and plant life. Many things had to be in readiness before animal life could be introduced.

T: The planet itself is alive in its own right. It's a living entity and we work with it to create vibrations that will work in this place. We deduce what kind of radiation and vibration this entity (Earth) has and then we create physical shells that will protect the essences from the radiation of this place, amongst other things. Not just radiation, but many other vibrations that will exist here and perpetuate themselves here.

D: *Are there any other life forms there?*

T: The vibration from above ... from beyond the physical is alive. But we're here to primarily colonize with the human form. We could do the whole thing. We have done this on occasion, but not here on Earth. We're here to work with other species to create the human form.

D: *I was wondering about plants, a food source set into place.*

T: Yes, there is. It has been populated with lower life forms like cells and bacteria, all the way up to the plant forms, as well as some fishes and some ocean-type beings. But primarily we work with other species to create higher physical shells for essences beyond. Primarily we work with humans.

D: *Have they been brought to the planet yet?*

T: At this stage, no. It happens rather rapidly. Once the base of the planet has been established for its ability to support life, we're able to populate it rather quickly with whatever is necessary.

D: *So the animals are brought from somewhere else, or how did that happen?*

T: Some species are created and some are brought from other places, and some are hybridized as well. They're a familiar type of a thing you might see place to place. It just kind of depends on the species.

This entire story has been told in my books *Keepers of the Garden* and *The Custodians*. It is always interesting to me to have the same story given again and again through several clients. This is validation that there must be truth in this story of our beginning.

D: *You sound like you've been doing this for a long time. Is there anyone who tells you where to go and what to do?*

T: Not specifically any *one*. It's like a collective. We have a rather tight knit connection with one another. We're not as isolated as humans are in their shells.

D: *They think they're all alone.* (Yes) *And it's different for you?*

T: That is correct. There is a sense of self and a sense of identity, but it's not as isolated as the human existence.

D: *So when you come to Earth and work with the creation of the human shells, you are there a long time?* (Yes) *You're able to see many changes, animals, plants, the whole thing?* (Yes) *So once they get the humans established, is there a plan for that?*

T: Yes, there is a lot of programming that's done. They're given a huge capacity for inner knowingness, but it's sort of by design that they don't get to access it as much as they know they could. And it's another—I don't know a polite way to say it—cosmic experiment. We're always working with creation. We're always trying new things everywhere. That's what the universe is: always expanding.

D: *Once the human forms have been created, they can't live without souls. Is that correct?*

T: That's correct.

D: *What do you intend to do about that? Do you have plans?*

T: How does a shell take on insoulment? *(Yes)* That is up to that *individual* essence, what we call "soul," and they will often determine how a shell unfolds and shapes itself as well. They help to create the vibration of the individual shell.

D: *Well, after you do all of this, do you stay on the Earth or decide to go back?*

T: Most of the time we go back. We do this all the time, and some are "watchers" and just kind of hang out and remain behind. But usually by an unknowing agreement that they do such a thing. In my case, I didn't know that I was going to be left behind. I didn't see it coming. There was an attack and those that got away were able to escape, but not able to come back and look for anybody that was left behind. That is what I believe happened.

D: *Tell me what happened?*

T: There were some primitives, programmed humans, if you will, humanoids, and their programming defragmented and they attacked. And they didn't understand how to use the technology that was left behind. Many of us escaped, but I did not.

This sounded familiar to me. I believe it is the same event that Bartholomew told of the first humans in my book *The Convoluted Universe, Book One.* They wanted the miraculous machines and technology for themselves. But after they killed the creator beings they found they did not have the knowledge of how to use the devices. So their progress stopped and began to go backwards.

D: *So you stayed behind?*

T: Yes. In Earth rotation, in Earth time, in linear time, I stayed behind a very long time. I would be almost eternal in Earth years.

D: *There was no way you could go back?* (No) *How did you feel about that?*

T: I didn't like it at all. I spent a very long time contemplating the light and being able to create. Spending more time fending off primitives. And then not just fending them off, but trying to teach them. Trying to reprogram them so that their programming wasn't so overwhelming. And that I'd be able to basically give them some of the gifts that I have. But it was not always easy. They didn't trust because of their programming. Their lack of trust created attacks.—It made it easier to not think about where I came from.

It was time to bring the session back to Tim, the human on the bed that all this was coming through. "Do you realize you are speaking through a human body now as you're talking to me?" (Yes) "The body we call Tim?" (Yes) "Is this one of the forms you took on when you stayed?"

T: No. My physical form ultimately passed long ago, but by Earth years it would be unimaginable how long it did stay.

D: *You stayed on Earth and went through many other physical forms during other lifetimes. Would that be right?*

T: I have come back since that first lifetime here, yes.

D: *So your essence eventually entered into Tim.*

T: That's correct.

D: *Why did you decide to enter the physical body of Tim? Did you have a contract or what?*

T: There are many things that have been left undone, things that needed to be finished—not just completed—but also *commenced* as well.

D: *So you decided to come into the body of Tim as a baby?*

T: Yes. Actually prior to the formation of his body. I chose his situation and this body because I knew it would be a strong one, and it was.

D: *It's a body you could use to fulfill your purposes?* (Yes) *Has this body accumulated karma? That's one of the things we were wondering about, if he had karma he hadn't repaid.*

T: No, not necessarily. I think that humans are trying to understand, but the programming originally is rather limiting. One of the things that he could do if he chose to, is just to rewrite the programming, and that's all karma is. It's not, to use vernacular, as intense as humans want to make it. And I think that would be something that he should know because for whatever reason, he's bought into the intensity of somebody else's beliefs, religious beliefs, if you will.

D: *So he does have the power to create. He can create anything he wants in his life. You know that's possible, don't you?*

T: Absolutely.

D: *But he's forgotten he can do it.*

T: Yes, part of the trip to being human is the agreement to amnesia.

D: *I guess it would be too complicated otherwise.* (Laugh)

T: Not necessarily. It's just programming, and we could arrange otherwise. But it does make it simpler for the original design.

D: *But would it be possible to reawaken this ability to create?*

T: Oh, absolutely!

D: *Because there are many things he wants to do with his life.*

T: Yes. There's a sense of danger that he has bought into, partially based on some of the lessons that I had to go through.

D: *In the other lives?*

T: Yes. But it's part of the present and only the brave and the adventurous can move the process forward. He is brave and adventurous, but he definitely is afraid in his heart on some of this.

D: *Isn't the time now to reawaken these abilities?*

T: Yes. The timing is wonderful, but he has some things that are well beyond what your recorded history would understand. And some of these things could be conceived as threats.

D: *But he wants to create a good life for himself. A good career, and there's no threat in that. Just to have a happy life.*

T: Part of his contract was to be more than that though. I think he needs to get over his fears. It's the biggest thing that gets in a human's way. He'll be safe. He's always worried about danger. He's always worried about uncovering some of these truths and what bringing them forward might mean, but that isn't necessarily something he has to worry about. We can take care of that.—If he

319

spent more time contemplating the light, he would contact it. It would actually call to him, but he has trouble trusting that this contact will be made. And it's not for me to tell him. He needs to discover it, himself.

It was time to ask the inevitable question: "What is my purpose?" Tim had a career, but he felt he should be doing something else. He wanted advice. He was told of many possibilities that he could pursue. "If he were to dedicate himself to what he knows in his heart, he can make his way in your space and time in your culture. If he were to just decide and make up his mind that this is what he was going to do, and he was going to do it no matter what, these other things would just nicely fall away."

D: *Now he will realize this is another part of himself, and he has created in the past. He can create anything he wants. He just needs confidence, doesn't he?*

T: Yes, there's an aspect I had trouble working through as my time as a creator, where I believed that I was betrayed into staying here. But in fact, it was something I had agreed to from a higher perspective that I didn't remember somehow. I thought I knew everything. I thought I was all knowing. That was something, somehow, that got by me. And when I was here, I was actually the last of my kind here and spent many Earth years here on my own. And I focused very much on what I considered betrayal of being left here. And it took many, many years to overcome the betrayal and realize that it was actually something I had agreed to. I created my own reality, and Tim still remembers that betrayal and he has attracted some betrayal in his present life. I think he just needs to focus on what he needs to create rather than focusing on fear or what he doesn't want to create. Instead of focusing on the betrayal, focus on the fact that he created it for the lessons that he needs to learn. He can then move forward with focusing on what he really wants rather than what he doesn't want. Because, as we both know, if you focus on anything, you're going to attract it, whether you want it or not.

D: *Is this part of the fear that he feels in the pit of his stomach?*

T: Yes. He somehow believes that he shouldn't be using what he learned from ancient times, that it is somehow not proper. Somewhere along the way he made an agreement to not use skills that he took lifetimes to learn. As if the need to tie his arm behind his back is some sort of badge of honor. He needs to just untie his arms and use every resource available to him.—He doesn't like to make decisions. But if he decides he can make something work, he can make it work. There's not a lot of drama about it, but he does like to bring forth a lot of drama with regards to some of these decisions. And he likes to wait a long time. I guess he knows that he's eternal in a certain sense, when he's not in his physical body. But he is in another and so he tends to wait an awfully long time before he makes decisions. Sometimes it benefits him, but sometimes it doesn't.

I asked the SC to look inside Tim's body to see if there was anything we needed to be concerned about. He didn't have any physical complaints, but I thought it never does any harm to check. However, they couldn't find anything wrong. "He is a fine specimen. A good shell, too. These things weren't designed for a long duration. That was part of the original design. They can be programmed to last a lot longer than most imagine in this current era. You can create the body you want to inhabit."

Tim's parting message: He knows a lot, but the more you know, the more you don't know. And there are certain things that he will know if he just pursues them, and sometimes the greatest failure is to not do something at all. And he just needs to get on with it.

Chapter 23

SEPARATING FROM THE SOURCE

When Brenda came off the cloud she was noticeably emotional, so I wanted to know what she was seeing that would cause this. She said it was like a city, yet one that she had never seen before. Very beautiful, pure white, with buildings that were very smooth. They almost glistened, like marble. Then she focused on one building that sat higher than the others, "Beautiful. Very fluid-looking, no sharp edges, very smooth." There was no vegetation, just this very white, almost pearlescent building. "It's very big. Now I'm seeing it from a different point of view. There are two huge, white columns on the front. And I look inside and it's a big, open space. It's in the shape of—almost in the shape of a leaf, pointed on both ends—an oval! Beautiful, very fluid-looking. The ceiling is a dome that is open at the very top, which doesn't make sense. Architecturally, I don't know how it would stand." Then she was inside the room and saw lights all around the room, almost like orbs.

Then I asked her to perceive herself. She sighed, "It's interesting. I don't get a sense of up or down when you say that. I don't have a sense of myself. I feel like I'm in a sphere. I don't understand." I encouraged her to talk about it because when the client is talking it becomes clearer. "I'm in a sphere of color; it's very—swirly. There's lots of blues and greens; some yellows. And I feel like little electric impulses are going through my body. It doesn't feel unpleasant, but I feel like there's no up or down, so it's a tiny bit disorienting. (Pause) I'm going somewhere.—This is a place where you go to go someplace else. It's a transport station. You go there, and then you go somewhere else." She then became emotional and started to cry softly. I asked what was causing the emotion.

B: I'm not sure. I'm not upset; I'm not scared or sad, it's just.... The emotion feels very big. This place is just a little overwhelming. Everything is in spheres; they're all spheres. The room that I'm in isn't a perfect round—it's an oval. Now I'm looking around more. On the sides, there are many of these spheres. They almost look like crystal balls, but they're very fluid. The spheres are probably two feet, maybe three feet across. They're all around the room, within the same plane. It keeps shifting, so it doesn't make sense to me, but these spheres are like amplifiers. It's a source of power, or a source of energy. Interesting, they're trying to be very gentle, like, "Okay, just look at the spheres."—Now this place feels different. It's the same shape, but the ceiling's not open. It's not white anymore; it's a darker room. Not that it's a bad thing, it's just that it's not as lit. So it feels more enclosed. And there are these glowing spheres all the way around the room, everywhere I look. They're on the same level. And they all beam across to the other ones, and you are in the middle. (A deep breath.) It's definitely a transport station.

I was trying to find out if there was anybody in charge. Was there any way to differentiate between all these spheres? How would you know where to go? She said she couldn't distinguish anyone. Then a gasp as she had a revelation. In a whisper she said, "Gosh, it's like you *know*! It's like when you go here, and you stand here, then it feels like it's already programmed." Her body began to shake, "When you ask me the question, I get an answer in my head, but I can't see them in this room. So when you asked what you're supposed to do, I heard, 'We will take you there.'"

D: *Ask them where are they supposed to take you?*

B: (Aloud) Where are we going? (Pause, then becoming emotional.) Into the Sun! The Sun's not exactly what we think it is. You actually go into the middle of it, and then you come out the other side, and it's not *our* Sun. It's the Sun of all Suns. It's the center Sun of all Suns. (Sobbing softly) It's where we have all come from. (Sobbing) It's home!

D: *Well, if that was home, what are you doing in this place?*

B: They're like outer stations, they call them. You go to the outer station.

D: *And had you come there from somewhere else?*

B: Yes, from the Sun. It's like when you're in the Sun, it's a pool. You have to come to the outer station to take form.

D: *So when you leave the Sun and go to the outer station, you are just these spheres?*

B: (Whisper) Oh, my gosh! Yes, that's it because you don't have form. I was seeing it the other direction. But yes, yes, that's it. When you're in the Sun you have no form. It's like in stages; when you come out you don't have form, so there are certain things that you have to do. It's almost like you coalesce; you come together. (All of this was said with the sense of surprise, of discovering something.) The pieces come together to make a form which you are in, now. And you can't do it all at once. It's almost like it's in stages. You have to go to this one place first, and then it coalesces. And then you go.

D: *So when you're with this light, this Sun, you don't have any form at all?*

B: No, it's like the sea. It's funny because it's very bright, but it's not hot. But it's moving. You would think it would be chaotic, but it's not.

D: *You said it is not the Sun of our solar system.*

B: No. It's the Sun of all Suns.

This is the way many of my clients have described the Source or God.

D: *Then why do you leave that to go to these outer stations?*

B: Because we want to. (Laugh) That's so funny; *because we want to.* It's almost like we're little children or something. It's very light, and very blissful. Yes, it's almost like when you're a little kid and you want to go explore. And there's so much excitement around it. It just makes your heart dance like a little child. It's playing, so you want to go play.

D: *And they let you do this? They let you leave?*

B: It's not even "let." It's so interesting because when you say "they let you," it's like we all decide, and we go. (Laugh)

D: *And then you go to the outer station and become this sphere as your first form?*

B: Actually, you start to take form before you even hit the outer station. It's so interesting! I see the Sun, and there's like these beautiful fingers of light coming out. And they're just beautiful! It's like these fingers of light come out, and then they start to come together into this amazing moving shape of color. And then they come to these orbs of light.

D: *Then it finally forms into an orb.*

B: Exactly! Yes.

D: *And then you're there on the outer station, and they say it's time to go somewhere else?*

B: Exactly. And that's when the energy starts to ....

She appeared to be watching something, and she found it interesting. The problem would be her ability to describe it.

B: The first time you start to feel separate. A sense of yourself. It's so interesting. It's weird. It's almost like you feel a sense of boundary, whereas before you *felt* no boundary—it was just all expanse. And then you feel almost like the outer edges of yourself.

D: *You began to feel separate?*

B: Well because you feel smaller. (Laugh) It's so interesting because I don't have a sense of we, or you, or I. But it's when the sense of self first starts to feel its own identity. Which is not really; it's an illusion. It's when the illusion first starts, but it's like a necessary tool that you have to have. I've never felt this way before. When you're at the Sun, you do feel like children. It's wise—it's the wisest thing you've ever felt in your life, but also the most joyful and innocent. It's a combination of wisdom and innocence, and so it's almost like a way of protection. It's almost like, "As you go forth, children, you must have some protection." And so to do that you must have some sense of self. And I don't have a sense of how long this takes, but it's a process. So then you go, and you start to feel a sense of self. Really, for me it feels like the first time.

D: *So this is part of the process before you can leave the transport station.*

B: Exactly.

D: *Then you're going to go explore.*

B: You can go anywhere.

D: *Do you know where you're going to go?*

B: Where am I? Right now? I went to Earth. I chose Earth. Oh! But I didn't choose it first!—I went someplace blue. Blue? Oh, my gosh! I don't see location. They're saying you went to the blue place to gather knowledge first. Oh, it's so interesting! There are all these different levels at all these different places. And there aren't really any levels, but the place I picked was very physical. But to go there, there were certain things you had to know. It's like tools. It's like you go to school. And all I'm seeing when I asked is blue, like the blue planet. It's a physical place, but they don't mean Earth. It's the blue planet. Ocean, it feels like.

Many other clients have described coming from a beautiful water planet, where they were experiencing lives as different types of sea creatures. They had no responsibility and such freedom that they didn't want to leave.

B: I'm observing as if watching a movie. I don't feel like I'm there, it feels like I'm watching something. I don't feel any emotion attached to it, but I see oceans, I see whales, and I see dolphins. I'm breathing underwater. It doesn't feel like water, it feels thicker than water. It feels like some kind of medium. It's very fluid, it's heavier than air, but it's not as heavy as water. It's not cold, it feels smooth, it feels silky, and when you look around it actually sparkles a little bit. I feel fluid, and I don't feel my shape. I don't feel like a dolphin or a whale. I see dolphins and whales. It's odd, but it's almost as if you had some silken cloth and you pulled it through the water, that would be me. I have some substance. I'm a little more dense than what's around me, but I have a hard time describing. I can't see myself, but I feel very fluid. And everything is swimming. There's nothing walking around on two legs.

D: *You don't see any land?* (No) *So what do you have to do at that blue place?*

B: What they said is, "You're coded." They used the word "code." Coded with what? And I heard, "It's all a step in creating the form." It must be coded, and it must be coded in a fluid place. And it's all through vibration. They didn't say "vibration," they said it's all "energy."

She began having difficulty finding the correct words to describe this. This is a common occurrence. I told her to do the best she could.

B: You get coded, they said. And then everything is built from the fluid. As you progress you go through the fluid place. And this fluid place is very blue. And I can see forms that look like whales; but it's not really a whale, it kind of looks like that. And I can hear tones like the dolphins toning. Alright, one is coming up to me right now and they're bouncing the tones back and forth. And I'm being built. That's an interesting word to us: *built*. It feels very clinical when I say that, and I'm not attached to the word. It's so interesting, it's like my body's being built.

D: *Is that part of the coding you were talking about?* (Exactly.) *So they have to take the essence that you were, in other words, and then make it into something more solid?*

B: Exactly! And that's where it's done for me. That's where I am built, or where I *was* built. It's so interesting the way I'm seeing it because it's very matter of fact, like this is just the way it is. It's all done through toning, like these tones are coming through.

She had difficulty explaining what she was seeing. She said, "It's so odd, it feels like a science fiction movie." Apparently they were building a human form, and it was done with tones. She saw herself with others coming out of the water as full-sized people, not little infants. They were walking out of the water as fully developed people, and there were many of them. The exception was that they did not have all of their "details" yet. They all looked the same, legs, arms, bodies, but with no defining features. "Now I'm actually seeing it mature before my very eyes. Now the people are getting hair and eyes. They are being created.—Yet I don't see anybody doing it."

D: *So what are you going to do with the form now, once it is created?*

B: Now we get the knowledge. Now we go into this—it feels more like a structure, it doesn't feel out in nature any more. There are people there, a building, even though I don't recognize the building. It feels very matter of fact, and yes, this is the way it is done. You go in here and—it feels like it's happening very fast, but I don't have a sense of time.

D: *Let me ask you a question before you go any further. Why did they make your form look like a human? It could look like anything, couldn't it?*

B: Because I chose Earth. Yes, it could have been anything.

D: *But in this case everyone looked like humans?*

B: That's a very good question. Let me really, really look. I immediately said "human" because it's the same size and height—arms, legs, head, torso. But no, we're not. It *looks* like it could be human, but they don't come into form like a human does. It's the way they're made. So they're made differently like we saw. They're not born like a human, so it's not a human. It's interesting; it's almost like that's the best shape for you to take for what you're doing—what they're doing.

D: *All right. So now you're inside this building, and you said there you get knowledge.*

B: Yes. There's a table and there are papers on the table, and people sitting around the table. It's like there are plans or something on the table, the papers. And the table is lit from beneath. And the people that I'm looking at look like .... All different kinds of beings! Oh, wow! It's interesting because the basic shape is human – arms, legs, torso, head, eyes – that is the same. But there are certain things that are different so you know they're not a human form. Like one person, their eyes are different; there are no eyelids, no eyelashes. There are several people sitting around this table; they do have clothes on. It's like I'm observing, I'm being shown this.

D: *What is their purpose with the papers?*

B: It's so funny because when I ask this—well, of course! You know! This is where the plan is made. The plan for where you're going next. There are seven of us that just walked in the room.

D: *There are seven in your group?*

B: Exactly! There are seven of us that came out of the water together. And now it's on to this next place. The worst thing is I don't see where we're going. (Sigh) This is where you go and you talk about it. It's like the decisions have already been made, and this is where they tell you.

D: *What did they tell you?*

B: They said I was going to Earth.

D: *Did you know what Earth was?*

B: No. I feel really weird because .... You don't logically get from one place to another in this place. I'm looking at it from a direction, and they're being very gentle with me, I can tell. It's like they're saying, "Within your understanding we have to show it to you this way, so that you can get an idea of what is happening." Okay, so I'm in a form. And then all of a sudden I'm formless, and I'm not sure where I am.

D: *Can you ask them why you have to go to Earth? Why that place?*

B: They're trying to show me in a way that I'll understand. It's almost like everything vibrates in harmony, and colors come off of it. It's like I'm seeing things from far away. I'm seeing many planets. And the weird thing is I don't even recognize ours. Like I don't recognize Mercury or Venus or the Sun. But I'm seeing all these planets, and it's like an orchestra—they're all vibrating in harmony. And it's very fluid, it moves. So they're showing me everything is going in harmony. Then when I look over and they show me Earth—Earth right now is out of tune. It's like a piano that needs to be tuned. Earth is not in tune, it's gotten flat.

D: *It's out of tune, out of harmony with the rest.* (Yes!) *It's very noticeable then.*

B: Very! When I see it from far away it's like everything is in harmony. Even though I don't hear it, it feels almost musical. It does! It feels like it vibrates, even though everything's not vibrating exactly the same. But they're in harmony like an orchestra, all these different instruments playing. They're all playing the same tune, or the same song, and they're all in harmony together. When they had me turn to look at the Earth—it would be like the most gorgeous orchestra you've ever heard in your entire life. And if someone went in there and played a piano that was out of tune, you would hear it. So it's standing out. It's noticeable in the orchestra of the whole of all the galaxies of everything that ever was—there's a flat spot. Now I saw—it's funny because I keep going further and further and further and further and further back in my perspective—so as I see, in our corner of this huge amount of space, Earth is flat. We're not the only place that's flat—there are some others *way* far away—but now I'm zooming up closer. In all of the universes that are close to us, Earth is noticeably ....

D: *The main one that's causing a problem.*

B: Exactly! It's out of tune. Out of harmony. It feels so *flat*. So we're going to help re-tune it.

D: *How do you feel about doing that?*

B: Excited. And the other thing is that the outcome is not sure. We don't know whether we can. Other places where we've gone before, we were very sure. You could go in, you just need to do this and this and this and this, and it'll pop right back. I just got a flash that we're not exactly sure.

D: *So you've had other lives where you've done things like that?*

B: Yes. We tune.

D: *Do you know how you're going to do this?*

B: I see color. It's all in the color, it's in the vibration of the color.—There are more, I'm not the only one. It's a "we." Oh, my gosh! There have been several before me, several after me—it's a "we." Now I'm seeing the web. It's a blanket, it's a web around the Earth. And it's like there are many tools. It's all in the vibration. There is beauty in the simplicity of it. It's not that easy, but it's like if everybody could sing. These tones, these high, beautiful color tone vibrations. Some places feel like they're under tar, like a thick sludge. It's not about wiping the tar—they're trying to show me a visual, an example. Some people get caught up in trying to clean it by trying to take the tar off of it—that's not how you do it. What you do is, you go in on the inside and you change the vibration, and then the tar transforms. It's not about wiping away or cleaning; it's changing it from one thing to another.

D: *So you're going to Earth. Do you go into a body, or how are you going to make these changes?*

B: Gosh, I wasn't in a body first.—I'm seeing the Earth, and around the Earth—it's different than I thought. It feels almost as if you had some fabric, or a blanket. But it's not as heavy as a blanket. It's woven though because I can see there's order to it. It feels like grids, or graph paper, but it's fluid, and it's around the Earth. And there are more than one—there are many layers of this fabric, or this substance, that's around the Earth. And where I'm seeing myself first is within those. And within *those* it's almost like funnels come off of there. It's like there's a big fabric over the top of the Earth, and there's a funnel that comes down to a point under the Earth. And when it's healthy and it's happy naturally, they just appear all over the Earth at different times, different places. And it feels very organic and very fluid. And they look like combs. It goes down, and there are these points. It goes into the Earth, and kind of recycles back through. And it's all moving. And the surface of the Earth feels permeable. So there are certain places on the Earth that have gotten hard. It almost feels dead; it feels suffocated.

D: *It's hard to penetrate?*

B: Yes! That's exactly the word. It's hard to penetrate. And since it's hard to penetrate, we now need to go down under the Earth, under the surface, and do it on the surface. We can no longer do it from above. And there are many, there are many.

D: *How are you going to do it on the surface?*

B: You bring that energy—okay, I can see it now. When we were above the Earth, we were like points of light like amplifiers, or activators. The energy comes in and comes to these points of light, and then it amplifies and is directed to the Earth. Now it's been necessary to bring that amplification closer to the Earth, so it's stronger. So those points of light have now moved down onto the planet so it will now become stronger because it must penetrate further in. So it is going into the Earth, down deep under the surface of the Earth. Before it worked from above. It can't be done that way anymore, it's too thick.—There are still the island of the people, the beings that are out there on the grid, but some of us are here on the planet.

I wanted to know if she was aware that she was speaking through a physical human body, and she reluctantly acknowledged that she sometimes was aware. So I asked when she decided to enter a physical body. If she was doing such an important job without a body, why was it necessary?

B: There was an agreement made. I was looking at the human body that I'm in. And I was asking, "Have I always been in this human body?" And the "I" that's speaking has not always been in this human body. I came in later. It was an agreement. That's a little confusing for me.

D: *Let's see if we can explain it. You mean the "I" that is speaking is not the one that was born into the body?*

B: No. I came in later. (Pause) The human language is not set up for this.

D: *I know. I've been told many times that the language is not sufficient.*

B: You asked if I was born in this human body, and I feel like I was not. But I have memories of it. I have memories from the beginning. It's not like there were no memories. But it's like it was not necessary for me to be here in the beginning of this human body. I came in later. I came in when the consciousness—It's so interesting to look at because it's not like we're separate, but it's like a part of you that's not quite as developed. Then I asked myself why didn't I just come down early, but I was busy someplace else. So it's almost like you send a part of you down. Because "I" wasn't needed when I was a child, or when this body was a child. I needed the body when the body was more developed.

D: *The other part was there as a child?*

B: Exactly. So it's like part of you comes down—and I don't want to make light of it. I don't want to make it sound like a robot. But the more underdeveloped part of you comes down and learns all the lessons from the beginning, and has all those experiences. It's like when you go to a doctor—you go to a regular doctor first, and then you go to the specialist later. You know what I mean? Then the specialist part of you comes in. And so the specialist part is the person who is speaking now, who was called to come in because the specialist part has the skills. So "I" who am talking wasn't born in this body, but a part of me was. So there's this agreement and you kind of merge into and then become. It's not like there are two beings in this body. That's not it at all.

D: *It's a merging of the two.*

B: Right. Merger is a good word.

D: *About how old was the body when this happened?*

B: Twelve.

D: *So the merger took place at twelve years old.* (Yes) *Did an incident or anything happen at that time?*

Brenda began to get emotional. When that happens I know we have hit something important. So I gently encouraged her to talk about it, and tell me what was bothering her. With a deep sigh, she continued:

B: I had it backwards. It's a little confusing in my head because I'm seeing it from two different perspectives. I'm seeing it from the child that was born. I don't understand that part. It's so interesting because I'm trying to find the *I*, and there is no *I*. It's like I'm just observing where the emotion came from. And it's because I was struggling to define *I*, and I can't. Then I just backed up a little bit, and just observed. And I observed Brenda as a child, and then with the being that was really a custodian type—I don't know if that's really the right word—but a person who came....

D: *Was that the one she saw as an imaginary friend?*

Brenda had discussed this in the interview. As a child she had an imaginary friend who was very real to her. This is not uncommon. Many children have these, and although they are invisible to everyone else, they interact with them. My oldest daughter had one and she even insisted that I set her a place at the table, and asked me to take her hand when we crossed the street. I didn't encourage it or discourage it. I knew it was real to her. She called her "Julia," so when my second daughter was born, I named her Julia because I was so used to hearing that name. The "friend" disappeared at that time. Some parents have told me they thought their children were going crazy when they talked about (and to) an invisible friend. I tell them not to worry, what is occurring is perfectly natural and the "friend" will eventually disappear. When Brenda's left, she felt very alone and abandoned. This was one of her questions. She wanted an explanation of what was happening as a child.

B: When she was little. Yes, I was one of them. The light beings.

D: *So it's like a little caretaker?*

B: Exactly! It was more than that though. It was toning the body. Many of the human forms, when the soul comes in, they're not calibrated at a rate that can actually withstand a higher vibrational being coming in. So when the baby came in, it was calibrated from the very beginning. It's almost like I'm seeing tapping on feet, which is so odd. It's like these vibrational patterns were imprinted all through the body, and the bone, the cellular system, from the very beginning. So it's a calibration. And the bodies are chosen very carefully to acquire the tools that are necessary to perform the job later. So when the soul comes in—I'm just seeing it straightforward—that is when the custodian comes down. There is some consciousness there, but it's not the full consciousness. The light being has not been born within that body yet. There's a soul there, yes, but it's just a bit of the soul. The soul is a huge oversoul, and a tiny bit comes in, and it's being prepared. It's being molded. And it's all part of it. So that wasn't actually me. It was part of me, but it wasn't all of me. So the custodian came down—not a custodian, a caretaker—a caretaker came down and helped prepare the body. The body has to be prepared for the higher vibrations because many times in the past when we've done this, when the higher vibrational being comes into a body, the body can't handle it, and it's short-circuited.

D: *I've heard that before, that sometimes the body, the baby, will die.*

B: That's happened! So we're very careful to calibrate it and then put the body in a place—it's almost like nested. We come back and check, and make sure the body is progressing now as it should be. And there has to be a certain kind of mind. The electrical impulses in the brain are different. There are more areas. I've seen the back part of the brain, it's different there. There's more activity there in the beginning. It's like electrical impulses are put there. Then it's observed, and then it's progressed. And then we slowly start bringing in more light. I see it as a very, very light blue light being brought in from different places into the body. The feet. Looks like the collar bone.

337

The back of the neck, the top of the head, the third eye area, under the places by the nose—interesting! Places by the ears. And so light is brought in gradually, slowly over time. Impulses are being used, and there's also different sequences of symbols.

D: *Like an activation is taking place?*

B: Yes, within the body. Then there's a point where it's all decided, and this soul is contacted, and asked. It's not separate when I say it's contacted, but there's an agreement that is made to go forward. And then we come in.

D: *What is the agreement? To allow the other part to come in?*

B: Like, "Are you ready? Does it feel right?" When the soul first comes in, and when we first make the agreement, everything is in alignment. As a soul starts to develop on the Earth, things change. The soul might have chosen another path. The soul might want to go someplace else. The soul might not want to go there anymore, so we have to ask again. Sometimes those contracts are broken; sometimes something happens in the life that's not foreseen. Earth is the wildcard—you never know what's going to happen when you get here.

D: *And they have free will.*

B: They have free will, so anything can happen. So we come back and we talk, and we ask whether it's still appropriate; whether they're still in agreement.

Much of this was explained in my book *The Three Waves of Volunteers.* Part of the saving of the human race from itself was the entering of new and pure souls into human bodies. Souls that had never known or accumulated karma, and thus were not stuck. This can relate to the ET experiences many people think are negative. The new soul has an energy that is totally alien to the human experience, so it cannot enter all at once. When this was tried in the past it resulted in the abortion of the baby. So it had to be done more slowly, in gradual intervals, so the body could adjust before the full energy came in later. This would explain the repeated visitations by ETs, extraterrestrials because their job is to keep monitoring the bodies and checking them to see if everything is functioning correctly. Thus the implants or monitors were put into the body to keep track of the person. This also explains the decrease in abduction reports because the work has now been finished. The souls entered (the 3 waves that I discovered), and there are enough now on Earth to accomplish the job, so there is no need for any more. Most of the abduction cases you hear about took place several years ago. Or they are checkups that are being routinely performed to make sure the body is functioning correctly in this strange and often hostile environment.

This would also explain the hybridization program that many have described as negative. The producing of bodies or vehicles that would be receptive to the high energy of the incoming souls without damage. A combination of genes, but more importantly a blending of the energies so the soul could live in the body. It is amazing that many of the people I work with say they don't feel they belong here, that this is not their home. Then while under trance they are revealed to either be a first-timer who has come directly from the Source, or an alien energy or light being that has never been in a human body before.

(Continuing)

D: *Is this what happened when she had that experience when she was about 10 or 12?* (She had visitations in her room at night that she thought were ET related.) *At the time it happened she thought it was a negative experience.*

B: At the time the human mind doesn't know. The human mind isn't fully aware of it at that point. At that stage in her life she wasn't ready to receive that information. We brought everything now that we could to make her comfortable. And we brought her friend back that she knew when she was younger.

D: *During the experience she said she remembered not being able to move.*

B: Yes, it's interesting. We do it as gently as we can, and many times we do it when the person is asleep. She was awake, which is the way it was supposed to be. She was developed enough that she could handle that much. It happened the way it was supposed to. It's almost like anesthesia where you put the person out so they can't move. But it's a pleasant place, and they come out of it not really remembering. Or you remember a good dream or whatever. It's not meant to be some place scary. She had a very strong-willed, very strong mind, and so when it started to happen, she chose to be awake.

D: *Sometimes people perceive it as negative.*

B: Yes because from a child's point of view she couldn't move, and it felt invasive. But it wasn't.

D: *She said it felt like things were being done to the physical body.*

B: Well, it was. The light being was moving in. It's like the final calibration. Not the final one, but the one that must be done before the other energy moves in. There are certain things that have to be done to prepare.

D: *What she perceived as entities around her—are they the ones that helped with this?*

B: Yes. And they were put in a form that she could understand at that time.

D: *Because you know on Earth we talk about ETs. People don't understand what they are.*

B: No, and I see it now.

D: *Is this part of their job to help with this whole process?*

B: Yes. One of them is very good at what he does, he can feel the body. He feels the body and brings it into perfect calibration and alignment with the light being that's moving in. The light being comes into the human body, so then when the human body wakes up in the morning, they won't even notice any difference. It's a perfect harmonic merging.

D: *Except they feel there's something they're supposed to do.*

B: Yes because that's when it starts to kick in.

D: *There are many people that remember experiences like this, and they perceive them as negative. They don't understand what's happening.*

B: The Earth is a very negative place. Not always—it doesn't have to be. But it's harder to stay in the positive, especially for the very—I don't want to use the word "powerful"—but for the ones who are sensitive. If there is a place of confusion and they reach up for a stream of energy, since there are so many negative streams that are so powerful, it's easy to become in alignment with that stream of thought. We have to consciously reach for the stream of light, for the one of love because here on Earth, the automatic one is fear.

D: *So what they perceive as negative is really not.*

B: Right. Exactly.

D: *There is something more happening, and it is an agreement that the person makes before they come in.*

B: It's all part of it, and it's all very good.

D: *There are many people that I have worked with who said they feel violated. They feel like something was done to them without their permission.*

B: No, that's not it at all. Their permission was given. It's a protection device for a child. You wouldn't show children a horrible movie because they wouldn't understand it— they don't know that it's not real. You protect them. You show them Disney movies. And then when they get 16 or 17, they can see it because you could explain it to them— that it's not real. And so there are certain things that are put in place as protection.

D: *All right. But now the merger has taken place and this being of light is inside of her, isn't it?* (Yes)

Brenda had noticed that her psychic abilities were being reawakened. She was beginning to see who she is. This was one of the things she wanted to know about. "It's taken a long time, hasn't it?"

B: Yes. There were many things that had to be done first.

Of course, another one of her questions was about her purpose. What was she supposed to be doing with her life? What was the plan?

B: It's the Earth. She must bring in the higher vibration and anchor it into the Earth. She's coded to do that. She has it in her.
D: *Is this why she was mentally given the information about the crystals?*
B: Yes, they assist her. The crystals amplify it and make it easier. The crystals are one with her; the crystals listen to her, and she listens to the crystals. The crystals are alive; the crystals are another force. It's a whole different world. It's a whole different force field that needs to be used. It's been around here forever on this planet. Crystals are an energy force that are beyond your wildest imagination. You don't know how to use them; you have forgotten. Actually, the power has been taken away. Other civilizations misused the power, so it was taken away.
D: *So now we have to get the knowledge back.*
B: Many of the crystals are sleeping. Some of the crystals on this planet are still active. But they can be, and they're meant to be, reawakened. And you reawaken through vibration. The vibration can be done many different ways. It can be done by focusing on intent, and she knows how to do this. Reaching up into those gridlines, and there are many levels—there's not just one. She's only seen one. There are many, many layers of these energy fields around the Earth. The one she must reach out to is the farthest— it's the purple one. She needs to remember to work with the purple one. She's been working with the green one. Of course, white is always there, but the purple one is the

transformation. And then you bring that in and it resonates with the bones in your body as well. And then it starts a vibrational pattern that is then directed into the Earth, and awakens the sleeping stones.

D: *In my work I was told that the body is part crystalline, too.*

B: Your teachers here would say that the heart is crystalline, which is true. But the entire body is crystalline.

D: *This is why it vibrates, like you said earlier?*

B: Exactly. That is why more is to be given to her.

D: *But her path is to work with stones that help with the vibrations of the Earth.*

B: Right. And there will be others that will be helping her. As she's working with the Earth, it'll start to change the vibration, and people become disoriented. It's interesting, if you give people a job, if you tell them to help raise the vibration of the Earth, by them being directed to do that they can't help but then raise the vibration within themselves. So it's important to know that some people won't do it for themselves. Instead of saying, "I can help you raise your vibrations," you could bring people together and say, "We really need to go and heal the planet over here." And then in doing that, the people are helping raise their vibrations.

D: *You said this can cause disorientation?*

B: Not with the people that are doing this work. As the vibration of the Earth starts to rise, everything starts to change. So for the people who are disoriented and they don't know what to do, and they're not in resonance, or they're not on the same plane when you're saying you need to raise their vibration within them, ask them to help others. Because if they help others in any way—if they help an animal, if they heal a plant, if they feel like they're helping others, or helping the planet, then it raises their vibration. It's pretty simple.—Her main focus is bringing people together to direct the vibration into the Earth that could no longer get through.

D: *She was working with healing.*

B: That's a sidebar.—When she gets larger groups together to bring that energy into the Earth, it's far greater than one person alone. If one or two people as the core then bring others in, it amplifies even more.

D: *And they can help with the combined energy.*

B: Yes. Everybody has something to share, and everybody's energy is a little bit different. So when it comes together it's like an orchestra. And it's just beautiful. And so then the orchestra, all the pieces come together because everybody adds their own unique part. So really, the more the better.

D: *And we want to bring the Earth back into harmony.*

B: It must be. It goes in both directions. And as you do it in yourself, within your immediate family, or within your group, and then you do it for the Earth, then it goes out into the Universe. It's all a part of it.

D: *Everything affects everything else. Things are really speeding up. More and more people are waking up to their abilities, aren't they?*

B: There's no other way. They must; now is the time. There is no more grace period. When there used to be, we used to be given some time. The time is now.

D: *I have worked a lot with what we call UFOs and ETs, but it's getting more complicated than people think.*

B: Oh, it's so much more. They've been around forever. They've been forever a part of the evolution of this planet.

D: *So when these people are having these experiences, they're actually being activated.*

B: Yes, exactly. The body has to be calibrated to a higher vibrational level so that the other energies can come in and work through them.

D: *I've also been told those that are too uncomfortable with it, you just release them from the program.*

B: Oh, exactly. Because of the free will on this planet they can make choices in their young lives and go on a totally different path. And that's perfectly acceptable. And then they are released from the contract. And it's fine.

D: *Because some of them say they think it's too negative, and they want out.*

B: They get on that stream of thought of negativity, or the fear—and sometimes that's part of their path.

D: *That's what I'm told. You don't want those type of people in the program anyway, and you can release them if they want to be let out.*

B: Exactly. At any time, yes.

Chapter 24

TOO MUCH TOO SOON

When Tonya came into the scene she felt she was in outer space because there was nothing but emptiness. It was not uncomfortable, but she couldn't see anything. She decided to move downwards instead of going out further into space. Nothing seemed to change until she suddenly felt that she couldn't move at all. "I want to say I'm in some kind of a capsule. I don't know where I am, but I'm enclosed in something.—I don't have a body. I can't seem to move forward, up or down. It's all this dark speckles.—I feel like I haven't been born. That doesn't make any sense.—I haven't made up my mind what I want to be.—I feel like I'm inside something, but it is something I'm a part of, or I made and I ... don't know what I want to be, so I don't have direction."

D: *You mean nobody has told you what you're supposed to do or where to go or anything?*

T: I hear *you*, but I don't hear anyone else talk to me or tell me anything. It's up to me.

D: *So you have a choice? You can do anything you want? Is that what you mean?* (Yes) *That's important. Many people don't have a choice. They have to do what they're told.*

T: I've done all of that. I've paid my dues. I now have choices I can make myself.—Now I don't know what I'm going to do.

D: *How do you perceive yourself?*

347

T: I'm a spot of some kind of energy or some kind of thought process ... because I'm thinking. I don't have any physical features. I am just surrounded by this mass of stuff to work with.—But I'm stuck. I don't know what I want to do. I don't know what direction to go. (Frustrated)

D: *Do you want to do something different or something you haven't done before?*

T: Yes. Something more than I've done before ... something that means more. The other time was something I had to do. Now I want to do something outside of myself. (Crying) I don't know how to explain it.

D: *The other ones were like assignments you had to do?*

T: Yes. Finish up materials or finish up jobs I hadn't completed. I did most of it, yes, I guess I have all the basics done.—I've been here a long time ... a long time. (Whispering and crying.) Yet there are still things to do. —I just don't know what I want to do.

D: *Do you have any ideas, any options that you can think about?*

T: Yes, but it affects so many people if I do what I want to do.—It's getting lighter. It's not quite so dark anymore.

D: *What is it you want to do that would affect so many people?*

T: I want to be part of the change. Part of the influence ... the change for the better. I want to go back for that .... It has to do with a cycle. I want to be there for the beginning of the new cycle and be a part of it.

D: *Did anybody tell you it's coming, or do you just know it?*

T: Both. I've been told and now I feel it. The end of the cycle ... the beginning of a new cycle ... a whole new kind of life.

D: *That sounds really awesome ... really big. Did they say why the cycle had to end?*

T: As all things have to come to an end. When things are lived out, it's lived out. It's about over and a new cycle will start. Things never stay the same. They are always changing, but this is a big change. This is cycles within cycles within cycles.

D: *Different than the other ones?*

T: Different for this place.

D: *Which place are we talking about?*

T: For the Earth.

D: *So cycles have happened for other places, but this is a big move for this area?*

T: Yes. There's so much that's happened here. I've lived through some of it. I helped. I've been through different phases of it. You know the phases ... and yet, I'm afraid of how it could end. It's not ready to end yet, but it's almost there. The cycle isn't complete, and it's not finished with what it should do, and so much depends on it. People have to change and I want to be part of that. I want to help with the change, and it scares me.

D: *Why does it scare you?*

T: Because, what if I'm not good at it?

D: *I think if you want something so badly, you will be good at it. You have the desire, don't you?* (Tonya crying, Yes.) *You said you had been there through other phases of it?*

T: Yes, and I fucked them up ... excuse my language.

D: *What happened? Tell me about it.*

T: The cycle of this planet. I was aggressive in my desires to change things too quickly, and that's where I am now. I'm afraid of being too aggressive, and yet I get frustrated.

D: *What did you do at that time?*

T: I introduced things too quickly. Introduced changes in thought ... biological changes.

D: *What time periods were those?*

T: When life was young. It was different than it is now. There are so many different times, I can't remember them all.—Thoughts ... because you could influence the thought in that period of time. I was different than now. I want to say it was a milky substance. A thought was like a milky substance. It was easier to influence. It was joined together ... it was a milky substance. Am I making sense?

(Irritated at herself.) You see, things visually were not like it is now. Today there are angles and sharp points and black spots and thought processes are just awful. It makes so many bad things. It's not pure like it was.

D: *By milky substances, it flowed smoother?*

T: Yes, more complete in itself. It wasn't individualized by itself. Thought processes... individual. You were individual as individuals. See yourself as an individual, not so much as a player on a team. You were you.

D: *They weren't ready to understand it yet?*

T: No. Anger. It was anger among each other. Emotions that were not part of what they originally had. The change was a little too abrupt.

D: *You mean you introduced a new way of thinking that they weren't ready for?*

T: Yes. It wasn't just me either. I was with a group, but it was still me because I was part of the group. It made them aware of things that they weren't aware of before. Kind of like Adam and Eve. Suddenly they were aware of the differences. I wanted them to be ready. I wanted to move it along. I wanted to say I helped, but it was too soon. Anger was not something that they had before. There was abuse. It didn't dissipate. It rolled into something worse. They began to hurt each other. We should have known they weren't ready.

D: *How could you know?*

T: Because we were far more advanced than they were. At least that's how we saw ourselves.

D: *You didn't know how people and human nature would react. You went into it with good intentions.*

T: Yes, but there was still evil involved, now I see. This was what *we* wanted to do. This wasn't thought out enough. We weren't considerate enough.

D: *Were you physical then?*

T: We did not come down at that time. We were in a mental state. We were physical, but we didn't come down. It was influence by our mental state. We came down later on.

D: *So you decided to stop it because it was getting out of hand?*

T: Yes, but it was too late. We couldn't change it back, and over time it escalated.

D: *Then nobody punished you, or told you you shouldn't be doing this?*

T: You're punished, in a way. I mean, when you know you cause something, it's still there. No one had to point a finger at you and say, "Look what you've done." You know what you've done. But you still have to make up for your mistakes. If you've added two and two and you've got five, you're going to have to correct it.

D: *You said that at another time you did come down?*

T: Later. It was later. I guess in Earth years, it was quite a long time later, but we did come back down.

D: *You and the same group?*

T: Yes. That time we mingled with them as we were. Physical, yes. It was time for them to accept and they could accept, so we came down in that state. Life was different when it was a milky cloud time. It wasn't the same. It was physical, but it wasn't as physical. It was a slightly altered state. I can't explain it. I can feel the difference, but I can't explain it.—When I came down, it was different than the other time. This time the world was more physical as well, not that they weren't physical before. (Frustrated.)

I think she meant it was more solid.

D: *Did you make mistakes again?*

T: Yes. I got involved in a physical manner.—Sex.

D: *Why did you do that?*

T: Why do you do anything? You don't think properly.

D: *You wanted to do something you hadn't experienced before?*

351

T: Yes, but it wasn't the right thing to do. It was not time. It was not proper. It was not right.

D: *Did the rest of the group do the same thing?*

T: Some, but not all, no. Most of them did not. I think there were three of us who had to stay. I don't know where the other two are.

D: *Why did they make you stay?*

T: Because I couldn't go back. I changed my own vibration by doing it ... by getting involved. Because I interacted with the people, they are now part of my vibration.

D: *Oh, now I understand. They lowered your vibration because they were denser?* (Yes) *You were supposed to help them in a different way.*

T: Yes. By demonstrating, by showing them things, by teaching. I was doing that, but then I got too involved.

D: *So what happened in that lifetime? Did you stay there?*

T: Stayed there and was eventually killed actually. Somebody became jealous. I don't know exactly. I don't really remember, but somebody became jealous, and killed me. But that was all right. It was time to go.

D: *But everybody makes mistakes. Nobody's perfect. That's how we learn.—You said you wanted to help people?*

T: This change that is coming. There's going to be a change. So much depends on how much people have changed within themselves. It could be a huge change for many, many people, or it could be a change for just a few people. And the others won't know that this has gone on because they're not aware of it. That's why it's so important for more people to be aware.

D: *They all have their free will, so that's why it can affect everybody in a different way?*

T: Right. I guess I'm just afraid that I don't know the right way to do it. I want somebody to help me. Actually there's so much I could do, or I think so anyway. I just wish I had someone to do it with.

D: *Have you lived other lifetimes as a human?*

T: Oh, many.

D: *These other lives, did you just live normal lifetimes?*

T: Normal basically. Some lives are very good. Some lives are very sheltered. Some lives were just pulled in and I didn't want to talk to anybody.

D: *So you had to experience many things. You weren't always in a position where you could dramatically affect people.* (No) *So when you made that mistake, you had to keep returning to Earth in physical bodies.*

T: I did ... quite often at different time periods.

D: *But now it's getting ready for something very important. Do you think you're ready to do something like this?*

T: I want to be ready. I've always wanted to do it by myself until lately. Now I don't know. I feel I need somebody to bounce something off of. Somebody I can work with so that I can find out if they think it makes sense or work at a certain point, and do it with me.

D: *Can you ask someone if they can come and talk with you before you make a decision?*

T: I have asked someone.—I don't know his name. He's been with me a long time. I know him, but I don't know him. I don't see a face on him, but I feel a presence.

D: *What are you asking?*

T: For him to become physical ... come down. I've spent my whole life talking in my head ... talking and not getting answers that way. I want somebody that I can relate to.— Will he come down? I don't care how he does it, just to come down and talk and be with me.

D: *So you won't be alone.* (Yes) *Did they tell you how you were supposed to influence people or help with this change?*

T: Just to be myself. I guess I thought it was going to be more complicated. They think I can do it.

D: *So the main thing is to be on Earth when all this is happening?* (Yes) *You said there would be many people going in a different direction.*

T: It depends on where you're tuned. What do you want? Where are you tuned to? Who is it you think you are? All

353

those things are questions that will lead you to where you are going. If you understand all the things that are out there and all the things you are. But people still don't seem to get it. They still are closed up. You can't make them see. No matter what you do, you can't make people see.

D: *If you were to talk to them, what would you tell them that they need to see?*

T: That they're not physical. They're not who they think they are when they look in the mirror. That they are anything they can imagine. That they are a part of a whole different life than what the Earth presents to you. So individualized, so separated, so split. You've got to go there, but you've got to come back. They're not coming back to where they should be. They're staying individualized. They're thinking they are an individual, when they're back together. I can't explain.

D: *They see themselves as an individual.*

T: Cut off. That's how I sort of feel, too because I feel cut off from what I'm supposed to do. So I still have that part in me, too.

D: *So you're supposed to show people that they aren't individuals?*

T: That's what I want to do. That you're all part of a whole. I don't know how to do that.

D: *So how did you come to Earth to make this change?*

T: I remember coming down as a walk-in for a very short period of time. I believe I was in a man's body in England. I work so much on the other side when they pass over, but they have such set ideas and sometimes it takes a long time before they realize where they are. It was in war time ... so many died. The confusion makes you more afraid when you pass over. It makes the self harder to find. The shell's off and is so thick and heavy with fear that it's hard for them to find out who they are. And it takes a long time on the other side to break through that. I thought maybe I could help on this side, and so I did. I took over the body for, I don't know, three months. The original soul decided to leave it and not take it anymore. He couldn't take the death. He did not like seeing the death. That's what I wanted to do. I wanted to see if I could make a difference on this side before they passed over. And some yes, some no, so I went back again. I went back and came here as a physical person to continue.—I wanted to be some kind of light or some kind of help or some kind of interpreter. I didn't know how exactly I was going to do it, but I wanted to be here for the changes.

D: *Is this when you decided to come into the body that became Tonya?* (Yes) *You came as a baby that time.*

T: Yes. My parents were good people. They were gentle people. They would give me the room I needed. The opportunity was available at the time and I was in a hurry. Things would start to happen. More people were aware of UFOs, if nothing else. I thought this would be a shoo-in, but it wasn't.

D: (Laugh) *It never is, is it?*

Tonya was one of those rare people who remembers everything from her birth and her childhood. Usually those very early memories of the other side and the birth etc. are forgotten when one enters the baby's body. Her parents didn't discourage the memories, and even encouraged her to remember and talk about them.

T: I forgot some of the lives, but the ones I remember usually have to do with people I know in this life. A couple of my lives, I've had friends that I have in this life. I've been able to identify them.—I did not forget because I didn't want to be cut off. I wanted the lessons. I wanted to remain connected as much as I could, and I seemed to be able to do it.

D: *Do you think you are helping to influence people?*

355

T: Sometimes I don't even realize how much. Sometimes I think not at all, but I guess I am.

D: *Do you realize anything is happening now to the Earth, now that you're here?*

T: Yes. I can feel the changes. And many people do. I'm not the only one. Many people know that things are going on. Many things are changing. That's what I want to be a part of. I feel like I'm missing something.

D: *What do you mean?*

T: I feel so closed in. I don't know exactly. I feel tight and closed in. (She became uncomfortable.) I know there are others here. Where are they? (Crying) Where are they? Why am I closed off? That's why I feel closed off. I don't know where they are.

I decided to call forth the SC and I asked it why it chose to bring this information forth for Tonya to see.

T: That's where she feels she is. If that's where you feel you are, that's what you see. Not to waste time. Condense and get it over with.

I asked about her purpose in this lifetime, and the SC indicated that the time was not right to know. She would know later. "She's impatient. That's why her life has been so tough. She's impatient to get stuff done. She's doing things. More than she knows. We think we're nothing sometimes." They didn't want to give her any advice at this time. "Go on with what you're doing. It will come. The answers she needs. The answers she's looking for. They will come to her. The books she needs, and the places she needs to go. They will come if she needs to do it.—Changes are coming. She will be happy. She will be pleased with the changes, but there is a little time yet. In Earth years, your time, it seems like forever, but it's such a short moment away. Everything is going to change in the world ... quick changes.—There are vibrational changes that will change the attitudes and minds of people. It depends on what their weaknesses are. Those weaknesses will become stronger unfortunately, and their strengths will become stronger as well. For it will vibrate at the rate it will affect them, and how they are affecting the vibration. How they vibrate will be exaggerated. Exhilarated. So there are many ... it's very similar to death. Where you vibrate from is death, or death of the body is where you go to."

When people die and go to the spirit side they can only go to those places that match their vibration. There are different levels of learning, and they are each more advanced according to your development. You always hope that you will at least go back to the same vibration that you left. You don't want to have to go to a lower frequency and then climb back up. But you can never go higher until your vibration is equal to that level. I assumed the SC was making a comparison between that state and moving to the equivalent vibration when the changes come. This is one reason why the very negative people will not be able to move to the New Earth. They cannot change their vibration that quickly. It has to be a gradual process.

D: *There are many places you can go on the other side, aren't there?*

T: Yes, there are. Some go only by themselves, if that's what they see; some with groups.

D: *You can never go where you're not vibrating at the same frequency. Is that right?*

T: Yes, and that is what will happen in this part. At this Earth time, too, there are vibrations going on and where you are and who you are and what you vibrate at will affect what happens to you and where you will go.

D: *You said some people are vibrating at a lower frequency?*

T: They have hard times.

D: *More of the negative frequency?*

T: Yes, and that is sad because it is so unnecessary.

D: *They won't even know what's happening.*

T: No. (Deep sigh and distress over it.)

357

D: *Will this affect the physical Earth?*

T: Yes. The more negative Earth will respond ... the changes ... the violent changes ... so unnecessary.

D: *What kind of physical changes? I've been told that many catastrophes are going to continue. Is that true?*

T: Yes ... slowly, but they will continue. The Earth will cleanse itself, too. You know that. It has to. It has a life of its own, as well. It's real. It is taking on all of these changes in itself, as well with each person that changes, that is living on its Earth and living in its system. It will react to that system ... each system ... in its way.

D: *Those that are vibrating at a positive level, how do their lives change?*

T: If there is death of the body, it will be a lightening kind of feeling. A light ... the veil will be thinner. It won't be a frightening, scary thing for them. They'll find themselves on the other side with ease. Some will be taken to other places. So many different situations ... some will stay on the Earth. Some will survive ... not many though, but those that don't and they still are negative ... (Deep sigh) ... they find themselves somewhere else, or they find themselves on the negative side of the Earth.—It's a change, as I said; it will change into many different aspects. There will be a darker side. There will be a lighter side. There will be an out of this Earth side. There will be a dimensional side. There are so many different changes that will happen. It's like a starburst. There's still matter. There's all that energy. There's fiery hot energy, some cold energy. Just so many different levels.

D: *So many things can happen at your different vibration?* (Yes) *I have heard the negative part will be for those that have created that part?* (Yes) *So others of us will go somewhere else?*

T: Either physical; others in spirit. The body may die off.

D: (I knew she had been talking about the New Earth.) *I've been told so much and it's still confusing.*

T: It is confusing. It's confusing for us, too because there are so many different possibilities. It depends on how many people are aware at the time of transition. That can determine which kind of life is more prevalent.

D: *I have been told there are many people, like Tonya, that have come in to help with this.* (Yes) *And just by being here, she is doing a lot, isn't she?*

T: Yes, and all are. All the young ones are much more different than the old ones. The old ones unfortunately, are the ones that are still in positions that are damaging not only the Earth, but the souls of people.

Going on to her questions. Some have been omitted because they were not relevant to this book. "She felt she's had contact with ETs. Can you tell her anything about that?

T: She has been a so-called ET. She has been a gray though not one of the smaller ones ... one of the larger grays.

D: *I know the difference between the two.* (Yes) *She knew from an earlier age that she had contact with them.*

T: Yes. They have often made contact with her and she with them.

D: *Why were they still contacting her?*

T: There were things to do.

D: *What kind of things?*

T: We cannot say at this time. (She was smiling, so I knew it couldn't be something bad.) Experiences that deal with the future.

D: *Is she still having contact with them?*

T: Oh, yes ... not so much out-of-body, but she can think with them and they can talk to her. She will continue to have contact. They have said to her, "We will come back for you in the end."

D: *What does that mean?*

T: We will come back for her in the end. (Laugh)

D: *Do you mean to help her when she gets ready to cross over?*

T: We cannot say at this time. (Smiling.)
D: *I have found in my work with the ETs that they are positive, good people.*
T: Oh, yes.

No matter how I tried to reword the questions, they wouldn't supply any more information, just that she would know in time.

Physical: Sometimes a problem with blood sugar because she doesn't eat when she should or eats too much when she does. It will not hurt her, but she should be aware of it.

D: *What happens when we don't eat at the times we are supposed to?*
T: It puts stress on the body ... makes you more tired, makes you more disconnected ... or out too much and not in enough.
D: *What do you mean, out too much and not in enough?*
T: She has a tendency sometimes to not fully come back as much as she should.
D: *Do you mean she is doing this constantly during the day?*
T: No, usually at night and then when she wakes up.—Not eating when you're supposed to ... there is a strain in the body, especially when you're doing certain kinds of work: physical work or spiritual mental work. They both put a strain on the body. It affects the sugar level. She is an irregular eater. The body is a little confused because her mind is a little confused. Like I say, she is out there more than most people. She is still functioning, but she does have to be careful and pay attention.

Message: She knows she is never alone, and she's always accepted and she knows basically who she is ... just to have patience. That is not her virtue. That's something she's lacked from many lives, is patience. Patience is so necessary when things do not just depend on one entity, and she knows this, but she wants to hurry things along. She cannot hurry things. She can help change them, but she cannot hurry them.

Energy

Chapter 25

THE PINK ENERGY FROM
THE CRYSTAL PLANET

When Anna came into the scene she floated down to what she called a "star." When she got to the surface it was quite rocky, but with large formations of crystals. They were huge, clear, beautiful crystals, almost making a mountain shape. "They are big ... bigger than me. The atmosphere is blue, and the ground seems blue as the sky. The crystals look like mountains and there are large ones like a crystal cluster with smaller ones mixed in. I am on a flat, blue surface. Everything seems to be a blue tint. It's as if it's a crystal mountain range, and there is a flat, blue land on the ground in front of me." I asked her how she perceived her body, and she said it was transparent. "It's a very beautiful clear, not white, transparent. And there's something pink around me. The inside of me is a pink structure that is surrounded by a transparent bright, soft colored skin. I can see the pink in my hands and there's a pink line going up my arm and up into my chest where it's larger, and then down through my legs. I know I have arms and legs, but I have a hard time seeing them."

D: *Is the pink that goes through your body like a circulatory system?*
A: That's kind of the idea that it looks like, yes. The skin, the outside, the see-through, is as if it's transparent, but light.
D: *What is your face like? How do you perceive that?*
A: It feels like I don't have any hair. (Chuckle) I can feel my face, and it feels a little different. My eyes are different.

They are moved more towards the sides of my head. My nose is different, and I don't think I have any ears.

Even though the body seems strange, she was comfortable with it, and the crystal place seemed very familiar. "I feel the blue. It's almost a silky, sandy feeling on the ground that is blue. And as I stand, I can feel that something in the ground is coming up through my feet and connecting with whatever this pink is inside. Energy coming through my feet where they're touching the ground. It feels wonderful. It feels right. It's familiar. I feel like I should probably move. I want to see more of where I'm at. All I'm seeing right now is this wrap around center area of this blue. It's not sand. It's more silky, more like a silk. It's more connected than a piece of silk would be. But it's not a solid piece of anything. It moves when I move my feet, and my feet are transparent."

As she looked around she became aware of something. "There are others over to my left, around the mountains, around these crystals. Others that are looking at me."

D: *Other beings like you?* (Yes) *So you're not alone there, are you?*

A: No, I'm not alone. They're standing back a bit but they're looking at me. It looks like maybe eight.

D: *Do you recognize these beings?*

A: Yes, they are just like me.

D: *So these are beings that you know?*

A: Yes. I see one noticing me who seems ... Oh! The pink is brightening. I think it's a greeting. A "Hello" inside this one. I felt it's a ... him. And I feel like I am lighting up as well. It's a happy feeling. He is walking towards me. He wants to take me over towards the others. We are walking and the ground is all blue. We don't have anything on our feet or clothing, but it feels normal. He is holding onto my left arm, and we're walking happy. I can't tell he's smiling, but I know he's happy because he's bright pink inside. I'm happy. (Laugh) We're going to the others and there's a square building that they're standing in front of. It looks like a house with two white pillars right in the center ... no, they're two large crystals in the center. Now I'm looking at the others and everyone is lighting up. And I feel like I'm getting brighter than any of them. (Chuckle) I feel like I'm *home!* It's a wonderful feeling! I feel like I've been gone, but they're welcoming me. And there are others I can see coming from further to the left. There are the eight and I know them very closely.

D: *Do they want to take you inside the building?*

A: I think that's what they want to do. They're not speaking. The pink that runs through us is lighting up to each other, and we are welcoming each other that way.

D: *Communicating in that way rather than with words?*

A: Yes. I feel it very, very strongly, and all through here (the middle part of her body) is just bright.—I'm going inside and I'm looking at these pillars, these crystals on each side of the entrance. I don't know how high they are, but probably fifteen feet high ... just straight, not clustered like the mountains.

When she entered the building the ground seemed to go downward in a deep slope. "It looks like I'm inside of a spinning top ... a slope. I'm standing on the edge of this slope, and he's with me holding my arm. And the others are there. I'm not sure if I'm supposed to slide down this slope. (Chuckle) It looks as if it's silver and brown that comes to a point and that's not much area to maneuver around. He's urging me to slide. Okay, I want to make sure he comes with me.—Yeah, he's coming. Wow! We went and I slid. I thought we would be stuck, but there was a hole in the middle to slide through. And I dropped and he dropped after me. (Laugh) So we're both here.

D: *Where's here?*

A: It's blue again. I feel he is talking to me, rather than hearing him. "Come ... come with me. Everything's okay. We welcome you."

D: *Ask him where we are.*

A: A hall? I don't know what kind of hall. He's taking me in. There are many others here. We must be underneath the building. The one I fell through. There are many others here. We all look the same. Now they're starting to light themselves, too. It's a big group. I feel I'm being welcomed back. (She started to sob softly.) There are too many to count. It's some kind of wide, round room.

D: *Ask him, "What is this place?"*

A: I think I need to ask someone else. He keeps saying I've returned. He seems very excited. I think I need to ask someone else. There are many here so I will do that.— Now I'm having both of my hands taken. Oh, we are all joining hands. I am sharing through my hands to them and they are sharing to the ones that are holding hands and so on.

D: *What are you sharing?*

A: Everything ... everything ... they have access to all of my pink insides, my energy that's making me who I am. I can give that to them through my hands. But also my thoughts and my feelings. I can see them pulsing in a *big* circle. We're holding hands and I spread it to the one next to me, and it is spread on and on and on.

D: *Are they also sharing with you?*

A: They're not right now.

D: *Mostly they're sharing you?*

A: Yes, we're sharing. It makes me feel good to be doing this. My energy has information that I'm giving them.

D: *What are they going to do with the information?*

A: They're using it. They're going to keep it in order to ... oh, they're learning. They want to know mistakes. They're wanting to know the kind of mistakes they could avoid with this information ... that they have not made that they could avoid.

D: *Mistakes that you have made?*

A: The mistakes that I have seen in other people.

D: *So not necessarily what you may have done, but what you have watched?*

A: Yes. They're looking for something on a grander scale. Not just my personal mistakes... mistakes of the planet. They don't want to make the same mistakes that I've seen. They don't want to make mistakes that will hurt this place.

D: *Where they are? Do you mean it's a different place?*

A: I'm on a star and I was watching mistakes, like cataclysmic mistakes. Big mistakes. They want to know as much as they can so they can avoid these mistakes. This is a very peaceful, beautiful, light filled, blue place.

D: *Do they mean mistakes that have happened on Earth?* (Yes) *Then they know you have come from Earth, so you have seen many things.*

A: Yes, and many times I have been on Earth a long time.

D: *But you said this place was your home.*

A: (Sadly) It is and I can feel it.

D: *Why did you leave if it was such a beautiful place?*

A: I wanted to help. I feel there are so many of us, but I feel as if we are all one and connected. And the pink energy that is within us is all connected. We are all sharing it through each other as we hold hands.

D: *But you decided to leave that beautiful place and come to Earth?*

A: Yes. I wanted to help. No one wants to make the same mistakes here that have happened on Earth, to disrupt this peace. It needs to stay this way.

D: *It sounds like a beautiful place where there wouldn't be any mistakes.*

A: It is. It's very beautiful and no one feels as if anything is going to happen. I think this was *my* own idea to go to Earth. This is what I wanted to give them.

D: *Did anybody tell you to go?*

A: No, they supported me. We share it through this area (motioning to her abdomen). We share a support.

D: *How did you know that Earth needed help?*

A: The crystals can transmit signals.

D: *So they were picking up signals from Earth?*

A: No. The crystals can transmit signals, but no, not from Earth. They've transmitted a signal from somewhere else.

D: *But you decided to go. Did the others want to go, too?*

A: No ... no. (Laugh) And I have a hard time with that. I know that everything will be okay, and everything will be the same. They're supportive. They're not giving me a hard time. There's one that I'm very close to and it's going to be very difficult.

D: *But you said that when you started out on this journey to Earth, you lived many lives?*

A: (Sadly) I've been on Earth for a very long time.

D: *You couldn't just go and live one life and report back?*

A: No, it's too far. The way I go to Earth was through help with the crystals.

D: *What do you mean?*

A: The crystals were able to change the pink to where I was a continuous bright white light. And my energy began to change. The crystals helped me to do this.

D: *So all the energy went?*

A: No. The blue ground actually energizes, but it also can pull it out. The pink energy is filling me and it leaves me cloudy but translucent ... but bright when the pink is gone.

D: *So only a portion, a part of you, went to Earth? Is that what you mean?*

A: Yes. I left my inner energy there to be filled with something different.

D: *And you decided when you got to Earth, you had to live many, many different lives?*

A: Yes, I needed to. I wanted to make sure that we were not as complicated, that it would never be this way. But I see now that couldn't be the reason that I went because it could not happen like that here.

D: *Explain.*

A: I went to help. I started to gather information of Earth and I started to believe that I was storing this information to help save my home so that it wouldn't become a disaster such as Earth has become, but I didn't need to do that. That wasn't the purpose. I didn't know I was doing that, but I have been doing that. The purpose was to help.

D: *The real purpose was to help the people?*

A: To help the planet ... I am not feeling necessarily, the people. The planet.

D: *You said you left the main part of your energy there? (Yes) Do you have access to draw that energy if you need it? Is there still a connection with it?*

A: Yes, it's still there. I became a shell of light that traveled and came here, but, yes, it's still there. I still call upon it. I do call upon it. It will always be there if I need it.

D: *When you came to Earth and had all these many lives, were all of them supposed to be helping the planet?*

A: I'm supposed to be helping. That's the reason I came to Earth ... to help. I started gathering negative events to bring back for some reason. At some point I started to gather cataclysmic events, things I don't want to happen at home. I've been gathering this information inside, but I don't need to bring that information back to them.

D: *You mean, for some reason, you started collecting the negative events rather than the positive?*

A: Not only negative. Unknowingly, I was trying to gather this information to bring back because I had seen the terrible things that had happened here, and I don't want that to ever happen at home. So I started collecting things that I thought would help, so that it would never be that way. But we don't need any of that. We're all one.—I've been gone a long time. I know many traumatic events and this makes me afraid that this could happen at home. And I almost would think on a cellular level because I don't realize. And the fear of it happening there was known that I've seen so many deaths.

D: *But you've also had many positive experiences?* (Yes) *It hasn't all been the negative things.*

A: No, and that is all within me. I was sharing all of that with them. Everything.

I thought it was time to bring the session back to the client. "Do you know you're speaking through a human body now when you're talking to me?"

A: Yes, but I see myself in this other form.

D: *You've gone through many other lives, why did you decide to come into the body of Anna?*

A: It was timing and I had to take the opportunity of the timing to come back. It was pretty quick, but the timing was right.

D: *Why is the timing so important?*

A: I knew that I had to be born right at this exact time. The time has to be exact when you come back to Earth. The exact moment, and my exact moment was very quickly after I left the last life.

D: *So you left one life and went right into another one? They were very close together?*

A: Yes. I didn't take time to rest.

D: *It's usually good to rest between lives, isn't it?*

A: Yes, especially if you have something traumatic. I wanted to come back. I had to catch the right moment, that I wanted to be *me*, and it had to happen right then. And I wanted to help people at this time.

D: *It was just a fast turnaround?*

A: I knew what I wanted and I was ready.

D: *But Anna has had some difficult times in this life, hasn't she?*

A: Yes. Lessons learned. Different. This life I came in to focus on people, not the planet.

Anna had been working in hospitals as a hospice nurse taking care of people who were dying. But she stopped doing that. "Was it too much, too hard or what?"

A: No longer able to care. No longer able to touch and care for them as they passed. Not what she wanted.

She had become confused because she didn't know what she was supposed to be doing. This was causing physical problems. I knew the SC had come in without being called, so I asked it to advise Anna. "She needs to be healing ... move. Move from herself and then to her family, then to others. First, she must heal before she can heal the others. She must heal herself first. She needs to stop being drawn to negative events. There is no problem with her Star. There is no problem with her home. They will be fine. She needs to let go of the fear that there will be something wrong there. She comes from the beautiful place with the crystals. She needs to learn how to access the energy from these crystals. She will be able to do this if she wishes to do so." Anna was living in her mother's house with her children. She was told to stay there for the time being. "She's in a place where she is able to learn these abilities without the negativity of the world feeding on her."

Because the SC said she must heal herself first, I asked it to look inside the body and see what it could find. The doctors had found many things wrong. It first concentrated on Anna's heart. "There is one major area in the middle of the heart that is having a hard time with the blood flow. She lost her heart when she stopped helping people pass. She needs to be aware of this. She needs to remember this." The SC said it could repair it and began working on it. "We are concentrating energy to the center. It feels as if we're pressing down. There is a valve. The center of the heart is open. The blood is flowing back and forth. The valve is letting blood freely flow and it is not meant to do that. We are using energy to push down to heal this to make it close. It is not able to close on its own." Anna began to take deep breaths. "There was blood flowing back and forth from the heart causing the bottom to become larger than the top. Now that it's closing, the blood will not flow back and forth any longer. It is repaired. It is not too enlarged that it cannot become normal size again."

I asked about her brain. The doctors said there was something wrong there. The SC looked inside and saw there were areas that looked as if scar tissue had formed. This had been caused by the blood flow in her heart. "No major part of the brain is affected by these. She should be fine with this scar tissue here. It shouldn't create any problem with any future plans."

D: *Can you remove the scar tissue? I have seen you do it before.*

A: We are trying to. Collectively, sometimes the scar tissue will pull off. That is what we are attempting. The center of her brain, the scar tissue must be dissolved. No damage has occurred that will interfere with anything. She has a good brain. Everything is functional. She doesn't need to worry about the brain.—She felt the need to heal and did not use her natural resources to do so. That is what she should do; use her stones and crystals. She can ask directly. She has access to all knowledge of this. It comes from where she is from. All of this information is already there. She can ask and know instantly. When she holds the crystals she will know.

Anna had come with a long list of physical complaints. She had also been having pain in her hips and legs. I knew what the SC would say, but I wanted *it* to tell her.

A: She is taking too much medication. She continues to heal. She will not have this discomfort anymore. It is only a forward motion she needs to take. She should not be in need of any pain medication as long as she's going in the direction she should be and using the stones and crystals. She has been closed for quite a while now. Her nausea is because she is sick with herself. She is sick with who she has become. The nausea and the aches and other things are nudges from us. She has genuinely lost her way and has been in desperate need of help to find this. The rest of her body is fine. (Cysts on her ovaries.) Now that she has given *birth* to her new purpose she will know that she can contact the energy she left at home and that will give her the answers. The depression she is experiencing is from her own making. She needs to come off the depression medication more slowly because she will be ready to run after a new mission. And as she does that, the pills will go. The depression pill is the only one that must be taken off slowly. It will be fine to stop the other medications. The thyroid is not a problem. She is fine. She is ready to speak and listen so she can stop taking this pill.

D: *I'm always hesitant to tell people to stop taking medications.*

A: If she wants, she can come off of them slower, but she is okay to stop. She doesn't need to return to the doctors. They make it worse for her. They bring negativity to her. They make her speak more negativities. She needs to speak in the positive.

D: *When we began the session, why didn't you take her to a past life?*

A: She went to the Star. She needed to be grounded. She needed to see home. She needed to know that her home is safe. Her going back to her home has created a feeling of safety in her that she has needed for a long time. She starts to doubt and starts to wonder, and we let her know.

Anna had a question about an unusual experience that she thought had to do with ETs or some unusual type of beings. She and some friends had seen the beings coming toward them across a field at night.

A: She was in a place that is frequently visited by some of us. It is a place of healing. It is a place where we take samples. We came here, *we* meaning *they.* I am not one of them. We came here to take samples. She and her friends happened to be there. So we changed form and waited for them to leave.

D: *I thought so because she said she first had a glimpse of a different type of being, and they changed form to be something that wouldn't be frightening?* (Yes) *But she and her friends weren't supposed to be there?*

A: No. They were just there at the same time.

D: *What kind of samplings were they taking?*

A: They were taking water samplings. The springs that they were at, the water that they were at, leads down in the earth for miles. They were taking samples of these rocks that are down into the deep parts of the earth. And this was a very accessible way to get them. The heat ... they are looking for new places to find things we all use. It is a natural spot we go to. There are many different things found down in the earth in that area.

D: *I know in the past they have taken samples of humans to see how the body is functioning. Is that correct?*

A: Yes. There is never any harm or intent. It is only the fear. There is no one out here to hurt. There is no way. It is not allowed. We cannot harm. The only beings that you will see are to monitor that you are okay. When you enter into a trance-like state we can heal you without pain, but oftentimes we need to take people to heal them. As they do have important work and they are not waking up to that. But we are not ready to let them die from this life yet.

D: *That's what I always say, "All they are doing is taking care of their own."* (Yes) *To make sure they are safe here because they do get caught up in these Earth things. Just the way Anna did.*

A: Yes, it is easy to do. There are many, many who have come from different homes, who have gotten caught up and lost, too. She has to remember who she is, and where her home is. That will keep her grounded and positive.

Parting message: Remember just to remember. Remember your home. Remember everyone is there for you. We are all here. You feel as though you ask and you do not receive, but that is not always. We do hear. You just need to listen and be positive and open yourself up so you can receive the answers.

***

D: *Can I ask you a question?* (Yes) *We are having all these terrible storms and tornadoes happening here one right after another. A weather phenomenon of nature.*

We had experienced the most tornadoes ever recorded in one month, and the deadliest. In May 2011, Joplin, Mo. had been devastated. "Is there a reason why this is increasing at this time? (June 2011)"

A: Yes. The Earth is repairing itself. You are seeing small signs now. The Earth will go into full repair mode. The physical Earth will repair itself after its energy leaves.

D: *What do you mean, "After the energy leaves?"*

A: It is as if you are a body, and you do not want to be in your body when you die. You have a choice to leave your body before it happens. The Earth energy does not want to be here when it changes, after it goes through all of its healing. There is going to be tremendous changes, uprooting, and pain for the Earth. The Earth's energy will leave to another plane before it starts having injury. It does not want to. It's had enough.

D: *Does this go along with what you've told me about the New Earth?*

A: This is the New Earth.

D: *So it is leaving? I always tell people it's evolving. It's going into its next incarnation.* (Yes) *Will it repair itself then?*

A: Yes. There will be tornadoes. There will be earthquakes. It will completely be rearranged by the time it's done and the Earth has had enough. The Earth does not want to stay in that. It will still exist. It just doesn't want to stay, as you wouldn't stay with a body that is suffering as it is dying.

D: *But if it's going to remain, won't there have to be an energy there to keep the old Earth alive, if I am using the right words?*

A: The energy leaving is not planning on going back to that old Earth. It will be a place that can be inhabited, but it will not be as of that Earth. That Earth will be a more dormant area. It will not be alive anymore.

D: *That part of the Earth is dying?* (Yes) *What about those left behind in that part?*

A: They will be suffering what the Earth has decided it does not want to suffer. They will be left. They will not be punished. They will not be judged. They will continue onwards when they pass.

D: *Because I've been told they can't change fast enough to go with the New Earth.*

A: No, they cannot.

D: *All of this is so complicated.*

A: It is. It is a process that the Earth has been wanting for so very long. It is tired of being picked on. So those of you that are going to be inhabiting the New Earth, you need to be gentle and you need to take care and you will because there will be no other way. That is what you will carry with you.

D: *So that's why we've been having all these storms and damage.*

A: This is just the beginning. It's going to get much worse, and when it does, the Earth's energy will leave. And at that time, those who are ready to leave will leave with it. Those who are aware, are going to be able to move with the energy of the Earth. They will be able to go. They will not have to stay behind as long as they don't start creating doubt and fear. That is what will keep them behind. You are feeling the changes of the energy of the Earth. The energy of the Earth is speeding up and trying to leave. It doesn't want to suffer any more. We are part of that Earth. We are tempered for this Earth and we are also continuing to speed up to go with it.

D: *When this happens, when the energy of the Earth does move to the New plane, will we notice a difference when we go with it?*

A: Yes, we will notice a difference. It will be a more spiritual energy. It will be a more light energy. You will feel more weightlessness, no more negativity. There will be no more earthquakes, no more tornadoes. It will be very evident there has been a change.

D: *But many people won't even be aware it's happening, I guess?*

A: No, those who are behind will not. They will be suffering with the Earth's body.

D: *You've told me before that, "Nobody really knows what's going to happen because it's never happened before."*

A: No, it hasn't. The Earth has had so many life forms on it and it has been a planet that was able to support so many life forms that it has taken so much abuse. It is a living thing just like we are, a living being, and it is tired. It is ready to pass over. It will still exist, as it always has, but it will not exist as a physical. Everyone is excited. Everyone feels for this Earth. Everyone who has watched, has seen the pain that this Earth has gone through. Everyone wants the Earth to succeed, but also the people, of course. Everyone would want the best scenario to be that way, but those who are feeling changes are in tune to the Earth. They are feeling the Earth changing. They will be able to go when the Earth goes.

D: *I'm told it is going to be a beautiful place.*

A: Yes. There will be no more pain on the Earth ... no more pain for us.

D: *I guess we will continue our work though.*

379

A: Yes, we will but it will be from a different point of view completely. The negativity will not exist. There are many who are wondering, many wanting to know "when." It is speeding up. We are seeing these things, these storms, seeing the effects from these and the oceans on the Earth, on the ground. These are signs that the Earth is going to continually get worse.

D: *It won't affect us anyway?*

A: No. It won't.

D: *Then there's no reason for fear.*

A: No, not at all. Fear is what will hold you back from transferring with the Earth.

I have written a great deal about the New Earth in my book, *The Three Waves of Volunteers and the New Earth.*

Chapter 26

CREATING ENERGY

This session was done in my hotel room in Laughlin, Nevada, when I was there speaking at the UFO Conference in 2008.

Connie didn't wait for the entire induction. She was already there immediately. She began describing a large domed building, and beautiful patterns inside the dome.

C: I'm standing on the floor looking up at the ceiling. There are star shapes and gold patterns on the ceiling coming through the green glass.—Now it's changing and moving.—I'm out in space somewhere, where all these patterns keep coming in and out. Designs and waves of motions and colors and lights. It's like I'm part of it. Oh, it feels wonderful! It's beautiful.

D: *Are you part of the designs or part of the space or what?*

C: It's like I'm creating all of these different colors and designs and patterns and waves, that flow in and out. But I feel like it's also my *body.*

D: *What do you mean?*

C: It's like it's part of my body that I am. My body is light and waves, and it passes in and out. But always a clear blue sky color is in the center. It's like pulses going up, and I'm creating the patterns. I'm the pattern and the creator at the same time. Oh, it's a wonderful feeling! There's even rainbows that come around. It's gorgeous.

D: *Do you have any desire to go and do anything?*

C: No. I just want to play with it.

I was trying to get her to go somewhere and see a past life. But she was enjoying this.

C: See how bright I can make the blue colors coming down. It's gorgeous. And every once and a while there are little flashes. Clear white light that comes in. Looks like a flashlight. It's me. I'm sending out these waves and lights.

D: *Do you get the feeling you're by yourself, or are there others with you?*

C: I feel like I'm by myself, and yet I'm not alone. But there's really no sense of.... There are no voices or sounds ... although there could be. I have the feeling that other energies can create the same thing. It's a wonderful feeling. Peaceful. Quiet. Like you're part of it and you're surrounded in it. Not thinking. It's just letting it come and go as it wants to.

D: *Could you direct it if you wanted to?*

C: I think I can. But I don't feel like doing that. Just letting it be. Like waves of ocean coming over you, or the wind.

D: *Just a part of everything.* (Yes) *Do you feel like you've been there a long time or what?*

C: Yes, I feel like it always has been something like this. It's always been something you can touch into and feel.

I knew I had to move this somehow because she was quite content to stay there.

D: *But you don't have any desire to go and do anything else.* (No) *So you don't have a body of any kind, do you?*

C: No. There's no body. It's as if the colors and the waves and the patterns are what you are. You know what it is. You know what you are. You know there's no limit to it. No restrictions. It's like you're suspended, but you're not suspended. It's *very* hard to explain.

D: *But the main thing is it's a good feeling, and you can use it, if you wanted to. Otherwise it's just a good place to be.*

(Pause) *Do you come to a time when you want to leave that place?*

C: I guess if I started thinking about something. It's not *I. It* wants to change. (Pause) It's almost as though constantly in motion, and yet you're still.

D: *Like being a stillness within the motion or what?*

C: Yes. Like you're in motion and yet you're not in motion. You're steady.

D: *But you said, it's possible it might want to change?*

C: Well, if you start taking it in and sending it back out, it's different.

D: *But you said* it *wants to change. I was wondering why you used that word.*

C: Well because there's no *thing* in it. There's no mass of it. It just *is.* There's no identity.

D: *That's why you call it "it"?* (Yes.) *But you said, if you send out something in a direction, it would decide to follow it?* (Right) *What do you mean by that?*

C: Because then it can start using it and create something with it.

D: *Otherwise, it just flows and it has no direction.*

C: It's like an idea, and you start to build on that idea.

D: *Where does the idea come from?*

C: It's already there. You just grasp it.

D: *So every possibility is there? Would that be a good way to say it?*

C: I think so.

D: *So you said, if something starts to go in a different direction, you can follow it?*

C: Yes because you can go in any direction you want. You can go in a circle. There's no limit. I guess you could say it's like something that just is, and you can follow it. And when you're done with it, you can go back and do something else.

D: *You return to that place then.*

C: Wherever. Or create a new place.

D: *But if you become curious, what do you create?*

C: Well, you take something, and it's like clay. And you start shaping it, and see what it becomes. But if it's a color that you find, it becomes that color. And you can just shape it.

D: *Let's do that and see what happens.* (Pause) *Do you think of a color or what?*

C: Yes. I have a yellow color, kind of a pale yellow. And I'm making a fan out of it. I'm shaping it into ... like a feathery fan. And it's light. And it has little white stripes in it. And now it just goes out. And now I'm using it to make waves. Like you're fanning it back and forth. And now I want to reshape it into butterfly wings. Now there's some orange.

D: *That sounds like fun just to be able to create things.* (Yes.) *When you create these things, do they remain?*

C: As long as I want them to.

D: *Become solid?*

C: Hmm, a little. I gave it to the light.

D: *It stays there as long as you want it to?* (Yes.) *Then what happens?*

C: Then I just let it go out wherever it wants to go.

D: *So it remains solid in that way.*

C: Not solid like a solid heavy object would be, but it goes into a dimension where it would be seen by others.

D: *So it doesn't just dissipate?*

C: No because I created it, and so I want to send it out as a gift. I want to send it out so others can see that I created it. It's beautiful. Yellow. A beautiful feathery fan. And now it's leaving and it's going away. And I'm not sad about it because I can do it again.

D: *I was thinking that if you created it, if you took your attention away from it, it would dissipate.*

C: Well, that's what you do when you let it go. You just say, "That's it."

D: *And it doesn't just dissolve into nothing again.*

C: I *could* make it dissolve. But since I created it, I want others to see it.

D: *So that makes you happy to do that.* (Yes.) *Do you just think it, and it becomes real out of all this energy?*

C: What I'm feeling is that there's a part of the wave ... you are the wave. And you see the wave. You ride the wave of all the colors and patterns and motions. And when you decide you want to *touch* something, you just go for a ride with it and create something out of it. But you don't keep it because it's a shared thing. You send it out. And let it become as long as you want it to become.

D: *And these waves are the energies?*

C: Yes. The waves are constantly in motion. And they're colors and they're lights. Oh! And now I'm creating a galaxy! Oh, wow! It's a wheel. And it has these arms that reach out like little rivulets. And it's making this circle, and it's going out as light. And then as it moves in a circular motion, it's picking up other colors from the waves that are around *it.*

D: *Did you just decide that would be something interesting to create?*

C: Oh, it was always there. I saw this movement, and I decided to make something else out of it. And that became a galaxy.

D: *Oh. A galaxy is difficult, isn't it?*

C: No, not when you're creating it. You can start it out and whatever ... it's not about size. It's just about thinking how you want it to look. And then you just let it go. And if you want it to grow big or small, you just ... it's not about the size.

D: *But when you create the galaxy, do you create all the little parts that are in it?*

C: No, it can grow as it wants to grow.

D: *Oh, it takes over by itself?*

C: Yes. It becomes its own light.

D: *Because I was thinking that a galaxy has planets and stars.*

C: Well, there are all different sizes. But you don't determine what size when you're creating these galaxies. It takes on its own light, and it's however *they* want to be.

D: *I thought maybe you had to create all the little planets and the stars.*

C: No, there's somebody else doing that.

D: *You mean you start out with the galaxy and someone else takes over?* (Yes) *And you said it becomes alive, and it can do anything it wants.*

C: That's right because it becomes its own thought. And its own way of learning what *it* wants to do. It's like you are the starter, and it creates its own design. You give it the idea, and then it will express itself, and how much it wants to be. What it wants to contain.

D: *It takes on its own life?* (Right) *So you don't control it any more at all?*

C: No. This isn't about controlling anything. This is about just going out and having fun. And just riding out the waves. And that's all that's out there. I see its program. You can go anywhere, anytime, and do anything you want. It's wonderful.

D: *Then you said somebody else, or some other energy like yourself, takes care of the other part?*

C: Well, when it comes to galaxies because there's so much to it, everybody has a different role in it. So you start it out, and then you let somebody else do what they want to do.

D: *Oh, so they can step in and play also.*

C: Yes. When you create little *puffs* of things, it's one thing. But when you're creating something that's going to involve other life ... other energies ... other ... oh, it's hard to explain. It's like you're creating a community, and you're not the only one adding to that community. So the galaxy is actually a community, and others must contribute to it. Galaxies aren't always made. But when you do, it's a responsibility to add.... It's like the colors of the rainbow. Everybody has a different energy.

D: *But once you create something like* that, *then you have a responsibility for it.*

C: Oh, sure, you have a responsibility to see that whatever you do with it, you're sending it out. But you're always sending it out as a love, as a gift because it came from *you,* but you don't put any need to it.

D: *Then others think, "Well, this is a good idea. I'll do something else with it."*

C: Yes because that's what you do. You let it go. And it is not your responsibility to know who or what or how it was received wherever it goes. Because there's no limits. And somebody else can reshape it, once you've let it go.

D: *But galaxies end up with planets and eventually....*

C: Well, I was talking about the group who has done everything. I wasn't talking about the galaxies. The galaxy, again, is a *huge* effort by the other minds that are out there. And so, when a galaxy suddenly becomes available to create for others, then everybody has an over-role to create in it.

D: *Because I was thinking, once you start having planets within galaxies, then there are separate lifeforms, aren't there?*

C: That's true. But not all galaxies have planets. Some galaxies are just huge spiral entities that spin and spin and spin. They don't have to have planets.

D: *They're an entity by themself?* (Yes.) *What would be the purpose then? Or do they have a purpose if they're just spinning?*

C: The purpose can be to show what galaxies can do. It doesn't have to have life. It can just be like a star pattern. Like a comet that streaks through the sky. It can be a galaxy. It doesn't have to contain life. It can contain other things.

D: *What other things can it contain?*

C: Well, it can contain other beginnings of waves, of motion, that can go out and create again as a universe somewhere else.

D: *But it sounds like it is alive.*

C: It's alive, but not life as you know it.

D: *So when you create these, you are actually creating something that is alive. Does that make sense?*

C: Yes, it makes sense for what *we're* doing. (Laugh)

D: *So when you create it, it becomes alive and you let it go.*

C: I become the force. A force. I said "galaxy," because it spirals like galaxies are recognized. But it is a force into itself. And it has its own mind, but it does not have to have life. There are galaxies that contain lifeforms that want to continue on because now they are developing and redeveloping *all the time.* But a galaxy that has its own mind can just *be* without doing anything. It doesn't have to have life in it because it's life itself.

D: *I see. That means that you are part of the creator force? Would that be a good way to put it?* (Yes*) But there are all kinds of forces out there.*

C: Oh, anything. Whatever you can imagine, that's what you give it.

D: *But some people when they create things like this, sometimes it can be used in the wrong way, can't it?*

C: There's no right or wrong. It's all about just creating, and enjoying playing with energy. But energy is like waves, like ocean waves. Currents that take you here and there. They're constantly moving and traveling. But you're always at home because you never leave.

D: *What do you consider "home"?*

C: The Source.

D: *How do you see that Source?* (Pause) *How do you comprehend it?*

C: The Source is like ... you are the sum and substance of that Source. You are part *of* the Source. And when you are riding in waves of the motion of the ideas, you are always connected to the Source. So you know you are always home, whenever you want to be, but you are also always going out and riding the waves of *life.* And it's not life, it's motion. It's alive, but it's not life as in *your* life. It doesn't have an end. It can go on and on and on and on forever.

D: *So that is what you consider to be the Source?* (Yes) *And do you go out from that when you want to create?*

C: Yes. You go out and you create something for yourself. You create a place that you want to stay. Or you can create nothing. You can do whatever you want wherever you want.

D: *Does someone tell you when it's time to leave the Source?*

C: No. You are the sum and substance of everything that is. Therefore, you choose how you want it to be, or you choose nothing. Doing these things that it wants to do. But you don't have to create. There is no such thing as "having to do" anything.

D: *Then you said when you create, there is no right, there is no wrong.* (No) *It's just the way it's used or what? I'm trying to understand.* (Pause) *Because you know I'm speaking from a human perspective. You know that, don't you?*

C: Yes. But I am not present in a humanness. (Laugh)

D: *I know. That's what I'm trying to understand.*

C: (Loud laugh) Well, we are all sum and substance of each other. And there is no such thing as right or wrong. There is just existing. There is just being. You can choose not to be, but that's not wrong. You can choose to create. That's not wrong. (Emphatic) There is no right or wrong. There is just one constant *forever.* (Had difficulty explaining.) There is one constant forever, that allows who or whatever that is in that constant, to do whatever it wants to do. But yet there is no ... I do not want to say "judgment." I'm wanting to say that everything is in perfect order.

D: *But you know when people become human, they do use energy in ways that are not so good, don't they?*

C: Right. But that's because everything has a right to be what it wants to be. Everything serves a purpose. Everything that is there, every single wave of creation.

Every energy creation is saying that, "This is what I want to see, what I want to be." But it's all energy. And therefore it can never be right or wrong because all energy is the sum and substance of everything. It's only the judgment by human beings that makes it right or wrong. They put a label to it. And there is no such thing as labels in the All, in the universe, in the creation, in the place. In the place where *all* are at home.

D: *But what about when humans hurt each other? When they're in physical bodies?*

C: That is what they had decided to create.

D: *Do they have to pay anything back whenever they hurt other people? Are there any rules about things like that?*

C: If they're setting up the rules like that to give it creation, yes. When you are creating, if you create rules, then, of course, you have to follow them.

D: *You have to play by those rules then.*

C: Yes. This is why not every galaxy that is created contains lifeforms or planets because the galaxy wants to be pure light, pure energy. Expressing down into humanness is the lowest form of expression in many ways.

D: *It's a very low form?*

C: Yes, it's a low form. And yet it is a perfect picture heading back home. The Source always wants to see what it looks like. And so it gives everything to its all, to go out and be anything it wants to be. When you set up lifeforms with rules, then that's where the problems come in. It creates the problem by creating conditions and rules.

D: *But humans think there have to be rules and regulations, don't they?*

C: That's right because that's the way they create their soul situation.

D: *But if being a human is the densest, the lowest, why do energies like you decide to be humans?*

C: I guess you could just say because we want to see what it looks like. (We laughed)

D: *Because you do come into bodies and become humans, don't you?*

I was trying to bring the session around to Connie, the human.

C: Yes, and this is part of what you created. When you shape the clay, you can shape it into (big sigh) what you call "aliens," but they're not aliens and they're not ETs. They are just a thoughtform that wants to be seen. It's an idea.

D: *So they don't have to all look alike.*

C: No, no. Flowers don't look alike. Trees don't look alike. It's just a different energy pattern wave that some energy wave created. Energy waves create each other.

D: *But they work together to do that, don't they?*

C: Right. Especially when you want to create something huge as a galaxy with planets.

D: *Without cooperation, I guess it would be chaos, wouldn't it?*

C: Well, there has to be chaos, too.

D: *What do you mean?*

C: When you're creating something and you send it out, and another thought idea decides to take it apart and *really* add stuff to it, this is kind of chaos.

D: *So it's in the formative stage. Is that right?*

C: Right. And then when it's done with the chaos, some other light wave can take it and reshape it into something more. It's not solid, but it's more contained. It has its own shape. Do you know what I'm saying?

D: *Yes, I think I understand.*

C: Very often because it's a mix of so many things, it doesn't know what shape it wants to be ultimately in that life.

D: *It's still trying to decide.*

C: Right, right. It wants to just exist from the Source, so you can be and do. It's so exciting! (Laugh) And so that's why there is no judgment of right or wrong. The Source says, "Just create and let me see everything that can *ever, ever* be imagined. Ever, ever designed."

D: *No limitations to anything.*

C: No. There are no limits attached to this. It is the unbroken circle.

D: *Well, I've heard the expression, "The dreamer dreams the dream." Is this going along with what you're saying?* (Yes, yes.) *Because I've been told that all of Earth and all the people on it are just a dream.*

This is discussed in my other *Convoluted* books.

C: (Smugly) That's right! That's right.

D: *I'm trying to understand that more.* (Pause) *I've always wanted to know, "Who is the dreamer?"*

C: (Laugh) Well, you can be the dream or the dreamer. You can be both. At the same time.

D: *That's why it's more complicated.*

C: That's right because the human, the densest form of understanding, can't understand. That's because it's been allowed to not understand. But everything is being allowed to be anything that anything can be. You see, that's why there is no such thing as learning because everything is all. All is all. Everything exists within and out. And therefore everything that has ever been shown, ever been known, is always liked and appreciated. No matter what it is.

D: *Because whenever I was told, the dreamer dreams the dream, I was trying to figure out, "Who was the dreamer?"* (Laugh) *So we are* both *then.*

C: We are the sum and substance of *all* expression.

D: *One question I have always asked that they would never answer, was, "What would happen if the dreamer wakes up?"*

C: That's a good question.

D: *If we are just all a dream. What do you think?*

C: Because the dream is not a dream in the sense that you perceive it, a dream. (Pause) We again are the sum and substance of All. Let us say, that a wave comes out from the Source because that's how the Source sends out its thoughts. A wave. And that wave says, "I wish to create a certain thing." And that wave says, "I want to be a dreamer. And I want to be a dreamer for as long as I wish to dream." You could have set a pattern of a limit. Not time, but a limit.

D: *In that way the dreamer is like a creator.*

C: That's right. And when that wave has finished being a dreamer, then in a sense it will wake up.

D: *Then what happens to the dream that it created, if it wakes up?*

C: Well, the dreamer wakes up, and then starts over again. Everything has a beginning, in the sense that the wave goes out. That is the beginning of the wave from Source. And it could go on *forever*, as long as it wants to dream. Until it wants to go back and start all over again. But it's always a circle. And so the symbols in the circle show you that you can stay, then you wish to start as a new wave. And you go off, and you limit yourself to *one thing*. That's the dream of the dreamer.

D: *But then does the dream continue to exist, or does it dissipate and dissolve, when the dreamer has its limits and wakes up?*

C: It depends on how the dreamer wanted to end it. And renew itself. It doesn't have to be a dream.

D: *But all the parts, the components of the dream just return to another type of energy.* (Right) *So nothing is ever destroyed.* (No, no.) *I think that is what people worry about. Do they just cease to exist?*

C: No. Nothing's ever.... What creation means ... you start out as a wave, again. And then you decide that this is a limitation. Again, it is the universal mind. And every little wave that goes out—and I say "little," because it actually does start out as a small wave of "idea." I guess I can say it that way. Then you take on colors and whatever you are creating, as you go out. You actually are, in a sense, the dreamer. You put a limitation on how far out you want to go with that particular idea. When you decide to end that idea, you can also say, "I want to begin again right here." And go from there in a different direction.

D: *You can go off and do something else then.*

C: Right. Each wave is a dreamer. And it says it is designing. Dreaming and designing are almost the very same thing. Let's say ten waves go out. Each has its own idea of how it wants to dream the dream. And where it wants to stop. Because, in order to recreate you have to have a sort of conclusion to that particular wave. But then it reinforces itself, and you set it in its motion in another way.

D: *That's what I was trying to understand. I guess I was thinking if a dreamer were dreaming and we were part of its dream and its existence, that it had control over us. It's a feeling of vulnerability, I guess.*

C: Right. In a sense, you could say that. But then maybe as that dreamer is dreaming *you*, you had already decided to be part of that dream, before it dreamt it.

I laughed. I decided that we had gone as deep into this morass as we could without bending my poor mind any further. So I decided to focus on Connie, the client, and hopefully bring us back onto familiar ground.

D: *But are you aware that you are speaking through a physical body right now?*

C: Yes, in a way because I feel the shivering of it.

D: *But why did you decide to come down and enter a physical body? If you had all of this power, if that's the right word?*

C: (Sigh) Because it is a deciding ... making a moment. You see, in the source of All, in the wave of all energy, in the true matrix of the true light of everything—I don't know if

I'll be able to explain this.—It is again about, "What would that feel like?" Because the Source, in its infinity, says, "I want this wave to go out and show me something different." It gives you the idea, "Go create, and go create what comes to you." And when you create what comes to you, the Source says, "Ah!" You never actually ever repeat, in even the tiniest detail, the same thing again. That's what creation is all about. It's creating. It's like in the human world, where we are in this moment in time. You could sit in the same place every day looking at the same mountain, and you would never, never see it in the same way every day for the rest of your life.

D: Hmm. Even though we think we do.

C: That's right! But that's because you're in this density that limits you to thinking that's what your limit is. And your limit isn't that. It's limitless. You are *forever!!*

D: (Laugh) *But in this case, you decided to enter the body that we call "Connie"?* (Yes.) *And to experience something through her?* (Yes.) *And have you also experienced other human bodies?*

C: Oh, yes! Many times.

D: *All for different lessons. Is that right?*

C: Well, you see ... it happens. But they're not really lessons. They're expressions of all that can possibly be there. They're expressions in the densest, densest form. And this is why this body, Connie, likes miniatures because she sees in the miniature scale the reality of the Source. Because that's what human beings are. At one time Earth had giants because that's what giants wanted to be. And you could walk on a bigger planet. Earth is a very small, small planet.

D: *I've heard that.*

C: Oh, yes, yes, yes. And so to humans because Earth is small, the Earth is everything. The Earth is density. It is in a way, a struggle for you. But that's because, again, that's what you all designed it to be. Rarely does one person, or one wave—I would rather say "wave" because that's what we are—design this Earth for one person to experience. It's a community.

D: *A community of beings or energies.*

C: That's right. And so when there are galaxies out there that have no planets, it's because there's a community that's agreeing that this should be a galaxy that doesn't have beings, humans. Otherwise it should just be pure light circling and circling. Until somebody decides to make a galaxy with planets out of it. We shape it. Have you ever played in a sandbox? *(Yes)* You take a big sandbox and you go and create all kinds of things. Whatever you feel like doing. You leave the sandbox, and somebody else comes along and reshapes it. You left it because you enjoyed it and now you're finished with it. And when you leave, somebody else comes and they reshape it to what they want to enjoy. That's kind of like the patterns of the universe. This is why a wave can go out, and say, "This is what I'm creating for a while." And send it out, and let somebody—another wave—take it over and reshape it.

D: *With our limited minds we try to understand these things.*

C: And you cannot think with the mind.

D: *But you said that's why Connie likes to work with miniatures?*

C: Right because she sees the world as it can be, when it is in small scale in other places. (Chuckle) There are beings who live in a world smaller than this human.

D: *I've heard that. It is said there are no limitations. It just goes from the macrocosm to the microcosm, and back again.*

C: Right. But your planet Earth is unique in that it shows you, for instance, the fairy kingdom, the devas. They are very small, but they live in a world just like humans. Except that they live differently because they're lighter, but they're smaller, aren't they?

D: *Yes, they are.*

C: She believes in the devas and the angel kingdom. Everybody knows that they really do exist, and are beginning to accept them now. And she will show people that it's safe to believe that because she has always believed in them since she was a child.—So planet Earth, in its densest form, gives clues to everything that's here, what it's really like. And this is why you have always been taught to pay attention to nature because nature has the clues to your answers.

D: *I'm not sure if I should call you the subconscious. Is it all right if I refer to you like that?*

C: That's okay. I don't have a name.

D: *But I always have to label something.*

C: That's okay. We know. Dolores, we understand very well how you work. And you are working *perfectly* in your expression. And you are an expression of a beautiful light. And you will be around for a long time because you are not only doing what is *necessary* around the world, but wherever you go you leave a deposit of your essence.

D: *I've been told that before. They said that's why it's important for me to travel to certain places.*

C: You must always continue because of your essence. You are carrying what we would call "a person of white light." Wherever you go, whoever you touch, whoever you work on in sessions, you are giving them *more* than you realize. More than *they* realize. You are passing on a dream. *You* are the dreaming dreamer. And you are fully awake. And when you give your presence to them, everyone that you touch, when you hug them or you shake their hands, you are passing on something special.

D: *I'm doing my job.*

C: You are ... it's not a job. It's your love, and you are planting seeds. Do you know what a seed is?

D: *Well, I keep saying that maybe I plant a few seeds.*

C: You are planting seeds. When you gave your lecture yesterday—or whenever that was (at the UFO Conference)—and you hesitated. The universe—we call it the universe—was saying to you, "Go ahead." And there was a certain amount of people sitting there who said,

"Yes." There was a consciousness voice that was sending back to you the thought, "Go ahead. It's safe right now for you to say it."

D: *It's time for people to know these things.*

C: Right. And it was correct. You were doing what you were being told to do. You are a beautiful light for the world. And you're going around planting your seeds. And guess what? You are the way-shower of those who will come right after you, and continue in a different method of work that will help because you're planting seeds. They could harvest them for you.

D: *That's why I'm trying to teach the method.*

C: That's exactly right.

D: *They won't all get it, but some will.*

C: Right. And it isn't just what you're teaching. It's others who will come along and realize ... you are making a name for yourself that is being recognized, not just for the *type* of work that you are doing, but it's allowing others to do *their* type of work. It isn't your path, but it's theirs. And they will harvest your seeds. Do you understand that? *(Yes)* Oh, good! I'm so happy!—But we are finished.

It had been enough time and I intended to bring Connie back anyway. But the SC informed me that the body was uncomfortable. But first I wanted to thank it for the help and information.

C: You are most blessed welcome. Please always continue your work. We know that you have a very busy schedule, but we are taking care of you. And we will keep your body healthy for you, for as long as it is time for you to continue this work. But it is good that you are sharing your lessons, and teaching people because the work must carry on.

Chapter 27

AN ENERGY BEING

When Luanna came off the cloud she saw a strange landscape. The terrain was just jagged peaks, some very tall and some small. The entire ground was covered with these, nothing else. "Their color is light brown with sparkles, like they're crystals. All jagged and sharp." I wondered how anyone would be able to move and walk on such a surface. She said she was not standing, she was flying, floating, looking down on this. "Peaks are too sharp. Everything is too sharp. It's like the crystals are peaks in the other peaks, and they are the same shapes as the jagged peaks. They are long and shiny and pointy. There are some little bitty ones and some bigger ones. And there are many reflections of light bouncing everywhere. Some of the peaks are so tall they are mostly in the clouds."

I asked her to become aware of her body, or how she perceived herself. "I guess I must have a body because I don't want to step on those sharp peaks. I can notice sensation. I notice warm spots and cold spots, and I can notice breeze and I can notice seeing.—I'm paying attention now to look between the peaks and crystals. If I look closer to the surface, it's not static... there are things that move. It's sort of like pieces of a cloud except that they're not white or gray. And then when they shine more and when they move they sort of glide around, and they change shapes, but they're not a cloud."

D: *What do you think they are?*
L: When I first landed here I thought it was empty, but I'm seeing it's not. They're almost like blobs that shine.

399

They're not definite and they can roll around between things, but they can also float. They're like blobs, but some of them are little bitty blobs and some are bigger blobs, and they are not a definite shape. They are sort of like a cloud, except that a cloud is more wispy.

D: *Are those the only forms of life that you can detect?*

L: No. There are actually little bitty, bitty things that crawl on the surfaces. They are sort of like the blobs, but they are much smaller. There's movement everywhere.

D: *Do you think you can communicate with these blobs? Do you think they are sentient beings that would be able to know things?*

L: Yes, they know things.—There's like a memory of inner soap bubbles. Except that they are all different shapes and sizes ... integrated.

D: *Well, what about yourself? Do you think you look like one of them?*

L: (Laugh) That's what I wonder. I can certainly float and I can certainly change positions. I don't have a sense of what I look like. I feel things like warm and cold.—I can change form ... can change size easily.—These others are floating around, or crawling. Some of them are so close to the surface that they're on it. I don't know if I'm like them or not.

D: *You can find out. The information is there. Are you like the other ones?* (No) *How are you different?*

L: They're like a simpler life form ... it's like a transition. It's not like a body. It's not pure light either. And I just stopped here, and I'm not like that exactly. (A sudden revelation.) I'm on a mission! This is like a resting place.—It's a place in-between. I am on my journey home, and this is just a resting place.

D: *You're more evolved and they are simpler?* (Yes) *And you think you're on your way home?* (Yes) *What do you mean?*

L: (Whispering) It's where I live.

D: *You've been somewhere else?* (Yes) *Tell me about it. Where were you?*

L: On Earth. I'm not going back there. That's why I'm at this resting place before going home to get purified. All done on Earth.

D: *Are you glad to get away from there?*

L: No, I miss the beauty, but I don't want to go back there.— I miss home. Home ... there's nothing jagged. There's nothing harsh. We all know. We all love. I miss home, but this is okay to be in this place. This is just a place to stop at. I don't know exactly why I stopped here except to take care of a curiosity. I didn't know about places like this. You know that on Earth they call them "amoeba." Except some of them are very tiny and some are huge and they are intelligent. They can merge with one another. They can change shapes. They can grow. They can shrink. It's kind of nice to be like that. Maybe that's why on Earth I like water so much.

D: *But it's good to just be nothing for a while, isn't it?*

L: Yes. It's definitely nice.

I decided to condense time and move her ahead to when she arrived back home. I asked her what it was like. "It's really beautiful and it's shiny, and many things are blue and green and gold."

D: *Objects or just colors?*

L: Well, the objects *are* colors. It's like anything can be touched and felt, so there's no difference. It's solid, but also you can go right through it, so it does have all kinds of spaces. It can make a ship that can travel very far that's made out of particular light. And they can make beautiful things if we have memories of where we've been, and we create.

D: *You have to have memories before you can create something?* (Yes)

401

She was marveling at and was in awe of the magnificent things she saw that were being created. She sighed deeply. "It's so safe and so beautiful here. I missed it." She began to cry.

D: *But you went to Earth for a reason, didn't you?*

L: We wanted that, and we all went to that beautiful, beautiful place. We would like for them to know what we know, and to feel what we feel.

D: *But you know when people come to Earth, they forget, don't they?*

L: Some of them forget. Some of them don't.

D: *Is it easier when they forget?*

L: No, it's harder because they get so sucked into everything. They suffer and get stuck. No, it's easier to remember. If they're brave enough to tell people ... but some of them get scared. Some of them know they are not going to be believed, and some of them just forget. But it's so beautiful there, and we also go to Earth and enjoy those places, so that we can collect memories, so we can be more creative, so we can do more for others.

D: *So you have to go and experience in the physical to have the memories?* (Yes) *Without that you couldn't create? Is that what you mean?*

L: We can create. That's what we are. We're creators of light, and yet we also can enrich as much of the planet as a whole. See, there's connection to everywhere there. It's not like people think. On Earth people accept it, but there are different planets that are not the same. On those everyone knows that it's easy to send the messages. It's easy to connect. It's easy to move on. It's easy to travel. It's easy.

D: *Because they haven't forgotten what they are supposed to do.* (Yes) *But isn't that part of the test, to forget when you come to Earth?*

L: No. Actually I think that when we raise their consciousness on Earth more and more and more, they're going to remember. That's what all of us want to do for them there. So they will treat each other better, so that they will not have to suffer to learn their lessons. It's not necessary, but that's what has been done. It doesn't have to be.

D: *It's easier to simply remember without the suffering. Is that what you mean?* (Yes) *But humans don't listen, do they?*

L: No, not always.

I decided it was time to move. The only other place to explore would be the spirit side, but I wanted to get on to the therapy which I explore with the SC. "Do you know you're speaking through a body that's living now as Luanna?"

L: Yes. But this is my home in this lifetime.

D: *I was wondering if this was before she entered the body of Luanna.*

L: This is also before and also after.

D: *So after she finishes here she will go back to the same place?* (Yes) *But if she was so happy there and it is so beautiful there, why did she decide to come back as Luanna?*

L: Before Luanna it was a volunteering to go to Earth.

D: *So she's returned again and again.*

L: Yes, but Luanna is the last one. I know this. Because it's over after Luanna and she gets to go home again, just like I am home.

D: *So you think by that time she'll have finished all of her lessons?*

L: On Earth, yes ... not all of the lessons.

D: *Did she know coming in that this would be her last time?* (Yes) *It's been difficult, hasn't it?* (Yes) *Did she create those difficulties for a reason?*

L: Wanting to be as complete as possible.

D: *What do you mean? How can we be complete?*

403

L: When we go from this place of light and leave this galaxy, as we call it, and we go to other civilizations, as they could be called, then we take on some of their karma. And then we complete all our human karma from this journey.

D: *So Luanna has also been to other places besides Earth, and you're saying that you take on karma from other places?*

L: The karma that Luanna is completing is just from her human life.

D: *Then it's time to close that chapter?* (Yes) *She's learned everything that she can learn in those lives.*

L: Not only learn, but also contribute. For the reason of the trip was to contribute.

D: *What was she supposed to contribute?*

L: Teaching people how to think ... teaching people how to love ... teaching people how to care for one another ... teaching people how to have faith ... teaching people how to create peace ... teaching people how to overcome disease ... teaching people to be connected to nature ... teaching people that the essence of despair is connection ... teaching people that they can be with one another in harmony ... teaching people that war is something that could end a life.

D: *Those are all wonderful things, but when we come to Earth it becomes hard, doesn't it?*

L: Right. But there are so many of the other ones. See, some of us forget, but the other ones were not us. Those are new. They are just learning. Different levels. Different things to contribute ... different lessons to learn. And also some from different areas ... some have had more human lives. And actually there are also other ones from other galaxies that have come.

D: *Also there are ones who have been coming back again and again and again?* (Yes) *Are they the ones that are more stuck on the wheel of karma?*

L: Yes. And that's why "outsiders" come to help them.—
Many people want to be helped, but they put themselves
into their own boxes. They know they want to be helped;
it's just that they get so stuck in their point of view. They
get so stuck in their limitations of that moment in time and
their bodies, that they don't believe they have anything
else. They want to get help without doing anything
different. They think that is all there is, the body or that
food or that place or that sight. Luanna gets stuck at
times. She had other lifetimes that she also remembered.
This time she came to remember who she was and what
she can do. She's doing a good job, but not as good a job
as she would have liked.

It appeared that some of the volunteers are really old souls
who decided to come here to help also. They also seemed to
be new to the Earth's vibrations, and this caused them
problems. One of the main things that would distinguish them
from the first-timers would be that they have more experience.
Yet Luanna recognized that they all had to work together to
help those on Earth who were "stuck."

Chapter 28

UNKNOWN ENERGY

Joyce was hesitant to come off the cloud. After much persuasion she did, but what continued for several long minutes was a series of shapes, colors, structures, vibrations, etc. that did not make any sense to her. It had no continuity. As soon as she would focus on one object or shape or color, it would change to something else that was equally unidentifiable. I had a difficult time following this because I was trying to get her to stick to one thing so we could progress. The only thing that she was sure of was that she was not on Earth, maybe even in a different universe.

"I'm not in a place. I'm in the middle of some kind of floating vibration. More like a vibrational frequency." It kept shifting back and forth as though trying to form into something, but never quite succeeding. When I finally asked her to perceive her body, she said she did not think she had a body. "I feel I have a presence. I feel I have a soul entity, but I can't see a body.—I'm a Source energy." She was trying to sense or find life in some form, but all she could sense was movement, yet movement in an energy form she was unfamiliar with. "I see movement ... some type of a thing moving. It has some type of energy form to it. It's going somewhere. It's going to do something. It's in the process.— Now I'm seeing the backend of this, and it's some kind of energy field. It looks like the cut end of the bottom of a tree that has all these rings around it. And now I'm in the middle of this huge formation that looks like the bottom of a tree and it's just full of energy and rings. And I don't know why I'm here. It's encompassing my whole visual field. It's an energy field and I'm trying to connect with this strange new design, this thing that's here. What are you? Why am I looking at you? I don't know why you are showing me this. Do I have some connection to you? Why am I here?"

When the subject begins to ask questions, the answers will usually come. Sometimes I also ask "it" questions, but usually I just allow it to unfold by itself.

D: *What do you hear?*
J: They're showing me energy fields and telling me stuff. It's as if they are throwing me waves of these different colors. And these colors are things I understand.—It's turned itself into another design yet again.
D: *Why are you being shown all of this?*
J: I'm receiving the "glue" of the Earth. How it sticks together. It's showing its systems and response.
D: *What does that mean?*
J: Wow! Looks like some vast area where there is blue air holding itself to this area.—Why are you showing me this?—"You are seeing the energy field as no one else has seen it."
D: *Is that what it means? The glue that holds everything together?*
J: Yes. An energy field that is not yet known.—What should we call it?
D: *Ask them to explain it to you so we can understand?*
J: (She took a deep breath.) The random fields of substance yet unknown that generate quantum physics.
D: *So we can better understand quantum physics?*
J: Yes. A type of energy.—Tell me!
D: *The type of energy that holds the Earth and everything here together?*
J: Yes. They are showing me visual form. I wonder ... does anybody know this?
D: *Do you mean people have never seen the way it looks?*

J: This is different, they say.—The energy fields that are being emanated in front of me are so minute. They are down to such small, microscopic structures. They are saying this is where you need to know ... what? What do I need to know? (A deep breath as if frustrated.) Cycles of energy at this point. The frequencies are at a point yet unknown. Well, tell me!

D: *You wouldn't be showing it to her if you didn't want her to understand it.*

J: They are really showing it's just a symphony of overlaying tissues of energies and fields and vibrations. It's just minute, minute, and minute. (Asking someone.) But what about this?—They're showing me a cone. The cones that peak and I am in the inside of it, and I'm being moved around it. They are showing me the inside of this energy field and now the structures are interfacing like my fingers are here on the sides. (Hand motions.)

D: *Intertwining?*

J: Yes, intertwining.

D: *What does that represent?*

What followed was a series of complex symbolism that was difficult to understand. I decided it was time to call forth the SC to get more answers. Hopefully it would not answer in symbolism, but in words we could understand. I asked it why it chose those scenes for her to see?

J: Monopoly of efforts.

D: *What do you mean? We didn't go to other lives. We just went into energy fields. What does it have to do with Joyce?*

J: Says here, you do not understand.

D: *We are trying to understand. That's the point of asking these questions. Is there something Joyce has to do with the energies?*

J: They are her source to use.

D: *Is that the purpose of showing her what energy fields look like?*

J: They are beyond understanding at this time. The time will come. They will make sense.

D: *Do you want her to learn to use these energies?*

J: Hers is to let other people understand it first. The secret factor must be uncovered. It evades most inquisitions right now.

D: *But it was like she was being shown different energy fields.*

J: That was a magnificent example of Source.

D: *There are others that have been to the Source, and described it as a bright light. Is it the same thing?*

J: The Source evades comparison.

D: *Is this a different type of Source or one I am acquainted with?*

J: They are unified. They are the same.

D: *But you want her to know about this energy and about the Source?*

J: They are her life's blessings.—Formations evade her. They are endless. She will make sense of them soon.— The information source is unbelievable, yet to be discovered. She will be using this in a way unknown to this day.

She was not shown any past lives because the SC considered it to be ancient history, and she was to focus on her new work.

When we got to the physical questions I had the SC do a body scan because she had so many complaints. The first thing it focused on was her blood. It was too thick. This was caused by unhappiness in this life. The blood had to be thinned. So the SC went through the system. "I'm traveling through the cells ... through all the ligaments, making circles everywhere. I am going through every possible capillary circling, capturing the wrong, moving it out. Removing anything that causes disharmony. I am going through all the organs and all the cells. Must move fast. (She had already had surgery and parts removed.) It could have been fixed.—The heart is being taxed. It messed up.—The capillaries ... organs needing support. Fixing everything. Clean out those things. (She had been having trouble with her leg since she broke it. I wanted to know why it happened.) The speed at which you proceed must be reduced. Top speed must not be continued. We slowed her down. (They worked on the leg.) I'm going through the porous bones. They need help. I will make them like a tree. Structurally strong."

They also worked on her hip and spine. The heart was repaired. The source of injury to the heart was "lack of joy." This was one of the reasons she was working so hard, to cover it up. To keep herself busy.

Chapter 29

THE SUN

Terry had several physical complaints because she was neglecting her body while taking care of others. She was told she needed to love her body. "Deep inside she agreed to come, but she's still not completely complete. She still wants to go."

D: *Is it too big of a job? Is that why she wants to go?*
T: Sometimes.
D: *Because she said she's never felt at home here. She doesn't really want to be here.*
T: She feels that, but sometimes she loves this place. Sometimes she loves her work.
D: *She came for a reason, didn't she?*
T: She understands this, but to be successful she needs to be 100% in the light in the happiness.

They wanted her to continue with her healing practice. They said she was sometimes working with a very powerful universal energy. It produced very powerful results; however, "Her body's not strong enough for it right now. It can destroy her. She has to get stronger herself. It's too much energy. She will use it eventually and very soon. But it can destroy because it's too strong." She was then given advice on how to get her body in better shape. It talked about her diet. "She has to be more outside in the nature. That's when she gains her energy. She has to stop eating meat. It's not good for her body. And go on liquids. All raw food. Liquids." This is the same advice the SC gives everyone when we ask about diet.

413

D: *She said she wanted to get to the point where she didn't have to eat anything.*

T: That will be good for her. We will send guidance that will teach her how to do that. Not everybody can do that. Some people, it can destroy, but for her it will be good. Liquids.

D: *Her body will be able to maintain itself that way?* (Yes) *We don't want to do anything that will harm her at all. But then she will lose weight, won't she?* (Terry was overweight.)

T: This is not about the weight. This is about energy. How it will feel the body vibrate. Because the food that she's taking now may bring her vibration down. That's why she cannot handle the higher healing energy now.

D: *She said when she was born, the whole first year, she had problems with her digestive system. Why did that happen?*

T: Because somewhere in her lives she was with the light. She knows how to take energy from the universe.

D: *So when she came into this life, she thought she could do the same thing?*

T: Yes. (Laugh) When she came, her parents did not understand that. The first year was difficult and that's when she was sick, and then we had to adjust to her body. We understand totally she can live without food, but her mother ... there was so much concern about her.

D: *That's natural. Humans know that you have to have food. They wouldn't want the baby to starve. So now, she thinks she can go without eating?*

T: She will go, but she has to start all over again. She has to adjust her body first. Go on diet, exercise.

D: *Do it slow?*

T: Yes, she has to do it slow. She cannot do it fast. She has to bring the frequency of the whole into organs on different levels where they can take in everything the body needs from outside sources.

D: *She will gradually bring the body into balance. She said she does like to be outside to get energy from the Sun.*

T: Yes, the Sun is very good. She used to live on the Sun actually.

D: *Is that what I've been told is the Source, or is it different?*

T: This is the Source. That's also universal energy. It just comes from the Source.

D: *When she lived on the Sun, it was something different?*

T: Yes. When she lived on the Sun, she was free from food. She didn't understand it.

The volume on this tape was erratic, and difficult to transcribe.

D: *Did she have a physical body when she did that?* (Yes) *Is it possible to live on the Sun?*

T: Yes. It's very good there. It's inside just like on Earth. Inside of the planet.

D: *Oh? It's not on the surface.*

T: No. No.

D: *That's why people could live there without being burned?*

T: Yes. It's not hot. It's very comfortable.

D: *We think it's hot all the time.*

T: No, that's all mind. All mind ... illusions when we think it's hot. The frequency is very high on the surface, and we have a different frequency of our body. That's why we don't feel its heat. We don't live on the surface. We live inside and that is very good.

D: *They don't need food because they live off the energy.* (Yes) *And they have physical bodies that can do this?*

T: Yes, we have the same body as on the Earth.

D: *But it's just a different frequency?*

T: Very high.

D: *Are there cities underneath?*

T: There are. Civilizations, but it's not the tall buildings. It's the small ... close to God. They have light, and the sky is purple. It's beautiful. We don't have to eat because we live off the energy from the outside. It's very good there. There's lots of love there.

D: *So she will be able to remember the way the body was able to exist at that time?*

T: That's what I mean.

D: *As long as it won't hurt her. We don't want to do anything that will harm this body.—Is that why she didn't want to be here?*

T: Yes. We can fly there. I can fly if I want. If I want, I can walk.

D: *How is there a sky under there?*

T: Inside it is not day or night.

D: *We think of the sky as having an atmosphere.*

T: It's a purple, and I cannot see the stars. I love to watch the stars.

D: *Would it be like daytime all the time?* (Yes) *So when she came to Earth she missed that place.* (Yes) *But she has to live here now and finish her assignment, doesn't she?*

T: That's what she agreed.—She has to do that. If we don't have the Earth, the Sun will destroy, too. The Sun is the Earth's orbit star. The Sun will destroy, too.

D: *What about the other planets in our solar system?*

T: They will be affected.

D: *What happens on Earth affects everything?*

T: That will destroy the balance between the planets. But she agreed to come to the Earth to save your planet.

D: *So when she finishes this job, she won't have to come back again?*

T: That will be up to her.

They worked on her body. The doctors were wanting to operate on her knee, and "they" said she would be healed before any surgery could occur.

Parting message: Love your body and believe in yourself. Connect to the Source. And listen more to yourself when you teach the people because there's a message for you as well. We're always here. She's never alone.—She has to meditate. She has to remember any time she goes through the darkness.

Anytime she can come in to us. She has to find the time to stop ... to connect with us and then she will be okay.

I have had several cases where the clients said they wouldn't nurse when they were born. Of course, the doctors had to feed them intravenously until they could get the baby to cooperate. In these cases the SC always says they came from a planet or dimension where they did not need food, so they were not accustomed to consuming anything in order to survive. This is the way many extraterrestrials live. They do not need to consume anything, thus their organs have atrophied from non-use. They live off of light, and they say this light comes directly from Source. In *Legacy From the Stars* there was a story of some who have to have regular "light baths." They lie down in a container similar to a sarcophagus, and the intensity and color of the light indicates how much energy their bodies need. This method is also used on spaceships while traveling through space and the light is stored in crystals. So it is easy to understand how a soul coming from such an environment is confused when entering an earthly body that needs to consume solid food.

Some of my clients (including this one) have heard of people who do not have to eat. They live off of their breathing. I believe they are called "Breatharians." I am sure that yogis and people who are used to meditating and living an austere life have taught themselves to exist without food, but I didn't think it would be possible for the average human being. During this session Terry was told that it is possible but it takes a lot of discipline and she was not ready for that yet. However, after I had finished giving a lecture in Ireland, in September, 2011, a young woman came up to talk to me. She was pretty and thin and didn't look any different than anyone else. However, there was an exception. She said she had never consumed any food or water throughout her entire life, even as a baby or child. She did not have any need for it. I would have liked to spend more time asking her questions, but there were too many people all wanting to tell me their own experiences.

"Please sign my book. Please just one picture." So the opportunity was missed. It seems as though when I have a question the universe provides the answer. I had wondered whether these types of people exist and I was sent one. I am sure if there was one there must be more. The SC said in this session that they do exist. One of our friends at the lecture said afterwards, that would certainly make life easier (and cheaper) if you didn't have to be concerned with buying and preparing food. I suddenly thought it would also do away from elimination of food: urination and bowel movements. I wonder if their organs have atrophied from non-use like the ETs. The woman had told me that she never has gotten sick so there was no reason to go to the doctor. So apparently it would be difficult for medical personnel to even know about these types of people. I am sure that if I am meant to know more about this, then more information will be provided in the future.

***

Immediately after finishing my lecture and class tour in Europe, I went to India to speak at a conference at Pyramid Valley outside of Bangalore. One of the speakers said that she was able to stop eating in the 1990s, but deep meditation was involved in accomplishing it. She said there were at least 30,000 people on Earth who also do not have to consume food. However, I do not advise this for the average person because I think special circumstances have to be involved in order for the physical body to survive.

Chapter 30

ACTIVATION OF THE NEW LIGHT ENERGY

When Sherri came off the cloud she began describing a scene that was becoming more and more familiar to me. Many of my clients are no longer going to past lives when we have the session. They are going to a beautiful light that seems to be also a powerful energy. To me, I think it adds validity if many people describe the same things while they are in deep trance because they have no idea what I am uncovering.

S: I see a very beautiful light. It's yellowy gold, but as it pours out and bathes me, it becomes more like violet lavender light. It permeates my body ... my heart. (She was becoming emotional.) It feels so very good.

D: *Where does the light seem to be?*

S: In my eyes... in front of my face and up higher. It's everywhere. All I can see is the starlight. As I described it to you, it felt so good I wanted to cry.—Now I'm totally in the light. It just permeated me and now it's all over me. It feels very calm and soft, and my whole body just glows.

D: *How do you perceive your body?*

S: The body is like a little shell on the surface like the skin, but there's nothing else. It's really interesting because everything kind of melts away, so as I look into my body there's just light. And yet I know I have a body, but it's starlight ... it's big sunlight. At this point it's many colors, not one color anymore.—It's just the light, yet I know there are beings here, but I can't see anything but light or

419

feel anything but light. It would be interesting to see others. I know they're there.

D: *If you could see them, what would they look like?*

S: They'd look like light beings. They would look like me. There would be these little shells with light in them and around them. (She became emotional and began to cry.) OH, the light is very powerful! (In awe) Oh, it's beautiful. It's so pure. It just goes right through everything. Nothing can resist this.

She said it also seemed familiar as though she had experienced it before.

S: I'm kind of navigating here because it feels like this pouring energy goes forever. But in terms of this body, it keeps going deeper beyond the body. So I'm just aware of the light in my body, but there are others there and I'm just soaking in this light. I feel like it goes through me and it's going somewhere like the Earth or something. It pours through me. (Sobbing)

D: *Why does that make you emotional?*

S: Because that's all I really do is have energy pour through, and I thought I was different. (Crying) I had been here before, but I didn't see it as me. This is much bigger. This is everywhere. I can feel it. I feel it go into the earth.

D: *Do you feel this is an energy that you use?*

S: That's what I am. (Whispers) I am light. I am energy. I didn't know that before. I could feel it before, but I *am* this energy. I knew this light, but it seemed like it was more "out there," and coming through me, but this is different. This is just pure light. It's forever.

D: *Do you think you would be able to use it?*

S: I could use it any way. They trust me with this light.

D: *Ask them what that means.*

S: They love me very dearly and trust me to use this light. (Sobbing and astonished.) They are pure love. This is wonderful to see them.

D: *What do they look like?*
S: They are columns of light, but they feel very, very big and powerful and upright. And they know all about us. (Crying) I'm so thankful to be able to be with them. They are saying, "We want to help you and we *are* helping you." And I can feel one of them with a much lower voice wanting to speak through me.

I assured her it would be all right to allow them to do that, if she was willing because it is always easier to communicate directly. The voice became stronger as it began to speak.

S: We are pulsing light through you.
D: *What is the purpose of pulsing the light through Sherri?*
S: She is able to flow freely and give this light freely. It is all perfect. We have a group of stars, but it looks like one light. And we have harnessed this light into forms that will flow through people, and Sherri is one of them. The energy is making her body tingle. We had to prepare her. We had to make her able to feel okay so that we could come through this form like we are now. She is feeling it and it's a wonderful feeling.—It's so weird to talk and feel the body. We are of great heart. We speak through the heart. She is feeling it as peace in the heart. Without preparation she could never handle this much light ... never ... no, never. (Pause) I'm seeing the planet and I'm seeing not only the light going into the Earth. I am one of the individuals speaking through her now, and I am particularly interested in the atmosphere, and this light will go into the atmosphere. There is much in the atmosphere that needs correction and adjustment and especially the violet light she sees and the blue light and white light. And all the colors that are already on the Earth will be adjusted with this light. So I am helping to adjust the atmospheric light frequencies so the work she is doing has much more consciousness. But I wanted to

show her these bigger things this light is doing beyond the personal world she thinks she is working with.

D: *Because we are involved with the individuals.* (Yes) *But you're involved with the bigger picture?* (Yes) *What is wrong with the atmosphere that it needs correction?*

S: It's much more than all kinds of pollutions and thoughts and things like that. It's much more of a disturbance. These disturbances were in place for a very long time to keep things at a certain frequency so people could learn things. But those things are being lifted away and the light is literally dissolving the thickness and pollution, and congestion and negativity. And so is able to completely release the sounds of dissidence in the planet that have been here for a very long time.

D: *So it's more than manmade pollution? Thoughts and other things are also polluted?*

S: Yes. They are being cleared. We use sound and light frequencies. We speak to her through sound and she understands sound better than other modalities. She can use the sound more freely to help others.

D: *Because her job is not to work on the atmosphere. Her job is to help the individuals?*

S: Yes. We had to clear something in the atmosphere to help her use these energies and that's why I came in now. This will make it much, much easier to work with the energies. It was an atmospheric adjustment that needed to be done through you, Dolores.

D: *Oh, she couldn't have done it on her own?*

S: No. It would have taken longer.

They then proceeded to give instructions about how Sherri was to use the energy for healing. "She can place her hands on or above the body and make the sounds, and we will come through and help." She would instinctively know the sounds to make. It would be very natural for her, and then they would work through her, and use her as an instrument. I noticed Sherri's body had been jerking and jumping. They said they had been clearing and adjusting so her body would be able to handle and direct the energy. They sent pure light energy "going into all the cells and all the bone tissue, and it's filling up with light and that's just what she needed." Sherri had been having some problems with her internal organs, especially the bladder, so I asked about the cause.

S: She had a hard entry and she came in in pieces. And she had a spaceship aspect of metal that was embedded in her which we would like to remove. It was like a weight, a pressure pressing in on her.

D: *You mean when she came into this life? Did something happen to the space ship?*

S: Yes ... before her coming into this body. She was delivered and ... she came in pieces and when there's a problem getting through, this created a pressure on her bladder, physically recorded in her body as metal pressing against her.

D: *What do you mean, she came in as pieces?*

S: In your time and space she was delivered in pieces, in boxes, in cubes, in light cubes. Installations, as you would say, and there was a problem in one of the installations.

D: *I'm trying to understand new information I haven't heard before. Doesn't the soul enter in one piece?*

S: That is true. The soul does enter in one piece. The soul is ... I'm trying to convey this in language terms.

D: *Language is always a problem.*

S: It is like this light that she is experiencing. It's flowing everywhere. It's radiant. It has no boundaries. But this thing I'm talking about is the human vessel. It cannot handle as much light and so we gave it to her in installments. And some of the physical energies on the planet, which she was a part of, had to adapt to these new energies. And there was a problem in the pelvic region and she was not able to fully accept that much light, and it caused physical problems in that whole area.

D: *Is that one of the reasons she couldn't have any children?* (Yes) *You said you're working now to remove the metal there?*

S: The conditions. The metal was the container for this light. That is gone, but the impression of the metal on the physical vessel was imprinted with this experience.

D: *The heaviness that was the pressure.*

S: Yes. It's only a memory.

D: *Can you take it away?*

S: Yes, of course we can.

D: *I think I understand what you're talking about now. I've had it explained from other beings like you, although they used different terms. They say sometimes the energy has not been in the physical body, the human body, before. Is that correct?* (Yes) *And so it's too strong of an energy?*

S: We delivered this to many beings at the same time. This was not a unique energy.

D: *I've heard it explained before that the body couldn't handle the energy so it had to be done gradually.*

S: It did, and then sometimes it didn't go as we hoped. It had to be refined and redone, but it was a problem for her physical self.

D: *I've heard that sometimes when this is attempted, the baby will abort because there's too much energy.*

S: Yes. That was actually part of her experience, too, but she did not choose to leave. She came in with very bright light and she was able to stay in the body, but it was too much. There has to be an adjustment with the mother's body also. We hope to handle the energy that's coming in.

D: *In other cases you told me about, it had to be adjusted so the next time the baby would not abort. It would be able to be born, but it couldn't have all the energy at one time. Does that make sense?* (Yes) *I've heard it in different terms. I've never heard of it in pieces or installments.*

S: You talk about walk-ins, and walk-ins are installments.

D: *But I've found now that there are many different types of walk-ins.* (Yes.) *Nothing is as simple as people think it is.—But does this mean that Sherri has not had life in physical bodies on Earth before?*

S: She has not had lives before on Earth. She's had other experiences. She's had many experiences and has a vast, vast memory of beautiful and different places. She has known the water planet, and she has experienced other star systems, and she goes past solar systems. She understands light and other realms and she knows beyond the physical creation of the swirling origins of what is indescribable.

D: *That sounds like she was very advanced. She really didn't need to have the Earth experience.*

S: She came in at a difficult period for this kind of energy, but she wanted to do this very, very strongly. She deeply wanted to do this and she came with others. There are others like her here on Earth.

D: *I've spoken to many. I think I understand them better than most people do.*

S: (Whispered) You do.

D: *Did she decide on her own, or did others help her with the decision?*

S: No, they came as a group. They joined together and came together, although it was over a period of years. They were one group and there are many groups coming now.

D: *But they're all spread out where they don't know each other.*

S: No, they will know each other very soon again.

D: *That's why they had difficulty because they felt they were all alone.*

S: Yes, that is true.

D: *But why did she pick Earth? What made her decide to come here?*

S: It was an assignment. It was something agreed upon. We are a council and this energy was beyond the galaxy. It was a realm of awareness that wished to be generated into pulsing in stages into the many galaxies. And as it came through, it joined with an existing something that was in place, and it had a story that had not been told. It had information that had not been experienced yet. It was new and it had information that would help change what all of you are understanding now about what is happening on the Earth. But it is a much bigger change that is happening through many, many galaxies and many places. This is a huge change.

D: *So it's not just here on Earth?*

S: Correct.

D: *What is this change that is happening? You said it's new, and has not happened before.*

S: Yes. I am unable to describe it. It's just not available.

D: *I know it's always hard to find the words. Just do the best you can with what you have.*

S: Right. Right. What is being created has never been experienced before, and there are beings of understanding that will be placed with each being on Earth. And they will then be listening to this incredible amplification that they deeply know through their own systems, and we are doing this now as we speak. This is a large implantation ... if there is such a word. We are implanting and embedding. This light is actually going into the very solar plexus and root chakra of each being and it is forming a voice. That's why it's a V-shape in the body. See this as good because we can see how this is spreading and all beings will have this new facility to experience light through their system of beingness of bodiness, and they can speak to all things through this new energy. It is cone-shaped and it's placed in the lower body; the area Sherri has so much trouble with. What she was feeling was the anticipation of this placement.

D: *It's in that area?*

S: Yes, through the chakras. It is a large placement of a whole new communication, and it's like a light cone that's being placed in the body of each being of the planet. That was the purpose of today, to allow us to consciously be perceived as one of the things that people are helping to bring through. It's light, but it also has a shape. It's a vortex basically.

D: *It's being put in everyone?*

This definitely was new information. I wanted to understand it, so I wouldn't perceive it as negative.

S: Yes ... everyone ... animals, too.

D: *What is the purpose of putting that in everyone?*

S: It's a new communication system. It's a much more advanced way of using light.

D: *In the past there have been communication systems that were like instincts.*

S: Yes. Intuitions. These old ways are not as effective anymore. This is so new it doesn't even ... yes, the old systems will be useful, but they will not be as effective as this.

D: *So it was time to change?*

S: Yes. A whole new system installed installation.

D: *How will the individual perceive this?*

S: We've been seeing a lot of disturbance in that part of the body in many people. That was in preparation for this and now that it is being adapted and in place, many things can happen that people can do more easily. And not feel as physical discomfort or as insecurity or even financial. It's alleviating the old system of the backlog of pressure that has built up in the system. This is a much more advanced form of human embodiment in using this information that is being sent.

D: *I'm trying to understand how it operates and if the average person is going to notice any difference.*

S: Yes. It becomes activated.

D: *So it's there, but it's not activated in every person?*

S: No, it comes activated. It's just that everything has been preparation and now it has been embedded in place.

D: *But the person didn't know when this happened?*

S: It just happened. The preparation has been a long time coming, but the actual event is only in the last few days. (This session has held on July 11, 2009.)

This was a surprise. I knew I didn't feel any different. At least I didn't think I did.

D: *Did something happen to cause it to become activated now on the planet?*

S: It was time for this to happen. We've been working a very long time ... for this time.

D: *That's been very recent. That's why I wondered if anything triggered this.*

S: It was planned for.

D: *You said everyone will have one. Will everyone know it's there? Will they react to it?*

S: I see. I see. I see it as there, but from the human point of view, it will take some time.

D: *Will the people notice anything different?*

S: It will feel very different. They will not be angered, and be very able to be here in the planet energy. Not that they don't love being here now. It won't be so hard because they will have like little stars and little planets inside themselves that feel like home. And yet they can be here and be fully in this light ... this energy. Everyone will have this.

D: *So they won't feel like this is a different place? They won't have that feeling of wanting to go home anymore?*

S: Right. They are home.

D: *It's easier to adjust.*

S: Yes, this will feel wonderful.

Of course, my curiosity made me ask if this had been done to me also. She grinned as she answered, "Of course." They then asked if I could feel it. The only thing I had been aware of was a feeling of energy moving through me as they were putting it through her. I didn't know if this was what they meant. I asked, "We're going to be aware of energy?"

S: You'll feel it. You'll feel it more fully. You'll feel it like she felt that star sun energy, but you'll feel it in your own unique way, like each person will. But it will feel like home. It's like their own experience of these energies.

D: *You said it fills the cells of everyone, or is that just for her.*

S: The light was filling up every cell, but the cone is a soul connection device.

D: *It's a way to communicate?*

S: Right. There will be no more separation from the Force or God.

D: *Can this be used for healing, or is it a different type of thing?*

S: The energy is the same, but how each person uses it could be very different. It can be used in many ways.

D: *That's what I'm trying to understand. What about the negative people out there?*

S: We are working on that. (Pause) What are we doing with negative people? For those it might initially be perceived as disruptive, but what it can do is to fuse the negativity. They cannot control this. That is an aspect of God and so they are transformed by the spinning of this cone in their system until they release that energy that no longer can be in this light.

D: *Because the negativity can't exist in this light?*

S: It can't exist.

D: *But you said at first it will feel a little strange, disruptive to them?*

S: It would feel to them, but it's so much stronger than their wills. They would be unable, and it would start to feel like all they could do is go with it. They couldn't fight it. They couldn't control it.

D: *Does this go against the free will of the individual?*

S: This is where the negativity is thrown off and disperses. This is where it evaporates by the light, and free will is this light. (Pause) Oh, I see what you are saying. The free will. This was agreed upon long before anyone came into form, anything manifested. They were interested in experiencing this (free will), and they took it very far, many places and many possibilities. But it is a time ... you know how a top turns and it looks like it's still, but it's turning very fast? *(Yes)* That's what this feels like in the system. And this feeling is so powerful that it is going to stay balanced, and the accumulated consciousness of this negativity cannot throw this off balance. So, free will to explore is one thing, but the ability for everything to remember and hold this energy is much stronger than the free will to explore and develop what you call "karma, negativity." That was agreed upon long before in a time when such an imbalance had been created, that we put in place what would balance it again.

D: *So you think now is the time because of all the negativity the world has created?* (Yes) *It is definitely out of balance. Now it is time to do this to bring it back into balance?* (Yes) *The world was created with free will to see what it could do, but it can only go so far.—Well, does this mean karma will no longer exist?*

S: Right. It will no longer exist. It cannot keep creating itself over and over and over again endlessly. It was just an exploration.

D: *What about the karma people have that they've not paid back yet?*

S: That's what I meant about the evaporation. It is dispersed and evaporated. It does not exist.

D: *In my work, I'm always telling them to forgive and to let it go.*

S: That is very good.

D: *Is it no longer necessary to tell them that?*

S: I come from a perspective where I see how this changes everything, but on an individual level, that may still affect the way you can help people. You can remember this has been placed in everyone, and perhaps it will be so activated that you will find new ways to ... I don't think you'll be seeing so much of the old form. It is falling away. What you will be doing is helping people into the new form, and they won't be able to hold onto the old one much longer.

D: *Does this mean this will be the end of wars and all the negative things that have plagued the world?*

S: Absolutely. It is a very big plan and it is in place and this big change—let's see—it's happening everywhere. That's the thing. It's not just Earth. This is so big. It's transforming everything. This is the biggest change ... ever. This is much bigger than Earth, but Earth is a very big part of it.

I asked about the information I had been given about the New Earth and the Old Earth. And the splitting and the new world moving into a new dimension. And that some people would want to stay with the old ways and not change.

S: I don't see that. Maybe someone else needs to come in to talk to you about that. There are many of us here.—This energy is everywhere. I cannot see anything being able to exist in a destructive, violent, negative form. It cannot stand. Now maybe that is the New Earth you are referring to, but an old Earth ... I just don't see it.

I thought it was time to return to Sherri's questions, and many of them dealt with physical ailments. The SC went through the body correcting all the problems, but it had advice for Sherri. "She needs to let go of sadness." I wanted an explanation.

S: Sadness. Right now her heart is sad. She didn't understand her experience and she took it to heart.

D: *What experience?*

S: That she was a light being in a human experience. And she could not understand the human experience, and it was very hard on her *emotional* heart. She couldn't understand this at all.—It's more about her understanding the light as she has the light available and for her to use the light in all ways that she can imagine, and we will be working with her very fully. We always have been, and she's been very willing to assist us, but now, in particular because of this session, she will be able to be more open. Many doors will fly open and we will be able to pour this light through many of the interactions she has throughout the day and with people. She is here to help. She has to let go of the sadness and accept her role. She should never lose hope. There are always new possibilities.

Time and

Dimensions

Chapter 31

THE DEPOT

When Chandra first came off the cloud she saw a forest of very, very tall trees on the edge of a meadow. She noticed a spry leprechaun darting among the trees. But instead of coming down there she felt the need to fly away from Earth into space. There she saw darkness and stars as she floated weightless. She felt as though she was part of space as she identified with it totally. " It feels good. I'm going somewhere. I see something, but I can't make it out. It's dark. I see stars. I see something floating out in the middle of it. The shape ... a galaxy of some kind, but it looks like orangey brown particles, and I'm looking at it from far away. They're swirling.—I went closer to the particles. Now I feel like I am part of the particles in space."

D: *What does it feel like to be a part of it?*
C: They just seem to be moving in the same direction. They are very small, like sand. I feel I could be sitting on top of them and I'm being moved by the particles kind of like being on a merry-go-round. It's moving in a circle.—I see something on it.—I see a baby or a child with dark hair who is somehow part of the flying dust particles. It has very long, dark hair, like grown-up hair ... but it looks like a baby. It's just sitting on the sand particles looking happy. It knows me. It's is saying, "Hello! I'm your spirit guide. I'm here for you like you really want."
D: *It wants you to see it as a baby?*
C: It wants for me to look at it that way.

D: *Your guide can appear any way it wants to. Whatever way it's comfortable for you.*

C: Yes, it's the least threatened, I guess.—It says to follow it. I'm taking its hand, but it looks so silly following a baby.

D: *It doesn't make any difference. That's a safe way to look at it.—Can you see anything as you travel?*

C: Lights. It's blinding right now. Very bright. And we're moving through it.—My guide is going with me, right ahead of me. I feel happy. I feel like I'm moving very fast.—Well, it says we're here.

D: *Where is* here?

C: I'm in space again and it's pointing to a planet. I wonder if I can get any closer to it so it will be clearer. It looks green, a planet with green and white spots. And now we are getting closer and it looks like a grayish green light ball. My guide wants me to go there. There's something for me to see.—Now there's gray, dark sand and there might be other beings. She's walking with me on the gray black sand towards a place there.—There's not much to see here. Even the sky is kind of dark ... there's no Sun. Not like it's night ....

There were some gray buildings made out of granite, and she went inside. The floor was like marble and a lot of glass and some mirrors. Even though it appeared empty she knew there were people there that she couldn't see. I asked her to become aware of her body. "I see a body. It's flesh, but it's a peach color and it has long arms, long legs ... it's not me. It looks human but it's kind of weird looking. It looks stretched out. My hands are very big ... big like sausages ... like very swollen, big hands."

D: *Are you wearing anything?* (No) *Do you have any hair?*

C: That's the weird thing. I can't really see my head. It's like this naked long, stretched out body, and up from the neck I can't see. Big hands ... little feet ... I don't think I have toes. And there are no female or male parts.

D: *Do you feel like you belong in that building?*
C: Yes, like I know I should be there. I work there.

When I asked what type of work she did, she answered, "I don't know. The room is very tall and there are these consoles along the wall. It's a circular room and there's something like computers. Some kind of machines.—It feels like I'm a tour guide. I just shuffle people in and out of that place. That's my job. Helping them go to where they are supposed to go.—It's like a train station. You go there before you go somewhere else.

D: *Do these people look like you?*
C: Everyone looks different. It's like an intergalactical place for travel people.
D: *And do you know where they're supposed to go?*
C: Most of the time. I don't decide where they go, but I help them get to where they are supposed to go. So they come in and they are disoriented, and I greet them, and then I somehow just know where they are supposed to go next. I feel something about their energy, and I take them to whatever room they have to go to get either some assignment, or if they are supposed to meet somebody else ... other people—friends—I guess would be better.—They all look different. Some of them look like beings of light. Those are in the council. Like they're in charge. And then some of them are all different ... like a science fiction scene. But sometimes it gets very crowded in there. There are many beings that go in and out, but somehow it's organized.
D: *So you have to process these, and tell them where to go?*
C: Yes, but it's not my decision where they go ... not my decision. I just help them get to where they are supposed to go.
D: *You just know this? You feel it? Is that what you mean?* (Yes) *Does it have anything to do with their frequency or their vibration?*

C: Yes, in a way. It's all different. And you just greet them and you help them get to the next step.

D: *Then somebody else takes over from there?* (Yes) *Have you been working there a long time?*

C: Oh, a while ... for a while.

D: *It sounds like it's a responsible position.*

C: Yes. (Undecided) Sometimes I'd rather be the one traveling.

D: *Do you have any choice about it?*

C: I don't ask. I don't dare ask. This is my assignment and this is my job and I don't mind it. I'm in a spot that's in-between. Like a depot, like a train station.

D: *And they're all coming in and going somewhere else.* (Yes) *And you wonder what else there is?* (Yes) *Is there any way you could find out?*

C: I have to ask one of the beings of light.

D: *Is it okay if we talk to them?* (Yes) *There's nothing wrong with being curious, is there?* (No) *Okay, ask them what you want to know.*

C: I'd like to know if people are out there. They said, "Yes."—They said that I do a pretty good job of helping people. I mind and I'm a good worker. And I will have a chance, but not yet.

D: *So you will have a chance to find out what's out there?*

C: That's what they said. I'm pretty happy.

D: *That means you will get to discover what it's like to travel?*

C: Yes. But more than travel ... exist differently.—I just know that when you go to different dimensions or a different existence you're ... how do you say? Like for example, you could be a different shape or *nothing*. And other dimensions have their different ways that you can perceive and know. So it's not just traveling, it's existing differently with different parameters. It depends on where you go, and I would very much like to go.

D: *Have you ever been anywhere?*

C: (Whispering) Have I ever been anywhere? (Loud) Besides here? Besides the depot? He says, "Yes." In places ... but in different times.

D: *What do they mean?*

C: They explain ... that I exist in different times already. Simultaneously.

D: *But you're not aware of these things?*

C: Now I am, or the fleshy, peachy being that I am ... now it knows ... (Confused) This is hard to explain.

D: *Is it okay if it knows?*

C: Yes, it's okay that it knows ... it raises its vibration by knowing.

D: *Because we don't want to do anything that will interfere with anything.*

C: They said it's okay now.—That light being is telling it about *me*. (Confused a bit.) That it's *me* ... that one of its existences right now is me ... Chandra.

D: *Why is it telling it that?*

C: Chandra is trying to reach out to them ... the light being and the fleshy thing. And it can kind of sense it and so they're communicating. They're not talking ... they're sharing ideas.

D: *Is it all right if Chandra knows these things now?*

C: Yes. I think she needs to know she's everywhere.

D: *Because we never want to do anything that's going to cause problems, but I was thinking information is not given unless it's time.*

C: Yes, that's true.

D: *Why is it important for her to know that now?*

C: There's always a desire to know everything that's out there, and it distracts her from what she's doing at the moment. The innate curiosity that she has, has her wishing for many things at the same time. She just needs to know that everything she wishes to experience she already is, and that the desire to experience everything is being fulfilled. Even though she is not aware of it. Just like her existence in what she calls a "depot," and the feeling of being stuck there, is not the only reality or existence that she has. There are other parts of her, you could say, living different lives.

D: *One thing she wanted to know, has she ever been part of nature?*

C: Yes. The grassy knoll that she saw earlier was her. (At the beginning when we first began the session.) She was the energy that was that part of it. A little being. A caretaker in a way, but also that knoll itself. Separate, but also of the same energy. A nature energy.

D: *Because she said she feels very close to nature.* (Yes) *We thought we were going to go to a past life and experience that. Why didn't that happen?*

C: She got to see what she wanted to see earlier, and she has a very clear picture of it still. She can go back to it whenever she wants to, when she needs comfort. And she needs to know, even though that was a very nice existence, it was time for it to cease. In order to evolve she had to leave that, or exist as something else. She experienced it, and she wished for it, too. She wished for it and she got what she wanted.—Then she wanted to be human. There's a part of her that was very curious to see what it would be like to be human.

D: *I'm trying to figure out how to word it. She had several lives being part of nature before becoming human?* (Yes) *Of course, I am wondering if they die or not.* (Laugh) *Do you understand what I mean?*

C: Well, that leprechaun still exists and it's still her. It never dies. It's still there. (The little creature that she saw darting among the trees.)

D: *He only exists in that form?*

C: Yes. It's hard to explain.

D: *Do the best you can.*

C: They're all there. The leprechaun is still there, which is her. And the being from the depot is still there, which is still her. She is everywhere she wants to be, which is in very many places, on certain levels or whichever existences she picks. Sometimes she is aware of it and sometimes she is not.

I had difficulty forming the questions to try to understand this better. "She is only aware of them when she focuses on them?"

C: It depends on the existence. For example, the leprechaun ... as a leprechaun she chose to be human. And the leprechaun is aware of that desire, and being a nature spirit, knows that it has occurred, let's just say.

D: *He is more aware than Chandra is?*

C: Yes. There are different levels of awareness and it depends on the existence. It's the same being, but each is allowed to know what they need to know.

D: *But they can't be aware of the whole thing, the whole picture. Is that what you mean?* (Yes) *It would be too much to handle?*

C: Yes. For example, the being in the depot was told this information that it exists in different dimensions because of its desire to experience in other levels. So it was told that it already is. Had it not asked, it would not know.

D: *Is that being able to understand?*

C: It was more to appease or comfort the being. It was to raise its existence. Its frequency is now a little bit lighter or higher for knowing that, but you cannot force ... you can only answer the questions when they are asked. If it hadn't asked, it wouldn't have known that it already existed in other places.

D: *So this would make it feel better to know that it wasn't trapped right there?* (Yes) *So it could continue with its job knowing that it was also able to experience other things.* (Yes) *So a little knowledge helps as each one continues its own life. So what we call "other past lives" are not appropriate to know about.*

C: Not always so.

D: *Because they are not at that level of development?*

C: Exactly. The being in the depot, you would say, was the lower frequency.

D: *Did I interfere with its development by ....*

C: No. In fact, it has been helped.

D: *Because I don't want to interfere with anybody's evolvement.*

C: No. One of the purposes or goals of all beings is to raise their vibrations to come closer to the Source. And in the knowledge that has been given to that being, the vibration has changed.

D: *So it has helped in its evolvement then?* (Yes) *Then am I correct in thinking that eventually to return to Source all of these parts have to come together at some time?* (Yes) *So they would all have to eventually raise their vibrations, wouldn't they?*

C: Yes, just like the leprechaun. His was a different vibration ... a different frequency. But it requested the experience of being human because it knew it would help his evolution.

D: *You know in my work, I'm used to taking people to the appropriate past life and finding the answers to their questions. This is what we thought we were going to experience, and it didn't happen.* (Laugh) *At least not a "normal" past life.*

C: It's very important to know that all the frequencies need to be raised of all beings, not just the human, but of everything that is All.

D: *At this time?*

C: Particularly.

D: *Why is it important for Chandra to have this information today?*

C: Her vibration is raising itself.

D: *So her answers are not to be found by going back and reliving a past life?*

C: No, not at the moment. She wants to know what to do. She's asking about her work situation.

D: *That was one of her main questions. She's not happy in the job she has.*

C: Well, you know she had a very good life as a leprechaun. It's much different being a human. Sometimes it's harder, in a way. It was much easier being a leprechaun. She has nostalgia for nature and connecting with nature because she knows she's of that originally. And longs for, not only the reconnection, but her type of life that was much easier. Much simpler. Less complicated, and leprechauns don't have to work the way humans do.

The SC thought about what advice to give Chandra, and finally decided to advise her to do healing. "She can work with nature, but eventually I see her as a healer. She's resisting, but ultimately she's a healer. She knows this. When she just talks to people they feel better. She can tell everyone where there's something wrong. There's energy around a person that she can read. She needs to develop that skill. If she can develop the skill to see a person's aura, she will be able to help them in a greater capacity. If she develops this skill she will be a very great healer. She will help many people.—She could also work with the Earth. It would be very easy for her to do that. She's already part of the earth, and her friends and other nature spirits would work with her. It would be very easy for her to do it.

D: *Does she have any contract to have any children?* (One of her questions.)

C: No, and she must stop worrying about that. She has another path this time.

***

Chandra wanted to know about an unusual incident she had experienced. She was driving on the freeway and she looked in her rearview mirror and saw a car crash behind her.

When she looked around there was nothing there. I asked if "they" could explain the incident.

C: She was temporarily living in a different parallel existence. Time had overlapped at that certain point, and she saw something that happened on another plane that had gotten ... let's just say "crossed." The two parts of existence crossed at that point. And the car moved from one point of existence to the other point where she was, but then dissolved—not the right word.

D: *Dissipated?*

C: Yes. Thank you!

D: *Because it didn't belong in this dimension?* (Yes) *That sounds like things other people have told me about where other dimensions sometimes overlap.*

C: Yes, they all think they are making it up.

D: *But there was no connection with her. She just happened to be at the right place?*

C: That's correct.

***

Physical: "When she was born she had a skin problem all over her body. (Something like eczema or psoriasis.) And it persisted all of her life, but now she has only a few small places on her body. What caused that? Why was she born with this all over her body?"

C: She has a matrix of that body riddled with ... I'm seeing ... it is a kind of energy and that affects her physical body. It clings to the matrix and that causes the psoriasis to appear ... almost like a rash.

D: *It's much worse than a rash though.*

C: Think of a rash as an energy form, and the matrix that creates her physical body ....

D: *Can you explain what you mean by the matrix?*

C: The matrix is a network of energy lines that come together that forms itself into the human body. It extends out of her body and you can't see it ... well, some people can see it, but it's about six or seven feet around the physical body, like a grid system that forms the body. And on this grid system she has what would be ... an energy that comes as a kind of a rash that has grown on this matrix or this grid. A system that forms her body and manifests itself as psoriasis. Almost like a shell ... in energy terms that is like the matrix. It is very difficult to explain. It would look like a grid system if you were to see it.

D: *Is this what the physical body really looks like?*

C: Well, on an energy level. The physical body is the physical body, but there are many (having a hard time explaining) ... there is a reason why the physical body looks the way it does because of the grid or matrix that everyone is born into. And the matrix is what determines the physical body as it appears in her dimension. Right now we are clearing the matrix of this ... I can only describe it to you as a rash.

D: *When you said this matrix extends out from the body, would that be what people see as the aura?*

C: No. It's separate. The matrix exists solely for the purpose of creating the physical body. The aura is energy of the body. Think of it as a multitask system. You have a mold and when you fill the mold—in this case you have energy at a certain frequency that creates a human form. In this nature a grid is like the mold.

D: *Then it doesn't become alive until the soul enters?*

C: No. It starts once conception happens, and it's always changing, which is evident because the human body is constantly changing. And it's not affected by the other energies of the human, as the aura. They are all into play with each other. The main purpose of the matrix is to create a building ... it's like the shell.

D: *So whenever the soul leaves the body, the matrix starts dissolving?*

C: Yes because there is no need for the physical body anymore.

D: *Can we help her with this psoriasis?*

C: Yes. What I have described to you as a rash is actually more like energy that has decided to cling itself to her matrix. It's almost like going along for the free ride. It's found her matrix very hospitable, and decided to stick around and has manifested itself as psoriasis.

D: *Even though it's causing problems, it doesn't know it.* (Yes) *To me it sounds like what I call an "elemental" energy.*

C: That is correct.

D: *They have no emotions or feelings.*

C: That is correct. But for some reason they like to stick around her matrix.

D: *They are attracted to it.* (Yes) *The same type of energy is attracted to buildings and places.*

C: Yes, and this is very beneficial for her to know this, so that she will begin to understand the way the physical body functions or exists, so that she can be a better healer.

The SC then quickly cleared the energy so that the psoriasis could be healed. "We have removed it with a blessing, so that the energy does not return. The body is now free and clear."

❧ — ‥ •❖➣❀━❉❖━ ━❉❖━❀❧❦❀‥ • ━ ◗

The energetic or etheric body, which provides the formative and sustaining pattern for the physical body, is experienced as *light*. Is this the matrix?

In Robert Winterhalter's book, "The Healing Christ," (published by Ozark Mountain Publishing) he gives a very plausible explanation when he was talking about the miracles of Jesus in the Bible:

Peter, James, and John witnessed the transfiguration of Jesus as an actual event. (Mark 9:2-3 (parallel passages: Matthew 17:1-2; Luke 9:28-29. This is commonly referred to as "The Transfiguration of Christ.") They could not explain it. Yet the event is consistent with the findings of modern scientists that everything visible can be converted to energy, and that the universe is awash in energy. It also agrees with the experience of many of us in the healing field, who have seen light surrounding people.

We can no longer believe that Moses and Jesus were unique in being enfolded in white light. These were natural phenomena and not supernatural. With the advance of knowledge, however, we have gained more than we have lost. These accounts of Moses' and Jesus' appearance are based on fact. The energetic or etheric body, which provides the formative and sustaining pattern for the physical body, is experienced as light. This is what the apostles saw, and it fits closely with the meaning of the Greek term for "transfigured."

James Eden, in his book, "Energetic Healing," gives corroborating evidence for the reality of the energetic body. Also, Kendall Johnson, who worked with Thelma Moss at UCLA, writes:

"Our experiments with radiation field photography and the Kirlian effect have led us to the conclusion that there is in each living organism an energy matrix or template that provides an underlying structure for its material body. The corona or edge effect that we have observed is the telltale evidence of that matrix."

The light, then, has always been present in all of us, though hitherto unknown and unrecognized. Knowing this, some of Jesus' statements take on new meaning. He not only declared, "I am the light of the world," (John 8:12; 9:5), but also, "You are the light of the world." (Matthew 5:14) Both in a literal and figurative sense, he knew how to "let the light shine."

Chapter 32

THE VILLAGE THAT IS OUT OF TIME

The first thing that Lucy saw was tall mountains covered in trees, and a village nestled in a valley. She announced, "I'm coming down between the trees to the floor of the valley, to the path that leads to the village. There's a path, but you have to know where it is. The village is hidden. You can't see it unless you know where it is. It is protected on all sides by tall mountains. Trees go down the mountains, and in the valley, the canopy of the trees covers the village. You have to know where it is. I go back and forth there. I talk to the people that stay there. I don't stay there. I find out what they have been doing, their reports, their investigations, their studies. I give advice. I point new directions. They don't travel up. I don't know why. I'm not the only one that does this, but I travel up."

D: *What do you mean by* up?
L: When I come to the village, I come down like from a cloud. When I come back up, I go back up like to a cloud, but it's not a cloud. It's not a ship either. It's just there.
D: *I thought you meant it was from the top of the mountain, but that's not the way it is.*
L: No. It's like I come to a ship that's not a ship. I don't know what it is.
D: *What does it look like?*
L: On the outside it's kind of grayish, porous looking, but on the inside it's another *space* ... a dimension. The outside is just a camouflage of the inside. An approximation of where I go from the outside to the inside. It's not seen

449

easily from below, but if it were seen it would look like, I guess, what some would call a "ship," but it's not a ship. It's a camouflage. It looks like a form of something, but when you go through it, you're no longer in that dimension. You're in this space.

So sometimes what people think are UFOs are actually portals or doorways to other dimensions. They are just disguised to resemble something else.

D: *So you can go through without opening a door or anything?*
L: Yes, it's like a membrane and you just go through it.
D: *Is this where you are from?*
L: Now ... yes.
D: *How do you perceive your body?*
L: Down below, human, but it's like camouflage.
D: *Another kind of camouflage.*
L: Right. Up above, inside, is a light. I can feel the outline of a body, but it's not with form ... light. A light body. Consciousness contained within energy.
D: *So it's not one solid light? Is that what you mean?*
L: Many colored lights.
D: *Then when you go to the village, you take on a human form?*
L: Yes. Cover it with a human form. It's a very thin covering so that it's easier to walk among, talk among. Most of the others are like me, too. They're here. Some are from there, and they wouldn't understand.
D: *What do you mean? Are these the people in the village you're talking about?*
L: The people in the village are like me, but the people that are not like me don't know that because we look like them. So when I come to visit, I have to look like them so nobody is afraid.
D: *But the other ones live there among them?*
L: Yes, and they don't know.

D: *Is that their job to stay there with them?*

L: Staying there, training them, learning and teaching them.

D: *What do the other people look like?*

L: They look like humans. The women and the men wear the same kind of clothes. Long shirt like things of fabric woven from natural stalks, grasses. But a soft, long shirt down to the knees and thin pants under, sandals.

D: *These people are native to that village?*

L: No, this village isn't a village that people settled. It's like a place they come to share between villages ... between groups of people, between places ... a meeting ground.

D: *They don't live there all the time?*

L: Somebody's always there, but the people are coming and going. It makes it easier for us to move in among them and to be their teachers. They have memories of us being their teachers for a long time.

D: *They come there to stay for a short period of time?*

L: Some short ... some long, depending on what they are learning. Those learning how to grow things, how to heal things, how to make things, each takes a different amount of time.

D: *Do each of your group teach something different?*

L: We all know what everyone else knows, but some are better at teaching certain things than others. We can visualize what we try to teach others better because they learn from showing as well as telling.

D: *Then when these people are taught, do they go back to their villages?* (Yes) *Do they have a memory of what has happened?*

L: Yes, they do.

D: *Do they know where they have gone?*

L: Yes. They have been selected by their village to come here. Sometimes villages send the same people. Sometimes they send different people for the different times of the year, but there's a constant coming and going. Different people in the village coming for different things. It's very much like a living library.

451

D: *That would be a good way to describe it. So when these people go to their homes, the people there understand what's happening?*

L: Yes. They know they've gone to this place like a school. Only sometimes they actually make the things they bring back, so maybe they can make them in their towns, villages. Sometimes it's drawings they bring back ... different things.

D: *So they become like the teachers in those villages?*

L: Inventors, teachers, helpers, doctors, healers.

D: *Would anyone try to come there if they weren't supposed to?*

L: No. No one has ever tried. They know if they want to come, all they have to do is ask.

D: *I was thinking if somebody tried to follow one of them.*

L: Sometimes children try to follow them, but children are not ready for this. These are adults ... some older people, who are learning the techniques of the mind so they can pass on what they have learned. Mind to mind doesn't describe it very well. Sometimes children try to follow, but there's protection around this place in the valley and only those who should be there can go through the door. They can't find it otherwise. It is protected. Even if they were standing right in front of it, they wouldn't know it unless they could go through it. It's a special place. It's out of time.

D: *What do you mean?*

L: It exists in the valley, but it's not in time. It's in space, but not in time.

D: *But this valley is an actual place, isn't it?*

L: The valley is, but the village is out of time. It's *in* that space and part of that space, but not in that time. Those who come to the village, when they walk through the door, they move out of time. And when they walk back out, they're back in their time.

D: *They don't realize this, do they?*

L: No, only those like us know that they are out of time. There's no reason for them to know this. And how would you explain it?

D: *To the average person it wouldn't make any sense.*

L: To some people, the older ones that live in what they call "modern times." All different times come here. Those that come in modern times understand the concept of space and time. Others ... it's too difficult.

D: *I was thinking this was just one time period.* (No) *So when you said they were going back and forth, you meant they come from other time periods?*

L: Yes. When they're in the village, it seems as if they're all living in the same time, even though they actually come from different times. They're all dressed alike, but they are all from different times, different seasons. They exist together in that space and on some level they all understand this even if they don't understand why. "What is this place?" It's not threatening. It's not frightening. It's natural. They come to learn and when they are done learning, they go home and they do what they have learned to do.

D: *Do they forget about being there?*

L: No, but they can't describe it to anyone that asks. They would just say, "You know, it's like a school. I met with these people. We learned these things. We went to the field and they showed me how to plant it. We went to a laboratory and they showed me how to use this."

D: *Some people, if they came from way in the past, would be very primitive, wouldn't they?* (Yes.) *So they're only taught what they can handle.* (Yes) *And other people that came from more advanced time periods?*

L: They return with drawings. They return with samples of what they want to create in their time.

D: *But the ones from the modern times would have more knowledge and be more intelligent.*

L: Intelligence is an interesting thing. Primitive people are not necessarily less intelligent. What we refer to as primitive isn't really primitive. They are much more aware of the spiritual context, aware of the world around them. They understand "All is one." No, the ones who are not ready for this learning would not even know this place.

D: *But even the more advanced ones in time....*

L: They think they are having a very vivid dream. It's kind of funny ... the dream within the dream.

D: *They wake up and make drawings?*

L: Yes, they come back with the drawings or the music in their mind, or a picture in their head.

D: *Aha! So they can reproduce the drawings and they can invent whatever it is?*

L: Yes. Pretty clever!

D: *It sounds like a very good place.* (We laughed.) *But you're one of those that go there and teach?* (Pause) *Or what do you do there?*

L: I observe. I listen. I walk among them, and if there is a question needing an answer, I absorb that, then they get what they need to know. But mostly I just observe and feel how it feels, if it's in balance. Learning is harder to do when you're out of balance. So people there, whether they're part of us or part of there, they still have to be balanced. They still have to be smooth and calm and clear.

D: *Were you ever one of the teachers?*

L: I have been ... mostly because it's kind of fun to do, but only for certain things.

D: *Did you have a specialty?*

L: The various healing arts that had to do with the mind and body connection. Sinking into the deeper layers of consciousness and then weaving those back and forth, inner versus outer, layers of consciousness. Sometimes there are snags, bundles where energy collects instead of moving freely and smoothly. And the sound is discordant instead of harmonious, and you have to know how to smooth that out so the physical body and the mental body can work together. I watched others working with the energies and if they got stuck—particularly if they were in the middle of something—and they got stuck with smoothing the energies out, then I showed them how to smooth it.

D: *You used to teach it and now you're just observing it?*

L: Right. At some point you can let your students become the teachers. And so they feel more confident when I am letting them do their work, but they know I'm there if they need me.

D: *You said sometimes they get stuck because there are tangles between the energies of the mind and the body?*

L: Yes, sometimes the mind interferes with the body and they create tangles of energy that are too difficult to unravel. They are so tangled up they can't be cut. They have to be smoothed, help them unravel.

D: *What do you tell them to do when they run across things like that?*

L: I don't tell them. I show them. I move it with my mind.

D: *Can you explain it?*

L: I don't know. I move it with my energy. My energy reaches out to their energy, blends with it, dances with it, and sweetly unravels it to where it seeks its *like* kind and then the energy withdraws from it.

D: *Then when your energy withdraws from it, it remains? It's not tangled anymore? You don't have to be there constantly?*

L: No, no. When they get stuck working with whomever it is that's come for healing.

D: *Then you smooth it out and you step back?* (Yes) *But it remains?*

L: Yes, it remains smooth when I've finished and the teacher is sometimes joined with me. Sometimes not ... sometimes just watching to see how I do it and then they touch it when it's finished to see how it feels.—It's the combination of the energy and the mind and the body where the two blend together ... very complicated. The

455

mind has a different kind of energy than the body. Blending the two together to harmony is important for longevity. To keep the body alive as long as you want to be alive and to keep it healthy. And sometimes things happen to the body. Sometimes things happen to the mind. Something damages, traumatizes, inflicts discordant energy into the mind. And because the mind is connected to the body, the mind and the body become entangled, bundled up into these knots that have to be smoothed out.

D: *And of course, the person doesn't realize any of this has happened.*

L: No, you have to know how to *see* this energy ... a deep level of seeing.

D: *What would it look like if you saw it?*

L: Threads of energy, different colors, different thicknesses, thick, thin, tiny, large but all jumbled together into balls, like tangled yarn. Each has a purpose though, and when it's entangled, its energy is not going where it's supposed to go.

D: *So your job is more or less making sure they are doing it correctly?* (Right.) *And then use the energy of your mind if it's not working like it's supposed to.*

L: Right, and to go in and unravel and smooth and then gently withdraw without trauma to either the mind or the body. Tricky, very tricky to establish that balance.

D: *You said you're observing but you also apply the energy?*

L: Both. I apply the energy to the people coming if the teachers working with them cannot. If they get stuck. I go directly to the source of where it's coming from.

D: *Do you work with them for quite a while?*

L: I go in and out. Sometimes I'm there, and it feels like time doesn't work in that place the same way it does outside of it. So it may be only a few minutes, and when you step out of that place, it may have been days, weeks, and months.

D: *You said it was out of time because people are coming from all the different time periods, as we perceive them.*

L: I don't know time as well. Time is different for me. Time exists in that particular space, but not for me. The place where I come from has no time. I know what time I'm in when I'm out of there, but when I come back there's no time.

D: *But you know time does exist in other places?*

L: Time runs differently in places. Some slow, some fast, some heavy, some light. Time is like a river. Sometimes it's fast moving. Sometimes it's slow and not consistent. —There are many places out of time.

D: (That was a surprise.) *There are?* (Yes.) *On Earth or just other places?*

L: Everywhere. Everywhere throughout the Universe. There are places out of time. How else would we get there instantly?

D: *Well, I know they say people travel by thought.* (Especially extraterrestrials.) *Is that what you mean?*

L: Yes, similar. Thought is energy. Everything travels with energy as energy. It's all energy. It's the fine tuning of the energy, the density of the energy, different times, different spaces throughout the Universe. Like windows into time and space, like doorways.

D: *You said there are places all over the Earth that are out of time?*

L: Yes. People very rarely ... people stumble across them, but because they're out of time, they're usually protected. It's very hard. You could walk right through some of these places and not know it's there because you are not in time with it.

D: *Not vibrating at the same frequency?*

L: Right, like a vibration, if you're not vibrating at that time. There's a mountain on an island. I'm not sure about the geography, but you walk between the rocks, a sliver of space in these large, large boulders. You have to know right where that sliver is. You walk through it and into this opening in the mountain, and you're out of time.

D: *I wonder if they would feel anything or see anything.*

L: Oh, yes, they see and feel sometimes, depending on what they are in tune with. There are places that can take them to other places. They don't stay there in the mountain. They go to other places, but if their vibration, their energy, does not match, they can't go anywhere. They don't even see it. They don't even know it's there.

D: *Would they know something was happening?*

L: They know something has happened. They don't always understand it. Some that do remember don't really want to talk about it. It's strange to them.

D: *It's almost like they have traveled into another dimension.*

L: Yes. The Universe is full of these places.

D: *But if the Universe is full of these "puddles"—it's not really a puddle, a window. Is there any danger of them going in and not being able to find their way back?*

L: Never. Your energy is always tuned to where you started, so you always come back to the right time. The energy always knows where it comes from.

D: *So you can't go there and get lost.*

L: No, you can't go there and get lost. If you panic and you're afraid—and sometimes people are—all you have to do is say, "Take me home." And the minute you say *home* or think *home*, or visualize *home*, you are where you started. And maybe time has passed, maybe time hasn't. It depends on what "pool" you're in.

D: *What pool?*

L: What place.

D: *But they can go someplace that would look totally different than when they first started out.*

L: Yes, and some of them do.

D: *That might be frightening to someone.*

L: They must have been ready for it or they wouldn't have been able to vibrate to it. They wouldn't match the energy. They can't go where the energy doesn't match.

And even if it is surprising or confusing or difficult for them to understand, on some level they do understand. And any discomfort, panic, whatever, subsides almost immediately.

This sounded very similar to portals through time and dimensions that have been reported in my other *Convoluted Universe* books.

D: *So, on some level they asked for that experience?*

L: Yes. Sometimes they think they've had a strange dream because it's easier to think of it as a dream.

D: *There wouldn't be any stability if they could do this all the time.*

L: Right, but no, no one can do this all of the time. When you need to do it, perhaps when you want to do it, if your desire matches your energy. You can do it for curiosity. Curiosity is what leads you forward to move.

D: *Curiosity is a very good, strong emotion.*

L: Very strong, but curiosity is a very light, light emotion. It's light. Explore.—If the person has asked on another level and they are ready for it, it can happen. There's an agreement among the others as well within them that this would be a good thing. So you see it's impossible to abuse or misuse this gift, this natural ability, that we all have. If they attempt to pervert it, energy dissipates in them and they can't get it back until they've created the clearance. There are all kinds of safeguards built into this. The energy protects itself.

D: *I have heard that you could go somewhere and get lost.*

L: No, I don't think it's possible to get lost. Even those who think they are, I think that's panic more than anything else. The minute they calm down and think of where they came from, they're back. The thought, the visual image, brings them back.

D: *They don't stay too long in these places, do they?*

L: Well, you're out of time, so it may be minutes and it may be months, and in their own time it may be minutes. Very much like, sometimes you can have a dream of an entire lifetime in one night, but when you wake up the next morning, it's only been overnight. You've moved out of time. Time works differently outside here.

D: *But that place where you came from, you said it was camouflaged to look like a ship.* (Yes.) *You said you entered a different dimension?* (Right.) *By just going through the wall of the ship or what?*

L: Yes, it's just camouflage. The minute you go through it you're in another space.

D: *This is very similar to what you are talking about.* (Yes) *Is it correct that when you go back into that dimension, that would be your "home"?*

L: Yes, I guess it would be like where I stay. I travel a lot. Home is wherever I am. I'm never "not home." I travel through space, through time. Depending on the energy I take, that's where I go back to. That other dimension is a temporary home, but home is even deeper than that. Home is a bigger space .... Oh, how do you describe space and time? (Frustrated.) It's outside space/time. I move in and out and when I move back through that camouflage and into space, that's a nice place to be. It's a real space. It's beautiful. It feels good. It's a time that we can be together in a little bit more conscious, less physical, more light body, but beyond. Light body is not the end to that. There's more, but beyond that it encompasses more than the limitations of a physical body, whether it's a light physical body or a regular physical body. Does that make sense?

D: *Yes, that makes sense to me, but then I investigate more of this than the average person.* (She laughed.) *But would these places be the same things as "portals"?*

L: Yes. Portals, doorways, windows ... wormhole is not appropriate.

D: *That is something different.* (Yes) *How do you define a wormhole?*

L: I don't. I don't go there. Wormholes are a mess! I don't like messing with them. They're difficult. They're heavy. They're amateurish.

D: *Okay.* (Laugh) *But portals are very similar to what you are talking about.*

L: Very similar. People would walk right through it and not know it was there, and they walked right through a door or a portal or a window. They don't know it's there because they aren't aligned to it, attuned to it, aware of it. It would look like nothing. They would not know it was there.

D: *I've also been told that the difference between a portal and a window is that you can look through a window, but you can't travel through.* (Yes, yes.) *Seeing into another dimension, another time, but not actually traveling there?*

L: Yes. It depends on what your intent is, whether it's a window or a portal. It can be a portal. If your intent is to observe, it's a window; if your intent is to travel, it's a portal. Like there's a doorway.

D: *And when you're inside, it's like being in a physical place.* (Yes) *But I was also told that you can't bring any physical objects back with you.*

L: No, that's why you have to come back in the mind or as a dream. That's why most people think it's a dream, an inspiration. Even though they made a physical representation, like they have made a new instrument or a new painting there. They can't take it from there. But they recreate it when they get back home.

D: *So what I have been told is accurate.* (Yes) *But is this what you mostly do, travel to observe and to teach?*

L: Yes, and then I have my times that I join other groups, where I'm learning new things from the places they've been to. We share what we learned when we traveled.

D: *So you never know it all?*

L: (Emphasized.) No! We all keep learning. It's very interesting. We are all learning together and sharing together, and sometimes someone wants to go to the places I've been because they want to see for themselves. And that's fine, too. That's why I say, "When we go down we blend in." Wherever we go we blend in. I don't even need to go into this alien stuff. Some of the alien stuff is ridiculous!

D: *That's okay because I've worked with it and I think I understand more than the average person.*

L: I bet you do. I'm sure you do. You understand what is behind the beingness. You understand the beings. And you understand sometimes the mirrors that reflect back to the people that see them?

D: *I call it overlays – what's another word?*

L: Masks.

D: *Something to make them think they have seen something that's not really there.*

L: Yes, screen memories.

D: *That's the word. Screen memories are overlays. Is that what you mean?*

L: Yes. It's done to protect. It's also done because sometimes, vision is wide ... and sometimes there are people who ... that's too much wideness.

D: *They can't handle it.* (No) *Their mind isn't equipped to handle it.*

L: The concepts, the context, the constructs, even the imagery, you have to build it like you're weaving a tapestry. And the more you work on a tapestry, the more it moves from a two-dimensional to a three-dimensional to a four-dimensional. Just like weaving a virtual reality that you see on the videos. It's the same thing and some people can only handle the two-dimensional. Some can handle the three-dimensional and the four-dimensional and more.

D: *I've been told that the aliens, the ETs or whatever you want to call them, are very gentle about this because they know what the person can handle.*

L: Yes. They are very gentle.

D: *And sometimes a person thinks they saw one thing and that's not at all what they saw.*

L: Yes, and that's okay.

D: *But sometimes they remember it with fear.*

L: Yes, and that's puzzling. That's something that got lost in the translation. Like the energy between the mind and body got tangled and that needs to be unraveled. And sometimes it has to be unraveled in sleep to take that fear away.

D: *I have worked with this for so long that I know there's nothing negative there. It's all in the person's perception of it.*

L: Yes, and that's why it's tangled because the mind is not comprehending the something else that was not there and makes it fearful. And so that becomes entangled with the real memory and the real experience, and so the created one causes the body to react. It's very sensitive. If people only knew how sensitive the body was to the mind. So you have to correct it, move it.

I understand this concept in my work with healing illnesses. The body is very sensitive to what the mind creates and this causes illness and disease. The body is only reacting. Thoughts are extremely powerful.

D: *It is my understanding that the aliens or ETs are just another form of life that the soul is experiencing.*

L: Yes, yes, and they take the form that they choose. And if they are physical, they have the form of where they are from. So many people throughout the universe, and in different times as well as space. There are so many different types.

D: *But have you ever lived in a physical body?*

L: Many times.

D: *So you haven't always been the observer, the light body.*

L: I move in and out. Are you aware that more than one consciousness can share a body?

D: *I'm not sure.*

L: As there are consciousness having many lifetimes, many experiences, here, there, everywhere. Your awareness can move in and out of those so that you are experiencing life here, life there, in different places and spaces of times. So when you slip—it's like slipping—you're slipping into that time, then you're living in that time, the physical body or whatever form it is. But your awareness, your consciousness, can also slip out, but life keeps going. Your consciousness is there and here.

D: *People talk about possession ....*

L: No, no, no, no. I don't believe in possession. I honestly think that people ... you know what I think that is? When people feel possessed, it's their own fear that has literally manifested.

D: *I believe that. Fear is very powerful.*

L: You can literally create. If you can create anything, then you can create fear. It takes form just as love takes form.

D: *But you were talking about two consciousness sharing a body. I've had cases where something would just enter... to just observe.*

These cases are reported in my other *Convoluted Universe* books.

L: Observe. That's all they can do. They are not the indwelling soul that is there.

D: *Two souls are not allowed to be in a body.*

L: No, no, they are observing.—Yes, I have lived in physical bodies. Physical lives, different places, different times. Human form is more available throughout the universe, multiverse, whatever you call it. Human form is more often found than not. Maybe a few tweaks and twitches different, but it's a template.

D: *I heard it's more practical: the torso, the head and the appendages.*

L: Symmetrical? Symmetry. Everything in this world has symmetry: plants, animals, the air, the water, everything has symmetry. When it's out of symmetry, out of discord, it's damaged. It has to be repaired, renewed and replenished.

D: *That's part of your job?* (Yes)

This was all very interesting, but it was time to bring the session back to the therapy that Lucy came to me for. "Are you aware that you're talking through a physical human at this time?"

L: Yes because I am part of this human.

D: *We thought we were going back to a past life, and I guess it was a past life.* (Laugh)

L: Past, present, future, no time.

D: *Of course, Lucy is not aware of you, is she?* (Laugh.)

L: Somewhat. The observer, the part that pays attention and notices that there's gentleness, wholeness right there, right there, where she can sense it. She's very good at sensing.

D: *She's done a wonderful job doing the same things you were doing ... teaching.*

L: In some respects, yes, definitely teaching. She knows her stuff when she teaches. That's why I'm able to be here because we are intoned, we are connected, we are a part aligned. She has helped many people with her work, but she doesn't really know. You never know. If you throw a pebble into the pool, you have no idea how far those ripples go out and that's okay. She doesn't need to. She doesn't particularly want to. Only if it causes harm is it a problem.—You never know until you go to the next level and look back.

We went through some of her questions, until we came to the "eternal" question: What is my purpose? They said it was time for her to be the experiencer, be on the other side of it.

465

She had been a teacher for so long, it was time to relax and enjoy life, to have fun.

L: She doesn't have to teach anymore. She can just *be* and some people can learn by just being around her. She really is a pretty good listener. Now comes the fun. Now the more joy, the more peace, the more balance brings to her life, the more the "New Earth," as you have called it. The New Earth is already there. It just has to become solid. Just bring in the joy and have *fun!*

Physical: She was born with a dislocated hip that caused a lot of problems when she was very young, and she had surgery to correct it. But then the problem came back when she was an adult and she had a hip replacement.

L: Miserable pain, miserable past life where there was no surgery. There was no way out of it. The pain lasted forever. It never went away, and it got worse and worse and worse. And eventually she "thought" herself to death. Not the same as suicide, but she "thought" herself to death. She willed herself to die. The pain was too much. What she didn't realize is that because she was in pain when she left, she took that pain with her. That's why it's much better to solve it before you go. You settle it. You make sure you are not in pain, whether it's physical, mental, or emotional because you take that pain with you. Sometimes it's easy to heal in another place, but sometimes it sticks like glue. Sometimes on the spirit side it can be healed very quickly. And sometimes it's so embedded, so unraveled that a piece of it, parts of it continue to travel with your consciousness as you move in different times, lives.

D: *I call it the "residue" people carry.*

L: Exactly. The residue carries with you, and so the physical form approximates that residue.

D: *That's what I deal with.* *It causes illnesses in this lifetime.* (Right.)

The hip problem had been caused by several falls in other past lives, so it was not just one incident. I asked what made it come back in this life, and I received the same answer I have heard many times: fear of moving forward. Especially into "unchartered territory." "The Mobia Strip, as she refers to it, the weaving of the physical, emotional and spiritual. The subconscious mind is really, mostly, concerned with the physical." They said it was healed.

L: She has already been shown a number of times in dreams, how she can literally transmute that metal back to the bone. (The hip replacement.) But that's too much for her to do right now.

D: *You have told me before that you can't do much with metal; it is very hard to get that out of the body.*

L: It is, and what we have done is seal the metal, so that it does not create hardship to her body. Metal emits energy that is harmful on some level. It is an interference of the body's physical energy. Hers is sealed, so it will not cause any problem. Her concern is that she was told that she would possibly have to have surgery again because it only lasts fifteen to twenty years, and hers is getting close to that. It's not going to be a problem.

D: *The doctors put that suggestion into her mind.*

L: Yes, and there's her little subconscious mind lapping it up like a kitten to cream. (Laugh) That's okay. We can reassure her, but it's sealed now so that it doesn't cause problems. She won't have to fear having that surgery

Parting message: No fear, no pain, no sorrow, no grief, just joy!

Chapter 33

THE EMBODIMENT OF AN ASPECT

Heather went to a life where she was some type of alien being, definitely not human, a dwarf with thick short hands and arms. He was going to the place where he worked or where he received his work assignments. The place was full of hundreds of other strange looking beings, all appearing different from each other. "Their appearance doesn't matter. I can barely even see that. I see them more as the function of the work that we do together." The place was a big auditorium with many tiers of seats. There was a podium in the middle and the tiers formed a circle around it. "The closer you are to the podium the responsibility increases, and the vibratory rate increases. No one's position is higher than the others. Everyone has an equal respect, equal say. We're all consulting together. We're all putting our ideas together and deciding things which the council acts on. The council is the ten people in the middle. This is more than just for my country, my place of origin. It's for the galaxy. That's why there are so many different kinds of people. But this is only one site, one organization. We represent the energy for our area, one part of the galaxy. And other people come there and attend. They represent the council and they go to another place where the council is bigger. And so they represent what we decide here to the bigger council. The ideas and agreements."

D: *Do these ten look different than the others?*
H: When I look at them I see them looking like a pillar of light. I can't see a being in there. I can only see pure light. And my sense is that they're beyond embodiment in

any form. They are beyond form.—My body can hold massive degrees of energy, and I use it to move from place to place to go someplace to do my work. But in my normal off time I don't have to limit myself to that body. I just sort of sit in meditation. And it can sit without breathing or eating or drinking. When I'm in my off time, my body just sits. I can leave my body very easily without maintaining it for long periods of time. That's my preferred state. My preferred state is non-body. But when I go to do this work, it's like I put on my body because I get a call. We still have a vibratory rate where we embody, but it's much lighter.—The second tier people actually flicker in and out. We stay in that body and hold the energy. The first tier doesn't even bother with that. They're just completely out of any body, any form—they just don't have any body.

D: *They're just completely energy then.* (Yes) *Your body will stay alive while it is just sitting there?*

H: It doesn't seem to breathe, and the organs go dormant almost. So you don't need water, you don't *need*. It doesn't matter too much to me. It's almost like I'm shut off waiting for my work.

D: *So the body maintains itself without having the soul or spirit in it.*

H: Yes, and yet I can come back at any time and make everything move again.

D: *When you're in that auditorium building, I was wondering about the purpose of the meeting.*

H: It's galactic and interglactic decisions. One of the people in the middle always starts the question. And each person has their input. And the people in the upper tiers are observing. They are not at the level to participate.

D: *What type of work are you sent to do?*

H: I work with planetary bodies. Surveys. It's measuring the spiritual readiness and cultural feelings of planets, and the planet itself. I have to go there, and I have to feel the energy of that place at that time. Like a survey, but I'm mingling with the planet, and a lot of information gathering. I work with planets and people, individuals. Because we work very, very fast, I see each person lightning fast.

D: *Is that place close to Earth, or does it have any connection to Earth?*

H: My actual ship can go anywhere, so we can be close to Earth. The place with the auditorium is far away across the galaxy, but it's still related to the galaxy that this planet is in. When I come to Earth, I have to embody an aspect of myself here. Other places are lighter, and I can go and get the information I need just in my etheric body. Go and come back. But with Earth I stayed longer.

D: *So you are doing this at the same time you have an aspect of yourself in an Earth body?*

H: Yes, and the rest of me is in the dwarf body.

D: *This aspect that is on Earth, is that the one I am speaking to known as Heather?* (Yes) *That is the aspect you sent to Earth?* (Yes) *It has to be an aspect because the energy is too strong?*

H: Yes. And because I only do as much as I need to do. (Laugh) That's kind of funny. Because this body that sits in the spaceship is regulating every part that goes out. So it's multitasking many different surveys at once with aspects. And each planet needs different energy, different levels of embodiment, in order to get the information we need.

D: *You can do more with all these different aspects, than just going as an individual.*

H: Right. So even when we put an aspect and go in our little bodies—or in my case, my little body in the chair. That's just one aspect reporting there, while there's still the surveying going on, on different planets and things at the same time.

D: *So when did your aspect enter the body of Heather? When did you send the aspect to Earth?*

H: It was arranged when she died.

D: *What do you mean?*

H: She died right after she was born because the body was very small, and another aspect was born.

D: *So you mean she actually died at that time, and the original spirit left?*

H: Aspect. It was still me, still *one* of me. And the other one of me who stayed didn't want to go through the birth of a human.

D: *Because sometimes that's an unpleasant experience.*

H: And also it was a small aspect portion that was born, for the safety of the mother and the baby. And then it was like it took five of the beings squishing. That's not exactly right, but assisting. And they couldn't do that while the baby was in the womb of the mother. So once the body was in the incubator they could assist me to enter safely then. The me that's the *more* aspect, the bigger, the faster, intense, brighter aspect to enter.

D: *So this would have been too hard on the mother.*

H: When they tried it, the babies died, so they knew they had to wait. It was too intense. The baby would die in the womb when they tried it in the past. Something had to be adjusted so that life can continue in that body.

D: *It had to be a small part to come into the body of Heather. Why did you want an aspect to come to Earth?*

H: The thought that comes is, it was an assignment. There would be no question. I was just handed that, and I am of service. And there's no question. It is my glory, it is my honor and privilege to serve the Center.

D: *I keep thinking of reincarnation. Has this personality we know as Heather had other lifetimes on Earth? Or is there a way of explaining this if we're speaking to this other aspect?*

H: This dwarf person has embodied at key times for assignment. I don't, in my consciousness, access other people's lives. I can, but it's confusing. Once I go above that, then it isn't Heather's lives. It becomes everyone's, and then it's not relevant to me. I was on assignment during that time that they say Jesus Christ was here. It was really three aspects, and they were spread in other bodies. Also we come in when there are major spiritual changes afoot. And there are ones we don't have in history here that I came for. There was a major change during a pharaoh. That would be one, and Buddha's time. It has to do with the people in the circle. I hold something, and all of us do. Many of us in these circles have our assignments around the time of embodiment for them for key times. We all work together and have our roles to play for holding the energy for a shifting with the spiritual atmosphere of a planet.

D: *Is this why you have sent this aspect now at this time because of the things that are going to happen?*

H: Yes. And we do it on other planets, too. We all go together on other planets as well because we amplify the spiritual energy of a planet at key times. In the same way that, at this time, this entire auditorium is embodied on Earth to change the spiritual energy on Earth. They all are here to work together to change the spiritual energy of this planet, and this plane. More than just this planet.

D: *She wanted to know her purpose. What is she supposed to be doing?*

H: There is no other work or purpose, and we know only this work.

D: *She thinks she is using the energy to change people's DNA.*

H: Yes, that is the work. It is the spiritual work. The human and all species have to change at this time. Must change, will change or leave. Her presence is called for, period. Her light will draw more people like a lighthouse.— Considering the material that we have to work with, we created a strong body because we have very strong bodies. We chose this body carefully to have dense bones. Most of her DNA on the male side is not standard issue human DNA, so that she could hold the energy. We received assistance from a more embodied group than we are, to physically implant and change our DNA. The father was a smokescreen for the mother for the conception to be logical, but we did not require too much of his material. Some of his physical strength and controlling bone DNA, was what he contributed. That is why we chose him.

Parting message: Heather is dearly loved. And we honor her for the separation difficulty of being embodied here on this Earth. We fully appreciate the difficulty and we await her return.

Chapter 34

CHANGING DNA

Ned was a troubled young man. More of a wanderer, he was traveling from place to place, still trying to "find" himself, yet not feeling at home anywhere. He caught up with me in Hawaii where we had this session. When he first came off the cloud he saw water, but it didn't appear like normal water. It was pink and sparkly. Then he said he was in the water, yet it didn't feel like water.

N: I'm in the water. I don't know where the surface of the water is, though. It's pink and sparkly and it feels really good on my skin, too. It feels like it's mixed with air, or something. I don't know how to say it. Maybe if I was outside of it, it would feel wet. But I don't think it's possible to be outside of it where I am right now.

D: *Why don't you think it's possible to be outside of it?*

N; Because it surrounds the whole planet.

D: *Then you don't think it's really water?*

N: He doesn't have the word to describe it. Water is a close enough metaphor. I'm in it, but it's part of me, too. I'm in an individuated experience inside of it, and there's something about what it is that's in me that connects me to it. But there is a distinguishment between them. It really feels good being here. I miss it a lot.

I asked him how he perceived himself.

N: I have skin. I have a membrane surrounding me that's kind of a grayish-blue.

D: *Then you feel like you're no longer a part of that substance you call "water"?*

N: No, I think that is in charge of keeping everything the way it should be so we can exist there like we do. And my responsibility is not as high, but my evolution isn't, either.

D: *So you could be part of this pink, sparkly substance?*

N: Yes. They love me there. I'm not developed enough to help be part of what holds it together so that I can experience inside more—the recipient of the experience.

D: *So you couldn't stay in that part all the time?*

N: Part of it that's related to the physical aspect, but it's not what I would describe as physical. I'm supposed to see this for some reason. They brought me here to show me.

D: *Who brought you there?*

N: (Nervous laugh) I don't know what they are. They're kind of scary, and funny, too.

D: *How did they bring you there?*

N: They chose me there, and I was just there.—I'm excited about going somewhere. They're trying to tell me I don't want to go, and I'm saying I want to go. I'm asking to go, and they're trying to tell me that I don't want to, and I'm saying I do.

D: *Where do you want to go?*

N: To Earth. They're saying, I don't know what it's going to be like, and I'm going to be scared. There was going to be experiences of stagnancy and non-growth for a long time. But it's really important that I am the one choosing to go. Which is why they're trying to discourage me—I don't think they believe me that I really do want to go.

D: *Why do you want to go?*

N: To help! There are difficulties there right now. It's complicated.

D: *How do you know these things?*

N: They're giving me that knowledge. I trust them.

D: *Even though they're strange looking, you do trust them.*

N: Yeah. (Nervous laugh) They are kind of scary, though. I know that if they thought me to not be there, I would stop existing. So there's some kind of fear element that is not justified for me to feel because that's just the part of me that isn't evolved.

D: *So this planet where you are is not Earth?*

N: (Laugh) No. It's a lot bigger. It has many orders of magnitude of dimensional development above what Ned understands as here now, though. Dimension is the most accurate term he knows to describe it.

D: *But if you're so happy there, wouldn't it be like a shock, or going backwards, to come to Earth?*

N: (Laugh) Like jumping in cold water. But it's fun.

D: *Are they trying to tell you what it would be like?*

N: Yeah. I don't get to always have fun. I think I can always make it fun, though. They think it's funny that I would think that.—My physical body won't be equipped with the physical abilities I'm used to enjoying and taking for granted right now.

D: *Any specific abilities that you won't have on Earth?*

N: Dematerializing, and you can't move things with the mind. That doesn't exist there yet. If enough of us go, we can teach that, but it's not there right now.

D: *Is it important to teach something like that?*

N: When it's asked to be taught. He wants to know it again.

D: *Then you're giving up a lot. Are you given a choice whether you want to go or not?*

N: Yeah. I don't know why I know that there's the opportunity to go, but I feel like I wouldn't be in front of them if I didn't know about the opportunity and ask it. I don't think that many of us know that this is even a possibility to regress back to a stage of a lower DNA template, though.

D: *Because usually you think about progressing, not going backwards.*

N: Yeah, there are a lot of difficulties and challenges with a higher level of spiritual evolution in a physical body that has a very large amount of dormancy with the DNA development. We can rebuild them, though.

D: *What do you mean, you can rebuild?*

N: They seem to want me to know that the only way we're going to be able to heal Earth through the path it's on is because the combination of our soul template inside the broken DNA template of the human body—which is like it is, not because it was meant to be that way. There was a lot of meddling to make it so. But our spirit can heal the DNA template itself, and make it available to everyone if we work on healing ourselves.

D: *You said the template was broken, the DNA was meddled with. What do you mean?*

N: The ones—I don't know why they're doing that—they're behaving in a way that is exactly opposite with how the Universe works, and they don't understand it.

D: *Do you mean the humans on Earth?*

N: No, the ones that are meddling with them. Some of the humans are, though, but that was just genetic stuff.

D: *Back in the very beginning, you mean?*

N: Yeah. People didn't choose that end, though—they were messed with.

D: *So the template was broken. (Yes) And you think it's one of your jobs to repair that?*

N: To heal me so we can all heal.

D: *Sounds like a big job.*

N: Yeah. There's a lot to do to make us all look outside of ourselves for things that we would consider important.

D: *So by coming into a physical body—although you say it's regressing—your spirit, your soul, will be able to change or repair the DNA?*

N: Yeah, apparently. They say we can actually manifest from the top down to physically change the template available to everyone. There are many of us here.

D: *So by doing it to one, it affects many? (Yes) How would that happen?*

N: Because the morphogenetic fields are all linked together.

D: *I thought you would have to go into each one and change each individual.*

N: That is what I do for me to heal my field template, and the contribution of that helps everyone else choose into that possibility, if they choose. Otherwise, they can't choose it until they get to this state naturally. The problem—it seems like Earth won't get there if something isn't done. It's on a path going the opposite direction because of all the meddling.

D: *It wouldn't just evolve there naturally.—You said there are many that are coming with this mission, if you want to call it a mission.*

N: Yes, it is. It's long. They don't think it's funny; I do. They're not laughing, though. They don't know why I think it's funny when a large group of beings decide to go opposite the law of One.

D: *They were going the wrong way.*

N: Yes. On Earth that's what they're doing.

D: *What do you think would happen of all of you didn't come to help?*

N: The time matrix would collapse here, as their soul groups would be undifferentiated for a long period of time. It would not be their ideal situation to create.

D: *By the matrix collapsing, do you mean the entire planet would just be destroyed?*

N: The whole harmonic universe that Earth is a schoolyard for. Everything is connected. It's a very limited state of consciousness needed to be experienced to perceive separation—and distance, even.

D: *So that's why it was important for all of you to come. But I've heard there are many others coming with other agendas.*

N: Oh, yes. They're cool, too. You'll like them. Some of them are here. I don't really know how many, though. They are all here to help. They chose it. We all did. We all chose it. Many people here seem to think they don't choose into the choosings they've chosen. They do, though. (Laugh)

D: *Well, these beings, these entities, are they the ones that are kind of in charge to tell people what to do?*

N: They're holding everything together. They're doing their best, and they give everyone an allowance of permission to create what they choose, even if it's not what is best for everyone else.

D: *They allow everyone on that planet?*

N: Everywhere. Everywhere in the whole time matrix.

D: *So they have a great deal of power?* (Yes) *It's like they're in charge of the whole thing.*

N: Not in charge—that's what they have become.

I asked if he, as a spirit, had ever been on Earth before. He responded that he had been on Earth, but had not always been the being we were speaking to. "It took a long time to earn that."

D: *You mean you evolved?*

N: Yes. I didn't pass through Earth for that lesson. But when I came, there was a place similar to it. It no longer exists, though. It was destroyed.

He then seemed uncomfortable and didn't want to talk about it. I told him he didn't have to if it upset him.

N: That's why I wanted to come back because that's not something that anyone wants to have happen. You always want to feel like your home is there for you. But if you miss what you have, you can go create it again.

D: *Were you there at the time it happened?*

N: No. But I knew many people that were there when that happened. I'm still here, though. I'm in a differentiated experience of consciousness outside of it, so I wasn't a part of the collapse. Or I left just before it happened. I don't have a name for it. It was a long time ago.

D: *But it affected the planet Earth?*

N: Yes! It *did* affect this dimensional level. Yes, it did. There might be physical remnants that are still there.

He said he evolved into this being after the collapse.

D: *You were just learning lessons of different types.*
N: Yeah. I would not describe them as fun, for the most part. —We've had to hide for a long time.
D: *Why did you have to hide?*
N: I don't like to die. It's not that fun. So we hide. It's better to experience things that make you smile.—And then he evolved until he was this other entity which was highly evolved. It took many, many lives to evolve to that point. The Earth life occurred after that entity.
D: *You would think after all of that, that he wouldn't want to come back.*
N: It hurts my heart to see Earth like it is, and think that, after passing through a similar experience, I couldn't try to do something. I'm existing anyway; I might as well exist where it's effective.
D: *But you were happy in the other water place. (Oh, yeah!) Then it was a step backwards to come back to Earth.*
N: No, it looks like it at one level. It's a big step forwards, though. Because the human DNA template is pretty amazing for what can happen in a third dimension, with the potential of it. It's almost all inactive right now.
D: *Have you had dealings with the others that were coming back to do the same thing? You said there were many.*
N: Yeah, he knows some of them, too. (Laugh) We've found each other, many of us. That's crazy. No, it's not! Why people make friends is due to many agreements they have to come together for a reason. You don't remember though. That makes it hard sometimes.

I thought it was time to get to the therapy part of the session, so I asked him if he was aware he was speaking through a physical body.

N: Yeah! Mostly when I go to sleep, though. Otherwise, it just seems like that is what I am—just that. The body. That's what they all try to tell us, though—the ones that know more.

D: *What do you mean?*

N: It seems like the majority of the problems with Earth are the beings that understand manifestation mechanics have had their information contorted so badly that they don't know that these mechanics are for everyone, and that everyone can create whatever they want. And you don't have to make everyone fight amongst themselves, and eliminate themselves, so that you can have their limited stuff because that's not why we're here.

This part that I was communicating with seemed to have a great deal of knowledge, but I didn't know if it would be able to supply the answers to Ned's questions. I asked it if I should call in the subconscious, or if it had the information we could use.

N: Some of it. He's rebuilt some of it; he doesn't have it all, though.

He then agreed that I should ask the subconscious to come forth. He was limited to a certain degree in his ability to answer the questions. I then thanked him because he did give us a lot of information. It said that it appreciated talking to me. I then called in the SC, and the first question I always ask is why it chose that particular lifetime to look at.

N: He's ready to know that. He knows he's not from here.

D: *He doesn't know it on a conscious level, does he?*

N: He thinks he does, but he thinks people are feeding him stories sometimes.

D: *Do you want to tell him about it.*

N: The word that will help him know is (Phonetic) Oro-feen. (Orophine?)

D: *Orophine? What does that mean?*

N: It's where he came from. I'm sure he will understand. It's the name of the soul group essence of the beings there.

D: *Orophine. I've never heard that name before.*

N: They're pretty high up.

D: *So he didn't have to come back. He could have just stayed there and kept evolving higher and higher, couldn't he?*

N: Yes. Due to some higher contractual obligations, he has a tendency to allow himself to feel obligated, rather than choosing and wanting into the process that he's in.

D: *But it makes it more difficult to come into a physical body and forget all these things. To know you have all these powers, and then all of a sudden you don't have anything but just a physical body.* (Yeah) *It's pretty frustrating, isn't it?*

N: Yeah, that's a word that can be used sometimes. Ned doesn't like that word at all, though. (Laugh) It has bad implications for the physical. He needs to know he did choose it all. He tries to act like he doesn't know what to do next, and that he doesn't know enough yet. Which is really ironic. He'll probably laugh later when he hears that.

D: *He does seem to be kind of wandering right now, not really knowing what he wants to do.*

N: Yeah, he punishes himself a lot. The way to word it so he'll understand is, he acclimated his neurology to emotional spikes that tend to come when he does something that he's not supposed to do. Which is useful for the most part because being subservient to authority is not conducive to his mission. But he does things that don't make any sense sometimes. (Laugh) Even when people who love him tell him to do something, sometimes he does the opposite, just because he thinks that's what he's supposed to do.

D: *But you said this is the way his neurological system is set up.*

N: Yes, but he chose that. He needed to distance himself with an illusion of separation from authority. You could say he has trouble with authority. It was harder before. He's working to be more open now. He knows he doesn't do nearly what he could, though.—You need to work on strand five now because strand four is fully rebuilt. Six is too far to look ahead to right now.

D: *What do you mean by those numbers?*

N: His DNA template that's physically manifest. He has four that are rebuilt; he thinks he's still in three though. He misinterprets things from not understanding a lot.

D: *So his DNA is already being rebuilt?*

N: Yes, many of you are. We're all making it possible for each other to rebuild that. So fourth strand is what we're working on right now.

D: *That's what I've heard, that the DNA has to change if we're going to make the shift.*

N: Yes. Everyone is really doing a great job, too. We all are.

D: *Is everyone's DNA changing?*

N: Yes. It's subtle, and it's more of a template change than a physical one. But it will be manifest for them when they're ready.—Five and six he has active from birth, but they're not ... the potential is there. Because six still has a lot of knots, and when sound travels through it, it's not all resonating in a harmonious manner, but it's still there. He tries to. But he doesn't understand the out-of-body thing yet. Right now it's just a game, and fun. He needs to learn how to utilize it as a tool to help others. Right now he's just playing. But he uses it to confirm information, which is helpful.

D: *What is the ultimate goal of this DNA, if you're going by these numbers?*

N: So that everyone can have avatar-level embodiment of their unconsciousness in the physical density, you could say.

D: *How high is it supposed to go?*

N: Twelve.

D: *Is that possible for the human?*

N: Yes! That's why it's such an amazing experience because there hasn't been a twelve-strand DNA template seeding before in this time matrix. It's very important!

D: *There are some people teaching that you can change immediately to twelve.*

N: Yes, their information sources are very, very flawed, though. They're channeling it from places that don't have their best interest in mind.

D: *So it is* gradually *happening. Is that where we're at right now, four and five?*

N: Ned's working on five; he's almost done here. The other indigos are working between four and five, and some are beyond six, actually. There are three avatars right now on the planet. And one of them has seven fully active. His name and identity are hidden though—it's not important to know who.

D: *I've been told many times we're not supposed to know who these people are.*

N: We're not. They have to hide.

D: *Because it could be dangerous to them.* (Yes) *But how does this make the body feel as the DNA is changing? What effects does this have on the body? Can we tell when it's happening?*

N: Your body's emotional system is your feedback point. So if you feel things that make you feel more of what you enjoy feeling, that help you feel emotions that you choose, if you can distance yourself from the emotion, you can call those good. Pejorative terms are not useful in most cases, but if you feel good emotions more often than not, it means you are directly on the path you're supposed to be on. The positive are feedback for when you're doing the things that you agreed to do. However, the negative emotions should not be confused sometimes because they're necessary to provide a distinction level so you can understand when the good ones are there.

D: *Is this changing of the DNA affecting the body physically?*

N: Yes, it feels like joy to have that happen. Experiences here described as peak experiences are usually activation points. And dealing with the emotional fallout afterwards is sometimes very interesting for him because he doesn't always perceive it as a good experience.

D: *I have heard that many people who are coming in for the first time have trouble dealing with emotions.*

N: Yes, very often.

D: *It really frightens them to feel it.*

N: Yes. But he's just used to the pattern of running away and hiding when external pressures manifest; which is necessary because before if he didn't run away and hide, he would get killed again. And that puts an obstacle on the level of progress that can happen in a single incarnation.

I asked what Ned's purpose was, what he was supposed to be doing during this time on Earth.

N: He's been given many gifts and he needs to share that without reservation. He wants to be judged in a positive way, and he doesn't understand fully that's not even the point because everyone is going to judge, no matter what. Especially if they're at a lower level of awareness development. He's been given many gifts, and he just needs to use them.

D: *But what path do you want him to take?*

N: Healing. He knows. He can stand between two worlds in a sense, which is helpful because he can bring to people who would not seek it, something that will help them. Because he can translate that into the medium of the technology currently available. Which, for some bizarre reason because it's external and complex, gives more credibility when it's actually less useful for people in a big picture development. He has information of things to create. And everyone that he needs to help create are already there in his life. He's still seeking other people to enable him to do this. And he knows—and there are three people who know him that know this, too—that all they need to do is do it.

D: *So the people are already in place.*

N: Yes, it's time to put the books down, and go ahead and do it. He can choose anyone he would like, but there are at least three separate creations he can manifest with others that will bring an extraordinary level of benefit to everyone.

D: *What are those three levels?*

N: (Laugh) It's a funny joke.

D: *What's the joke?*

N: Keylontic neurolarcrustic (?) (Phonetic: ner-o-lar-krewstic) biosymbaligismistics (?) (Phonetic: bio-sim-bul-ij-izm-ist-iks)

Was his intellectual arrogance having fun with me? http://www.bibliotecapleyades.net/voyagers/esp I thought the word he was using sounded a bit like chelation. He then spelled it: K-E-Y-L-O-N-T-I-C. There is a website for a Keylontic dictionary www.bibliotecapleyades.net/voyagers/esp voyagersindex.htm

N: It's the mechanics of matter manifestation and consciousness ascension. He's been given this information. He does appreciate it, and he does try to share it, and he chooses to feel distanced from people for knowing it. But he has been given this info. The information is there—he needs to create the device. It's a deflection of it.

D: *So it'll be a device.*

N: Yes. He and the entity known as James (his friend) are supposed to do it together. They spend too much time just enjoying it, though. And enjoying knowing what they know. The only reason to know that is to do it, though.

D: *They're just treading water.*

N: (Laugh) Yes, they are. Treading water—I like that.

D: *Well, that's one project. What are the other two?*

N: He can do them all. I think it would serve him more to only have one presented right now.

D: *To focus on one at a time?*

N: Yes. He already knows the others. They're already written down. They're manifest physically as knowledge, so he knows the steps to take. The first one he would describe as biofeedback software interface. In real time analysis—real time is a bizarre term—and light and sound. The ionized water is a very good idea, too.—That's enough for now. He chooses to feel overwhelmed in abundance, which he can create with knowledge. So it tends to impede his progress in movement.

D: *Ned did bring up the subject of doing healing.*

N: This device will facilitate that greatly because it will mean much less time and effort expenditure in the moment to cause healing to happen. And it's just one extra thing to add into the tool box. It's a big tool, though.

D: *He's been having a lot of fun playing at being human.*

N: Yes, this is an amazing body to have. There are many benefits to the human body.

Chapter 35

THE COLOR OF DNA

At first Susan saw doves and a fountain that was surrounded by a mist. She became aware as she moved into it that the mist was more of an energetic or magnetic field. Then she saw that her body was also not normal. "I know I'm there, but there's no body, if that makes any sense. I don't feel a body. I feel a form of some kind, but I don't feel arms and legs and feet. But I know I'm there in a form."

D: *What does that magnetic field feel like?*
S: I think I'm floating above it, but I'm in it at the same time. It feels like my brain's at rest, and I just have a knowingness without thinking about it. It's very peaceful.
D: *Do you want to move further or do you want to stay in that magnetic field?*
S: I feel like I'm going up. I'm being drawn up out of the mist in the field.
D: *What do you see as you are drawn up?*
S: A white X. I am going through the center of the X and I'm standing on white clouds. Very interesting standing on clouds.
D: *Is anyone else around or is it just you?*
S: Just me. I now have feet and a white robe "thing" ... not really material. Probably light, but it has a form to it like a loose robe. Above me is a goldish light. It's not warm and it's not cold. It's just very comforting. Very peaceful.—The light is emitting something. It's going across my forehead and shoulders, and it's making me

really warm. It's a good feeling. And I feel all this is interesting. Like my physical body is lying down here. All the pain is going out of it, and all the tension is relaxing. But yet, I'm up here in the light at the same time.

D: *That's okay. Let's concentrate on that part up there and see what it's doing.*

S: Oh, the light is moving from the front of my forehead around to the back of my head, and it feels like it's doing something. I can't describe exactly what it's doing. Maybe expanding my head like there are no bones there. It opened it all up like there are no real skull bones. Now the light is going all the way through me to my feet. It feels like an energy. It's right through the core. It's right through the middle. Not radiating to the sides, just right to the core ... through the middle.—Now I see something like a tunnel. It's right above me. I'm in a tube or a tunnel with clouds, with really beautiful gold sunlight shining down the tube.

D: *When that light, that energy was going through the body, what was it doing?*

S: Opening up the vibrations so I could go into the tunnel ... the tube.—The light is getting larger and it's filling up the whole tube. It's not clouds anymore. It's gold yellow light. It has a life of consciousness. It's not just color. I'm just immersed in the middle of it now. It's all around. It feels like there's a waterfall coming out of the center, flowing over the top all the way down. It's not water though, but it looks like water coming out of some kind of a pottery or something made out of gold. It's just flowing around me and it's shimmering. It's pink and it's blue and it's lavender, green and sparkly. Like an opaque pot or urn with something flowing out of it.

D: *What is the purpose of it flowing over you like that?*

S: I'm hearing words like "immersing-cleansing-blessing-welcoming." Whatever this is, it's very significant. It feels really very good. "An infusion of knowledge," they're saying, but it is a necessary step right now. It's a step from the physical world to the etheric world or the higher realm. They're showing me something that looks like a twisted up DNA of something ... and they're spreading it out wider. They're making the DNA chains wider. They're so narrow. They're making them very wide now so it can possibly carry more little fibrous hairs with information of bits of dewdrops on them. They're going sideways, which in your language would be horizontal like the horizon.

D: *They're stretching it out that way?* (Yes) *You said this is like an infusion of knowledge and information?*

S: They said an infusion of knowledge ... a pouring out of knowledge.

D: *Does this represent the DNA?*

S: They're telling me it's color bands ... the DNA ... we never thought to look for.

D: *Is that what they mean? Color bands ... in the DNA?*

S: In the DNA ... and they're quite thick actually. They're not fine. They're like layers. Layers of ... I want to say "clouds" to me, but that's not the right word. But that's the only word I can come up with. It's layers of this cloud, misty stuff and there are colors in it.

D: *At first you said they were wispy.*

S: Yes, but they're gone and now they're bands of color. Makes no sense, but they look like each band is one and a half feet tall. They layer on each other. And each one is a different color. They say it's a necessary process, and this is how it works. This is the higher ... they're either saying "realm" or "consciousness." This is how this all works.

D: *That's what I'm trying to understand. What do they mean? How the higher consciousness works?*

S: They are saying it's ALL forms. This is how ALL forms work. Even leaves have DNA, and even leaves have processes of forms. We can't understand that here, but on their side, it's all forms. Everything has a form, and everything has a formula. And this is how it is, and this is what should be followed.

D: *What do you mean by a "form" ... do you mean a shape?*

S: No, no space ... it's a process. It's just how the process is.

D: *I think of a leaf having a certain shape and the body having a certain shape.*

S: But you have to get to the "finite," not the shape. This is what forms the form. The form you see is the leaf, but this is behind the form. This is what forms the form, and this is the laws, and this is how it is.

D: *But you said it has to do with formulas, too?*

S: Yes ... that's how it's all set up. It's just process ... just how it is ... the process.

D: *Does it all go back to the genetics, the DNA? Is that the core ... the main part?*

S: No, it all goes back to the ALL, the one, the light. This is his outpouring. It outpours this way. It's like the flowing ... like the pot or urn with the light and the mist. This is the ALL outpouring. This is how it outpours.

D: *How it creates?* (Yes) *But you did say you were talking about the DNA. That's a part of the creation process ... if I'm using the right words.*

S: They're saying, "If you wish." (Laughing loudly.)

D: (She continued to laugh loudly.) *If they have better words, I'd think they could use them.*

S: No, they're saying for you to go ahead ... they're saying, "Yeah, if you wish, go ahead."

D: *We try to understand it in the words we know. They may have better words to help us understand.*

S: They are thinking we are doing a good job with this, but I think we understand that.

D: *So the DNA is wider and composed of colors.*

S: Yes, and that's very interesting that there are colors.

D: *This is something that scientists can't see?*

S: Not in their current evolution, but they are coming close. They're coming close to this, but there is fear of exclaiming this ... for fear of ridicule.

D: *They are now discovering more and more genes and their genetic patterning. And that has more to do with colors? Is that what you mean?*

S: It's the color of life. That's what they're saying. "It's the color of life." I love the thought: the color of life. Everything has a code and the code is equal to a color which gives it its life code, and it's simply the process they follow or is to be followed. They're showing me a red cardinal and it's just sitting there. And it's saying, "It's the code I followed."

D: *The red was very important for that creature?*

S: Yes ... that life. The creature is saying the color was the lesson, but it's not just the color. It's an energy that it's spinning, and that's the lesson ... and they're sending it. There's something ancient that spins that way.

D: *And that was the code? Does that also have to do with the formula?* (Yes) *The code of the color. Is that all part of the formula?*

S: Color is part of the formula, but part of the code. That's part of the lesson.

D: *So the colors are very important?*

S: It's important, but it's just what it is ... the outpouring from the ALL. It's how its consciousness can relay all (She seemed confused.) ... can relate to everything else ... what it does. (Maybe: It's how its consciousness can relay to everything else what it does.)

D: *So it has to do more with color than anything else. This is how the information is transmitted? It creates something?*

S: Yes, but it's all one. It's not separate pieces. It's all shaped into one. It's a color. It's a lesson. It's a vibration and it's a movement, all at the same time.

D: *Then each one is individual and that's what creates a different form, a different creature?*

S: If you wish, yes.

D: *I'm just trying to understand with my limited abilities.*

S: Yes ... it's very overwhelming and beautiful. I understand it, but I don't understand it. I see how it works, but I don't think that I would ever understand it. But I'm seeing how it works.

D: *You don't think you'd be able to explain it?*

S: They're saying, "We have explained it. This is the explanation of it."

That didn't help much. I thought it was still as clear as mud. I was going to keep pressing for more explanation.

D: *But you said the DNA ... you saw the different colors blending into each other.*

S: And they're much wider than we see. It's really wide.

D: *I guess what you see is even beyond microscopic. Do the colors go in any certain order when you see them with the DNA?*

S: I see red first. Red seems to be the basis at the bottom, and it's a cloudy red. And then it gets much clearer and the band gets thicker ... coming up from the bottom. And the next color looks black, but it's not. It's so purple it looks black. Then it goes into a beautiful purple color and it stays that same color. And it goes up to the next one ... best way I can explain it is a goldish, reddish orange. It's not gold. It's not red. It's not orange. I don't know this color. It's a blending together. And it moves. This one has movement in it ... lots of movement.

D: *Each color has movement?*

S: Each color has movement, but they move in and out of each other. Oh, I saw something like this once.—They have a plexiglass container and it has maybe colored oils and water. And they flash back and forth, but they infuse one another and that's an energy form. That's a building block. That is definitely a building block to life.

D: *So these colors don't remain separated in these bands?*

S: Not in this band. The red did and the purple, but the gold/orange/red one moves in a continuous motion. But this one has something to do with life. Life has several meanings. It has consciousness. It's movement. It's awareness-knowingness. It's all of that into one. You can't pick one piece out. It wouldn't work. It would be flattened, so it takes all of those to make this form and this is the creation form. It is definitely a creation form.

D: *Are there other colors above the gold/red/orange one?*

S: There are other colors. They're not very clear, but mostly it's just a pristine white after that. A very pristine ... oh, white's not even the right word because it has life to it.

D: *But this is what is in the DNA? This is what causes life?*

S: That's what they're showing me, yes. But it's wide. It's so amazingly wide! I would never think it would be that wide. It's different colors and different life forms. Some I can almost name, but if I say a color, it disappears, so ....

D: *Different combinations of colors?*

S: Source of combination ... source of life, it says, and it's always in movement.

D: *This is what creates the different forms, the combination of the colors?*

S: Yes. The combination of the colors creates the form and the laws it goes by.

D: *For instance, you were talking about the bird and the leaf and the human, they would each be a different combination of colors?*

S: Almost definitely. But still, it's all one and the same but the different combinations are what makes it the chosen lesson.

D: *And this all comes from the ALL? But doesn't it continue on from there? Once one thing is created, doesn't it recreate itself?*

S: It is replicated, yes.

D: *So it doesn't have to come from the ALL each time, when it replicates itself?*

S: No, everything comes from the ALL. If it has a form of life and a consciousness and a movement, it comes from the ALL every time. You see, you could do that now with replication, but you see it ... life without life. You can copy something, but it has no life ... only a copy.

D: *Would it be alive?*
S: It would be alive like your sheep ... Dolly?
D: *The clone?*

Dolly, the sheep, was not the first clone, but she was the most famous. She was produced in 1996 from a cell taken from another sheep's udder. However, she only lived six years, dying in 2003. There is a continuing debate about whether she died so young because she was a clone. When her DNA was examined in 1999 it was found to be actually *older* than her body. She did give birth to four lambs over her life span, but I could not find any research about whether they also died young.

S: Yes. It is alive. It moves, but yet the life is missing. It is life, but it's life without force. It is alive but it is like a paper doll. You have a form and can cut-out the form and hook it over the shoulders and you have something that looks like life, but it's not life. Yet it's very pretty, but it does not contain the source.
D: *But like the sheep, for instance. It is able to replicate itself.*
S: Not a clone sheep. Not at this time. On a cellular level inside the tubes in the laboratory. No, not at this time. We see the cell's moving; however, within the cell, the source is not there. It's an empty cell.
D: *I thought they said that Dolly, the sheep, could become pregnant and have a lamb. I think of that as replicating itself. Isn't that true?*
S: We are having a discussion over this. They say, no, and some say *possibly*, so they are divided over this. (Chuckle) Like I'm watching a panel of people saying yes, but they're ... (Chuckling) ... oh, it's funny. Looks like a bunch of philosophers up there.—They're agreeing that they are short-lived offspring.
D: *Yes, but that is physical. We can see it.*

S: Yes, but it still has no source. It has no source to it, it has no source at all. Oh, what they're trying to get across is that there's no spirit lesson. There's no spirit. It's an empty shell. ... Very interesting.

D: *I always thought that no matter how it was created, a spirit could be assigned to it and come into it.*

S: Well, that makes sense. Okay, they just said that some will, some won't. Proper people? Oh, it's like your ethical farmers. Some will have that? (Speaking to someone else.) Okay, they're showing me so I can understand this better. It's the difference between a commercial operation and a small ethical, spiritual operation. So in essence, both can exist.

D: *So they can have offspring?*

S: And that's a bad intention on the one side. They are talking about creator gods on the other side. That would be the ethical spiritual ... the right people? Then on this other side, they equate that to corporations with mass production.

D: *And those are the ones that are not doing it correctly, you mean?*

S: They are just showing me empty cells. The cell is just a white sac/circle. But on the other side, there's the cell and there's the color and there's movement and there's a burst of white light in those cells. So they would be the ethical ... they would be doing it right. Those would be the offspring of the source.

D: *Then in that case, life would be allowed to enter if they were doing it ethically?*

S: Possibly ... possibly. It's a probability.

D: *That's what's confusing because they show us these animals and they seem to be alive and they are reproducing.*

S: For all intents and purpose, it is alive. Like different degrees of color. There is the difference in the degrees of colors and tones. The one side is definitely the creator God that has the ethics. The other side, I hesitate to say this, but they are using more intention. The other side has intentions for some kind of a purpose.

D: *Good intentions are the most important thing of all.*

S: Intention comes from the light.

This reminded me of a client in her forties that described an unusual experience. She had been trying to get pregnant and had tried everything. The doctors decided to attempt in vitro fertilization by implanting her eggs into her uterus. When they took her eggs and examined them under the microscope they were like empty shells with nothing inside. They had never seen anything like it. They finally used donor eggs and hormones, and she was able to have her daughter. This was the first time I had ever heard of eggs that were like empty shells until we had this session with Susan discussing cloning. Interesting!!

D: *But when they're reproducing these animals by cloning, they say they are doing it to have food for people.*

S: The other side of the food is that it won't be very good for you. It will show them faith but it will not fill their need. But on the side with the Creator God, this side is allowing this animal to have its evolution and its spirit and its lesson. It's very important for all things. They both have intention, but one has a higher intention than the other side. It's like the other side is just following the steps. They aren't moving up the ladder. They're just following steps, like they're clones themselves. There isn't any judgment on it though. "They" say it's just the intentions and there is space for both.

D: *I have also heard that they have cloned human beings.*

S: True.

D: *I thought they have done that for a while.*

S: (Laughing.) Thousands and thousands of years!

D: *Does that mean the cloned human is different?*

S: Somewhat. They aren't original forms, but there can only be few original forms.

D: *The cloned human is alive, it moves. But is it alive like the other people?*

She misunderstood. I was referring to other humans, but she thought I meant the Source [or whatever].

S: The original ... the originators? No, no. The originators are above all of us. They are pure light, however they agree to share their light.

D: *The light is what makes the creature alive ... gives it life?*

S: It's what gives the creature the chance to evolve, and to reach back to the higher beginning.

D: *I've always thought that the shell didn't matter. It was just a vehicle to use on the Earth.*

S: (Almost nonchalantly.) True, it's just dressing.

D: *And if the soul or the spirit decided to enter one of those clones, it would come into it just to have an available vehicle.*

S: They're thinking. We have a group of philosophers. (Laugh)

D: *Because the spirit and the soul come from the Source. It comes from light.*

S: Well, you see, it all comes from the same place.

D: *So wouldn't that come into the cloned human?*

S: They're talking about different degrees of lessons so ... they're saying, yes, in theory, it all works. (Giggles) It's all the same. It just depends on the degree of the lessons. It's about degrees in lessons ... degrees. Degrees of the lessons. On the other side, you have the people whose intention is just to follow a process. Maybe they don't know that they can ... No, it's divided. One side is all full of light and evolution, and the other side is just following a process. It's like a blank process. They just keep turning out the same things.

D: *Just trying to see what they can do?*

S: Yes. The creators are like an assembly line of creators. They don't have the same vibration of the other side. The creator god side has so much of the force. The word is: light, love, creation. And the other side is just going through the process of blank ... just blank.

D: *Of just curiosity?*

S: Not even curiosity. It's like they're just doing it.

D: *So that will make a difference in what they do create?* (Yes) *We are told that we can create our own reality. We can create things.*

S: There's a process that we do create. We do create *through* that process, yes.

D: *But that's different than creating life. That's what you mean?*

S: You can still create life, but one has more life force than the other one does. Does that mean they're both alive? Yes, they're both alive. It's the difference in a blade of grass. A blade of grass is a blade of grass, but one side has a different code that it comes with. It evolves and draws to it sunlight and water and nurturing and love. The other side is a blade of grass, but it's just a blade of grass. It's going to go through the coding, but it will never prosper like the one with the sunlight and the water and the love. But yes, they're both alive and they're both blades of grass. And one will go on and evolve into something else, a better blade of grass, and one will die as a blade of grass.

D: *That goes along with scientists now genetically altering plants.*

S: Yes, it does. Now we're at the source of this. You can create a corn kernel but they are not the same. They're not the same.

D: *Going back ... you said the colors are the main building blocks, I guess, of life. Are these colors very essential?* (Yes) *I've also hear that sound has a lot to do with it, too. Do you see that?*

S: It's the vibration, yes. It's the movement that starts the life force process into movement. It's that piece that starts the movement. It's like a river that never stops. It starts with a little tiny arc and it just builds and builds, and soon there are just waves and waves and waves of this vibration that just moves and never stops. It moves all the way through. It never stops!

D: *It's eternal that way.*

S: That's a good word.

I thought it was time to start asking Susan's questions. I asked permission to do so. "We are at your service." I wanted to know why this information was brought through. Why did they want Susan to know these things?

S: We chose this lesson for her to show her that she's on the other side. She's on the creator God side. She does create good things. What she needs to understand is that she will always keep evolving. She's always accepted into the higher. She's from the higher. There's only the higher for her.

D: *When we begin a session, we always think we are going to go back into past lives. You didn't want to take her to anything like that?*

S: That's not important. She knows that. It is what it is. This one needs to spend more time in the future. She's been given such abilities for the future. We need to help her unlock the part where she understands the future because she needs to spend more time creating the future.

Before I even had a chance to bring up her physical complaints the SC began to look inside her body, and decide what needed to be done.

S: Where we're looking at right now, inside, there's a code in there that needs to be removed because it's not the truth.

It's in her abdomen. That's a second station. They call it a power center.

Susan had been having problems in that area: colon spasms and bleeding clots.

D: *It's below the solar plexus.*
S: Oh, yes. It's the power.—We're moving that very gently now. She has a lot of trauma in this area ... just scar tissue.
D: *You can heal it, can't you?*
S: It's not even a healing. We're just going to remove it, but it does need to be gently. It is a sensitive code that we need to remove in a very specific way. It may take a little bit because there is a process. There are steps that need to be followed so as to not harm the body.
D: *What kind of a code is there that is not necessary?*
S: Oh, it was implanted there for a reason. It needed to be a safety measure for this one. She's far too advanced ... far, far, far too advanced.
D: *When was it put there?*
S: As soon as she hit this place.
D: *When she came into this body?*
S: After she was here. Far too advanced. It's a stop gap measure and it was put there to protect her. The information would not have been looked on favorably in the past evolution of where your planet was. It would not have been accepted. It would not have been favorable. It would have done her harm.
D: *So it was to keep her from saying too much?*
S: Yes. She was born into people who did not understand. They're in their rights. They are. They do what they did. They did their lessons, but they did not understand.—She doesn't need that anymore. That's been fulfilled. The past is the past.
D: *She thought she'd released it, but I don't think she has.*

S: She understands that she hasn't released it. She doesn't understand why she hasn't released it. This child has done work. We have helped her. She has really done work, but what she doesn't understand is that it wasn't hers to release. It's ours and now we feel secure that we will take this when this is done. She doesn't need to hold on to this.

D: *So you say that can be removed?*

S: We are removing it as we speak. It's very delicate. There are many layers ... many, many layers.—It must be done very gently in a very distinct manner at certain level of tissue, and beyond tissue. Takes a lot of work.

While they were doing that work I asked about the other parts of her body. They told me before that I could ask questions while they were working. She had been in a car accident and she thought her memory had been affected by a head injury.

S: We see circles in the brain that were not there. We see the tissue is not the same.—We're calling in someone to work on the tissue right now. There's a new group coming to this job. She's part of a very new group ... very rare ... very few of them that will be giving the instruction for the future.—We've called in someone. They're working there now.—There's a group we've called in, not to repair these tissues. Our job is the lower code. This is a group that has been assigned to her that will be coming in with the future information for her. So we have separate groups. We have two that are here right now and one group will be coming in at a different time. To help with the future work, yes. It's all very important. That is what she assigned on to do. She agreed. Yes, she did.

D: *But yet, she says she never wanted to be here.*

S: She wanted to come! She wanted to come in the beginning, but there were circumstances that were not fulfilled. And it made it very, very, very difficult for one with such life force that has a greater understanding of the

All things. That's very difficult for a person that comes from that space to incur. She often says she cannot comprehend the cruelty and the killing, and she would never be able to comprehend it, but she adapted quite well. She's fine.

D: *She said she had a near death experience when she was seven.*

Susan had almost drowned, and she remembered leaving her body.

S: Yes, we needed to call her home because of these unforeseen circumstances. She thought she was going to stay on Earth, but we called her home, and we were able to set things right, as it were, and send her back. She did not want to come back. She did not understand.

D: *But she had a contract, didn't she?*

S: We all have contracts! We all, no matter what side we're at ... we all have contracts.

D: *And she couldn't get out of it?*

S: No. There's no getting out.

D: *So that's what happened when she was seven, just to get her straightened out?*

S: Yes, and there's much more than she saw. She might have been forgetting or fading, but she had to be reminded that there was much more. She has to know that there is a struggle. There has always been a struggle. She does not want to believe in light and dark or shadow. Yes, they are all different lessons of different degrees. They are all choices and we wanted to show her that this is very real and this is evolution. And this is how evolution has been going on for billions of years, not even a time frame. We're talking your terms. But she needs to know there has always been a choice, and you play all the choices and everyone plays all the choices. On every level there is, you play out all of the choices. There's no judgment; it's just choices. Once we showed her that, we showed her the possibility of this pristine place that she wants to be in, and she wants everyone to be in. We showed her that this is a possibility.—We also want her to know the true expanse that she is. She is not this little person on this little grain of sand. She is much bigger, and yes, she does struggle with the ego. It's almost like a curse for people here. You have ego for a reason. If you don't have ego, you don't go forward. It's part of the life force. It's what keeps you going.

When talking about her purpose, they said she would not like to hear this assignment. She was to speak before larger groups of people even though this was something she was afraid of. "We will be of assistance. She needs to understand that the group's not even there. It's bigger than just people sitting in the chairs. It's not about numbers. It's about souls."

As I finished the questions, I said that Susan knew most of the answers herself already.

S: People always do. They just don't want to believe what they hear. We talk to you constantly. Dialogue is ongoing. You hear it in your head. You hear it in your soul, what people call their "soul fabric." We are here. They're never alone. They don't need to feel abandoned. So many feel abandoned. We would never abandon them. They're never alone. It's an assignment. We're a sign-on. We have arms all around you. You are very protected. We're here. We've always been here. We do not go anywhere. We are assigned to you, and will stay with you. And we wish this is what human people could understand, the general masses. We are assigned to you. We will never leave or abandon you. We are here for you.

Chapter 36

WORKING WITH THE SYSTEMS OF EARTH

Henry wanted to explore a strange incident. In 2005 as he was going to sleep, he heard the words, "Your father is dying" and he went to a spacecraft. He had no other memories and wanted to explore it. I took him back to the night of the event when he was in his home in West Virginia. He was getting ready to go to bed, and described the ritual of turning off the lights, opening a window to let fresh air in, and getting under the covers. He had just dozed off when he heard a voice in his head, "Come. Your father's dying.—So I left." I asked him to explain how he left. "I guess when I decided to go, I was there. Instantaneously.—A different galaxy."

D: *What do you see that makes you think it's a different galaxy?*
H: It's just a knowing. I don't actually see it because I went there.—He's waiting.

What he saw next was very difficult for him to describe because it was not like anything he had ever seen before. He did not find it repulsive, just difficult to describe. "Trying to see it is my problem." He was standing next to a bed where a strange looking being was lying. "Colors. Brilliant colors. It's not skin like ours. Around the head, similar to feathers like a bird, but not that. Similar to hair, but not that either. It's short, maybe an inch or two long. It's part of the body. Brilliant colors." When he looked at himself he saw that he looked the same. I asked if he could describe its face. "That part is difficult. It's hard to explain. He has eyes, yes, similar to ours. Bird-like. Feathered. The hands are something like this." There was much confusion as he held up two fingers and described what appeared to be three appendages on the hand. There were no clothes. He mentioned that someone was standing next to him by the bed.

D: *Is this the person who brought you there?*

H: No. That was the messenger. He brings the people here that he feels are a part of this group. He's on a mission. We're not exactly the same.

D: *What do you mean?*

H: Strange ... that I was there in my room. It's me. The body that I have there on Earth, and the consciousness there on Earth ... was so *upset* at this being strange. And it was like being in a different body. It is very normal to be there now looking at it. I was on a mission there. The mission is this group. This group of beings.

D: *Is that a planet where you are right now, or what?*

H: It's not a planet, no. A condition of space. It's like a .... (He had difficulty.)

D: *Do you want them to help you explain it? Or can you understand it?*

H: Getting it to here is the problem.—It is a part of a universe, and it isn't. It's part of a place, and it isn't. It's in a completely different realm of existence. It's not bad, or any different than this place on Earth where you are. It's a place where the *functions* are waiting to develop. Planets we develop. Our mission is to develop. To develop planets and develop different forms of life on them. We take a planet, and populate it with different forms.

D: *Do you create the planet to begin with?*

H: No, the planet is created. We create the forms for the planet. The planets come into existence in a particular universe. They become habitable to different lifeforms. When we do this, we do this on a particular planet. There are others who do it for other planets that are very different from Earth.

D: *Different lifeforms?*

H: Different types of lifeforms that we actually create.

D: *So all the planets have different kinds. Is that what you mean?*

H: Yes. And we go to Earth to learn. When you do create these things, they take on a personality of their own. And these particular forms did take a personality on their own.

D: *Is that what is intended?*

H: No, actually it wasn't intended. Don't know why that was given to do this. But these forms are very ... they're not destructive, they're unpredictable. And it's beyond our belief structures and how we function. In order to manipulate—or not manipulate, but to—integrate into some form of a system, so they can be placed on different planets. And one of the things in my past lives, we go to a planet that has this type of personality and learn how to deal with it. And how to restructure it.

D: *Do you mean whenever the beings or the creatures are created to inhabit a planet, they are not supposed to have a personality?*

H: Oh, no, no. It isn't that so much as they have ... let's see how to describe how they form. First, we can develop forms of life. But we become responsible for those forms of life that we develop. And sometimes it gets out of hand, and it isn't going well with those particular forms. So consequently, we have to go *learn* how to handle some forms, if we create them. I suspect that we are nothing more than students doing this process.

D: *So in the beginning, whenever these are created, you don't know which way they're going to go?*

H: We're in a learning process of how to do that. At least this group is. I guess, yes, the father, the main man, is the one that's dying. He's the one in charge. He's the one who creates, and is guiding us through the process. What he does is send us each to different places, to live, to understand.

D: *Other planets besides Earth?*

H: Yes, in different places like that, yes. Because these are the places that have been developed by others. And so the beings on these planets go through the processes of growth.

D: *So whenever you first develop them, do you know how it's going to turn out?*

H: No. That's part of the lessons you need to learn. You create the lifeforms with the knowledge of what you have. However, if it turns out that they're not developed enough ... it is similar to your little children, when they first come out to be born. And they grow as children. And they need to learn how to work in a particular society as they proceed to grow. It's similar to that. And another thing I don't understand is, why they take on personalities of their own. You do understand that when they have these bodies and emotions, and they take on the personality, you're responsible for the development of the lifeforms, as such. But they have their own personalities. We don't have control of the personalities. We have to develop and understand how we work around those personalities. And show them so they can learn more than they do.

D: *But are you allowed to do that? To interfere with what they are doing?*

H: It's like showing them a different way. And they take up the different way. But to learn how to do that is another story.

D: *When you were first creating these lifeforms, do you start out with cells, or how do you do it?*

H: No, it's nothing like that.

D: *How do you create the lifeforms?*

H: Just by imaging them.

D: *Just in your minds?*

H: Something like that. No device or anything. You just create ... you have the *ability* to create lifeforms.

D: *Does anyone tell you to do this?*

H: No. It is part of the hierarchy of learning, through awareness of all things. And this is just one stage of that. One stage of that awareness as you're developing. It's like on Earth where Henry is learning development stages, where he's going. That's part of the lessons we need to project back because we had to simplify ourselves. And learn how to handle that from the simplifying up.

D: *And you said, where this is happening is not a planet. It's something else.*

H: Yes, it's something else. It's a place. It's a different dimension.

D: *So why was Henry called back there on that night?*

H: Because that leader ... something happened. We don't know what. All we know is he's dissipating in the energy. It is very unusual. We've never seen this before. It's unlikely something like that would occur. It's as if your God on your planet would all of a sudden not be there. Such an energy would dissipate. And we don't know why he's dissipating. There's something else that's going on.

D: *So that's why Henry was called back there?*

H: Exactly. And why I was there to escort him. Everybody came back.—Hang on a minute. (Pause) Wait!—We're now within a circle. Something's occurring that I can't describe.

D: *To the leader?*

H: To all of us together. Hang on a second so I can see. (Had difficulty finding the words.) It's a condition that exists in that dimension that there aren't any particular ways of communicating what is happening. Because none of this exists here on this planet. Nothing like this exists here.

D: *It's a different form of communication?*

H: No. It's an existence. Something shifts in the existence, is the best way I can describe it. (Big sigh) Wait one minute. (Pause) What I'm being directed to say is ... it's a phase from an adjustment to the existence of that system.

D: *Like a progression?*

H: Right. In everything is a progression. It never regresses. —They all have come back. And they're everywhere. There's a movement. I don't know what it is.

D: *Is it caused because the leader is dissipating?*

H: No, actually the leader is sort of dissipating.—As you know from your path, death is nothing more than the transition of one existence to another. So that's exactly what's happening here. The entire ... existence is dying again. I can't explain it.

D: *And it's being caused because the leader is going through a change?*

H: No. It's a transition for everybody. It's an event that's extremely important.—It's gone! Everything's gone! It is shifting. And it's shifting in a direction. I can't tell which direction it's shifting, but it's shifting into another layer. That's the best way to say it ... another layer.

D: *And they want everybody to be there to....*

H: To make that transition to that layer.

D: *To use their own energy to help this happen?*

H: No. Nobody has individual energy there. Everybody has an energy. Everybody *is* the energy there.

D: *They operate as a group?*

.   H: As one.

D: *Then why did Henry leave there? Apparently this is where he came from.*

H: Only one of many. Direction was there as one body.—It isn't that this is Henry's home. It is and it isn't. It is his body and it is not his body. And he's there as an extension from here. And that's as close as I can describe it to you. This is more of an extension.

D: *The body of Henry is an extension?*

H: Of there, yes. And even though he has evolved past it, he has to go through in order to develop the learning of what it's like to be from there, to what we determine to be, an extremely low level. And learning of these points, so that can now be expanded to the group. You understand, this is simultaneous. In other words, what he is doing here learning, is coming through and going there, and simultaneously happening there.

D: *So everything Henry learns in the body on Earth is....*

H: Simultaneously being sent to there.

D: *Being transmitted to that.*

H: Yes, that's about as close as I can get it.

D: *Is that part of the learning and trying to change the people, as you said?* (Pause) *Because you said you didn't like the way they were developing.*

H: Oh, the beings we created. Yes, it is the same. It's similar to being a teacher in an elementary school, and all the kids are in chaos. So you have to learn how to deal with the chaos, so they can come to you and learn, and move on.

D: *And one way to learn is to enter a body on Earth?*

H: Ah, yes. And experience it first hand, simultaneously doing it.

D: *So that is why Henry came to Earth?*

H: An aspect of Henry came to Earth, yes. Entered the physical body. Just one aspect. There are many aspects.

D: *Did he choose this, or was he told to do it?*

H: Told to do it. It's like if you're a part of ... to use an analogy. If you're a general over an army, and you say, "You go there, and you go there, and you go over there, and you go there." That's what you do because that's what you have to do. To come into a body to experience what it's like here. And the information is simultaneously being sent back.

D: *Has Henry been on Earth before in a physical body, or is this the first time?*

H: He is in the physical body this whole time. What I was going to explain to you is, when you do that ... (Big sigh). When that is done, it's a one way ticket, this direction. And not in a sense, that direction. So in other words, that is an entity unto itself. It's an extension of this.

D: *I guess we are used to thinking of an aspect coming and then returning again and again to Earth bodies. Either because of the building of karma or whatever.*

H: That's a system developed on Earth. That's a different system than is developed somewhere else.

D: *So Henry is not involved in that system?*

H: No, but you have to follow the rules of that system.

D: *So he was told to do this to help the people of Earth to develop. Is that correct?*

H: No. He is told to do this to *learn* the development, through the process, in order to transcribe that back. The development. Showing the development. But he had to understand how to do that by living it. So once you live it, then you can project it. Does that make sense?

D: *I'm trying to understand. I know it's very difficult to put concepts into our language.*

H: That's why we don't use language.

D: *It's easier mind to mind.*

H: Mind to mind, absolutely.

D: *I was thinking, you said it was a one way ticket. So when he's through with this life, he won't have to return.*

H: No. That's a necessary. He may come back to another level. In the past or in the future, in your terms. Or not even on this planet. It could be somewhere else.—The aspect of love, by the way, is very *strong* when you do this process. The aspect of love of the creatures you've created, has to be extremely strong. And compassion is love in form, just like it is on the planet Earth. And yes, what will occur, these creatures will develop and then transmute, and continue to grow and grow. And it's similar to what's going on on Earth right now.

D: *I've been told that love is the answer to everything. It's a powerful emotion.*

H: Yes, it is. Unconditional love, yes.

D: *Everything has to be created with that in mind, doesn't it?*

H: Well, the system where we are here—no, it's all one system. (Pause) It appears that the moment you, from this place, go in to create another system of some sort, you end up splitting it. So there's a plus or minus, so to speak. That's a two way system here, plus or minus. There are some that are four, five, six, eight, ten different systems. And this one happens to be what you call a "die" system. It's a plus or a minus. The Earth is plus or minus, hot or cold, good or evil, all those things.

D: *Two. A dual system.*

H: A dual system, thank you. Some are quad systems. Some are twelve systems. And that's way beyond comprehension. They are extremely complicated, compared to the dual system. That's why it's so hard to break it down. You'd have to work through here to get it. (He pointed to his head.)

D: *Through the brain? That's what I've been told. The mind has no concepts to understand some of these things.*

H: Right. It's like a person that's been blind from birth, and they all of a sudden can see. And you say, "This is a cup." And they go, "Huh?" And then they touch it, "Oh, yes, that's a cup." And then they have to relate that cup to the vision they just saw. And so on. It's a very difficult process, to get a blind person to see. In a sense, this is the same scenario because the people on Earth are blinded. They don't have that faculty or facility to see here, here, here and here at the same time. You have to develop a system to show them what it is.

D: *I like it when you give me analogies. They're much easier for us to understand.*

H: Yes, and it's hard. I have to think like an earthling in order to get the analogy correctly.

D: *Anyway, Henry was brought there that night to be part of this.*

H: Right. It's the death of a system that brought it into a transition into another system. He had to call it "death," because a dual system doesn't understand anything but that. That's the only way to explain it.

D: *But that place where he went that night, where you are right now, is that a physical existence?* (No) *But he saw these people as having physical bodies. He saw rather strange-looking bodies. Can you explain that?*

515

H: It is very strange-looking bodies compared to the dual system. Now, when you go there with the mental from here to that mental there.... In order to make the communication functional ... you bring a dual system into one, so therefore you create something that's going to be translatable into words. Something it can go back to and relate to.

D: *Something it can identify with.*

H: So you can identify, yes. It actually is understandable to human minds.

D: *So they don't actually have physical bodies.*

H: Not the way you know them. That was just something to show because he'd been there. (Confusion) Dual system time ... what you're calling "reincarnation," as such, is nothing more than.... Like you go someplace and you go to sleep, and you wake up. When you're sleeping it's one way, and when you wake up it's another way. According to Earth time, there may be the many millenniums, and you call it reincarnation.

D: *By going from body to body.*

H: From body to body. It's just nothing more than making a transition. From there to there and there to there. Taking up all this information and transmuting it to here, so these others can be created. And this life of a higher realm of knowing and understanding, tried to develop in the lower realm, and get the lower realms moving.

D: *I think we're at the point now when we're allowed more information. Even though it is still just little crumbs because we can't understand it all. But why did you want Henry to remember going there?*

H: So *you* could get the information.

D: *Me?* (Yes) *You had him remember so he could come here and give it to me?*

H: It seems that way. (Chuckle)

D: *But it's also important for him to know, isn't it?*

H: Oh, yes. He's learning more and more.

D: *Can you tell him what he's supposed to know from this experience?*

H: He's already got it. He just got it.

D: *So when he listens to the tape he will understand?*

H: Yes, I think so. One of the things he needed to understand, and others need to understand: this is a dual system. And there are more, like a four system, eight system, and a twelve system. That is way beyond your comprehension. Now Jane Roberts and Seth brought it out as clear as it can be, when he described the fifth dimension. This is the easiest way to describe this: Frame a picture of little cubes 90 degrees of each other in three dimensions. So you have these bunch of little cubes here, here and here and here and here. And when Seth said, "Hey, this is where you are, Jane. And another system is the next cube over. Now two or three cubes away from you, you have no idea what that's like. That system is completely different." And that's where we're going here. This system is completely different. It's hard to describe. And the only thing you can do to go from here, or as Seth said, "Where you are, Jane," is to go from this system, take a snapshot of the picture that you see. And bring it back here and try to put it together. And that's the best description found that I can describe ... during this process here. So when you go to five, ten, twelve, twenty-four and thirty-eight different systems, instead of just a dual, it's a whole different thing. A whole different way of thinking.

D: *One of my clients described when they were creating universes, that they all had different rules and regulations. Is that what you're talking about?* (Yes, yes, yes.) *Because in some of these other universes that they created, planets could be square. They could be oblong. They could be moving in totally different kinds of orbits. Yet they would be obeying different laws of physics than we have here.*

H: Every physicist in each cube is, in a sense, significantly different than any other physicist in other cubes.

D: *And they said that this universe obeys the laws of this universe, but the other universes have other laws?*

H: That is why one cannot go from this universe to that universe, and expect to survive. Unless it has its own universe carried with it.

D: *Which would be a little hard to do, wouldn't it?*

H: Oh, you can do it. But they can't stay there very long. It's hard. Seth brought that out. He said, "If you have a body from universe A, and you want to go to universe B, and you happen to do that. The different laws of *your* body is different from the law of *this* body, and you may not come back. You can implode physically.

D: *I've been told in other words, that the matrix of the body would be destroyed.*

H: Ah! Of the *body*. This is a body, this is the matrix. Yes, it could.

D: *Because the soul cannot be destroyed.* (No) *I was told that you could not bring anything back from one universe (or dimension?) to the other. The matrix would be destroyed. It couldn't exist.*

H: Well, the universe wouldn't be destroyed, but the form would be. That's a way that you can understand it.

At least I was back on familiar ground, even if I still didn't fully understand it, it was something I had discovered in the early days of my work. In my book *The Legend of Starcrash* the hunter found he was able to travel to an alternate universe and was able to bring back to his village the body of an unknown animal. It was a very unusual situation because you were not supposed to be able to do this without the matrix of the animal being destroyed. I assumed it was allowed because the village was starving and desperate for food. In my work I keep discovering unknown concepts. As the reporter I enjoy exploring these, and I also like it when it is unexpectedly confirmed by another client, as in this case. I know I still have many more pieces to put together before it makes sense, but at least I was keeping an open mind. I never knew what was around the next corner in my work.

D: *But you wanted me to have this information?*
H: Yes, pretty much.
D: *Because you know I get little pieces from here and there and I have to put it all together.*
H: That's right. We understand that.

I then thought I should ask some other questions and experiences that Henry wanted to know about. Yet this part said, "We're limited to ... our focus is only on what we do. We don't know the other part. That is a whole different thing." I then asked if it would be all right if I called in another part that could answer the questions. They said that would be very permissible. So I thanked them for the information they had supplied and I asked them to depart. Then I called forth the SC. The first thing I wanted was for it to explain more fully what Henry had experienced that night. It asked, "The one you just finished with?"

D: *Yes. Do that first. See if you can explain it. Then we'll move on to the other questions.*
H: It was the consciousness of other systems. And spoke through the conscious mind of the other systems and other developments. There are many developments going on, and different evolutions all the time.
D: *They sounded like they were part of the creator beings.*
H: They *are* the creator beings. Which is just another level. Many levels of life.

The sound suddenly disappeared as though some type of energy knocked it off the tape recording. There was a long pause, and then the SC continued.

H: They're multi-dimensional ... places that are multi-dimensional levels of beings. There are multi levels, dimensions within dimensions, within dimensions. And so, here on Earth, that aspect of the creator beings is one part of the dimensional aspect. Which everyone is attached to some lifeform or another.

D: *Why is it important for Henry to have this information at this time?*

H: For his development. He's developing constantly in many directions.

D: *He seems to be able to understand all of these things.*

H: Yes. We feel his stubbornness quite often.

I then wanted the SC to explain another strange experience that the other part couldn't. It happened at night when he said he went through space. He heard someone tell him, "Remember, you volunteered for this." And he entered a *huge* craft that had something like a shopping mall, and a holograph on the wall of many folders. "What happened that night?"

H: Exactly what he told you. But the folders are opening a little bit at a time, here and there.

D: *The folders that he saw?*

H: That he saw. The many folders over there. And they're being dissolved accordingly.

D: *What do the folders represent?*

H: Conditions and situations on probabilities of the planet. Each probability that comes into being, that particular folder will open, to do the process, whatever it takes. So this is a multi-dimensional situation because the probabilities and possibilities ... there is more than one timeline on this area. And there is more than one event occurring. And the events are occurring simultaneously. And therefore it depends on which timeline you're on, to which folder he's going to see to open.

D: *They give you the possibilities and probabilities?*

H: They give you the *result* of possibilities and probabilities.
     So if you open a folder, you push it in a different direction
     on that timeline.   But on this timeline you're doing
     something else.   And what's most important here, time is
     so simultaneous that this definitely is an illusion.
     However, there are many, many, many universes of
     illusion.   And you are in each and every one of them.
     Each is being played out accordingly.   So the folder
     depends on where you are. This is a different event, this is
     another event, and that's another event and that's another
     event. And each one when you open it ... each folder is a
     series of folders. So this line here has a series of folders
     becoming that timeline going on there and there. Past
     lives, yes, he's having time shifts.   The timeline shifts.
     And he's aware of them now because we made him aware
     of it. So he gets glimpses, and he'll move in and out of
     those time shifts.

        This goes along with another concept explained in the
     other *Convoluted* books. That is that every time we put energy
     into a decision and choose that possibility, which becomes our
     reality. But the energy put into the alternate possibility has to
     go somewhere, so anther alternate reality is created and another
     you is living that one. More mind-bending concepts.

D: *Why did you want him to be aware of it?*
H: It's part of his whole development.   And the people he
     touches.

        Henry was interacting with many people and "they"
     thought it was important that he continued to work with this.
     "He'll be directed. He just doesn't need to know everything.
     (Chuckle) He's like a wild horse, trying to hold him in with
     reins on him."

D: *Sometimes it's better not to know everything.*

H: Well, that could be dangerous. In that in some aspects it would kill him. He's already missed 23 events. He's had 23 different times he should have been dead. Each time was deflected. In some cases reinstated. He should have died, but he was reinstated.

D: *So it wasn't his time to go.*

H: It's not a matter of timing to go. It's just—how do you say this?—There was one incident when he was killed, and he was reinstated immediately. So there was no *gap* in-between when the body was dissipated and reinstated.

D: *What was that incident?*

H: We would rather not say. He knows what happened, but he doesn't know when.

D: *But he actually* did *die, and he was sent back immediately?*

H: He was reinstated.

D: *Because he had to stay here longer.*

H: Yes. He was reinstated ... it's a form. Sometimes you want to think of an accident. And of course, there's no such thing as an accident. But the point is the process and you have to not allow a break. Just allow a continuation. No break in it.—But the important thing here is—and he's learned this now. And we know that you have also.—It just depends on which way you're facing. You're learning processes here. And it's because it's a dual system. Now if you really like it complicated, go to a multi-dual system.

D: (Chuckle) *Yes, they said they couldn't explain a lot of that, and it would just confuse us anyway.*

H: It's terribly complicated. You don't have the brain ... the mind can do it, but the brain can't. The brain is not structured to do that.

D: *Let me ask you about when he was onboard the craft with the folders. Was that a physical craft?*

H: Oh, yes, very physical.

D: *So it wasn't like the other experience?*

H: No. This was a physical craft in this universe, yes.

D: *Why was he taken there? Did he have a connection with those people?*

H: That's another aspect of him. It's like this. (He held up his hand.) The fingers are aspects of the same one. (He held up each finger.) This one's different from that one.

D: *So that night he had to go back into that other body that was another aspect of himself?* (Yes) *But he remembered, so it was important.*

H: Yes, very much so. The craft he was on ... that's an ongoing thing right now. Your planet, as you well know, is going into this process of change. And he's just wanting to know—how do you say this?—He will know what to do when the time comes to do it. That's what the folders were all about. And again, if the folder is this way, and the folder is that way, they are the possibilities.

D: *I have told him that sometimes it's not time to have the information.*

H: Exactly, exactly. That's what your books are for. Somebody has to do it.—He has touched many different lives, and he doesn't know it. Just dropping a seed here, and making an explanation of a simple analogy. And you do the same thing. And it just spreads. And this planet at this time needs to know that. And now it's heading for a wild ride.

Chapter 37

THE HEALING OF ANN

DISCUSSION BEFORE SESSION

Ann had written to me, but the letter was so similar to many others I receive I did not pay much attention to it. Besides, I was busy traveling and lecturing. Then she called and said she had met my friend, Nina, and had a strange experience at her house, and Nina thought she ought to see me. I normally don't let anyone come to my house for sessions, but my car was completely shot and I was going to have to buy a new one. So I couldn't drive to Fayetteville and have the session at Nina's house. So finally I agreed that they could come to my home. (This was before I opened my office in town in 2003.) My daughter Nancy and I were also leaving for Europe in a few weeks, so I definitely didn't want to get involved with a local person at this time. I agreed out of courtesy to Nina because of our long friendship, but I did not think anything would come of seeing Ann.

On the phone Ann gave the impression of someone who had absolutely no knowledge of metaphysics, UFOs, or anything of that nature. That was why her experience with Nina was so strange. It had frightened her so much that she was sitting on the floor in her kitchen crying just before she decided to call me out of desperation. I could tell by asking her questions that she did not even have the basic understanding of the paranormal. Nina agreed to come with her to my house in October, 1999, and when they arrived we had a discussion at the dining room table while eating lunch.

Ann had several physical problems. She was an insulin dependent diabetic, was on heart medication (even though she was only in her early forties), and had been diagnosed with the early stages of throat cancer. The doctors had performed a biopsy and wanted to operate. She was also involved in a bad marriage.

Ann tried to describe what had happened that had triggered the unusual event. It occurred in September, just a month before. Nina is a practitioner of an energy work called "gentle touch," where she acts as a conduit for energy to help the person release any blockages in order to promote wellness. It is similar to Reiki and is done on a massage table. Ann had gone to Nina's house to visit and discuss her problems, including marriage troubles. During the conversation Nina offered to help her relax, and Ann was on the massage table when the incident occurred. All of this was totally new to Ann and she didn't even know what Reiki was. She was expecting to relax and maybe fall asleep because this often happens with any type of energy or massage work. Ann had had a hard day at work in the hospital emergency room where she worked as an aide, and was ready to relax. The room was totally dark except for the faint glow of a candle, to further induce relaxation.

Ann described what happened next, "I was relaxing because this was going to be like a massage, and all of a sudden I wasn't there anymore. I was, but I wasn't. Let me explain this to you. I knew that Nina was still around me, but at that same time I was also in another room somewhere else where these beings were all around me. And every one of the beings were touching me, on my arms or my legs. I wasn't really afraid of them. It was kind of a sense of ... curiosity. I was as curious about them, as they were about me. And I remembered that I was still on Nina's table, and I was able to tell Nina, 'Nina, remember everything I describe to you.' For an instance I was able to see Nina, but after I said that, Nina was gone. I was at two places at one time."

Ann then did her best to describe the beings she saw around her. "Their faces were all around me. They were like orange gel. Real thick, thick, thick gel. There was almost like a holographic-type face in there as well. It wasn't a real face. They never opened a mouth to talk to me, but I knew what they were saying. I don't know how to tell you. In my head I heard the voice, but nobody's lips were moving. Their faces were very warm. But this gel ... I remember I kept wanting to put my hand in it."

D: *To see if it were solid or liquid?*
A: I don't know. It just looked inviting. It looked *fun,* actually. (Laugh) But I was also skeptical and afraid. I wanted to, but I didn't. They kept telling me that they needed to remember love emotions. That I had an abundance of compassion, and they really enjoyed me. There were a whole bunch of them. There was a main person—not a person, a being—that was by my head. And there was all this machinery behind them. I really couldn't focus in on it, but I remember seeing there were knobs, there was color, there were buttons. And the light that was above my head was huge. It was massive, and perfectly round. It was up there like a surgery light, but even brighter. It didn't bother my eyes, I could look right into it. They told me to look into that light, and it would not hurt me. They would never hurt me, is what they told me.

I was looking into the light, and all of a sudden, a strobe starting going off really fast. And I didn't like that at all. It scared me because as I was lying there I thought they were trying to steal my emotions from me. And they were trying to steal my love, and that I would never have it again. They didn't say that, but I thought they were going to do that.

This is similar to the investigator in *The Custodians,* who thought they were going to steal her memories when they put a machine on her head onboard a craft. She found out it was actually like a duplicating machine. It was only recording, not removing them. This may have been what was happening to Ann.

A: They were adamant to make it known that they would *never* hurt me. And in fact, now I would fear humans more than I would them. Seriously, I feel that humans are more scarier monsters than they are. There are more communications we had, where they just flashed so much stuff in front of me. And it's so fast. And I can see quick formulas even in my mind's eye right now as I'm talking to you. I could almost write some of it down, but I can't put the whole thing down because it comes too fast. But I can see numbers, I can see signs.

I have heard this many times in the last few years, that people all over the world are receiving information on a subconscious level. Most of the time it appears as geometric symbols or strange signs that have no conscious meaning to them. They are receiving these in many unusual ways. Some say they are relaxing lying on a couch in their living room when a beam of light comes through the window aimed at their forehead. And they see symbols moving down the light into their mind. Others are expressing this by a strange compulsion to spend hours drawing unusual symbols. In my work with the ETs they say this is the transfer of information into the subconscious mind through the use of symbols because symbols contain entire blocks of information. The information is being subtly transferred to the brain on a cellular level. It is information the individual will need in the future as the Earth and mankind goes through the coming transformation. They will have the information when they need it, and they will not even be aware of where it came from. I was told, and this has been written in some of my other books, that this is the meaning of the Crop Circles. The symbols designed in the grain fields contain blocks of information that is transferred into the minds of anyone who sees the symbol. They do not have to be physically in the circles to receive the information, all they have to do is see the symbol.

Some of the information Ann was receiving she thought might be formulas. She had a limited education, leaving school after only the tenth grade and getting her GED later. So she had no conscious knowledge of chemistry. She served a few years in the Coast Guard as a paramedic.

We returned our attention to the experience, and she attempted to describe their appearance. "All of them looked just alike. Their hands were nothing like ours. There were four fingers, but not really a thumb. Yet their maneuverability with their fingers was very good. They could do anything with them. They were really touchy. Their fingers were not set like ours. If we could have taken our forefingers and spread them out a little bit more. If one of these came out more to the side. I'll never forget their hands. And they were all over me, so I will remember the hands. And their arms and their legs are *very* thin and skinny."

I wanted to understand this because some of the description did not fit any other aliens that my subjects have described. The idea of orange gelatin faces mystified me. She said she didn't think it was a mask, gelatin was the only thing that fit the description. "Thick, thick, thick, thick, real thick. But *in* that gel effect you could actually see almost a face, but not quite a face. And the rest of them is green. I hate saying this. I really do. It's my green aliens. It was caterpillar pea ugly green with radiances of a yellowish green around them on their skin. The skin itself was kind of a caterpillar greenish." She laughed at the absurdity of the mental picture. She didn't know how tall they were because she was lying down.

Ann explained that the beings were going through the same hand motions that Nina was when she was giving Ann energy on the massage table. Maybe they were imitating, or learning.

I didn't want to tell Ann too much about other cases I had examined, and Nina also was not saying much. We did not want to influence her. I knew she had not done any reading about this type of thing, and I wanted the information to be spontaneous when we had the session.

After the discussion we all went to the bedroom for the session. When Ann was in trance I took her back to the date when the event occurred at Nina's house. She returned immediately to the night, and repeated the conversation she was having with Nina and her husband Tom as they sat around the dining room table. Nina was nodding to indicate the situation was correct. To speed the events up I had her move forward in time.

A: We're walking. And we went through the garage, and into another small room. Smells like horses.

D: *Why does it smell like horses?*

A: (Laugh) Because there are horses. I can hear them.

Nina lives in the country and has a small stable next to the garage. Her workroom is next to the two. Nina had Ann get on her massage table so she could help her relax. Nina began to work on her head area, and then Ann appeared to be watching something. Then she asked very softly, almost in a whisper, "What is that?"

D: *What do you see?*

A: Ummm. A bunch of them ... several. No, they're not people. They're beings.

D: *How do you know they're not people?*

A: Because they don't look like us. They look different. They are *much* different. They're over here, touching my hands and my arms. They're on my legs.

D: *Can you feel it as they touch you?* (Oh, yes.) *If you can feel them touching you, they must be physical. Is that right?*

A: Oh, yes! (Carefully, as though she wanted to say it correctly.) They are touching me. And I am letting them touch me. I'm telling Nina to watch. I don't think she can see these people. I have to tell her what they look like.

D: *Tell me, what do they look like?*

A: Ooooh, they got spongy faces. Jelloey, spongy, orangey faces. They got eyes in there.

D: *What do their eyes look like?*

A: Kind of dark bubbly. Bubbles. Two bubbles. One on one side and one on the other. Dark. Not quite black.

D: *But you said the faces are kind of spongy?*

A: Well, in your understanding it would be spongy. Jello. Sort of smooth with a glimmer now and then of a rippling effect.

D: *Does their whole body look like that?*

A: No. Just the face. I can't see their whole body. The head is a greenish color ... and it has a strange yellowish-grayish color mixed in with it. They have long arms. Plastic looking. And they're just constantly feeling.

D: *Are they wearing anything?*

A: No. There's no man, there's no woman. There are no clothes. They don't need them. Their skin is protection. They're telling me they're not going to hurt me. They're telling me that I have emotion. Strong emotion, and they're learning from me.

D: *What are they learning from you?*

A: Love. They don't understand our love.

D: *Can you ask them some questions?* (Yes) *Tell them we're curious. Why don't they understand these emotions?*

A: (Pause, as though listening.) They're from a different universe that is technological, mechanical. It is on a higher vibrational level. They don't hurt each other. *We* hurt each other.

D: *Did they* ever *have emotions?*

A: Yes. Not like ours. Not like we understand. Theirs were completely different. Their emotion was in the understanding of education, progression, strength, until progression and strength got in the way. And through their generation growth pattern they put it to the back, and gained the strength and the growth, then the technology. And they forgot emotion because the generation pattern changed their molecular structure.

D: *Generation pattern? What do you mean?*

Somewhere in here the voice changed (as it always does) and I knew I was speaking to someone other than Ann. When this happens I always know I will be able to obtain answers that she could not possibly know.

A: Molecular structure. You don't understand, I have to change the words for you.

This meant that the entity would have to search through Ann's vocabulary to find the words nearest to what it was trying to convey. This is often difficult because many concepts are hard to explain using our understanding. They have told me many times that our language is insufficient. Often they have to resort to analogies or examples. The word "molecular" was pronounced a little differently.

D: *Do you mean molecular structure?*
A: Yes. Is that how you say it there?
D: *We say "molecular." It has to do with the molecules? Is that correct?*
A: Yes. It changes the brain wave patterns. It changes the sensors in the body. The chemistry in the body, to where it becomes more mechanical. It's very difficult to explain from this universe. Generation patterns. The generations as they progressed, their bodies changed. I am trying hard to explain this to you. You need to ask me better.
D: *All right. I'm trying to phrase the questions because Ann would like to know also. Why are you interacting with Ann in that room?*
A: Because she's very open. (Softly) Oh, wow! There are two at the same time, (Ann apparently was interjecting.)
D: *You can tell me so I can understand.*

A: Do you understand mental telepathy?

D: *Yes, I do.*

A: All right. We will speak to you through mental telepathy.

D: *I would rather have it in words. Is that all right?*

A: If it can be defined.

D: *If you can define it, or if you can give me analogies. Do you know what analogies are?*

A: Oh, yes. You live off this very much.

D: *You may not realize it, but I have a little black box here. Do you know what it is? It's a recorder that records words.*

These entities have often referred to my tape recorder as my little black box, so I used their terminology. They find it amusing that we have to resort to such primitive devices.

A: We record through light.

D: *Yes, and you people are always asking, "Why do I need a box to record the words?" We can't remember like you can. So we have to put the information in the box so I can play it back later.*

A: It is your lower technology.

D: *Yes, that's why I have to use words, instead of mental telepathy. So you can understand I have to have analogies. What do you mean, you record through light?*

A: We record and retain through light. Energy and pigmentation and light. It is penetrated into our body, and we put it in our remembrance. And that is where it is stored.

D: *Can you recall it any time you want?*

A: Oh, yes. We can magnify it at any time we want.

D: *But with me I have to have it in words because we are still in the lower ....*

A: I'll give them to you in words.

D: *I would appreciate that. So you chose to interact with Ann at that time because she is open? Is that what you said?*

A: Very much so.

D: *And you said you are communicating with her with mental telepathy?*

A: Very much so.

D: *Have you ever had contact with her before this night.* (No) *Did you just choose her at that time?*

A: She is excellent to our abilities.

D: *And you said you have come from another vibrational frequency?*

A: Yes. *I* am from the seventh plane. Which is a created universe from the seventh plane.

D: *That's why it's invisible to us, isn't it?*

A: Completely.

D: *Then as you are interacting with her, is she actually in two places at once?* (Yes) *Can you explain how that is done?*

A: Through change of vibration. It is a—I don't know how to choose your words.

D: *Try.* (Pause) *All we have is our language. We don't have your abilities.*

A: I am looking for the correct analogy. Your sleep pattern would be the closest thing we could relate to on this level. You are sleeping, you are here. As you sleep you would travel. This is the same as we use with her in her sleep pattern.

D: *Although she is not asleep at the time she is in that room.* (No) *It's also not a dream, either.* (No) *But can you interact with her physical body even though she is in ....*

A: (Interrupted) Mental.

D: *You're working with the mental body?*

A: Correct.

D: *Do you have any idea who I am and what I do?*

A: You're a teacher.

D: *Well, I have worked with many of your kind. Maybe not exactly your kind ....*

A: Yes, we know this.

D: *And they've allowed me to have knowledge when I've asked for it.*

A: Yes, we know this.

D: But I have never met your type of being before.

A: We know this. It has been many, many, many days. Much time has gone by. Your understanding of time is much different than ours. You are at a time frame and a level right now that you will be called. You are drawing near to many universes at this time. You are calling us, and we are coming.

D: Because I have interacted with many other types, but not one that fits your description.

A: I know this.

D: But you're positive, aren't you? (Oh, yes.) Because I wouldn't want anything to do with negative.

A: This is true. Your planet has had so much negative energy that it is very difficult for us to penetrate to your planet, to your universe. You have distracted this universe something terrible. You will be on a high destruction plane. We are looking for people at this time in your plane and in your universe that we can penetrate and help. We come not to harm.

Ever since this voice began it became more gravely sounding, deeper and rougher than Ann's normal voice. An old sound.

D: Are you speaking from onboard a craft, or are you on a planet?

A: I am on a plane level. Not a planet, but a plane. Your understanding of craftship is much different than our understanding of the concept of travel.

D: She said she could see some machinery in the background.

A: Yes, we had to take her to a level close to her understanding, where she would not be .... Oh, I don't know the word for your language. She would not be afraid.

D: Does this happen often, that people think they are onboard a craft, and actually they aren't?

A: Yes, quite often.

D: *Is your world that you come from a physical world, as we think of physical?*

A: Not as you understand the physical. In a sense, where we come from, we can gather as one unit if needed to be. Let me explain this a little bit further. If there are several of us that need to combine and join together for a further understanding, we can join into one body.

D: *I'm thinking of a group mind.*

A: Correct.

D: *But you can combine into one single entity?*

A: Correct. That is the unity.

D: *Would the entity appear similar to the way you do now, or would it be larger or ....*

A: No, no. There is no visual sight to it as you understand visual sight.

D: *Then why are you appearing to her with the orange faces and the green bodies?*

A: This is her understanding of us.

D: *Do you really appear that way?*

A: We can appear in any shape form that we need to appear to the individual.

D: *What is your normal appearance?*

A: We are an energy mass.

D: *That's what I was thinking it sounded like. Then on the place that you come from, you don't need physical things.*

A: Correct.

D: *But yet you did say you evolved technologically.*

A: Correct. There are many planets in each universal level and planes. Each one of these planets has their own beam structure. We have to manifest to that beam structure for their understanding. Without our technology, under-standing you at times would not be able to progress. You are a species, a being that is very low. You hurt one another. You inflict pain on one another. We are trying to help you.

D: *But you know it is not all of us.*

A: Correct. But there are so few of you that *do* understand that enlightened side.

D: *I'm trying to understand. You said you don't have the emotions anymore because you went in the other direction through technology.*

A: Yes. As a combined unit we can understand emotion.

D: *But if you had technology, I am thinking of physical things.*

A: Yes. That is your understanding. Technology is in the consumption of energy. The break up and split up of energy combined to a mass source.

D: *Did you at one time have a physical body?*

A: Yes, when we were at a lower plane. We evolved beyond that through our technology.

D: *But this was not the correct way to go?* (No) *If you had had a choice, which way would you have gone?*

A: That's a personal decision. Each entity has that choice.

D: *But I meant, if you had not gone to technology and become what you are, could you have gone in another direction?*

A: Yes, there are several choices to choose from.

D: *When you had a physical body, how did that appear?*

A: There is no one form of physical being. It is a choice.

D: *So you could all look different?* (Yes) *I'm so limited by what we think of as physical.*

A: Yes, you are. Your senses of touch, smell, hear and sight are very limited.

D: *That's why I am always trying to expand my understanding.*

A: I will try to help you. You are trying to think in a physical formation, and we are trying to project in an emotional.

D: *Is this one of the reasons you contacted Ann because you wanted to know how the emotions of the human being works?* (Yes, yes.) *It's complex, isn't it?* (Oh, yes.) *But we are a complex being.*

A: You are a funny being.

D: (Chuckle) *What do you mean?*

A: You beings, you find humor in the strangest ways.

D: *You have humor, too, don't you?*

A: Umm, not on your level of understanding.

D: *Well, what do you think is humorous?*

A: You beings.

D: (Laugh) *Observing us?*

A: Yes. We observe you as a whole unit.

D: *Yes, but yet we are not a group mind.*

A: (Suddenly) It is cold here.

D: *On our world, you mean?*

A: It is cold.

I didn't know if Ann was feeling cold in her physical body, or if the entity was experiencing cold from our world. I decided to play it safe and alleviate any physical symptoms. I then covered Ann with a blanket.

D: *Where you come from, can you control the temperatures better?*

A: There is not a temperature change as you have here.

D: *Well, if you communicate and work with Ann, the main thing is we do not want any harm to come to her.*

A: Never harm any being. We are here to help you. There is time for your information and knowledge. At this time it is not meant for you to have all information and knowledge. We have shared with Ann some information and knowledge. And there are certain times that we will increase that information and knowledge.

D: *I was told one time that all of my questions would never be answered because some knowledge was as poison rather than medicine.*

A: That is correct. You beings do not know how to put information into perspective to make a unity. I think I'm saying that word wrong.

D: *I think I understand what you mean, though. But they've told me if I ask the questions in the proper way they would try to answer.*

538

A: This is correct. What are you wanting to know?

D: *Ann said she was having many things flooding into her mind lately. (Yes) Although it frightened her at first, she said she seems to be getting formulas.*

A: Yes, that is correct. There are many formulas that are giving. Not all formulas are directed to a specific item, as you would say on your planet.

D: *What are the formulas to be used for?*

A: You have a lot of problems that you concentrate on. Illness.

D: *Yes, that seems to be a strange word to you.*

A: Yes. You do not know how to surpass this.

D: *We're trying.*

A: Yes, but you don't.

D: *Do the formulas you're giving her in her mind have to do with this illness?*

A: Some. We have given her pieces and bits of information. As time goes on we will tie it together. We cannot change the force of your world. We will not inflict that change on your force. You have to invite *us* for that change. It has to be a *mass* invitation.

D: *But couldn't she use the information to help others?*

A: They have to ask for the help.

D: *We know people that might be able to turn the formulas into medicine. (Yes, yes.) Would you be able to tell us some of these formulas so we can have them for the little black box?*

A: I can write them down for you. You do not understand my language. I have to write in yours.

I had the pen and notebook ready, and I uncovered Ann's hands. Then I placed the notebook in her hand. For several seconds she felt the paper, especially the metal spiral binding, as though it was an unusual object. "You have strange articles."

D: (Laugh) *Yes, it is. A piece of paper, and here's a pen. This is a writing instrument that we use.*

I put it in her other hand. She found the pen curious, and kept feeling both the pen and paper.

D: *That is a writing instrument, and this is what we write upon. It's called "paper." What do you think? Can you do this?*

A: You in your language have a formula.

Ann wrote on the notebook without opening her eyes. The entity explained that the formula dealt with chemistry, and someone familiar with chemistry would understand it. She then stopped abruptly.

A: This is the beginning simple basis, a curing all (carrying ?) element that penetrates to the red blood system of your species. It would enlarge the white blood cells so they would work in unity with the red blood cells that are ulcerated in cancered cells in your body. They would then be replenished to help.

D: *Would this be a formula for a medicine of some kind?* (Yes) *A liquid?*

A: No. It is a mass.

D: *Like a tablet?*

A: Tablet? I don't know tablet.

D: *A small thing that you would take through the mouth.* (Yes) *And a chemist looking at this could understand it.*

A: Some. Not all people are advanced. This will be researched.

D: *Do you have another formula?*

A: Not at this time.

I was taking the notebook and pen away from Ann, so I could cover her up again. She held it a little longer while feeling the spiral binding again. I explained, "That is metal that holds the pages together. It is a spiral on the edge."

A: I want to feel it.

D: *It holds the pages together so we can turn them. Write on one side and then the other.*

A: Why do you need to do this?

D: *We have to have something we can look at.*

A: Why do you not use your mind?

D: *We haven't gotten to the point we can go mind to mind.*

A: (Interrupted) Why?

D: *We're not advanced enough yet, I guess.*

A: You will be.—It is very cold here on your planet.

D: *Let's cover you up again. Don't worry, we won't keep you here too long. We will try to be as kind as we can because we do appreciate your help. Is it cold in this vibration? Is that what you mean?*

A: I am shaking. Yes, it's cold.

I started to give suggestions for her comfort, so she (and it) wouldn't feel the cold, but she interrupted just as I began. "It is gone. I read it."

D: *You read it?*

A: It is gone.

D: *The feeling of cold was in the body that we are communicating through.*

A: Correct.

D: *Are these the main things that you want to give her, the formulas for illness?*

A: Some. We want to learn from your people.

D: *What would the other formulas deal with that you want to give her?*

A: Craft. You call "aircraft." Your aircraft is polluting our system.

D: *Polluting your system?*

A: Your universe. And it is leaking into other universes. And we must put a stop to this.

D: *What do you mean? Our airplanes?*

541

A: Your .... I will try to find the words that you use. Your fuel.

D: *The fuel we use to power our machinery?*

A: Yes. Correct. You have resources here on your planet, as we speak, but you choose not to use them. These resources were given to you from our same creator, our same God, our same energy force. And your people have chosen not to use them.

D: *But you know we are just a small piece of the whole of humanity.*

A: You don't have much time.

D: *We don't have much say, though.*

A: Yes, you have all say. You have all choice.

D: *But we are not the ones in power.*

A: Yes, you are.

D: *I mean, we are not the ones that make the decisions for the world.*

A: Yes, you are. You are not working as a unit.

D: *That's true. We are all individuals.*

A: Correct. You separate your energies, your powers.

D: *That's why what we say isn't going to affect the ones in power. The ones that ....* (He interrupted: Yes.)

It was obvious that it would be impossible to argue with a being that was used to operating as a unit to accomplish what they wanted. He could not understand our limitations due to functioning as single units. Of course, he had a point. I have found this in my work (especially with Nostradamus), that when people cooperate together, their mind power is enormously increased. But how do you get this across to the average person, that they have such latent power?

D: *But you said the fuel is leaking into the other universes?*

A: (Emphatically) Yes! It dissipates into the air, which breaks into our molecular system, which is traveled through time and space.

D: *I guess we don't think of....*

542

A: No, you don't.

D: *You're talking about the other dimensions?* (Yes) *But what can we do about it?*

A: You can fix it. You have natural resources that are planted in your Earth's soils. You have plantation in your Earth's soils at this given time, that is also used for your medical medicine, as well. And you choose not to use these resources.

D: *A plant, you said?*

A: Yes. I do not know the name.

D: *What does it look like?*

A: It is ... (Pause) I do not know how to describe it in your language.

How do you describe something if you don't know the words and their meanings? The other entities have taken the information from my subject's brain and vocabulary. This entity seemed to have difficulty finding the proper comparisons.

D: *We have to know what it is before we know how to use it.*

A: It is pointy, quite pointy.

D: *The leaves?*

A: Yes. There are several sprout as the phalanges.

D: *Does it have a flower?*

A: It at times will. It has a strong odor. There are some of you who use this plant now, but you do not use it in a unit sense for your whole planet.

D: *What do we use it for?*

A: You intake it into your body. You breathe it.

D: *If it has a flower at times, what color is the flower? That might help us identify it.*

A: I don't know what you mean by color of your flower.

D: (How do I explain this?) *Ah. Well, the flower is the part that will usually make some seeds later. It has petals. We have colors like red, yellow, white. Do you have any colors in your spectrum where you live?*

A: We have spectrums, yes.

D: *You don't have colors like that?*

A: Not in your level of understanding.

D: *Because I'll have to have more information before we can understand what kind of a plant it is.*

A: Again, I will draw this for you.

D: *That's very good. Just give me a moment, and I'll get my archaic writing instruments out again. Because we can't look into your mind to get the picture.*

I got the notebook and pen out again and put them in Ann's hands.

A: I enjoy this.

He again was fingering the materials as though they were unknown and unfamiliar objects.

D: *What does it feel like to you?*

A: I cannot describe. (He began drawing a picture of a plant.) It feels different. I am not used to this substance.

D: *That does have pointy leaves. That's what we would call the "leaves." Are the points sharp?*

A: They do not hurt or inflict pain on you. They will *help* you. I did tell you this.

D: *Can you draw the flower?*

A: The flower?

D: *Yes, can you draw what that looks like? That will help us identify it. You said you don't know colors.*

A: The flower. (She was drawing it.)

D: *It has many petals. Is this a tall plant?*

A: Oh, yes, very tall. Much taller than you as a human.

D: *Then we're not looking for something low to the ground.*

A: No, it starts low. It grows tall. It is a very majestic plant. Although your people have trampled it.

D: *We don't know its value?*

A: Yes, some of your people do know its value. But many of your people fight.

D: *So this is the plant that we can use for medicine, and we can also use for fuel?*

A: Yes. Your resources are very limited. This is a plant structure that is not limited. It is plentiful all over your planet. And you do not choose to use so.

D: *We probably don't know it's useful.*

A: Yes, you have ones that do know. We have seen them and talked to them.

D: *So what part of the plant would be used for the fuel?*

A: The stem and the leaf. It will replenish itself. It was given to you.

D: *For that purpose?*

A: Correct. You have what you call ... your sight? To see. It is very good for one's sight to see. It is very good for many of your illnesses that you have created in your own planet, due to your resources that you have chosen to use. You are a planet of self-destruction and illness.

D: *We have caused these illnesses ourselves?*

A: Correct.

D: *I was thinking as I looked at this drawing. It's not a tree, is it? Because trees are taller than we are.*

A: No, it is a plant. We understand your tree life. This will grow in a ... how do you put it? Cluster form. We will give Ann the knowledge and the sight. This is what you call her, Ann?

D: *Yes. That's her name that we call her.*

A: We will associate that.

D: *We have to have names and labels.*

A: Yes, we realize that.—The one you call Ann, you have to strengthen her.

D: *That's what I was going to ask you about. She is experiencing some physical ailments.*

A: She has not come to us and asked for healing.

D: *Can you work with her?* (Yes) *Would it be all right if I told you that it is permissible to work with her body?*

A: No. She has to. We cannot force change any of your structures without your permission.

D: *What about going down her list? We want her to be* completely *healthy, don't we?*

A: Correct.

D: *What about the diabetes? (Pause) Do you know that* word? (No) *It has to do with sweet things that cause problems in the body. It makes the body go out of order.*

A: Sweet?

D: *Sweet. Sugar?*

A: This is a substance.

D: *It's a substance, and it sometimes causes an imbalance in the body.*

A: One moment. (Long pause) She will no longer have that.

D: *Can you make it go away?*

A: She has already asked.

D: *Because she has to give herself injections. Do you know what that is?*

A: She will no longer.

D: *Because no one likes to keep taking injections.*

A: She will no longer.

D: *You can bring that part into balance?*

A: It has already been done so.

D: *What if she doesn't realize this and still keeps taking the injections?*

A: You do not work as a whole unit on this universe.

D: *Will the doctors, the medical people, be able to see she no longer needs the injections?*

A: You will.

D: *Because the doctors say that if she stops the injections she will hurt herself.*

A: Correct. The one that you call "Ann".... One moment. (Long pause)

D: *What are you doing?*

A: I'm trying to become one with what you call "Ann."

D: *But no harm.*

A: We never inflict harm on your kind.

D: *And only a temporary fusing, so you can find out what's wrong with the body. Is that right?*

A: One moment. (Long pause) This that you call "pain" in the body that you mentioned.—*It is* gone.—Many of her physical problems are caused by putting wrong substances into her living body. Fuel intake.

D: *What she's eating or drinking?*

A: Correct.

D: *Can you show her what to eat?*

A: We do not eat substances as you do. It is up to her substance intake. What you call "fuel source."

D: *What is she taking as a substance intake that she shouldn't?*

A: One moment. (Long pause) This is very difficult to describe this.

D: *Does she eat it or drink it?*

A: It is a "eat." It is a substance. I cannot describe the substance. It is brown in color, of your color. I am understanding your spectrum.

D: *You can see the spectrum now.*

A: Correct. It is brown. A dark substance. It's a fleshy substance. It is of your animal. It is quite large to your proportion. It has ... four walking vessels. You use wrong chemicals. You chemicalize your flesh.

D: *And this is causing problems in her body?*

A: Correct.

D: *I think I know what it is you're talking about. It's a kind of an animal that we do eat.*

A: Yes, many of you do.

D: *Would it be correct to say it's a cow?*

A: I do not understand cow.

D: *A cow is a large animal. It has rather smooth skin. Sometimes they're brown, sometimes they're black. But they are large. (Yes) And we eat their meat. (Yes) This is the one she should stay away from? (Yes) Very good. Because I think she can do that and substitute other things. (Yes) I think this is going to help her a lot.*

A: She is helping us.

D: *Yes, and in return you want her to stay healthy.*

A: Correct.

D: *Then can you help her with these problems with her throat?*

I thought I had better try to help with all of her ailments since it was working so well.

A: One moment. (A very Long Pause)

D: *What's happening?*

A: It is done.

D: *Very good. Very good. Is it gone immediately, or will it be a gradual ....*

A: (Interrupted) Yes. It is gone.

D: *Then the body is returning to its proper state of complete balance and harmony, isn't it?*

A: Correct. You, *you,* as a human race, do not do this together.

D: *We try to do it in small groups sometimes.*

A: Hmmm. Very little. It takes much more.

D: *But we try to show people that their minds can control their bodies.*

A: Correct.—This one that you call "Ann," she can call upon us—in what your time structure, you say "daily." What is daily?

D: *Well, it's a little hard to explain. We have days because our planet revolves....*

A: (Interrupted) Are you speaking of Sun and moons?

D: *Yes. It goes around the Sun. During the day is when it's light....*

A: (Interrupted) She can call us upon every Sun that comes to the bright side of your moon, in your words.

Ann's voice had been so gravelly that it didn't sound anything like her normal voice.

D: *That's daily.*

A: Correct.

D: *When it becomes night, that's when the planet turns away from the Sun.*

A: Correct.

D: *Yes. But the main thing is, she has to live a life on this plane. So we don't want to do anything to interfere with that. We have to live in this physical world.*

A: We have come, not to interfere, but to assist you. We do not come to harm.

D: *She was afraid at first that you were going to take something away from her.*

A: That was never.

D: *Do you know that sometimes I use this information that I write about it?*

A: You are a teacher.

D: *Is it all right if I use the information that you tell me?*

A: Correct.

D: *This way more people will know about it.*

A: It is very good for your people to know and to learn to unite. You are a teacher. But you do not ask all the right questions.

D: *I don't have them in my mind yet. They have always told me the questions are more important than the answers.*

A: Correct.

D: *So just be patient with me.*

I then asked the entity to recede back to the seventh plane where he said he was from.

When Ann awakened she had absolutely no memory of the session. We attempted to explain what had happened, especially the parts about her physical condition. When she looked at the drawing of the plant she thought it looked like cannabis or marijuana. It has been said that this plant has many more uses and value than we recognize, especially since the government has classified it as a drug.

I told Ann that I would never tell anyone to stop taking medication, especially to stop insulin injections. But if they were correct and the diabetes condition had been removed, would it harm her to take shots if her body no longer needed them? I really did not want that responsibility. I needn't have worried because Ann said that she had to take her blood sugar reading every morning to indicate how much insulin she gave herself. Her blood sugar had been running around 300.

An amazing thing happened when she called me a few days later. When she took her blood sugar reading the next day it had dropped to the 80s. She did not give herself a shot. All day her husband kept asking her when she was going to take the injection. Her response was, "I don't need it anymore." That was a very important statement because it showed that her mental attitude had changed, and her belief system had clicked in. She *believed* that she no longer needed it.

Since she had been scheduled for throat surgery, she went back to her doctors at the VA hospital, and told them to take all the tests again, and to not ask her why. Later all of the tests came back negative. There was no sign of throat cancer, and her heart condition had improved to the point that she no longer needed medication. It has now been twelve years (in 2011) since we conducted this session. She has never had another insulin injection. Her blood sugar dropped from 300 to 80 and has never risen. Of course, the doctors have no answers. They wrote across her medical records, "We have no explanation for this case." She now tells everyone, "I *used* to be an insulin dependent diabetic."

Another thing happened that may have influenced her cure and would be more in line with my therapy work with the subconscious. Ann was in a bad marriage and this was causing her much stress. One of the main causes of diabetes that I have found is the lack of sweetness. Psychologically, the lack of love in the person's life. This would also account for the heart problems, the heart being the seat of the emotions. And the throat problems, being unable to express her feelings to the most important people in her life. Shortly after this session

Ann got a divorce, and she and her son have been living on their own. I know this was a very important contributing factor to the cure.

This was one of the most dramatic cases I had worked on at that time in 1999. Most of the cures that occur now during my work come from the intercession of the subject's subconscious mind when the subject understands the reason for the illness or physical symptoms. In Ann's case it was done through the intercession of an entity from another dimension. Yet it was bound by regulations. It could not interfere, but only performed the physical cures when it asked Ann's permission. So the entity from the seventh plane was also bound by the restriction of noninterference, and had to be sure that Ann really wanted to let the illnesses go. When it had her permission, the cures were instantaneous.

Chapter 38

THE BACKDROP PEOPLE

If this chapter doesn't bend your mind with its strange and new concept, then I don't think anything will.

Suzette came off the cloud standing outside of a forest of very large, tall trees. Rather like pine trees or cedars that were very old and huge. She was trying to see the Sun, but it seemed to be hidden by something like cloud cover. Then she discovered that it was not clouds, it was actually dirty air that was keeping the Sun from shining. She was worried about the trees dying because of the air. Then to her surprise, and mine, she saw dinosaurs. Some of them were large, like Tyrannosaurus Rex. She said they were smelling the air, and were worried. Something was not normal, and she was sensing it also.

There was also a surprise when I asked her about her body. She said it was ugly because it was covered with nasty matted brown hair. She felt male in midlife and was wearing an animal hide that came down from her shoulder. I asked if she was comfortable in that place, and she replied, "No! Because the sky... the air is gone. There's not going to be any life." So something unusual was definitely happening. I wanted to know if he had been comfortable there before this. "No. It's a struggle every day. Because of the beasts ... just to live is a struggle." These were the larger beasts, but also there were smaller ones that they ate. They used the hides from these after they clubbed them, and cut the hide off with a stone. Then they would dry the meat. I wondered why they would have to clothe themselves if they were covered with hair. He said, "For protection. There are smaller plants with thorns on them when you're going after the animals."

I wanted to know where he lived, and it sounded like he was describing a cave. "It's like looking at a tunnel in the stone. Like a hole. It just goes in and opens up. It goes further in but the tunnel lets in enough light." Then he saw there was a child in the tunnel. "This hole ... there's nothing else in there but the child, so I think I escaped to this place. I brought this child to this place." He had come from somewhere else. "It's unknown death. I know I have to protect this child from what's in the air. Death is coming. Death to the trees and death to the dinosaurs." He described the place he had come from as an open faced cave, where many people who looked like him lived. "They just don't think nothing bad's going to happen. They didn't believe me."

D: *How did you know something was coming?*
S: The trees and the dinosaurs told me.
D: *You can communicate with them?* (Uh-huh) *How do you do that?*
S: Just listen. They show me pictures. Death is coming.

No one else would listen, so he had taken the child and left. The other people just ignored him. The child was not born to him, but an orphan. They had traveled a long way from the original group before stopping and staying at the tunnel. He was hoping it would protect them. But now a new problem presented itself: he needed to feed the child. "I have to hunt. Everything's dying. Dinosaurs are falling. It's as if they can't breathe. It's choking the trees. They can't breathe either." It was not affecting him yet. "I'm low to the ground. It hasn't gotten down here yet.—I need to find food. I'm hurrying ... running through those plants that have thorns ... looking and looking.—I found something. It looks like a small pig or a big rat or something, and I club it." He took the food back to the tunnel.

A period of time must have passed, but of course, this primitive being would have no concept of time. "I come out and everything's dead. Everything's brown, but we're still alive. Some of the animals choked. The air was bad." I wondered if he had been in the ground a long time. "Must have been, but you can breathe again. Other animals that lived in the caves or were deep in the ground are coming back out. The ones in the water survived." So apparently, any creature that was underground was protected. "And the plants are coming back up through the roots. The air is starting to come back to the sky. Sun's starting to shine. It's warming the planet. It was cold when it came."

He decided to go back and see if any of the others had survived. He didn't want to, but thought he should. He took the female child with him. I condensed time and asked him what he found when he arrived there. "Death. They're all gone. Couldn't breathe." So because they were living in an open cave they couldn't escape the choking air. I asked what he was going to do now. "Just move on. Life will go on. I'll go and see what I can find ... anyone else. There might be others who survived underground."

Then I moved him forward to see if he ever found anyone else. Instead he saw: "A very bright light ... very bright light ... too white. In front of me." I immediately thought he had died and was journeying back to the Source, which is always described as a very bright light. If this was true I wanted to know what happened to him. How did he die in that lifetime? So I had him move to the last day of his life and asked him what he saw and what was happening. "I see a ship that's shiny. We are taken ... we are taken. The ship ... on my journey. It landed out there and we were taken. The ship was round and shiny." He was breathing deeply as if distressed.

D:	*How were you taken?*
S:	In a light ... there was a light around us and on the ship.
D:	*Can you see any people?*

S: Tall ... not hairy ... light skin ... white eyes ... white colored hair. They're not like us. They're not hairy like me ... I'm hairy.

This sounds very similar to the hairy creature described in Chapter 22 <u>The Creation of Humans</u>.

D: *Have they taken you on the ship?*
S: Yes, they treated me like a beast ... one of the animals. I'm the only one that looks like me. They're poking their long, skinny fingers, touching me.
D: *Can you communicate with them?*
S: I don't think you have to.
D: *That's why they treat you like a beast?* (Yes) *Maybe they don't know you can think.—Do you know where they're taking you?*
S: We see two stars. They're in the sky. There are windows all around me. There are lots of round cylinders ... lots of different colored lights.

This journey could have taken a long time, so I condensed time again and moved him ahead to when they finally arrived wherever they were taking him. He saw a city composed of crystals. "It's ... I'm home. (Deep sigh) Crystal ... everything's glass ... I'm home! They brought me back home. —I was supposed to be one of the beings. I chose to go to that place where I was so hairy. Now I'm back home."

D: *Do you still have the hairy body?*
S: As I'm walking it is falling away. The hair ... that role ... I'm changing back to what I was.
D: *You mean the body didn't have to die?* (No) *You just transformed back again?*
S: Yes. I'm a lot happier. I didn't like being hairy.
D: *Why did you choose it?*
S: I was to bring back this child. I was to save this child.
D: *Was she able to make the journey all right?*

S: I don't see her right now.

D: *But that was your job, to save her.* (Yes) *And this is home?* (Yes) *Do you know where it is? Do they call it anything?*

S: (Pause) I see a Z. I see an X. I don't understand the symbols.

D: *Maybe it will make sense to you later.—What is your body like now?*

S: It's wonderful! It's no body hair, tall, white skin, blond hair, blue eyes.

D: *Like the other ones on the ship?*

S: Yes. They were poking fun at me, back when I was hairy. It's better to be home with all the glass and all the crystals and all the lights.

D: *They were poking fun at you because you had forgotten?* (He laughed: Yes.) *When you went and experienced being hairy in that other place, were you born as a baby into that life? Or how did it happen?*

S: I think it was the normal process when I was born into that group of people, so it has to be accepted, but I was never accepted growing up. They didn't listen to me.

D: *They didn't understand you. And while you were there, you forgot about your home?* (Yes) *Forgot where you came from.—I think it's interesting that you didn't have to die to leave that place.*

S: We don't die.

He was just transformed back into his original state. Now that he was back where he felt he belonged, I wanted to know what type of work he did there.

S: We go in this place and make a diary of what we learned. A record of what we saw and what happened. And you energize with the crystals.

D: *How do you do that?*

557

S: All you have to do is touch them. There is sound, vibrations ... there is healing. Different lights, color, reflects through you.

D: *This brings you back to normal?*

S: Yes, you energize. You heal anything that needs fixing. It's so right and so peaceful there, and so beautiful because of the crystals.

D: *But you did decide to leave this place. To explore?*

S: That's our job. We have to go choose another job. We go where they need help. And I had to save that child. I couldn't save them all so I saved that child.

D: *You tried, but the others wouldn't listen. What was wrong with the air? From where you are now, do you know what was causing that?*

S: Yes. It was a multitude of volcanoes and everything that could go bad. Knocked the oxygen right out of the air; took the Sun away, and they just couldn't breathe. Nothing could breathe. Anything that was big, that took a lot of oxygen, they died. There was a lot of activity and people didn't survive and the big animals didn't survive. They didn't have protection.

D: *Did you know this was going to happen before you went there?*

S: Yes, in the crystal city I knew. But I didn't know when I was there.—It was just not comfortable with all of that hair. (I laughed.) But I had to have it to blend in.

D: *What are you going to do now? Are you going to stay there for a while?*

S: Yes, I am. I am going to check on my options.

D: *Are you going to have to go somewhere else?*

S: Yes. That's our job. We look at all the stuff and then decide.

D: *But you do have a choice, don't you?*

S: Yes, we have a choice.

D: *Do they show you these options?*

S: Oh, yes, when you're looking in the crystal. It's a big crystal, and it's like liquid. A little thicker than water.

And you can see the life of a person and what their job is and what they're doing. You just watch their whole life.

D: *But you know that humans have free will. Things can change, can't they?* (No) *Maybe you are seeing one possibility?*

S: You only see one path, what that person is meant to be there for.

D: *Yes? But sometimes people don't take that one path once they're in the body.*

S: Hmm ... creates chaos.

D: *Because you know they have free will, and sometimes they forget what they're there for, don't they?*

S: No. They just don't listen.

D: *You can come into the body with all good intentions about what you're supposed to do, but other things get in the way sometimes.*

S: It's like those people back at the cave, they're just people. They don't have a path. They're just people. *I* had a path. That child had a path.

D: *So if you choose an option, you don't go off that path? Is that what you mean?*

S: Yes. There's just so many in this room where the crystals are that choose a life or have a path. The rest of the people aren't sent here on a path.

D: *What are their lives for then?*

S: It's like a backdrop.

That was a strange statement. I had never heard that before.

D: *What do you mean?*

S: In a movie they paint something around the person so there's a backdrop.

D: *So the others don't really have purposes?*

S: Right. They come to live, breathe, work and die.

D: *Is there any hope that they might find a path, or are they a different kind of soul?*

S: They didn't choose. They're just here to be part of the backdrop. They're slaves. They're slaves that go from one star system to the next and they are used as a backdrop.

D: *Just to be there for these persons with a purpose.*

S: Yes. For you to learn, to stay on your path, you have to have these other people in your way, living beside you, but you're here for a lesson and they're here for a backdrop.

D: *Yes, but sometimes they create problems, to try to pull you off your path?* (Yes) *Is that part of their purpose, to distract you?* (Yes) *But when you're in your body, you don't know all these things, do you?*

S: Not all beings are the light source. Not all *light* beings are the light source. They're just here as energy to help us with our lessons, to create chaos or to work or just to live. Certain beings go to learn the lessons for the light Source. It's like you're just a higher being.

D: *Then the other ones, they don't evolve to become higher beings?*

S: No, they're just energy. Like making a movie where they use extras.

D: *But the ones on the path, the higher source, can they recognize each other out of all the mass of other people?* (Yes) *If we could do that, we wouldn't let things bother us so much, would we?*

S: That's right.

D: *If we knew they were there to add drama, I guess you would say?* (Yes) *But when you're looking at these options, you can see all the different lives you're going to go into.—You know that you're speaking through a human body right now, don't you?* (Yes) *It's probably one of the options you chose, the one we call "Suzette." Did you see that as an option before you came in?*

S: Yes. I only chose options where I could save someone.

D: *Why did you choose the life that was going to be Suzette?*

S: She will be used to surrender with children and higher light beings to teach. I won't be coming back to the crystal planet for a long time, so I have to teach. We have to get the life source higher vibration on this planet. She will be teaching life source children and animals.

D: *The animals are important also?*

S: Certain animals are a higher life source.

D: *So like the humans, many animals and insects are like the backdrop?* (Yes) *And certain ones are a higher vibration?*

S: Yes. There's so much pain on this planet.

Here Suzette expressed pain as she said her head hurt. I gave suggestions for well-being to remove the physical sensations.

S: There's too much pain. There's pain all around with the animals and with the plant life and in the water, and I have to help. I have to help teach these life sources that are of higher vibration so they can help the planet and help the animals and help the trees. I can't just leave. I have to stay here and help. (She moaned as if very frustrated.) Big job.

D: *Yes, it's a big job. But you're not alone. There are others coming to help, aren't there?*

S: Yes. You can feel it. You can feel the vibration.

D: *What is it you want Suzette to do to help?*

S: Teach the young. They came here, too, but everything is going to happen quicker. They're going to help sooner because there's only .... OH! My head hurts. (I gave suggestions again.)

D: *Why do they have to learn quicker?*

S: Time is short because of these lower beings. All they want to do is hurt each other. They want to destroy each other. They want to destroy the land, which hurts the animals, the trees and the water. And in short, you have to get to the youth so they can spread the words and help heal the planet.

D: *The adults are not going to be able to help?*

S: The higher source adults. The others have gone from doing their jobs as backdrops to being angry. They want to be angry at somebody or something and all they want to do is kill ... kill or hurt. (She winced in pain again.)

D: *Their being angry creates an emotion that is drawing energy. Is that what you mean?*

S: Yes. We ought to stop that.

D: *The negative type of energy that can hurt things.*

S: Yes, it can hurt the planet.

I asked about Suzette's purpose. "She is to work with the young people. Teaching, listening, understanding." She was told she didn't have to go out and look for people, the higher life sources would come to her. "People that know ... they know ... people know. She came to heal or to save." Suzette had said that since she was very, very little she was very angry at being sent back here, and she didn't understand this.

S: Yes, this job is big. She didn't want to come. This job is big! There's so much pain ... so much pain.

D: *But she chose to be here.*

S: Well, I think I needed to choose. They're sending life forces. We didn't get to choose this job. This is a big job. Many life forces have been sent here to save this planet. I would rather have stayed at the crystal city.

Suzette is very psychic in her present life. She can see things that are going to happen in the future.

S: I saw it clear back when I was hairy. I knew everybody was going to perish. I could see in every lifetime.

D: *Is Suzette supposed to use those abilities in this lifetime?*

S: Yes. Trust and teach. Higher spiritual thinking.

D: *She said people won't listen to her. They won't believe her.*

S: Just talk to the ones with the higher life source.—
Everything is speeding up. There's less time. That's why
we all had to come here. There's less time. We have to
save the planet.

D: *I've heard there are some that are not going to be able to
be saved.*

S: No. The backdrop people, but they're angry.

D: *The vibrations are changing. So the backdrop people will
stay with the old Earth?* (Yes) *And that's why they're
angry?*

S: Yes. It's like they're acting and they got a script and they
are playing this part, and their part is to destroy this
planet.

D: *They have anger about this?* (Yes) *But the planet cannot
be destroyed, can it?*

S: No. It can't be. It's just like when the dinosaurs died and
the trees died, but everything came back to life. Not the
dinosaurs or the trees, but they don't know that part of it.
But this is a beautiful planet. This is a beautiful home.
Not as pretty as the crystal place, but....

D: *Then the backdrop people will stay with the Earth going
through all the changes, the catastrophe part?*

S: Yes, they won't survive. They'll be gone. The others will
move on. This new place will be so beautiful. The
vibration will be so high and this will be a learning place.

D: *That's what I was trying to understand. It will separate
into two parts?*

S: Yes. It's like two levels, and the old Earth will be on one
level, and the new Earth will be on a higher level. But
they won't see each other, like they're in two time warps.

D: *That's what I've been told. One will not even be aware of
the other.* (Right)—*But you want to teach the children so
they can go to the new Earth?*

S: Yes. More with higher vibration can help save, and this
will be a teaching planet. There are other places that are
teaching, but this will be a teaching planet.

D: *So those that are left with the old Earth will live out their lives in a different way?* (Yes) *You said those people are not evolving at all?*

S: Yes. They're just like backdrop, you know, like paint a picture and paint somebody on it.

D: *So as the Earth goes through all the changes and catastrophes, there will be many people dying.*

S: Yes, yes. There will be a lot of that. (Matter-of-factly.)

D: *But they choose this before they come in anyway?*

S: No, not so much choose. They're kind of like slaves. They're taken from one place to another to do whatever they need to do there because they are just energy.

In this life Suzette had a memory of seeing two stars and she asked about this. "These two stars in the sky, is that the crystal city?"

S: You go toward the two stars. The crystal city's past there.

This was an interesting concept that opened up a different way of looking at the two Earths and the separating of the Old from the New. I was in the final editing of this chapter when I suddenly had a revelation. It is strange how many times you have to read something before it finally clicks. Maybe this is the way the mind works; it has to be exposed to something several times before it finally makes sense.

I thought the idea of Backdrop People was interesting and certainly a new concept, but then I saw more in what the SC was trying to convey. Many times at my lectures people want more information about the separation of the Old and New Earth, and those who will be left behind. I now think this concept holds some of the answers. They said most of us chose to come and experience life at this time and came with a higher purpose to help save the Earth. But, unbeknownst to us, other energies were also sent to Earth to play bit parts in our scenarios we have created, to act in our illusion. These were called the Backdrop People, who come to live, breathe, work and die, but have no real purpose other than to be the extras in our play; the backdrop to act against. They called them "slaves," but I think that is a rather harsh word. They are just energy and are taken from one star system to another to play their parts. Rather like the extras in a film who spend their entire lives playing that insignificant part and never getting to play the leading role. It reminds me of the movie *The Truman Story* where the young man spent his entire life living inside of a created illusion where actors played their parts, before he finally realized it wasn't real. The others were playing their parts very realistically and convincingly.

They said these people have become angry, but I think they have picked up that anger from associating with the negativity which surrounds them. And this negativity has increased their anger. This has created all the wars and catastrophes that is present now on the Earth. This would also account for the thousands of people who are killed in the various wars and natural catastrophes. They are there to provide the drama for our illusion. They said, "They are taken from one place to another to do whatever they need to do there because they are just energy." I think the only way to look at this is with all emotions removed. We wanted to experience certain events in our life, and these were the people hired by Central Casting to fill in the scenes. I am not saying this is true, but it's an interesting concept to ponder. More mind candy! Take it or leave it.

It is now my opinion that these are the ones who will be left with the Old Earth, the Backdrop People because they do not have a higher vibration or purpose. They teach us lessons by their mere presence, but they are not intended to evolve further. These are the ones who will be left behind. The ones who realize their higher purpose and raise their vibration and frequency will travel on to the New Earth. There will be those who came in knowing their mission and had high ideals, but they let the negativity of the others pull them down and influence them. Those will also have to stay with the other energy on the Old Earth as they separate. This is why it is important for us to realize that it is only an illusion and find our role in the creation of the New Earth, and our part in helping others find theirs. And not be sucked into the angry energy of the Backdrop People and be stuck on the Old Earth. This is why this is such an individual thing. Each must find their own way and reawaken to the purpose they came to fulfill.

This strange concept of backdrop people who were similar to extras in a movie left a lasting impression on me. Now when I'm in a crowded airport, cruise ship or busy city and I see all the bustling people going about their business seemingly oblivious of each other, I think "backdrop people." An interesting concept and one that probably has more significance than I realize.

Chapter 39

THE FRAGMENTS REUNITE

When I went to Santa Fe to teach my class at the Northwest New Mexico College in 2008, I stayed at a guest house in the country outside Santa Fe. The altitude bothered me the entire time I was there (10 days). I saw many clients at the guest house before going to El Rito (the other campus) for the class. The physical problems went away once I got back to Albuquerque and started home.

Pamela was already in a strange place when she came off the cloud.

P: Everything is sparkling. Everything is alive. Everything here knows. It is quite beautiful and quite alive. Quite real to me.

D: *What is sparkling in this place?*

P: Crystals. Everything knows, everything is alive, intelligent, always.

D: *Where are the crystals?*

P: Everywhere. They are like carpets, but they are also in the air. They hang in the air. The whole realm is light, but it is in crystals. Everything is glowing with very subtle colors.

D: *The crystals make colors?*

P: No, the light makes colors.

D: *Is this a physical place?*

P: No, it is a dimensional place. It is living energy.

D: *Sounds like it would be powerful energy.*

P: It is, but it is soft. It is very relaxing. It is strong, but it is not apart from me, so you don't feel it as aggressive.

D: *Become aware of yourself. Do you have a body, or what do you feel like?*

P: No, I am also that. Light.

D: *So you don't have a physical form?*

P: I can form one if I want to, but I have more of a form of light that is shaped a little bit like me.

D: *It sounds beautiful. And you don't have any reason to be solid or physical?*

P: I don't have much reason.

D: *You just like being the light and the energy then.*

P: I am. I am, yes.

D: *Are there others there with you? Or do you sense anybody else around?*

P: (Deep breath) I sense simultaneity. I sense that I am in a place where everything I have known is coming together. Everything that I have been and have known is in this place all at once. There is a convergence of light so all those crystals are all part of allness.

D: *You said, everything you have known. Does that mean in other lives, or what?*

P: Other lives and other dimensions, and just within God. I am feeling happy. I am wanting that closeness of everything coming together. This is allness. This is all of life, all at once.

D: *So it is a different place than the Spirit side where you go when you leave a physical body?*

P: This is a dimension on the Spirit side. This is a place I am just starting to know. I have seeds of it and those seeds like the crystals are all converging.

D: *Is this your first time to be there and experience it?*

P: I'm sorry, your question does not make sense.

D: *I just wondered if you had experienced it before.*

P: I have seeds and now it is unveiling.

D: *So it is time to really become aware of it then.*

P: It is time. It is time. I need to know that everything will come together at the right time, and I need to feel it in my body.

D: *So it is a different feeling than you have had before?*

P: Yes, this life. It feels very, very good. It is resonating and I am changing into this. (Deep breathing.) I seem to be absorbing direct knowledge rather than needing to know, more spontaneous in the moment. I know what to do and I feel safe, and I am relaxed. This is more where all of me is coming together all at once. Everything that I have been and known is coming together.

D: *You are seeing and feeling this energy for a reason. Are you supposed to do something with it?*

P: Focus on the gathering within myself. It is like I have called everything, all parts of me in all dimensions, together. And they come together and it is in that focus that everything unfolds.

D: *Is that what you mean by the "gathering"?*

P: Yes. All the fragments are moving towards me, towards one, now.

D: *Because I have been told that we do splinter or fragment into many different pieces and parts.*

P: Yes, I have been many things. The pieces are all coming together.

D: *So it is time to no longer be separate.* (Yes) *But when you were separate, you were learning many lessons, weren't you?*

P: I did, and I finished it. There is no reason for fragmentation any more.

D: *Why is this important for you to know this, that it is a coming together of all the fragments?*

P: It increases enjoyment and peace in my life. Enjoyment of everything. Everything.

D: *Did you have enjoyment before?*

P: I did, but it was within the fragments. The crystal pieces are coming together. They are fitting together. There are things that are happening within the coming together.

D: *What do you mean? We are trying to understand the process.*

P: (Sigh) I will remember more. I will have more power. My angelic nature is opening more to allowing myself to play. More abilities to use higher aspects of myself.

D: *Why is this happening at this time?*

P: (Sigh) Because it can.

D: *But Pamela does wonderful work with the energies.* (Pamela was an energy healer.)

P: It is not about Pamela. There are other beings coming into this one.

D: *What do you mean?*

P: Other beings, light beings coming also here.

D: *Is this part of the integration process?*

P: No, it is different. Integration allows for other beings to step in.

D: *It wasn't as easy for them to come in before?*

P: It was not necessary before. She did what she was asked to do. It is time for others to participate. She will allow it. They are here.

D: *Where did they come from?*

P: There is no *where.*

D: *My main concern is that they are positive.*

P: She is not concerned. These are her. These are higher aspects of herself.

D: *So they are all part of the integration process?*

P: Not integration of the crystals. These are different aspects of the light.

D: *So the other ones were more or less the aspects of the physical lives.*

P: They are aspects, yes, of fragmentation, individuality. This is not an aspect of fragmentation of the self. (Deep breathing.) These are aspects of gifts of God that have never fragmented. Her work will remain much the same. The energy will change to have more potency. More powerful, much more powerful.

D: *But you said this is a time right now. This is necessary?*

P: This is part of celebration. It is not part of need. This is part of love. She has fulfilled the needs. She wants to experience more of God. To expand and grow within the nature of God. This is something as a gift.

D: *She said she had the feeling that something has been happening to her, like an awakening of some kind.*

P: This is gradual and sudden both. This is a sudden change in vibrational capacity.

D: *Will these light beings be in her all the time, or will they come and go?*

P: All the time.

D: *Does she have to call on them when she does her work?* (No) *By using this energy, will her work be more effective in the healing?*

P: The purpose is not so much effectiveness, as it is explosion of flavor of God. She will definitely notice a difference when she works. Everyone is feeling it in a different way, and she has developed links to develop language and techniques to help people enjoy it and live it comfortably. She will help them to accept it.

D: *People come to her to be healed. Is this one of the things this energy will be used for?*

P: One of the things, yes. It is not mainly for the people. It is mainly for the Whole.

D: *Her development?*

P: Not her development, the Whole. It is a movement within the Whole.

D: *I want her to be able to understand this process when she awakens.*

P: The understanding is intelligent. There is always understanding. There is always compassion. There is a shift from individual mind to wholeness at this time.

D: *Is this happening everywhere?*

P: Everywhere where it is possible.

D: *Is this part of the vibration and frequency changes that are happening?* (Yes)

I explained that I knew about the new Earth and moving into a new dimension. She agreed that this was part of that process.

D: *Are other people also going to experience this?*

P: Yes, many, many are awakening now. Being aware of their wholeness. All parts of the Source that were suspended, are now integrating.

D: *As we move into this new dimension, everything has to come together? And more people are becoming aware that they are no longer separate?*

P: Yes. As more and more merge with the whole parts of themselves, it makes it easier for others to accept. They will feel more comfortable.

D: *For some people it is not a comfortable process, is it?*

P: They have chosen that. Some people choose to grow through uncomfortableness.

D: *As we integrate with the Whole, you said we will feel different?*

P: Everyone will feel different, everyone. Everyone will feel more comfortable with Wholeness. They will know something is happening to their soul.

D: *But we will still keep the physical body?*

P: For those who have need of such, it will happen. This is happening at the same time for those in the body and out of the body.

D: *The ones on the spirit side are also experiencing this?*

P: Yes, this has nothing to do with being in a body. It is time.

D: *Does it have to do with the development of the planet?*

P: It is not development of just this planet. It is development of the Whole, all, everything at once. The universe, everything is moving in a different mode.

D: *So there is no way it could be stopped or changed? Is it something that has to happen?*

P: It is God's choice.

I explained that I had heard that there would be two Earths, and on the old Earth, these things would not happen.

P: I am not connected to that. I am connected to the part that is moving into wholeness.

D: *But this is not like death, or the dying of the physical body, is it?*

P: Whether the physical bodies are here or not is not the question. Everyone experiences it the same in or out of the body, in or out of any consciousness, anywhere. It is not important to understand what is happening, only to enjoy it.

This sounded somewhat similar to the energy cone that was implanted in everyone in 2009. Chapter 30. I wonder if it is the same thing with different wording?

D: *If the integration process is just beginning now, what is it all going to lead to ultimately?*

P: A lifting into a unified whole. More wholeness can function within each individual. It is more like there is a thread, a kind of a unifying thread that is going to be coming into everything. Everything will feel more connected to everything else everywhere. Everywhere, everything will be lifted into another dimension.

D: *What will that other dimension be like? Can you tell us anything about it?*

P: It is like an interwoven fabric that suddenly aligns everything to awareness of essence.

D: *So when we reach that part, will we no longer have individuality?*

P: No, there will be individuality. There will be just more threads of unity available and functioning. Individuality is changing to some extent and there is more of an overlay of wholeness.

D: *How is the individuality changing?*

P: More of the fragmentation from more aspects are completing.

D: *So there will be no need to have physical lives anymore. Is that what you mean?*

P: There are no physical lives, so to speak, in reality. But there will be less scattering of experience.

D: *I am trying to understand. There are still people who are accumulating karma. Will that make a difference?*

P: I am not part of that flow. I don't know. I only know I am part of this fabric of Wholeness. I am part of what is coming together. It is happening now.

D: *Even though I know that time doesn't exist on your side, do you have any idea of how much longer it will take for everything to come together?*

P: According to our perspective, it has already happened. It is unfolding, but it has already occurred on inner levels. Life will move on pretty much the same. This energy is available to everyone, to be used in any way they want. That is the work. They will decide whether they want to be part of it or not. It is given to everyone, and they will make choices as they wish. It changes everything automatically. There is a lack in creation because of lack of wholeness. When there is more wholeness present, creation happens automatically.

D: *This is why I tell people to be careful what they ask for, be careful what they want to create because it seems to be happening faster.*

P: That is true.

D: *It used to take a long time.*

P: That was on purpose.

D: *The way Earth was you had to have time to be sure that was what you wanted.*

P: Yes, learning at certain curves needs to be slow.

D: *So now you can have it much faster.* (Yes) *But first you have to be sure what you want.*

P: But Wholeness provides the answer to what you want. It is only when you don't know what you want that the creation becomes confused. They don't create. The Wholeness creates. When there is enough wholeness functioning, all creations display individuality with purity. They just realize Wholeness is with them and the Wholeness functions to bring about everything that is exact uniquely them. Exactly and everything that they need. If they allow the link to hold the map of Wholeness that is coming in, then everything works automatically. In every plane in every way.

D: *So they can also make themselves healthy by using this energy?*

P: They don't use the energy. The energy uses them.

D: *Is there anything they have to do to contact this Wholeness?*

P: No. It is available, just not to resist it. The energy of Wholeness helps you to know what you want. The problem is that people do not know what they want.

I was looking for some type of ritual or process that an individual could use to call forth this energy for creation. Humans always like instructions. In *Convoluted Universe - Book Three,* Chapter 37, there is the chapter where the healing energy speaks and tells how it can be called upon at any time.

P: There are small ways that people suppress feeling worthy of being happy. It is mostly trust that is needed.

D: *We are used to asking our angels and our guides to help us create something.*

P: All the angels and all the guides are starting to link. There is a linking now so there is less individuality on all levels. It is like having all angels instead of one. There is less space between desire and support. It is an accelerant to the process. At this time, Pamela is linking to aspects of knowingness and those who have shared knowing. This is facilitating a linking.

D: *I want her to understand why she is being given this information.*

P: She is not needing information as much as process of connection with vast moving networks of people, grounding the change.

Pamela had a physical question she wanted information about. It had been a mystery for the last ten years. She said she would suddenly feel tingling in the body and then be unable to move. She would remain like this for quite some time (hours), and it would be disturbing to others around her who witnessed this.

P: These are parts of the fragments coming in. This was when the Wholeness opened.

When these incidents happened, Pamela was never afraid. She just wanted to understand what was happening because during those times she had to go and lie down until it passed.

P: This is a shift within the Wholeness, versus the completion of fragmentation.
D: *So another fragment would come in and blend together?*
P: Or more of the Wholeness was integrating. It would temporarily suspend and dis-coordinate.
D: *Of course, it was a little disconcerting because, even though she wasn't afraid, it would happen in public sometimes.*
P: She was always taken care of.
D: *It hasn't happened to her for a while, so is that part over?*
P: The Wholeness is more subtle and fragmentation is more complete. There are other kinds of things that will be happening. Energy changes that bring shifts in the body-mind that are temporary. There becomes little desire to care about the body and more desire to be with Spirit at that moment. There is a relief of the burden of caring.
D: *Will she notice anything physically at the time these things happen?*

P: A slight dis-coordination due to a shift in focus. She is getting better at staying connected. It is temporary, always temporary. Love is important because the process is love right now. As given, intelligence is far more functional than information. Those intelligences have now been linked to this one.

**

Another client mentioned something that sounded similar when "they" were talking about a Soul merge.

D: *Can you explain what that is?*
M: That's when a person opens more and more to their higher aspects. What happens is: the mind opens up and it seems like someone is coming into them. But the consciousness just expands so they are taking in more and more aspects of themselves.
D: *What does it feel like if something like that happens, so we will know what it is?*
M: It feels like they have more awareness. Actually, they feel lighter in Spirit and they might notice little personality changes. Maybe some likes or dislikes might change. But pretty soon, the one, the aspect that has expanded themselves, will get used to where they are and then know how to work more with this person. We all are on all levels growing.

**

Continuing with Pamela:

I wanted to know if we could have any information about the changes that the Earth would be going through before it went into the next dimension.

P: There are many possibilities in motion right now, and she is part of that process that is trying to unify everything into the best possible outcome. There are forces at work;

many, many matrices, many forces. Everyone will be taken care of everywhere, no matter what their circumstance. Everything is moving toward greater unity, however it looks on the outside.

Chapter 40

THE PICTURES

Dawn and her daughter, Alexis came to my office to have separate sessions. Dawn surprised me by giving me a packet of pictures and the CD they had been printed from. They said they had been taken in 2004, and they did not know what to do with them or who to give them to. They finally decided that they should give them to me, that I would know what to do with them. This was in 2006 and I have kept them, not knowing what book they should go into. At the time of the session it was difficult to understand. Finally, now in 2011, I think I more fully understand what the SC was trying to describe, and I think it is time to finally present them to others. It shows how much I have grown since 2006, and that my concepts have been broadened. I hope I am correct.

Dawn said they had been outside one night and saw an unusually bright object in the sky. At first they thought it was a star, but it was larger and brighter than any they had seen before. They pointed their camera at it and took a series of pictures. Then they watched as the object gradually faded away. When they had the film developed they were stunned. What was shown on the pictures was not at all what they saw that night. They saw a solid object, not one that moved, morphed and undulated as the one in the pictures.

Over the years people have sent me similar pictures, but they always related them to UFOs because they had no other explanation. I think these show that most of what people think of as unknown spaceships have other, even more complicated, explanations.

I conducted two sessions, one with each of them separately. The information that came through was similar, but I think the mother's (Dawn) had more description. We had gone through two past lives and was conversing with the SC. It had already helped with personal information and had worked on serious physical problems. Then I wanted to ask about the pictures:

D: *I wanted clarification. Dawn and her daughter, Alexis, brought these photographs to me yesterday, and they are really curious about them. Can you identify what is in the pictures?*

DA: It's the higher forces working with the planet. They're trying to keep it in balance. They're working with energy grids on both sides of the dimensions, this side and the other side.

D: *But in the picture, it almost looked like a physical object.*

DA: Yes, it's an entity. It's elastic. It can spread over a lot of territory by expanding. It just works on both sides. Working with the balancing of the planet, energy work, spreading goodness around the planet as it moves and it spreads, as it moves and it spreads, it moves and it spreads, almost like a mother's loving arms. It's all a part of the evolution, of the spirit and evolution of intellect, evolution of living awareness as you go out. This is what this does. This does this with more than just the Earth planet. This is its role and this is what it was created for. It goes and brings balance lovingly. It's a female energy ... smooth.

D: *She said when they saw it in the sky, it looked like a star.*

DA: Yes, camouflage.

D: *The thing in the pictures didn't show up until they were enlarged, and it seemed to change shape. That's why we thought it was a physical object of some kind.*

DA: The human eye and the physical human body is not on that vibrational level to be able to see it with the naked eye. You can feel it. Sensitive people can feel its presence, but they can't see behind its camouflage. But the camera picks it up.

D: *Why were they allowed to photograph it?*

DA: Because other people need to see it and know that things are under control, that things are   moving along on schedule.

D: *Is this the way it normally looks because it is like a "worm" shape?*

DA: Yes, it can change its shape and size depending on what it's doing. It accommodates itself to the environment it's working in and also the dimension it's working in, depending on the energy make-up of the dimension it's working in.

D: *It almost looks like it's organic.*

DA: No. It's a light being. It does have elasticity. It does have pre-moving roaming parts around it, seers that do the job, too. That rotate around it, that connect and intermesh and guide like in a distance type situation. And it's all parts of the whole of itself.

D: *Does it normally look like that, or is that just the way the camera picked it up?*

DA: It wouldn't normally look like that on this side, but through your atmosphere, in your dimension here, that's what it would normally look like. But maybe in another star system ... things are affected by their environment. It's like a thought is affected by the environment. How it looks depends on the effects of the dimension in the environment that it presents itself in. You can have a thought of a chair in one environment and it will look one way; you can have a thought of a chair in another dimension in another environment, and it'll look a different way. They won't look the same, even though it is the same thought or picture.

D: *What does it really look like? I mean ... what is real anyway ...* (Laugh) *in its normal state?*

DA: In its normal state when it's relaxing?

D: *Where it comes from, how does it appear?*

DA: Just a huge vapor ... HUGE vapor of light ... Huge vapor of light.

D: *Because Alexis said in her session that it was so big you couldn't comprehend it.* (Yes) *Does that make sense?*

DA: Yes, from our point it does because your Earth realm is a lot smaller than where it hangs out when it's in between jobs. It's all a matter of perspective.

D: *So it was here to help out?*

DA: That's what it does! Yes. It's a nurturer. It's nurtured of "Nurturer."

D: *But is it here to help with what's going on with the Earth at this time?*

DA: Yes. It spreads almost like a sack, an energy sack and it spreads out around the planet. As it goes through its changes and a lot of the negative energies that kind of wear holes in things, her love energy smooths this out, mends the holes, mends the tears, puts it back and readjusts the vibrations. As the vibrations of the Soul and Earth evolve, it wears and it tears, and this comes back and mends it like a sock and fine tunes that energy if it needs to move up. Everything moves faster as its energy rate increases.

D: *So it appears in the pictures as small, and you said it is huge. Is that because it was so far away from them or what?*

DA: It's huge in its own natural place of rest. But when it enters other dimensions and other solar systems, it accommodates and shifts its size. It may need to become real, real tiny if it's working in the tiny realm, or if it's in a medium size realm, it will accommodate and become the format in size to access successfully and interact with the planet it's working with. Or it can be real big. It's fluid. It's flexible. It can expand or it can become small.

D: *So they were just allowed to see it in that form?* (Yes) *You said people are supposed to know about this?*

DA: There are some people who are supposed to know about it, yes.

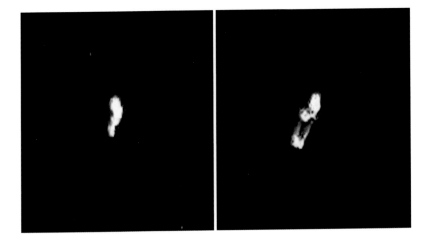

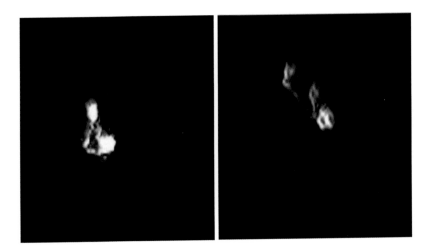

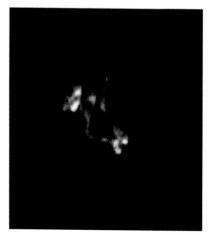 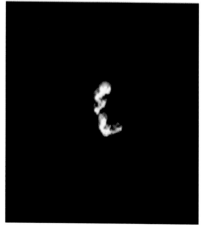

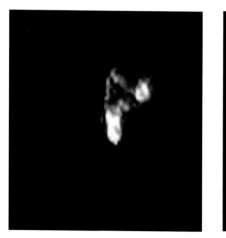 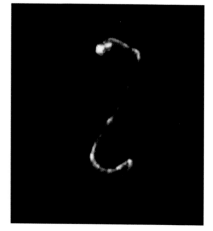

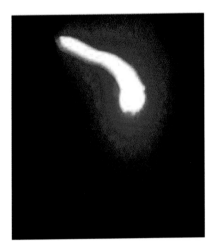 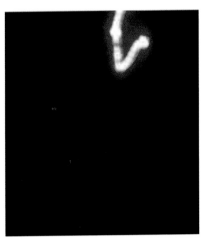

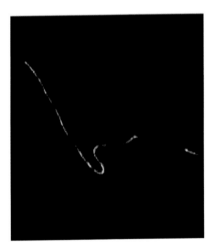 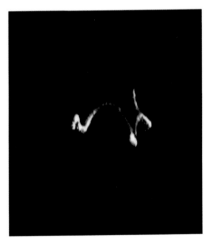

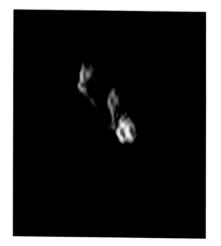
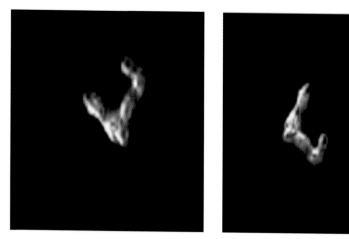

D: *Will I be able to use the pictures and try to explain this to people?*

DA: Yes. That's one of the reasons they came here.

D: *To show them to me?*

DA: Yes. They've been wondering for some time. They knew it was supposed to go somewhere to get the information out to people that needed to see it. It's going to give them a sense of security. There's going to always be those who won't understand it, and it might cause fear in them. But people that are ready to hear this and see this, it will instill in them a feeling of support. The support systems are there. The mechanisms are there. All is functioning as it needs to be. If you think that you are a soldier alone ... you are not. Just take a look at what's up there.

D: *When I showed my daughter, Julia, the pictures, she felt a tremendous amount of energy and vibration emanating from thems.* (Yes) *And she also started feeling that maybe it had something to do with DNA. Is that correct?*

DA: Well, it's working with all the energies to move the planet forward in its evolution, and they are all interconnected. How can I explain this? It affects the energy of the planet all the way down to the core, so it's going to hit all energy, the structure of all energy. It has to be raised as the planet evolves and moves higher in its evolution. The shift has to all come together and that's what this thing does, too. You raise the vibration on the outside, all the way down to the center ... out. The image that's in the sky works on the outside in.

In my book *The Convoluted Universe - Book Two,* there were two mentions of an energy force that would be directed toward the Earth in the early 2000s to help raise consciousness. This would penetrate to the very core of the Earth and affect every living thing (even plants and animals). Yet it would be invisible to human sight. Maybe this is associated with what Dawn photographed in 2004.

D: To the center of the Earth? (Right.) *It affects everything.*

DA: Right. It's like dust settling. It's almost like it creates an embryonic sac around it. The planet is growing.

D: This way the people, the animals, the plants, anything in its vicinity would also be affected? (Yes) *Then according to my daughter's theory, do you think it's affecting the DNA with the energy?*

DA: Yes because the DNA is energy. It's energy encoded in the physical matter. This is a good thing. This is light work and this is a part of the plan for the planet as well as us because we're the planet, too. The people on the planet are all part of the organism and it's all a part of the process. This is not the first time that this thing in the sky has performed this type of work. This is what it does. It comes when it's needed. That's its job description!

D: So it's helping with the evolution of the planet as we go into what we call the "New Earth" then?

DA: Yes. It's also a spirit builder, strengthener. So the photos need to get out so that the people will know, so they will feel protected in a sense and guided. Guided and protected.

D: In a sense we could call it the equivalent of God if we wanted to. Energy that strong?

DA: When you say God ... you mean....?

D: The Source. What you call the Source.

DA: Yes. Source. It's part of the One. It's part of the one that the One has created and sends out part of itself, even though it has female aspects to it because it is a nurturer, a soother. It stimulates change and growth and feeds that by keeping the energy environment in a situation where it naturally brings about evolution. It's part of the Source. It's that part of the Source that created. It's that HIGH. It's that advanced. It comes from Source. It's big. It's part of the Creator institution.

D: Institution?

DA: Yes. We all are Creators, going from smaller and up, up and up. When we've evolved, we become bigger and better Creators. We get bigger and better at it until you get to Source, which is number One, and that's our goal. To take what we've learned and bring it all back to Source. I don't know how to explain it.

D: *Oh, you're doing a good job. I understand. But during the session yesterday I was told to be prepared that many people are going to see the pictures and they're not going to understand. They're not going to believe.*

DA: But so many people don't believe or understand so many things anyway.

D: *And they'll think it's fake somehow. Most of them think of UFOs, ETs, so that's as far as their imagination can go.*

DA: Yes, and some of them don't even grasp that.

D: *At least we know it has nothing to do with anything like that.*

DA: No, it's not a UFO. No, no, no, no, no, it's not a UFO. It's higher than the angelic realms. It's kind of like an angel, in angelic realms. If you want to try to explain it to people to kind of understand, tell them they could look at it as a "super-sized" angel or something. (Laugh)

D: *I wanted to clarify it. If I'm going to work with people and talk about it, I'm going to have to understand. And you guys keep giving me more and more difficult concepts. I guess the world is ready.* (Laugh)

DA: There's always somebody who's ready, but things are held off until there's a big enough group that are ready. To where they get this information and it's more successful and quicker for it to spread out. When you come in and there's only one ready, it's going to be a lot harder and take a lot longer. More than if there's a group. So now there's a big enough group, and it's also going to cause scientists to think more about their theories when they see those pictures. Physicists will think more about relationships of light and energy when they see those pictures. It's not just going to affect people on a soul level where they are requesting advancement of their soul; it's going to also hit doctors on the science level in the world and physicists in the world. They'll even understand through their theories and their research. It'll be a gateway to them. It will open up a realm of understanding in the whole scheme of things. A deeper, bigger scheme of things just by them observing the photographs and applying the knowledge to it that they know, that they discover.

D: *Is there anything else you want me to know about this?*

DA: If there's anything that comes in, you'll definitely be told.

Chapter 41

FINIS

I was working under a deadline to finish this book. It had to be at the printers by a certain date because it was already in the distributor's catalog, and orders were being placed by bookstores. People were telling me that Amazon had announced that it was available. When I heard that I laughed, "I don't think so! It's still in my brain and my computer." It didn't help that I was writing it while on a lecture and class tour. It was putting a lot of pressure on me. We had just completed our annual Transformation Conference in June, 2011 in Arkansas. Everyone who has ever put on a large conference knows the amount of work that takes. Immediately afterwards, with little rest time, I was on a nationwide lecture and class tour giving classes all over the United States and Canada. Then I was only home for a week to get ready for the two month tour of Europe in August, ending at a very large conference in Bangalore, India in October, 2011. Then home for a week and off to six weeks in Singapore and Australia in November, 2011. Time was spent traveling from city to city, radio interviews, TV recordings, lectures, classes. Planes, trains, cars, until you truly don't know where you are. Every hotel looks alike, every airport looks alike, every lecture hall looks alike. Many times when I was ready to start a lecture, I would ask the audience, half-jokingly, "Where am I? What city am I in? What country am I in?" People are the same everywhere I go. The language and the accents are the only clue I have sometimes. My daughter said, "After a while you can't remember *when* something happened because time just blurs together. It becomes an *event* memory. It truly illustrates to me that time *is* an illusion. It is daytime in the country you are in and nighttime back home in Arkansas. Or, in some cases, it is today here and tomorrow (or yesterday) there. All this has to be taken into consideration when trying to communicate with the "real" world you left. It truly shows that time has no meaning (even though we are trapped within it).

So in the middle of all this I was trying to finish this book. I was using every bit of spare time I could find between events to work on my little laptop in my hotel room. Thank goodness for the new technology. Now I don't have to travel with reams of manuscript to edit. It can all be done with the little flashdrive.

I can still remember my first ventures into the world of computing when I got my first one in the 1980s. I wrote my first five books on the old fashioned manual typewriter, then moving on to the electric typewriter. We knew the real meaning of "cut and paste" in those days. The new invention of the computer was like a miracle revolution. I didn't have to retype each page if I found a mistake. You didn't have to mess with carriage returns and rolling the paper in. But I found good reason not to trust those first newfangled computers. They would too often eat my words and digest them to the point that they were never found again (except in my head). Many times, after working for hours on a chapter, I would push the "save" button and walk out of the room with my fingers crossed. I didn't know if it would save it or decide to eat it. In the latter I could see my words floating endlessly through the limbo. I would immediately print it out because it could always disappear at any time. At least it would be in paper form and I could touch it. The worst that could happen would be that I would have to type the whole thing again, but it was safe. Now several of my books can be stored on the little flashdrive device only a few inches long. I am sure that even more miraculous ways of storing information are in the development stages. But because of my early experiences with computers in the 1980s I am still suspicious, so I put it on paper as soon as possible.

So on this trip in 2011, I treasured every moment I could squeeze in to be alone and work on the book. I found the best way to get a book finished is to be closed up in a room in a foreign country. In my room the TV was all in a foreign language so it did no good to try to watch it. The only window in the room opened out onto rooftops, so I didn't even have beautiful scenery to distract me. Then I could totally immerse myself in the project. My daughter kept saying, "I don't want to put any more pressure on you, *but* that book has to be done by the time we get home in November."

On this trip we went to many different countries, many of which I have always wanted to see. I had such an attraction to some that I was positive I must have had a past life there. Yet when I arrived there, I was disappointed in that respect. The ancient ruins are interspersed with the city, and the modern overpowers the old. They are just that, ruins, and they are overshadowed and seem out of place among the modern buildings and bustling traffic. A few such as Stonehenge and New Grange, are set off by themselves. Yet even with them, they are ruins or mere skeletons of what they were intended to be. Even the Sphinx and the Great Pyramid are not as expected. The city of Cairo encroaches all the way up to them, and they are also mere shells and ruins of what they once were. I expected to feel something at the Colisseum in Rome, but it is sitting in the middle of the city with souvenir and food stalls all around the walls and surrounded by bustling traffic and noisy tourists. Even the grandeur of the Taj Mahal was not quite what I expected. It is a beautiful building, but the extreme poverty of India goes all the way up to the gates. The Parethenon in Athens is beautiful, but a mere shadow of what it once was, now a partially reconstructed ruin sitting on a hill above the city. Maccu Picchu is also special and has a powerful energy, yet it also is a ruin. Everywhere I have been, the tour guides always say the same thing, "We don't know how these were built. We don't know the real function. We don't know ... we don't know." Often their *official* explanation is implausible.

My regressions into past lives in these areas make more sense and supply more information. I have always been fascinated by the work of archeologists and their tedious work of bringing the past back to the light of day. Without them we would have no indication of the wonders of the past except from ancient documents. Yet I believe what they have uncovered is only a small fraction of what still remains hidden beneath the sands of time, beneath the waters of the oceans and deep within the mountains. There is much ancient history and knowledge that will probably never be uncovered. Yet I know it exists within the amazing computer called the "mind," and we are able to access this through deep trance hypnosis. This is what makes my work as a reporter and researcher of lost knowledge so exciting. I never know what the next session will uncover or disclose. It doesn't matter to me if it can be proven because I am not trying to convince anyone. My job is to get them to open their minds to other possibilities and probabilities. Others can focus on the proving part of it. My job is to open up new worlds of knowledge.

All my life I have had an unexplained attraction to anything ancient, especially Egyptian and Roman. As a child I devoured old books on these subjects, yet I didn't care about the text. I was fascinated by the pictures, especially the pictures of ancient hieroglyphics. In school I was very excited about ancient history and I became disinterested when it moved into modern history. I remember I had an extreme fascination with Pompeii. I read the book *The Last Days of Pompeii* by Sir Edward George Buliver-Lytton, and made a book report on it for school. When it was made into a movie (black and white in those days), I was disappointed because it had deviated from the story in the book. As a child I saw an old copy of it in the window of an old bookstore where I lived in St. Louis. I wanted my own copy so badly, but money was scarce during the Depression. I managed to save a dollar (mostly from turning in discarded Coke bottles found in the alley. I could get two cents a bottle) and walked many blocks to see if that would be enough to buy it. (In those days children were allowed to have adventures. You could walk, roller skate or ride your bike anywhere you wanted. There was not the fear that has been ingrained upon children today.) I can still remember the bitter disappointment when I found the old bookstore had been closed for years. So my precious book had to remain in the window, untouchable.

So you can imagine my excitement on this trip to Europe in September 2011, when I discovered I would have a few days off in Rome, and one of the sight-seeing tours would be an all day tour to Pompeii. I would be able to see it for myself. Would it stir any memories? Also I knew I would be including some past life regressions into one of my books and I wanted to see if the locale etc. matched what my clients had seen. My husband had seen it back in the 1950s when he was stationed onboard the USS Randolph, an aircraft carrier, that pulled into the port of Naples for a few days R&R. He said it was only a bunch of ruins and brought home a little booklet of pictures of statues etc. that had been excavated. Of course, it would not have had the same meaning to him as it had to me.

So after a long bus ride from Rome, we arrived to the same scene as all the other attractions: ruins (beautifully excavated and reconstructed), souvenir stalls, traffic and hundreds of tourists. The Mediterranean could be seen and Mount Vesuvius was still spewing smoke, foreshadowing the possibility of another eruption, but the grandeur of Pompeii was swallowed up by the modern. There is always the possibility that I may have experienced a past life there because of the extreme and unexplainable attraction, but at the actual site I felt nothing.

It goes along with the saying, "You can't go home again." Even in this life when I returned to where I grew up in St. Louis, everything was changed. Buildings had been demolished, a freeway had been constructed through my old neighborhood, everything seemed older and dirtier. Nothing resembled the memories I carry in my mind. So it is with past life memories, it is not the way we remember. We see it one way in regression, then another way in reality. You truly can't go home again. I think the closest we can come to it is with the feelings of *deja vu*. Everything is so old in Europe that many of the old structures still remain. In America when something is a hundred years old, it is often torn down and a parking lot built in its place. In Europe buildings hundreds of years old still remain. A friend of mine said he once went inside an ancient (still active) cathedral in England, and felt an overwhelming sense of sadness. He found an isolated corner and sat crying for a long time. He could not understand why it happened, but I know from my regression work that the place probably triggered a past life memory.

I have already reported one of my own experiences in the beginning of this book. My memory being awakened in Athens, but that was associated with a past life regression. I had another one happen spontaneously in England. I was walking to the entrance of the Tower of London, which I have seen many times with various friends. This time I was walking carefully, trying to maneuver the uneven cobblestones. As I looked down at my feet I had a glimpse that I was wearing a long simple brown dress and soft shoes. I heard in my head, "It was a lot harder when you had to wear those kind of shoes." It was like the voice was joking and referring to the fact that those shoes didn't have soles. The visual faded quickly, but I had the impression that I came there to the Tower of London on a regular basis. I was not one of the prisoners, but I had the feeling of a servant, maybe a scullery maid or something similar, a simple life. The whole impression lasted only a few minutes and faded quickly. Yet it left a lasting impression because it is rare for me to experience such visuals.

So I think it is true, we can't go home again. And we really don't need to. We can see that it only makes us sad because we can't recapture the same feelings. We can't bring back the same people and relive those experiences again. It can only be done through regression, and then we know we cannot remain there in the past (even in this lifetime). We can only take these experiences and use them to make this present life better and more meaningful.

There was a reality TV series a few years ago in America where they took families and isolated them in a simple hut with no modern conveniences at all. They had to live exactly as people lived a couple of hundred years ago. They had to grow their food, prepare it, forage in the woods, cut wood for heat and learn how to spin the cloth to make their own clothes. Even making candles for light, etc. The families were competing to see who could manage to do it and see who could continue the longest before giving in and wanting to return to the modern world. It seemed like a good idea, but there were things that were not accounted for. The people in the past had to live in those ways because that was the only way to survive. They didn't know anything else. But the modern families had been exposed throughout their lives to more advanced things, so they knew things could be done differently, more efficiently. They kept wanting to change things because they knew they could and they knew how. You cannot take something out of the mind that had been learned. So when we look at the past, we often look at it through modern eyes. We can never logically know how they thought, what emotions they felt, what their lives were really like, *unless* we use the deep level of hypnosis that I use. This is real time travel, where the person goes back through a time tunnel and *becomes* the other personality in every respect. This present lifetime no longer exists in their mind so it cannot influence their thinking and memories. They are there in time and experiencing history as it is occurring.

I have had several people offer me huge amounts of money to take them through many past lives in several sessions. I asked them why did they want to do that? They said it was just a curiosity, just a fun thing, just something to do. That is not the purpose of my work. It is not a curiosity experience. It is serious therapy designed to help alleviate physical, karmic and other problems that are interfering with the growth of the individual. I have usually found that the person who wants to experience many past lives as entertainment is not satisfied with their present life. They are looking for a form of escape. Some of these will dwell on who they were in that life and what happened to them, instead of living the present one. The purpose of my work is to have them discover the cause of their problems, understand them and incorporate the knowledge into the present one so they can live it to the best of their abilities. That is the reason they chose to be on Earth at the present time, to live life and understand it, not to escape from it. So I always refuse such offers because they are counterproductive. "They" have said many times that the person is sometimes not shown a past life during the session because they do not need to live in the past, but to focus on the present and the future. To focus on the past only keeps you tied to the past, and inhibits further soul growth.

There is a saying, "If you forget the mistakes of the past, you are doomed to repeat it." This is the value of studying history. But I see this statement as also referring to karma, national as well as personal because there is also karma between nations, countries. In this difficult school of Earth one of the requirements is to take a lesson or class, and if you don't do it correctly or learn the lesson, then you have to take it over again until you do pass and move on to the next grade. The universe doesn't care how long it takes you, you have eternity. But why take an eternity to learn one lesson, an eternity to be stuck in one grade while the others move on. I think the object would be to learn as fast as possible and graduate sooner. Learn from the lessons of the past and not have to repeat them. Then we can move on to the wonders of the many other schools that the Source has planned for us.

And so we come again to the end of another series of sessions that I hope compromised the thinking of some, twisted a few more minds like pretzels or lit a spark of curiosity that there may be possibilities out there never considered before. If so, then I have done my job as reporter, investigator, researcher of lost knowledge. So we will leave for now, as I ponder the countless piles of cases that will be put into future books. Maybe I will be able to stretch a few more minds in the process. In the meantime, keep searching, keep asking questions, keep thinking and searching for *your* own truth. There is more out there than can possibly be believed, and in this important time right now, the doors are being opened as more and more important and incomprehensible knowledge is being brought forth. Keep thinking for yourself. The doors are opening, and you will never be given more than you can handle. Trust, believe and explore!

Dolores Cannon, a regressive hypnotherapist and psychic researcher who records "Lost" knowledge, was born in 1931 in St. Louis, Missouri. She was educated and lived in St. Louis until her marriage in 1951 to a career Navy man. She spent the next 20 years traveling all over the world as a typical Navy wife, and raising her family. In 1970 her husband was discharged as a disabled veteran, and they retired to the hills of Arkansas. She then started her writing career and began selling her articles to various magazines and newspapers. She has been involved with hypnosis since 1968, and exclusively with past-life therapy and regression work since 1979. She has studied the various hypnosis methods and thus developed her own unique technique which enabled her to gain the most efficient release of information from her clients. Dolores is now teaching her unique technique of hypnosis all over the world.

In 1986 she expanded her investigations into the UFO field. She has done on-site studies of suspected UFO landings, and has investigated the Crop Circles in England. The majority of her work in this field has been the accumulation of evidence from suspected abductees through hypnosis.

Dolores is an international speaker who has lectured on all the continents of the world. Her fifteen books are translated into twenty languages. She has spoken to radio and television audiences worldwide. And articles about/by Dolores have appeared in several U.S. and international magazines and newspapers. Dolores was the first American and the first foreigner to receive the "Orpheus Award" in Bulgaria, for the highest advancement in the research of psychic phenomenon. She has received Outstanding Contribution and Lifetime Achievement awards from several hypnosis organizations.

Dolores has a very large family who keep her solidly balanced between the "real" world of her family and the "unseen" world of her work.

If you wish to correspond with Dolores about her work, private sessions or her training classes, please submit to the following address. (Please enclose a self-addressed stamped envelope for her reply.) Dolores Cannon, P.O. Box 754, Huntsville, AR, 72740, USA

Or email her at decannon@msn.com or through our Website: www.ozarkmt.com

Dolores Cannon
Conversations with Nostradamus,
  Volume I, II, III
Jesus and the Essenes
They Walked with Jesus
Between Death and Life
A Soul Remembers Hiroshima
Keepers of the Garden.
The Legend of Starcrash
The Custodians
The Convoluted Universe - Book One,
  Two, Three
Five Lives Remembered
The Three Waves of Volunteers and the
  New Earth
Stuart Wilson & Joanna Prentis
The Essenes - Children of the Light
Power of the Magdalene
Beyond Limitations
Atlantis and the New Consciousness
O.T. Bonnett, M.D./Greg Satre
Reincarnation: The View from Eternity
What I Learned After Medical School
Why Healing Happens
M. Don Schorn
Elder Gods of Antiquity
Legacy of the Elder Gods
Gardens of the Elder Gods
Reincarnation...Stepping Stones of Life
Aron Abrahamsen
Holiday in Heaven
Out of the Archives – Earth Changes
Sherri Cortland
Windows of Opportunity
Raising Our Vibrations for the New Age
Michael Dennis
Morning Coffee with God
God's Many Mansions
Nikki Pattillo
Children of the Stars
A Spiritual Evolution
Rev. Grant H. Pealer
Worlds Beyond Death
A Funny Thing Happened on the Way to
  Heaven
Maiya & Geoff Gray-Cobb
Angels - The Guardians of Your Destiny
Seeds of the Soul
Sture Lönnerstrand
I Have Lived Before
Arun & Sunanda Gandhi
The Forgotten Woman
Claire Doyle Beland
Luck Doesn't Happen by Chance
Max H. Flindt & Otto Binder
Mankind - Child of the Stars
James H. Kent

Past Life Memories As A Confederate
  Soldier
Dorothy Leon
Is Jehovah An E.T
Justine Alessi & M. E. McMillan
Rebirth of the Oracle
Donald L. Hicks
The Divinity Factor
Christine Ramos, RN
A Journey Into Being
Mary Letorney
Discover The Universe Within You
Debra Rayburn
Let's Get Natural With Herbs
Jodi Felice
The Enchanted Garden
Susan Mack & Natalia Krawetz
My Teachers Wear Fur Coats
Ronald Chapman
Seeing True
Rev. Keith Bender
The Despiritualized Church
Vara Humphreys
The Science of Knowledge
Karen Peebles
The Other Side of Suicide
Antoinette Lee Howard
Journey Through Fear
Julia Hanson
Awakening To Your Creation
Irene Lucas
Thirty Miracles in Thirty Days
Mandeep Khera
Why?
Robert Winterhalter
The Healing Christ
James Wawro
Ask Your Inner Voice
Tom Arbino
You Were Destined to be Together
Maureen McGill & Nola Davis
Live From the Other Side
Anita Holmes
TWIDDERS
Walter Pullen
Evolution of the Spirit
Cinnamon Crow
Teen Oracle
Chakra Zodiac Healing Oracle
Jack Churchward
Lifting the Veil on the Lost Continent of
  Mu
Guy Needler
The History of God
Dee Wallace/Jarrad Hewett
The Big E
Conscious Creation

For more information about any of the above titles, soon to be released titles,
or other items in our catalog, write or visit our website:
PO Box 754, Huntsville, AR 72740
www.ozarkmt.com